STATUTORY INTERPRETATION

MICHELLE SANSON

STATUTORY INTERPRETATION

MICHELLE SANSON

OXFORD
UNIVERSITY PRESS
AUSTRALIA & NEW ZEALAND

OXFORD
UNIVERSITY PRESS

Oxford University Press is a department of the University of Oxford. It furthers the University's objective of excellence in research, scholarship, and education by publishing worldwide. Oxford is a registered trademark of Oxford University Press in the UK and in certain other countries.

Published in Australia by
Oxford University Press
253 Normanby Road, South Melbourne, Victoria 3205, Australia

First published 2012
Reprinted 2012, 2013, 2014 (twice)

National Library of Australia Cataloguing-in-Publication data

Author: Sanson, Michelle.
Title: Statutory interpretation / Michelle Sanson.

ISBN: 9780195568684 (pbk.)

Notes: Includes index.
Subjects: Law—Australia—Interpretation and construction.

Dewey Number: 348.9402

Edited by Trischa Baker
Text design by eggplant communications
Typeset by diacriTech, Chennai, India
Proofread by Valina Rainer
Indexed by Julie King
Printed by Sheck Wah Tong

Foreword

The subject of statutory interpretation within any of the Commonwealth of Australia or state or territory jurisdictions is not one that arouses great enthusiasm. Neither is it a mandatory subject within the group of subjects prescribed by the Law Admissions Consultative Committee as part of a qualifying LLB or JD law degree (sometimes described as the Priestley requirements), and rarely appears even as an elective subject within the curriculum of most law degree programs.

Yet it is acknowledged by the judiciary, especially by the High Court of Australia, that an expertise in statutory interpretation is an essential part of the knowledge of all practising lawyers, and that statutory interpretation is a subject that needs greater exposure in any law school syllabus.

This importance has been emphasised by a quote incorporated in that long-standing introductory text, *Glanville Williams: Learning the Law*,[1] which refers to the following statement by Lord Steyne: 'the preponderance of enacted law over common law is increasing year by year … and the subject of interpretation has moved to the centre of the legal stage.'[2]

It is this acknowledgement that a preponderance of case decisions now involve an interpretation of disputed points of statutory interpretation that has led Dr Sanson to write a text wholly dedicated to this important topic.

Readers will discover that in this all-embracing publication the author has endeavoured to cover every aspect of the interpretation of statutes in a way that will arouse and retain the reader's interest, whether it be in resolving basic matters relating to statutory issues, or in more specialised instances such as construing legislative intent or the weight of prior interpretation, to cite just two examples in the text.

It has been my privilege to have known Dr Sanson from her time at the Law School where I was then Dean, at which time she had already commenced writing

1 A T H Smith (ed) *Glanville Williams: Learning the Law* (Sweet & Maxwell: Thomson Reuters, 14th ed, 2010) 121.

2 Lord Steyne, '*Pepper v Hart*, A Re-examination' (2001) 21(1) *Oxford Journal of Legal Studies* 59.

a basic text on International Trade Law before she had graduated, and to where, after a successful time in practice, she returned to become an outstanding law teacher.

She is now a member of the University of Western Sydney Law School, where she is still inspiring the enthusiasm of successive cohorts of law students. She also continues to make a major contribution as an author of legal textbooks, and I am sure *Statutory Interpretation* will become yet another highly regarded contribution to the lengthening list of her publications relating to the interpretation and explanation of legal topics.

Emeritus Professor David Barker AM

Table of Contents

Table of Cases

Table of Statutes

Commonwealth

Australian Capital Territory

New South Wales

Northern Territory

Queensland

South Australia

Tasmania

Victoria

Western Australia

United Kingdom

Preface

This book responds to a recognised need for lawyers to have improved skills in statutory interpretation. Our current lack of such skills is the result of a delayed response on the part of some legal educators to the significant proliferation of statutes as a source of law. In many cases law schools explicitly teach statutory interpretation only in the first year of law school, assuming that advanced skills in statutory interpretation will be imbibed, by osmosis, through the study of substantive law areas that are housed within statutory provisions. But anyone who has taught statutory interpretation in first year will readily acknowledge the difficulty in teaching a skill to students who have no prior knowledge of law. It is akin to teaching chess strategy without any pieces on the chessboard. Other law schools offer a later-year elective such as 'Advanced Legal Method' which, no doubt, is selected by those students who realise the importance of statutory interpretation. But having these skills is not 'elective'—it is essential.

It is pleasing to see that other law schools are already taking an integrated and holistic approach to their curriculum, including statutory interpretation. Provided each and every academic refreshes their own skills in statutory interpretation, it can be successfully embedded. However, statutory interpretation issues can only be covered as they arise in the context of the substantive law. It is submitted that, by adding a 'capstone' subject on statutory interpretation, students in their final semester before commencing practical legal training can integrate their knowledge of statutory interpretation and apply that knowledge in the context of scenarios from any area of law. This requires them to identify not only the statutory interpretation answers but also the issues themselves. Yes, the curriculum is full, but space needs to be made.

The gap in skills of statutory interpretation among Australian lawyers has become so dire that members of the judiciary have taken it upon themselves to seek change. In August 2007 two Victorian Supreme Court judges, Chief Justice Warren and Justice Maxwell, President of the Court of Appeal, wrote to the Law Admissions Consultative Committee (LACC) on this issue. Their submission was supported by Chief Justice Gleeson of the High Court and Chief Justice Spigelman of the Supreme Court of New South Wales. No doubt it would have the support of many other judges.

They wrote of the current lack of understanding of statutory interpretation displayed before the courts by practising lawyers. They endorsed the view that statutory interpretation is a distinct body of law, and proposed that it should have a substantive place in the legal curriculum rather than merely being taught indirectly in other subjects.

On LACC's request, the Council of Australian Law Deans (CALD) undertook a survey of how issues of statutory interpretation are presently taught, following which LACC developed a statement of the competencies reasonably expected of a law graduate in this area. This book has been written taking that statement into account, ensuring the salient matters are covered and additionally adopting active learning pedagogy to enhance student learning. It presupposes knowledge of the Priestley 11 subject areas. Readers new to law school are advised to first read Chapter 12 of *Connecting With Law* (Sanson, Anthony and Worswick, Oxford University Press, 2nd edn, 2010), written as an introduction to statutory interpretation for first-year law students.

The structure of this book is intentionally aligned with the length of a typical semester, and in addition to research and analysis of statutory interpretation rules and principles, it provides case scenarios and application exercises. Chapter 14 has been designed as a consolidating chapter to which readers will repeatedly refer. It contains a Statutory Interpretation Index (SII1) synthesising the book's rules of statutory interpretation, then embedding these in a set of four practical exercises.

The aim is to revitalise statutory interpretation, currently viewed by many students as a necessary evil, to make it a living, breathing, dynamic tool for understanding and applying the law.

Dr Michelle Sanson
September 2011

Acknowledgments

Thanks go to David Barker AM and the three anonymous reviewers for their constructive feedback. Thanks also to the Hon James Spigelman, the Hon Michael Kirby, Bernard Wright, Peter Rae, Joy Keast, Michelle Head, Katie Ridsdale and Trischa Mann.

Thanks to Gordon and Patricia Sanson, who most likely would consider statutes easier to interpret than daughters, and who cannot believe a whole book was written on the meaning of a few words.

CHAPTER 1

INTRODUCTION TO STATUTORY INTERPRETATION

We live in an exciting time of transition. The great commons of the common law are being engulfed by a tsunami of legislation.[1]

1 K Mason, 'The Intent of Legislators: How Judges Discern It and What They Do if They Find It', in *Statutory Interpretation: Principles and Pragmatism for a New Age* (Judicial Commission of New South Wales, 2007) 33 at 44.

Legislation is the predominant source of law applied by judges in the common law world today. This is because, even though the doctrine of precedent allows for the development of law by judges through cases, most areas of law are now set down in statutes, and cases primarily concerning their interpretation. Accordingly, advanced skills in statutory interpretation are essential for all legally trained persons. No longer is it adequate to have a vague memory of approaches to interpretation learned during first-year law.

Through legislation, Parliament communicates, to individuals and corporations alike, what it expects them to do and refrain from doing, and what procedures they must follow to effect certain outcomes. Being able to properly advise clients on the way legislation applies to their professional or personal circumstances can reduce the incidence of litigation, and being able to succinctly advocate for a particular interpretation during a court case can reduce the length, and therefore the cost, of hearings.

Statutory interpretation is not just one extra skill for lawyers to have. It is a central, essential skill—an area of law in itself.[2] James Spigelman, then Chief Justice of the Supreme Court of New South Wales, stated that 'the law of statutory interpretation has become the most important single aspect of legal practice. Significant areas of law are determined entirely by statute. No area of the law has escaped statutory modification'.[3] Michael Kirby, while a Justice of the High Court of Australia, said that 'we have well and truly entered the age of statutes … but we still need to wean lawyers from their love affair with the common law and judicial writings'.[4]

Statutes are, however, difficult to interpret. Indeed, they have been referred to as the 'most repellent form of written expression known to man'.[5] The written word is an essential but an imprecise means of communication. It is 'essential' because it is simply not feasible in a modern society to pass laws down from generation to generation by word of mouth, and it is 'imprecise' because words may be interpreted narrowly or broadly, or may have different meanings depending on the context in which they are used. The primary responsibility of the court becomes one of resolving a dispute over the meaning of words.

The role of the courts in statutory interpretation is limited by the separation of powers doctrine. A court cannot improve, rewrite, or develop a statute. Nor can it

---

2 J J Spigelman, 'The Poet's Rich Resource: Issues in Statutory Interpretation' (2001) 21 *Australian Bar Review* 224.

3 J J Spigelman, 'Statutory Interpretation and Human Rights', Address to the Pacific Judicial Conference, Vanuatu, 26 July 2005, www.lawlink.nsw.gov.au/lawlink/Supreme_Court/ll_sc.nsf/pages/SCO_speech_spigelman260705.

4 M Kirby 'ALJ @ 80: Past, Present and Future', Address at a conference to celebrate the 80th anniversary of the Australian Law Journal, Sydney, 16 March 2007, www.hcourt.gov.au/speeches/kirbyj/kirbyj_16mar07.pdf.

5 C Allen, 'The Literature of the Law', *Aspects of Justice*, Stevens & Sons Ltd, 1958 at 284.

apply the purpose of the legislation in isolation from a statutory provision giving effect to that purpose. As discussed in Chapter 3, a court must interpret the words used in a statute in the light of their context and purpose. A judge must work out what Parliament intended and give effect to it, even if the judge does not personally agree with the statute. The challenge, of course, is that what Parliament wants is not always clear and obvious.

Before proceeding it is worth noting that the words 'interpretation' and 'construction' are often used interchangeably.[6] This may be seen, for example, in the text of the new s 15AA of the *Acts Interpretation Act 1901* (Cth), which refers to 'interpretation' although the explanatory memorandum about it refers to 'construction' (construal). Is it necessary to interpret every statute, or can a statute in which the meaning is obvious simply be applied? This would appear to be the thrust of Gleeson CJ's extra-judicial comment: 'Unless the meaning of a legal text of any kind, whether it be a will, a contract, or an Act of Parliament, is self-evident, then the text requires interpretation'.[7]

Perhaps one would best use 'interpretation' to work out the meaning of a single word or phrase, and 'construction' to construe the meaning of a whole section or provision. Certainly neither term is used in everyday life—at home if we sat down with a good book we would not say we are 'interpreting' or 'construing' it—and at work, we may say we are 'analysing' data, 'reading' a report, 'perusing' a letter or 'applying' the terms of a contract but we would not usually say we were interpreting or construing these documents. Use of those words inherently suggests that what Parliament produces is either unclear (in need of interpretation) or incomplete (such that the meaning has to be constructed based on what is there). Neither flatters Parliament; perhaps in hindsight 'statutory application' would have been a more innocuous term.

History and evolution of statutory interpretation

Understanding how statutory interpretation evolved from our English origins assists in our understanding of the matrix of rules we use today, some derived from statute and others from common law cases. It must be borne in mind that, prior to the rise of parliament in England, the only form of statute was a decree from the monarch. The eleventh-century early beginnings of the common law following the Norman Conquest had almost nothing to do with statutes, and in the following century, during the reign of Henry II, the itinerant justices who travelled the realm dispensing the

6 *Wilson v Anderson* (2002) 213 CLR 401 per Gleeson CJ at [8].

7 M Gleeson, 'The Meaning of Legislation: Context, Purpose and Respect for Fundamental Rights', Address to Victoria Law Foundation, Melbourne, 31 July 2008.

King's justice were not applying statute law, or even a common law of England, but local customary laws. It was only when Henry II introduced a system of criminal procedures, including the Assize of Clarendon in 1166 and later the Assize of Northampton, followed closely by the writ system, that the beginnings of a coherent body of law could be seen. It would be another 130 years before a Model Parliament was held and a rudimentary system of passing bills through Parliament, followed by royal assent, arose.

It was not until the fourteenth century that the notion of parliamentary sovereignty, giving statute law superiority over common law, resulted from the gradual (and in the case of Charles I, brutal) reduction in the power of the monarch, and the dawning realisation by the courts in the 1530s that statutes were binding, and that there needed to be guidelines for interpreting them. Because statutes were seen as an affront to the common law, courts construed them narrowly. The 'literal' approach to statutory interpretation ostensibly flatters the Parliament by saying that the Parliament must mean what it says: if the meaning of the words was clear then the courts would apply that meaning regardless of the result; but it also protects the common law against excessive incursion by statutes. As long as formalism was the order of the day courts would only apply statutes whose meaning was clear on their face. If they were unclear then (with regret, they said) it was up to Parliament to enact amendments.

The golden rule and the mischief rule both emerged over time[8], but remember that courts would only use these rules when the ordinary meaning created an absurdity or repugnancy. The golden rule could only modify the words to the minimum extent necessary to address drafting errors, and the mischief rule allowed consideration of the mischief that was intended to be remedied but only where that mischief was evident from reading the Act as a whole. There was little reference to extrinsic materials, besides the common law.

For the English penal colony that became Australia, the absence of British judges in the early days meant that the beginnings of this Anglo-Saxon system were more military than civilian. And while the Australian legislature took a long time to develop, English statutes played a key role from the beginning. To use Paul Finn's expression, 'we were born to statutes'.[9]

As Blackstone wrote, colonists carried with them as much English law as was applicable to their new situation, including English statutes and the common law rules for their interpretation, as spelt out in the *Australian Courts Act 1828* (Imp). A proper court system was not implemented until Bigge's damning report on Governor Macquarie reached England, prompting passage of the *New South Wales Act 1823* (Imp) establishing the Supreme Court of New South Wales. The task of our first

8 This book assumes readers have an introductory understanding of statutory interpretation. Readers unfamiliar with the golden and mischief rules should refer to Chapter 9.

9 P Finn, 'Statutes and the Common Law' (1992) 22 *University of Western Australia Law Review* 7 at 8.

Chief Justice, Sir Francis Forbes—applying colonial practices and customs, without the benefit of colonial legislation, in the light of English statutes and common law 'as far as applicable'—could not have been an easy one.

Australia did not have a representative legislature, as opposed to an appointed Legislative Council, until after the *Australian Constitutions Act (No 1) 1842* (Imp). The independence of our legislature was also very late in blooming, due to the doctrine of repugnancy under which local laws that were inconsistent with English law were struck down by the Supreme Court. The repugnancy doctrine as set out in the *Colonial Laws Validity Act 1865* (Imp) applied right up until 1942 at the Commonwealth level, and until 1986 at the State level.[10] That makes for a legislature still in early adulthood at the turn of the twenty-first century. Little wonder that the rules of statutory interpretation are only now crystallising into something distinctly Australian.

The passage of interpretation legislation in the 1980s has set us on a path, with relatively little deviation between the Commonwealth, the states and territories, towards a coherent body of law relating to statutory interpretation. This book aims to synthesise that body of law and to present it in a structured manner. However, just as the obvious inconsistency in laws could not be hidden by Blackstone in his early commentaries, nor can obvious inconsistencies in approaches to statutory interpretation in Australia be clad over. Honesty is the best policy, so inconsistencies are identified and recommendations made where relevant. This is the most logical approach.

What then has been the approach of courts in Australia to interpreting statutes, over the past two centuries? For the greater part, indeed right up to the 1980s, courts were highly conservative, literal, and focused on replicating what could be expected from an English court. There was extreme deference to interpretations by English courts in analogous fact and statutory situations; English cases were cited as authorities with reverence. The four options for the treatment of legislation by the courts, set out over a century ago by legal scholar and former Dean of Harvard Law School Roscoe Pound, remain illustrative even now. He said that courts can:

1 treat statutes as a superior source of law, applying them fully in rule and in principle, and reasoning from them by analogy;
2 treat statutes as being on par with judge-made law, applying them fully and reasoning from them as one would with other judicial decisions;
3 give only direct effect to statutes, favouring a liberal, or broad interpretation; or
4 give only direct effect to statutes, favouring a strict, or narrow interpretation.

When Pound was writing, courts were positioned well and truly in the fourth category. Although he predicted that there was 'coming to be a science of legislation',[11]

10 *Statute of Westminster Act 1942* (Cth) and Australia Acts (1986).
11 R Pound, 'Common Law and Legislation' (1907–8) 21(6) *Harvard Law Review* 383 at 384.

he did acknowledge that courts tended to treat the common law as superior to legislation. His comment was that '[t]he proposition that statutes in derogation of the common law are to be construed strictly … assumes that legislation is something to be deprecated'.[12]

The role of the judiciary in interpreting legislation

Where have we come to today? Paul Finn is of the view that 'judicial treatment of statutes in this country falls into Pound's third and fourth categories',[13] although he considers that while all four have a place, none has 'exclusive sway'.[14] But in some ways we are in the first category, because it is well settled that Parliament can, by enacting legislation, override the common law. There are of course exceptions, such as the role of the High Court in determining the validity of legislation, and the presumption against parliamentary interference with fundamental rights except where express words are used. But on the whole it is recognised that legislation is both prolific and prevailing.

Additionally there has been, as seen in the first and second approaches, a degree of reasoning by analogy from statutes, such as in *R v L* (1991) 174 CLR 379 where, in finding a common law crime of rape in marriage, the High Court reasoned that the notion that

> by reason of marriage there is an irrevocable consent to sexual intercourse … is out of keeping … with recent changes in the criminal law of this country made by statute, which draw no distinction between a wife and other women in defining the offence of rape.

The High Court was reasoning by analogy from a statute to support its reasoning for change of a common law rule.

But what has been inconsistent is the degree to which statutory provisions have been applied. It cannot be said that they are applied 'fully' as in approaches 1 and 2, and sometimes they are applied broadly, as in 4, or narrowly, as in 3. There are rules that lead courts towards a narrow or broad construction of a statutory provision, such as the presumption that beneficial statutes will be broadly construed and penal provisions narrowly construed in favour of the citizen, but otherwise the inconsistency is largely in the approach taken by different judges.

---

12 Ibid at 387.

13 P Finn, 'Statutes and the Common Law' (1992) 22 *University of Western Australia Law Review* 7 at 19.

14 Ibid at 20.

Justice Spigelman has described it as a 'spectrum of judicial opinion':

> It is useful to think of a spectrum of judicial opinion ranging from strict literalism at one end to broadly based purposive interpretation at the other end. That such a spectrum exists, and that it is a wide spectrum, reflects the fact that there are a number of well established principles—like the literal rule, the golden rule and the mischief rule—which do not necessarily point in the same direction. The process of selecting which principle or rule should be given salience in a particular case is a matter of judgement about which reasonable minds can differ.[15]

If this were a book on jurimetrics a hundred pages could be dedicated to tracing judicial reasoning of various High Court judges, showing how their beliefs about the role of a judge in our system of government impacts on the decisions they make. As recently as June 2011, the time of writing, marked differences in approach can be seen for example in the decision of Justice Bell in *Jemena Gas Networks (NSW) Limited v Mine Subsidence Board* [2011] HCA 19. While the remainder of the High Court was willing to adjust the ordinary meaning of the words in the light of the statutory purpose, Bell J in dissent confined her interpretation to the ordinary grammatical meaning of the provision, saying, effectively, that the unreasonable result was caused by the unreasonable provision.

This strongly formalist approach may be contrasted with that of Justice Kirby, known colloquially as 'The Great Dissenter'. See for example his dissenting judgment in *Al-Kateb v Godwin* (2004) 219 CLR 562, where the High Court decided a human being could be held indefinitely in executive detention despite having committed no crime. Kirby J invoked a presumption in favour of liberty and against indefinite detention as a human right which could only be rebutted by express words, which he found were lacking.

There are arguments for and against legal formalism and judicial activism, and there are times when each is called for. A strictly formalist approach puts the onus back on Parliament to correct imperfections and injustice in legislation, and in solving statutory lacunae, the courts are facilitating Parliament's abdication of responsibility. There are also arguments about the separation of powers and the role of the courts. But equally, there is a need, if for no other reason than that the public should have confidence in the court system, to do whatever can be done, within the bounds of statutory interpretation, to do justice as between the parties. Particularly when values are involved, people often feel they know, intuitively, the 'right' outcome to a case. When reading the case exercises in this book, readers are asked to pay close attention

15 J J Spigelman, 'The Intolerable Wrestle: Developments in Statutory Interpretation', Address to the Australasian Conference of Planning and Environment Courts and Tribunals, 1 September 2010, 1.

to their intuitive response, and try to see how it influences their attempt to apply the rules of statutory interpretation to reach that outcome.

This discussion is not tending towards a suggestion that the rule of law be cast aside and judges reason based on fairness (as is still done in some international commercial disputes). It is simply recognising that judges, due to their inherent beliefs about the role of the judiciary, will tend towards different interpretations of statutory provisions. Where the result is that a case outcome may depend on who is on the bench as much as upon what is in the statute, then the rule of law is not best served. Whether an enduring resolution to this problem can be found, or whether it should be accepted as an inherent part of our system, has long been a matter of argument.

What would not be acceptable would be presentation of the outcome of an issue of statutory interpretation as if it were the only, right answer, as though statutory interpretation were akin to a mathematical formula:

$$\text{Issue} + \text{Rules} = \text{Outcome},$$

$$\textit{where}\ \text{Rules} = \frac{\langle \text{words/context} \times \text{purpose} \rangle - \text{maxims} + \text{presumptions}}{(\text{extrinsic materials} = \text{history} + \text{debates} + \text{dictionaries})}$$

This would not do for a court and it would not be a satisfactory response in statutory interpretation exercises. It is preferable to state the available approaches using the rules of statutory interpretation and identify which was chosen, and for what reason. This would assist law students and lawyers alike in understanding the modern approach to statutory interpretation being taken by the courts, and would perhaps enable them to engage in more depth with the bench on these matters. But might it open up judgments to appeal on the basis that the judge applied the wrong rules of statutory interpretation?

This raises the question of whether there is precedent in statutory interpretation. On the one hand, pronouncements of the High Court as to the correct approach to be taken should be followed by lower courts. But the interpretation of a word or phrase in one piece of legislation obviously cannot be used as an authoritative interpretation of another piece of legislation. At each instance, meaning depends not only on the words used, but the context in which they are used. This is the focus of Chapter 3 of this book. Essentially, the approach the court should take will depend on the statutory provision in question—and perhaps, even for conservative judges, the clearer the intention of Parliament and the principle underpinning the statute, the more comfortable they will be in taking an expansive approach, reading where necessary beyond the words, or even reading them as if additional words appeared (this is also considered in Chapter 5).

The time is ripe for the courts to develop a consistent approach to interpreting legislation, particularly in the light of common extra-judicial statements showing its importance. Here is one from former Chief Justice Murray Gleeson:

> Over the past 30 years, there has been a surge of legislative activity reaching into areas that once were occupied exclusively by lawyers' law ... [c]onsequently, applying legislation is now the largest part of the work of modern judges.[16]

Statutory interpretation is a complex task. It can be made more accessible if nation-wide codification is achieved through negotiation by the Standing Committee of Attorneys-General. This can be coupled with greater explanation of statutory interpretation in judgments, more regular and accessible training for lawyers and judges, and a greater focus in law schools.

Structure of this book

Having already discussed the evolution of statutory interpretation and some of the issues with the approaches taken by the judiciary, Chapter 2 focuses on the role of the legislature. It examines how statutes are created, with a view to understanding how the provisions that generate thought-provoking issues of statutory interpretation come about. There is a discussion of the plain English drafting movement, and a discussion of the pros and cons of comprehensive but incomprehensible legislation versus general vague legislation which is comprehensible but leaves a great deal of discretion in the hands of the judiciary.

Chapter 3 proceeds directly to the applicable legislation on the interpretation of legislation. The discussion focuses on the Commonwealth legislation but notes similarities and differences in the state and territory legislation. Chapter 4 goes to the crux of statutory interpretation—the cornerstone provision of the Interpretation Acts—governing the task of interpreting each statutory provision in the light of its context and purpose. This chapter considers what is included in the context, when it is considered, how to find the purpose, the reality of unstated purposes, multiple purposes and conflicting purposes. Chapter 5 continues with the related but distinct notion of intent, which, counter-intuitively, is an objective phenomenon rather than an investigation into the 'actual' intentions of the 'actual' Parliament that passed the 'actual' statute. Chapter 5 also looks at interpretive techniques which give courts a way to shrink or strain the meaning of statutory provisions in their effort to give effect to the purpose of the legislation.

16 M Gleeson, 'The Meaning of Legislation: Context, Purpose and Respect for Fundamental Rights' Address to Victoria Law Foundation, Melbourne, 31 July 2008, 4.

Chapter 6 considers all elements of statutory interpretation that can be found within the statute itself. These are referred to as intrinsic materials. They include everything from preambles, objects clauses, definition sections and syntax through to headings and margin notes. This discussion of the component parts of a statute is followed by discussion of the words themselves in Chapter 7. Chapter 8 then considers all elements of statutory interpretation that are external to the statute. These are referred to as extrinsic materials. Close attention is paid to the relevant legislative provisions, and different kinds of extrinsic materials are examined, along with examples of their use by the courts.

Chapter 9 returns to common law approaches, considering the degree to which the old Literal Rule, Golden Rule and Mischief Rule play a role today, and referring to the ongoing (albeit diminished) use of Latin maxims for interpretation. Chapter 10 focuses on common law statutory presumptions, some of which are strengthening rather than fading in the face of the modern statutory approach. Chapter 11 takes one of those presumptions—that Parliament does not intend to interfere with fundamental rights—and couples it with a recent legislative development in Victoria and the ACT of statutory bills of rights, whereby statutes are interpreted subject to human rights. Chapter 12 continues the theme to some extent by considering the application of international law in statutory interpretation, in relation both to the presumption that Parliament intends to legislate in conformity with international law and the unsettled place of customary international law and general principles of law.

Chapter 13 considers specific instruments, with the interpretation of delegated legislation and other instruments such as guidelines, rulings and so forth by quasi-legislative bodies such as the Australian Securities and Investments Commission (ASIC) as well as the interpretation of codes, and wills, deeds, contracts and agreements.

Chapter 14 brings the findings in the book together in a practical methodology for statutory interpretation. An attempt has been made to provide a first iteration of an index to the rules of statutory interpretation, referred to as Statutory Interpretation Index 1 ('SII1'). It goes on to provide a practical methodology for approaching complex questions of statutory interpretation, and includes a complete case scenario to which statutory interpretation rules are applied using the methodology. There are also four full practice scenarios, including facts, law, and materials such as second reading speeches and explanatory memoranda. They may be used in law schools which continue to 'embed' statutory interpretation across the curriculum. They are also appropriate for moot activities, with student groups acting for each party, and a further student group acting as judges. An assessment task could involve handing up written submissions ahead of oral argument, with students in the role of judges having to prepare a written judgment which is defended orally. Where these exercises are used in continuing legal education, outcomes reached by independent consideration can be compared with those of colleagues.

Most chapters also include smaller 'case exercises' in which major cases on statutory interpretation are disaggregated and presented as a problem scenario to the reader. The pedagogy behind this technique is to shift an otherwise passive adult learning method of reading into active learning in which the reader constructs their knowledge through attempting to apply their knowledge of relevant principles of statutory interpretation. Once the mind is made up, the reader is able to compare their interpretation with the interpretation reached in the real decision.

Guidelines for interpretation of this book

1 No book can be all things to all people. This is a book on statutory interpretation, and while cases relating to substantive areas of law are considered, they should not be treated as entire case summaries. Cases may have three or more key issues, and if only one of these is an issue of statutory interpretation, that is the issue focused upon. Similarly, cases may have numerous facts, and facts not material to the issue of statutory interpretation are excluded.

2 Case exercises are to illuminate the process of statutory interpretation. Accordingly, fact matrices are presented as being current or recently occurring when in reality, depending on when the case was decided, they may be anywhere up to 70 years old. This is to give a sense of immediacy, and there may be scenarios which present statutory provisions that have since been amended or repealed.

3 The focus of this book is on using illustrative examples of the application of the rules of statutory interpretation. It is not an encyclopaedic loose leaf service, so it does not footnote numerous cases on each point or attempt to cover the minutiae of rules which may have been used a hundred years ago by English courts.

4 The focus is on statutory interpretation in Australia. Where there is an Australian authority for a rule, it is used in preference to a preceding English authority. Similarly, where a High Court authority is available, it is used in preference to state court authorities. Finally, where a recent illustration of a statutory interpretation principle is available, it is given priority. Also, quotes from cases are given wherever possible and references contained within quotes have been omitted.

5 Readers must cast aside any pre-conceived notions about statutes being tedious and boring, or equating the experience of interpreting statutes to passing time in Siberia clothed in a hair shirt. Statutory interpretation can be fascinating if it is given a chance. Have faith.

CHAPTER 2

CREATION OF LEGISLATION

Understanding how legislation is drafted by the Executive and then created by Parliament—the mechanics *and* the dynamics—is essential to interpreting legislation. The discussion in this chapter focuses on Federal Parliament, recognising that the bicameral process is replicated in all jurisdictions except Queensland, which has just one House of Parliament. However in all jurisdictions the processes are similar. This chapter also focuses on primary legislation. Delegated legislation is the focus of Chapter 13.

Legislative power

It is noted at the outset that constitutions are the font of power for the legislature, executive and judicature. Federal legislative powers are limited to the enumerated heads of power in s 51 of the Commonwealth Constitution, with residual powers remaining with the states. There is a separation of powers but this does not mean a separation of *persons*—for example a government minister is both a Member of Parliament and a member of the Executive.

The legislature has the power to replace or significantly alter whole areas of common law (consider the effect of the *Civil Liability Act 2002* (NSW) on torts law for example) or create entirely new areas of law in response to changed community values. It can be responsive to potential threats arising from new technologies, such as bioterrorism or human cloning,[1] or drive changes in society through legislation. Discrimination law is one example.

Drafting styles

Before a proposed law can be moved in Parliament in the form of a Bill, it must be drafted completely. This differs, for example, from the way international treaties are made, where various options for some provisions are included in the draft. A decision must be made about the preferred form of the law that the Minister will put forward, bearing in mind the Minister's assessment of the likely support the bill will attract in that form.

In terms of drafting styles, there are two key approaches. The first involves drafting a general provision and leaving its scope for courts to determine. The most well known example of this drafting style was s 52 of the *Trade Practices Act 1974* (Cth), repealed in 2011. It provided quite simply that a corporation 'shall not engage in conduct

1 For a discussion see T Faunce, 'Health Legislation: Interpretation Coherent with Conscience and International Human Rights', in Corcoran, S and Bottomley, S (eds) *Interpreting Statutes* (Federation Press, 2005) 299.

that is misleading or deceptive'. Enormous volumes of litigation resulted from that provision, so that ultimately, virtually every civil dispute in contracts and torts included an alleged breach of s 52. The second drafting style is detailed, attempting to provide a clear and comprehensive law that will minimise the scope for judicial discretion in interpretation. Knowing that users of the legislation will seek to interpret legislative provisions to suit their own purposes, attempts are made to make the legislation as watertight as possible.

These approaches have been described by Lisbeth Campbell as 'fussy' versus 'fuzzy' drafting.[2] She aligns the former approach with the common law legal system and the latter with the civil law system: 'the civil tradition of legislative drafting favours openness and generality … while the common law tradition favour precision and particularity'.[3] The reason for the common law 'fussy' approach lies in history: rather than having Codes laying down the law, the bulk of law was derived from court decisions, and eighteenth-century courts viewed legislation as secondary to common law. Accordingly, to get courts to apply legislation to its full extent and not read it down, drafters had to be as clear and specific as possible.[4]

Each style has its pros and cons, summarised in the table below:

	Pros	**Cons**
Civil tradition	• Clear and easy to comprehend • Law is more accessible to lay people	• Judges have broad powers and discretion in applying the law • General principles lend themselves to varying interpretations which can create inconsistent case outcomes
Common law tradition	• Specific and detailed • Precise • Comprehensive • More certain • Judicial discretion is contained	• Complicated and elaborate provisions can be difficult to comprehend • Results in enormous amounts of law which is less accessible

As will be seen below, the passage of bills through Parliament is a process of compromise, and in some circumstances it may be preferable to get legislation passed, even if it includes vague language, than have the bill fail altogether. It just results in the courts having to determine the meaning of the otherwise indeterminate language. Often central concepts remain undefined in legislation, which leaves the courts to

2 See also Peter Bayne's discussion of 'fuzzy' drafting in the context of interpreting statutes on administrative law: P Bayne, 'Fuzzy Drafting and the Interpretation of Statutes in the Administrative State' (1992) 66 *Australian Law Journal* 523.

3 L Campbell, 'Legal Drafting Styles: Fuzzy or Fussy?' (1996) 3(2) *E Law Murdoch University Electronic Journal of Law*, www.murdoch.edu.au/elaw/issues/v3n2/campbell.html (accessed 23 June 2011) [1].

4 Ibid at [7].

settle upon the ambit of their meaning. For example 'import' is not defined in the *Customs Act 1901* (Cth) and 'assault' is not defined in the *Crimes Act 1900* (NSW). [5]

Plain English drafting

Statutes are not a popular form of prose. Few people would choose to settle down on a Sunday afternoon with the latest copy of the corporations law. It would be unusual for a non-lawyer to ponder a question and choose to look online to locate the relevant legislation in order to find out their legal rights and responsibilities. Instead, they might ask a lawyer friend, any friend with an opinion, visit a community law centre, phone a talk back radio station or google the topic online. Most would reach a conclusion as to whether they have a case or not before even visiting a lawyer's office to have their situation closely examined.

Not only does this attitude towards statutes have an impact on the general populace, but many lawyers also read statutes as a last resort, perhaps only when a text or encyclopaedia cannot provide a sufficiently meaningful explanation of what the statute says. As Michael Kirby has said, lawyers 'find the obligation to read Acts of Parliament, from beginning to end, so distasteful that they will do almost anything to postpone the labour'.[6] While there is a general expectation that a statute be read as a whole, it can reasonably be claimed that few lawyers in practice would habitually read beyond immediately relevant provisions and perhaps the definition sections.

It is a genuine difficulty, in a society where (a) ignorance of the law is no excuse and (b) legal advice costs money, to have laws that are incomprehensible except to those legally trained (and often even legal experts have differing views). Further, there is no system for seeking a declaration from the court as to whether an intended course of action is legal, commercial and private parties alike must simply take the risk that their legal advice was wrong.

There has in recent years been a shift towards 'plain English' drafting, based on the not unreasonable view that legislation should be comprehensible to the average person in society, who has basic education but does not have legal training. Plain English drafting favours a simple and straightforward style, using language that is direct and familiar, getting rid of unnecessary words, and avoiding long-winded and complicated sentences. The sections are shorter and the structure of legislation more user-friendly.

5 See the discussion in Miriam Gani, 'Codifying the Criminal Law: Issues of Interpretation' in Corcoran, S and Bottomley, S (eds) *Interpreting Statutes* (Federation Press, 2005) 197, 211.

6 M Kirby, 'Towards a Grand Theory of Interpretation: The Case of Statutes and Contracts' (2003) 24(2) *Statute Law Review* 95 at 96–7.

For example the *Acts Interpretation Act 1901* (Cth) was amended in 2011 to incorporate elements of plain English style. A 'simplified outline' of the Act was included at the start of the Act, giving an overview and introducing the structure of the Act. A general provision was included in s 2(2) that the application of the Act and any of its provisions is 'subject to a contrary intention' which saved having such a statement repeated throughout the provisions in the Act.[7] Definitions which were previously spread across several sections were grouped together in a new section 2B, and there was some tidying up of provisions which previously referred, for example, to the commencement of Acts which had been passed before 1937. The ACT Act goes so far as to replace the expression 'interpreting' with 'working out the meaning of'.[8]

In practice, it is extremely difficult to draft legislation in plain English. Bear in mind that a number of drafting conventions already exist, and assumptions are made as between legislative drafters and courts, meaning that drafters can anticipate how their provisions will be interpreted, and courts can infer what drafters were trying to achieve with their words. Where each does what the other expects of them, a symbiotic relationship prevails. To facilitate the drafting of statutes in plain English, it may be necessary to drop some of these conventions, and courts will therefore have less confidence in receiving the message sent by the drafters in their choice of statutory language. Additionally, where legislation that has been in force for some time is rewritten and passed in plain English, the challenge then becomes, is the new Act merely the old law in a new format, or has the substance of the provisions changed? This may generate additional litigation, since lawyers cannot advise clients with a degree of confidence until the new provisions are tested in the courts.

Section 15AC of the *Acts Interpretation Act 1901* (Cth) provides that: [9]

> Where:
>
> (a) an Act has expressed an idea in a particular form of words; and
>
> (b) a later Act appears to have expressed the same idea in a different form of words for the purpose of using a clearer style;
>
> the ideas shall not be taken to be different merely because different forms of words were used.

In *Commissioner of Taxation v Stone* (2005) 222 CLR 289 the Court considered income tax legislation in which, sixty years later, the legislation was redrafted in plain

---

7 This was already the case in s 4 of the *Interpretation Act 1984* (WA).

8 See s 138 of the *Legislation Act 2001* (ACT).

9 See for the states and territories: s 14C of the *Acts Interpretation Act 1954* (Qld), s 147 of the *Legislation Act 2001* (ACT) and s 62C of the *Interpretation Act* (NT).

English. The issue in the case was whether receipt of prize money, grants and sponsorship by Joanna Stone, a police officer who also competed professionally in javelin throwing, was assessable income for taxation purposes. Was she running a business in professional sport? The *Income Tax Assessment Act 1936* (Cth) had referred to income from personal exertion as including proceeds from any business. The *Income Tax Assessment Act 1997* (Cth) stated in s 1–3 that it covered the same provisions in a 'rewritten form' and that 'the ideas are not to be taken to be different just because different forms of words were used'. Kirby J considered that the plain English project had been left incomplete: 'To some extent it has complicated matters by the need to reconcile the 1997 Act and the 1936 Act. In particular circumstances, of which this is one, the consequence of the supposed simplification has been to produce an additional complication'.

In *Halwood Corporation Ltd v Roads Corporation* [1998] 2 VR 439 the Court of Appeal of the Supreme Court of Victoria, per Tadgell JA with Brooking and Ormiston JJA concurring, discussed the trend towards redrafting existing legislation in 'plain English'. This entailed replacing 'receive' with 'get', 'notify' with 'tell', 'required' with 'needed', 'discover' with 'find out', and finally 'shall' with 'must': at 445. It was this last alteration which the Court had issue with, seeing 'must not' as a blunt instrument compared with 'shall not'. The following comment was made by Tadgell JA at 445:

> According to the Hansard record of relevant ministerial remarks, the Bill for the Act was avowedly cast in 'plain English'. Despite that, Pt 5 is not free from ambiguity and some of its English words, while individually plain, do not readily reveal easily comprehensible concepts ... It seemed to be common ground that the Act suffers from inconsistency of language and a corresponding want of precision conducing to awkwardness of interpretation ... plain English alone achieves nothing: to be useful it must run in tandem with clear thought.

Ormiston JA at 452 stated:

> The vice, so far, of plain English is not so much in the concept as in its execution. It is no use redrafting statutes unless the person responsible for the redrafting has a complete understanding of what it is that has to be achieved. It is difficult enough to amend existing laws let alone to rephrase and reorganise statutory concepts which have been understood in a particular way over many years ... 'plain English' cannot simplify complex concepts and it is more frequently the need to simplify the concepts that is required rather than the use of 'modern' language. Again, well instructed minds can achieve that end but if the concepts are not to be changed, clarity will not always lead to brevity.

It makes sense that new laws be drafted from the outset in plain English, and judicial interpretation clarify their scope, rather than constantly referring back to the interpretation of the relevant provisions under the 'unplain' version of the statute and deciding whether they apply to the plain version or not. Over time, as plain English drafting becomes the norm, the courts will no doubt develop new conventions for interpreting legislation drafted in plain English, and those conventions will be referred in a future edition of this book.

Drafting conventions

Draft legislation takes a standard form. Ruth Sullivan has described it this way: 'An Act is a distinct literary genre, like a sonnet or a play. Like poets and playwrights, legislative drafters are constrained by a number of conventions, which interpreters rely on in determining the intended meaning of the text'.[10] Acts uniformly commence with a Long Title and the words 'the Parliament enacts', followed by the substantive clauses. They may be grouped, using headings such as Chapter, Part, Division and Subdivision, although the most common groups used in legislation these days is Parts and Divisions. At the end of the substantive clauses there may be Schedules.

Amending bills also have a standard format similar to the original Act, but typically the text of the amendments is included in Schedules to the amending Act. The format must for each amendment state 'Omit ... and Insert'. Where new sections are inserted, letters are used, from A to Z. So for example a new section between 10 and 11 becomes 10A rather than being the new 11 and the old 11 becoming 12. This assists with the interpretation task because one can look at how a particular numbered provision has been interpreted without it having change number several times over the years as new provisions are added.

Draft legislation must be in the exact form in which it will be passed, if it is passed, so it cannot include side comments explaining why specific provisions have been worded a certain way, nor can it provide alternatives in case the proposed wording is considered problematic. Instead, the explanations go in a separate, accompanying document, the explanatory memorandum.

In legislation, drafters use a variety of expressions to represent the relationship towards, or connection between, different entities, persons or things. For example 'with respect to', 'in relation to', 'by way of', 'by reason of', 'in connection with', 'as a consequence of', 'in accordance with', 'as a result of', 'the result of', 'by reference to', 'with regard to', 'in consideration of' and so on. Not infrequently the crux of a case turns on the scope of these expressions. But their scope cannot be objectively determined and defined because it depends on the context in which they are used.

---

10 R Sullivan, 'Statutory Interpretation in Canada: The Legacy of Elmer Driedger' in *Statutory Interpretation: Principles and Pragmatism for a New Age* (Judicial Commission of New South Wales, 2007) 105 at 116.

Accordingly, one cannot rely on the interpretation of a particular word or phrase from another case relating to another statute, or to another part of the same statute.

The political dimension

As each bill must be passed by both Houses[11] and assented to by the Governor-General (as the Queen's representative),[12] the composition of each House is relevant in understanding the compromise that is often involved in the successful enactment of new law.

The Senate has 76 elected Senators, including twelve per state and two per territory. The House of Representatives has 150 elected Members of Parliament, and the political party or coalition with majority support forms the Government. Their leader becomes the Prime Minister, appointed by the Governor-General, and other members in the leading party or coalition become the government ministers. Government ministers are both Members of Parliament and members of the Executive Government, administering a portfolio and sitting together with the Governor-General as the Federal Executive Council. Senior ministers form the Cabinet, whose decisions are legally ratified by the Federal Executive Council. The Governor-General appoints High Court judges on advice from the Federal Executive Council, showing the interplay between the three arms of government.

Members of Parliament tend to vote along party lines, which means that a government bill initiated in the House of Representatives has little problem passing in that House. However, over the past three decades governments have tended not to hold a majority in the Senate. Accordingly, much more compromise has been needed in the details of bills, with the views of opposition parties and minor parties being taken into account. In 2010 Campbell Sharman commented on the positive impact this has had on the Senate:

> It is not just that the party or parties in government do not control a partisan majority on the floor of the Senate, but that, for most of the period since 1955, governments have had to gain the support of one or more independent or minor party senators to pass measures through the Senate. From this lack of government control has sprung the independent role of the Senate in scrutinising legislation and in holding governments publicly accountable through the use of an extensive committee system.[13]

11 Except in Queensland which, as noted earlier, has a unicameral legislature (one house of Parliament).
12 In the case of the states, the relevant Governor assents to Acts.
13 C Sharman, 'The Representation of Small Parties and Independents', www.aph.gov.au/senate/pubs/pops/pop34/c13.htm.

Parliamentary procedures

Bills may be initiated in either the House of Representatives or the Senate, although typically they originate in the House of Representatives. Most bills are government bills (as opposed to Private Members' bills introduced by non-ministers) and are introduced by the Minister responsible for the relevant portfolio covering the subject matter of the proposed law. The bill is accompanied by an explanatory memorandum signed by the Minister, explaining the proposed law and summarising its contents.

Procedures for the passage of bills in both houses are very similar.[14] They include various stages, namely initiation, first reading,[15] second reading, referral (where relevant) to a committee for public consultation, consideration and advice, consideration in detail[16] (including proposed amendments), adoption, third reading, and transmission to the other House for concurrence (typically from the House to the Senate, but of course Senate bills go the other way). The bill may be returned to the House in which it originated 'as is' or with amendments. There may be some negotiation by way of messages between the Houses to address remaining issues. Once settled the bill is presented by the Attorney-General for assent by the Governor-General.[17] At the time of assent the Bill becomes an Act of Parliament, with the clauses and sub-clauses of the Bill becoming sections and subsections of the Act.

As a Bill passes through both Houses of Parliament amendments are frequently made. These must be relevant to the subject matter of the bill, as set out in the long title, and they must propose the omission of some words and the insertion of others. According to the Senate, approximately one-third of bills are amended.[18] Government amendments are usually prepared by government drafters, while non-government members are assisted by the clerk. Relevantly, as the bill passes between the Houses in negotiating amendments, agreed provisions may not be revisited, only those that remain unsettled. This may cause Parliament to consider matters at issue divorced

---

14 For more information on parliamentary practice and procedure see H Evans (ed) *Odger's Australian Senate Practice* (12th edn) at www.aph.gov.au/Senate/pubs/odgers/contents.htm and House of Representatives Practice (5th edn) at www.aph.gov.au/house/pubs/PRACTICE/index.htm.

15 Prior to the ready availability of printed copies of bills, all draft legislation was read out from start to finish in Parliament. In practice now, Members of Parliament will have received a printed copy before Parliament sits, so the process is a formality where it is simply stated, for example, 'The bill is read a first time'.

16 Although courts are exhorted to focus on the Act as a whole, Bills are by default considered in an established order, namely clauses in numerical order, the Schedules, then clauses that have been postponed, the preamble and then the title. It is only by leave that a Bill may be considered as a whole: see Standing Order 149 of the Commonwealth House of Representatives.

17 In the event of a deadlock, a double dissolution may occur, in which both Houses are dissolved. Elections are then held for both Houses and, if necessary, a joint sitting of both Houses occurs to vote on the Bill.

18 Senate, 'Brief Guides to Senate Procedure No. 9: Consideration of Legislation', www.aph.gov.au/Senate/pubs/guides/briefno09.htm.

from the Act as a whole, which can result in a change to a provision that does not sit well with the remainder of the legislation. As Hilary Penfold QC commented, 'Parliamentary amendments may be good for democracy but they are not good for the coherence of legislation'.[19]

Legislation example

While extreme examples of awkward legislative drafting are easy targets, and law students may scoff at ambiguous wording in legislation, the reality discussed above is that legislation involves compromise, and there is often little time to contemplate the finer points. As Mason AC has said, 'Judges may need to remind themselves that legislative drafters often work to produce gold from dross within particularly short timeframes'.[20] Amendments which occur as the Bill passes through Parliament may unsettle the balance of the legislation or create inconsistencies or impracticalities. Below is an example of a Commonwealth Act, tracing its experience, to show how amendments come about both prior to, and after, enactment.

Renewable Energy (Electricity) Act 2000 (Cth)

The impetus for this legislation came from a government promise made in 1997 to introduce a mandatory requirement that electricity retailers and large users source an additional two per cent of their electricity consumption from renewable energy. The aim was to increase the contribution of renewable energy generation to Australia's electricity supply. This is in the context that electricity generation is the largest single contributor to Australia's greenhouse gas emissions, accounting for over one-third of total emissions.

The Renewable Energy (Electricity) Bill 2000 was first introduced into the House of Representatives on 22 June 2000, where it was read for a first time. The Long Title was:

> A Bill for an Act for the establishment and administration of a scheme to encourage additional electricity generation from renewable energy sources, and for related purposes.

Clause 161 of the Bill had a standard provision on the making of regulations:

161 Regulations

19 H Penfold, 'Legislative Drafting and Statutory Interpretation' in *Statutory Interpretation: Principles and Pragmatism for a New Age* (Judicial Commission of New South Wales, 2007) 81 at 92.

20 K Mason, 'The Intent of Legislators: How Judges Discern It and What They Do if They Find It', in *Statutory Interpretation: Principles and Pragmatism for a New Age* (Judicial Commission of New South Wales, 2007) 33 at 33.

> The Governor-General may make regulations prescribing all matters:
>
> (a) required or permitted by this Act to be prescribed; or
> (b) necessary or convenient to be prescribed for carrying out or giving effect to this Act;
>
> and, in particular, may make regulations prescribing penalties not exceeding a fine of 50 penalty units for offences against the regulations.

The second reading was moved the same day but debate was adjourned. It took place on 29 June 2000, at which time the Bill was also read a third time and the Bill was sent to the Senate for concurrence.

The Senate already had notice of the Bill prior to its being formally sent from the House of Representatives—already, on 28 June 2000, the Senate had referred the Bill to a Standing Committee (the Environment, Communications, Information Technology and the Arts Reference Committee). The Committee held a hearing on 13 July 2000, and was addressed by various persons who had made submissions on the Bill. Reference was made to the amount of time that had already been expended on this Bill, including a technical working committee which took 15 months to reach a consensus, and a further five months for consensus with the states and other stakeholders. There was clear preference for the Bill to pass without delay, with provision for review after two or three years of operation. In the afternoon the Committee heard from the Honourable Peter Elliot Rae, Chairman of Renewable Energy Generators Australia Limited. Mr Rae stated, *inter alia*:

> The regulations are to be an important part—some people have said that the devil is in the detail in relation to this legislation. It is a matter of some concern that so much is to be in the regulations and so much of the effectiveness of this will depend on what is in the regulations. We do not want to see it held up in any way, we want to see the regulations being able to move forward, but we would like to see that the drafting of the regulations is a consultative process. There ought to be some representatives of the industry who will be affected by this who can participate.

The Senate received the Bill formally from the House of Representatives on 14 August 2000, when it was read for the first time. The second reading was moved the same day but debate was adjourned. The following day the Standing Committee report was tabled and it was resolved to publish the report.[21] The Bill was read a second time, after which it was considered in detail during the Committee Stage, on 28 August, 3, 4, 5, and 9 October, at which time it was reported by the Committee with amendments, and the report was adopted. The Bill was then formally read a third time and the Amended Bill returned to the House of Representatives for concurrence.

---

21 Environment, Communications, Information Technology and the Arts References Committee Report, August 2000. The report was in two volumes and included 33 submissions.

The Amended Bill contained 24 amendments. Amendment 23 provided:

> Clause 161, page 94 [after line 23], at the end of the clause, add:
>
> (2) Draft regulations must be made available for public comment for a period of not less than 30 days before the regulations are made.

In the House of Representatives on that same day, 9 October, the Bill with Senate amendments was reported. Some of the Senate amendments were accepted (Nos 3, 4, 8 to 16 and 21) and others rejected (Nos 1, 2, 5 to 7, 17 to 20, 22 and 23). In relation to No. 24, amendments were made in place of the Senate's purported amendments, and the Amended Bill was returned to the Senate for concurrence.

The reason for rejecting Amendment 23 was as follows:

> This amendment would substantially delay the implementation of this measure and as a result, the scheme would not be able to commence on 1 January 2001 ... A 30 day consultation process would substantially reduce the likelihood that the regulations for this measure could be tabled in the 2000 sitting period.

The following day, 10 October, the Bill was received into the Senate and further considered. The Bill was further considered by the Senate Committee on 11 October and 7 December, at which time the Committee reported back. The Senate resolved to insist upon some of its amendments disagreed upon by the House (Nos 1, 5, 6, 17 to 20 and 23) but not others (Nos 2 and 7), for which amended amendments were proposed. The proposed No 24 was rejected and another version proposed. The Bill was returned to the House of Representatives.

The same day, 7 December, the House of Representatives received the Bill, considered it further and resolved to agree to the amendments insisted upon by the Senate. Accordingly, the Bill passed all stages. On 21 December 2000 the Bill received Assent, making it an Act. It commenced 28 days later.

The final s 161 of *Renewable Energy (Electricity) Act 2000* (Cth) read:

> 161 Regulations
>
> (1) The Governor-General may make regulations prescribing all matters:
>
> (a) required or permitted by this Act to be prescribed; or
>
> (b) necessary or convenient to be prescribed for carrying out or giving effect to this Act;
>
> and, in particular, may make regulations prescribing penalties not exceeding a fine of 50 penalty units for offences against the regulations.
>
> (2) Draft regulations must be available for public comment for a period of not less than 30 days before the regulations are made.

Although the motivation for including public consultation on the regulations was well intended, it created problems in practice which necessitated amendment of the legislation.

This is because one aspect of the Renewable Energy (Electricity) Bill 2000 (Cth) was the creation of a 'Renewable Power Percentage'.

39 Regulations to specify renewable power percentage

(1) The *renewable power percentage* for a year is the percentage specified in the regulations.

The regulation specifying a percentage for a year must be made on or before 31 March in the year.

(2) If the regulations do not specify a percentage for a year, the percentage for the year is:
  (a) for the year commencing on 1 January 2001—0.24%; and
  (b) for any later year—the rate worked out using the formula:

$$\text{Renewable power percentage for the previous year} \times \frac{\text{Required GWh for the year}}{\text{Required GWh for the previous year}}$$

The challenge was that the percentage had to be specified by 31 March each year, and before the regulation could be made there had to be 30 days for public consultation. In practice, the data from the previous year could not be collated and analysed until the middle of February, and there was no time for analysis and drafting of regulations to meet the legislative timeframes. Therefore, the *Renewable Energy (Electricity) Amendment Act 2006* (Cth) provided:

190 Subsection 161(1)

Omit (1).

191 Subsection 161(2)

Repeal the subsection.

The Explanatory Memorandum to the Renewable Energy (Electricity) Amendment Bill 2006 (Cth) did not explain the reason for the change. It merely said:

Item 191—Subsection 161(2)

182. This item repeals subsection 161(2) of the Act which will expedite the regulation making process by removing the requirement for draft new or amended regulations to be made available for public comment for 30 days before they are made.

The amended legislation can work in a practical sense, but public consultation is no longer provided for. This may not in reality create too great a problem, as the main need for public consultation was on the regulations as they were first determined. But removal of public consultation may be a reflection of a preference by bureaucrats to decide the way forward, unburdened by the extra work and effort involved in consultation.

In conclusion, it can be seen that amendments made to draft legislation as it passes through Parliament, regardless of how well intentioned, may create unforeseen challenges in its implementation. We cannot blame this on parliamentarians, when we alone have the gift of hindsight.

Conclusion

It will never be possible to provide perfectly clear and uniform legislation, and perfectly uniform interpretation. Words are necessarily vague, and take on different meanings when they are applied in different contexts. Parliamentary compromises may be made during informal consultations that are not reflected in the Hansard records. As Gleeson CJ has said:

> Acts of Parliament often require interpretation. Their meaning is not always self-evident, and in any event the volume and complexity of legislation produces inconsistency and uncertainty. Whether it is described as a science or an art, statutory interpretation is of central importance to the daily work of all judges.[22]

In practice, issues arise not only from the lack of clarity in the rules, 'but also because those affected by them have a vested interest in misunderstanding and misinterpreting the rules so as to achieve a more palatable outcome for themselves ... Sincere or not, much legal debate is more a battle between conflicting 'try ons' rather than an impartial attempt to arrive at a consensus on public meanings'.[23] Barristers for each party will propose an interpretation the court should give a legislative provision, depending upon what best suits their client's interests. The court, however, is not limited to the interpretations presented to it, being free to decide on its own method of interpretation. This was stated by Kirby J in *Coleman v Power* (2004) 220 CLR 1 at [243]:

> [I]f parties do not address the interpretive point in argument (many do), that is their choice. It is not the judicial obligation to put specifically to parties, least of all well-resourced

22 M Gleeson, 'The Meaning of Legislation: Context, Purpose and Respect for Fundamental Rights' Address to Victoria Law Foundation, Melbourne, 31 July 2008, 5.

23 T Campbell, 'Ethical Interpretation and Democratic Positivism' in Corcoran, S and Bottomley, S (eds) *Interpreting Statutes* (Federation Press, 2005) 83, 90.

> governmental parties, every rule of statutory construction relevant to the performance of the judicial task. Subject to considerations of procedural fairness, this Court may adopt a construction of legislation that has not been argued by the parties, and a fortiori it is not restricted to the interpretive principles argued by their representatives.

The focus of the Court is on working out what Parliament meant, not on choosing between the interpretations the parties wish it meant. The Court must give effect to the will of Parliament even if to do so is personally repugnant to the judges themselves. As stated recently by French CJ in *Rowe v Electoral Commissioner* [2010] HCA 46 at [29]:

> If a law subject to constitutional challenge is a law within the legislative competency of the Parliament that enacts it, the question whether it is a good law or a bad law is a matter for the Parliament and, ultimately, the people to whom the members of the Parliament are accountable.

The courts do not always please Parliament with their conclusions. But, of course, if Parliament is not satisfied with the court's interpretation of a statute, it can always pass amending legislation.

CHAPTER 3

INTERPRETATION LEGISLATION

In accordance with the doctrine of parliamentary sovereignty, any rules set down by Parliament prevail over any conflicting common law rules of statutory interpretation. It is therefore appropriate to cover the Interpretation Acts before common law rules, noting that in practice the Interpretation Acts in many respects align with the common law approaches. It should be noted, however, that while the legislature can pass legislation saying how the courts should interpret statutes, it cannot interfere with that interpretation by the courts.[1] Legislation can be passed prospectively to get around problematic interpretation, but this does not change the actual interpretation in the specific case that drew Parliament's attention to the fact that its legislation was not being interpreted in the intended manner.

The Federal Parliament and the parliaments of each state and territory have passed interpretation legislation as follows:

- *Acts Interpretation Act 1901* (Cth)
- *Legislation Act 2001* (ACT)
- *Interpretation Act 1987* (NSW)
- *Interpretation of Legislation Act 1984* (Vic)
- *Acts Interpretation Act 1954* (Qld)
- *Interpretation Act 1984* (WA)
- *Acts Interpretation Act 1915* (SA)
- *Acts Interpretation Act 1931* (Tas)
- *Interpretation Act* (NT)

These Acts are referred to countless times in this book. For ease of reference, 'the Queensland Interpretation Act' or the 'ACT Interpretation Act' is a reference to the Acts listed above. As will be seen in this chapter, the Interpretation Acts are mostly uniform across all jurisdictions in Australia. Needless to say, each Interpretation Act should be used to interpret Acts in its own jurisdiction—the Commonwealth Act is used to interpret Federal legislation, the New South Wales Act to interpret New South Wales legislation, and so on. Note that while the years of the above acts may suggest their provisions have been in place for some decades, in practice some provisions have been updated quite recently. For example the Commonwealth Act was significantly amended as recently as December 2011.

Additionally, the Interpretation Acts apply equally to primary and delegated legislation—see s 136 of the ACT Act, s 46 of the Cth Act, s 2 of the *Legislative Instruments Act 2003* (Cth), s 5 of the NSW Act, s 4 of the NT Act, s 3A of the SA Act, s 4 of the Tas Act, s 4 of the Vic Act, and s 3 of the WA Act. In Queensland see *Statutory Instruments Act 1992* (Qld), Schedule 1, which lists the provisions of the

1 See generally the discussion in T Campbell, 'Ethical Interpretation and Democratic Positivism' in Corcoran, S and Bottomley, S (eds) *Interpreting Statutes* (Federation Press, 2005) 83, 86.

Interpretation Act that apply to statutory instruments. If forms of delegated legislation are not covered, then the common law rules will apply.[2]

The Interpretation Acts perform two main functions. First, they contain generic provisions which apply in all legislation unless the legislation specifies otherwise. As Gleeson CJ stated in *Attorney-General (Qld) v Australian Industrial Relations Commission* (2002) 213 CLR 485 at [7]:

> The *Acts Interpretation Act 1901* (Cth) is, according to its long title, an Act for the interpretation of Acts of Parliament and for shortening their language. It shortens the language of Acts of Parliament by making it unnecessary for Parliament to enact elaborate and repetitive provisions anticipating possible uncertainties and declaring the legislative intention on those points.

Second, the Interpretation Acts contain instructions to the courts to consider the purpose of the legislation and, where relevant, extrinsic materials.

Gleeson CJ has made these extrajudicial comments on the above two purposes of the Interpretation Acts:

> Some of the principles according to which a court looks for the meaning of a statute are themselves contained in legislation, either in the form of a general interpretation Act, or in specific interpretation provisions in a particular statute. General interpretation Acts serve two main purposes. For drafting convenience, they set out certain ground rules, such as a provision that, unless the contrary intention appears, certain words will have a particular meaning or effect. This saves unnecessary repetition and explanation. More significantly for present purposes, such Acts also state general rules to be applied in finding the meaning of statutes. Parliament enacts legislation upon an assumption that the meaning of what it says will be understood in accordance with those general rules. Interpretation Acts set out the working assumptions according to which legislation is framed by Parliament, and applied by the courts. In addition, the courts themselves have developed principles of interpretation, based on logic, common sense and experience. Those principles are known to drafters of legislation.[3]

The generic provisions in each of the Interpretation Acts are the focus of the present chapter—some are also considered in Chapter 6 on intrinsic materials. Due to their significance, the requirement to consider the 'purpose' of legislation is given individual treatment in Chapter 4, and the option to consider 'extrinsic materials' is considered in Chapter 8. Subsidiary common law principles are covered in several chapters, but mainly Chapters 9 and 10.

---

2 See D Pearce and S Argument *Delegated Legislation in Australia* (3rd edn, 2005) [25.15].

3 M Gleeson, 'The Meaning of Legislation: Context, Purpose and Respect for Fundamental Rights' Address to Victoria Law Foundation, Melbourne, 31 July 2008, 7.

There is a general provision in s 2(2) of the newly amended Commonwealth Act which states that the Act and any of its provisions apply unless a contrary intention appears in a specific Act. In state and territory Acts it is still more common for such a phrase to appear in each separate provision.

Gender

Although it may seem obvious to modern readers that legislation is addressed equally to people of different gender, in reality gender-neutral language is a relatively recent development. Accordingly, several Acts still use 'he', and to avoid any uncertainty about whether legislation is directed to males only, the Interpretation Acts provide that 'he' includes 'she' and vice versa.

Section 23(a) of the Commonwealth Act simply provides that 'words importing a gender include every other gender'. See also s 8(a) of the NSW Act, s 37(a) of the Vic Act, s 32B of the Qld Act, s 26(a) and (ab) of the SA Act, s 10(a) of the WA Act, s 24A of the Tas Act, s 145(a) of the ACT Act, and s24(1) of the NT Act.

Age

The new s 37A of the Commonwealth Act, which mirrors the previous provision in s 25E, provides:[4]

> For the purposes of any Act, unless the contrary intention appears, the time at which a person attains a particular age expressed in years is the commencement of the relevant anniversary of the date of the birth of that person.

As an example, a person who has already been alive for 18 years turns 18 at 12.00.01 am on the 18th anniversary of their birth. The NT Act goes on to specify that, where a person is born on 29 February in a leap year, the anniversary of their birth is taken to be 28 February in any years that are not leap years: see s 30(3).

Number

It may seem obvious that where a legislative provision makes it an offence to discharge a bomb in a supermarket, it would also cover discharging more than one bomb, but the Interpretation Acts cover the issue expressly. Section s 23(b) of the Commonwealth Act provides that 'words in the singular number include the plural and words in the plural number include the singular'. This means, for example, that 'any person' is to be read as 'any person or persons'.

---

4 See also s 37 of the NSW Act, s 38 of the Qld Act, s 149 of the ACT Act and s 30(1) of the NT Act.

Similar provisions exist in the states and territories. See s 8(b) and (c) of the NSW Act, s 37(c) and (d) of the Vic Act, s 32C of the Qld Act, s 26(b) and (c) of the SA Act, s 10(c) of the WA Act, s 24(d) of the Tas Act, s 145(b) of the ACT Act, and s 24(2) of the NT Act. The NT Act, s 24A, also specifies that where an Act refers to a range of numbers, words or things, those at the beginning and end are included in the range. This would mean, for example, that 'from 18 to 25 years of age' would include both 18 and 25 years of age.

Distance

The Interpretation Acts provide that where an Act specifies that something must be say 500 km from a certain place, or within 50 km of a certain place, this distance is measured in a straight line (colloquially, 'as the crow flies') and not according to distance calculated by driving on roads, which may bend, rise and dip, or require left and right turns. See s 35 of the Commonwealth Act:

> In the measurement of any distance for the purposes of any Act, that distance shall, unless the contrary intention appears, be measured in a straight line on a horizontal plane.

There is a similar provision in most of the states and territories: see s 38 of the NSW Act; s 43 of the Vic Act, s 28 of the SA Act, s 65 of the WA Act, s 28 of the Tas Act, s 150 of the ACT Act and s 27 of the NT Act. An exception is the Queensland Act, which provides in s 37 that distance is to be measured along the shortest road ordinarily used for travelling, unless there is a contrary intention that it should be measured in a straight line on a horizontal plane or in another way.

Time

If an Act refers to a time, it means the standard or legal time in the place where the legislation applies. Section 37 of the Commonwealth Act provides:

> Where in an Act any reference to time occurs, such time shall, unless it is otherwise specifically stated, be deemed in each State or part of the Commonwealth to mean the standard or legal time in that State or part of the Commonwealth.

So for example in New South Wales legislation, the time is NSW time, including if relevant any adjustment for daylight savings. Section 4 of the *Summer Time Act 1972* (Vic) is verbose, and warrants quoting as an example:

> Notwithstanding anything in any enactment, regulation, by-law, rule, proclamation, Order in Council, order or notice, or in any contract or agreement (whether made orally or in writing),

> or in any deed or other instrument, where any time or period of time is prescribed, specified or stipulated as the time at which, or the period of time for which or during which, or any part of which, the doing of any act matter or thing is required, permitted or forbidden, that time, period of time, or part of a period of time, as the case may be, shall, with respect to any period during which summer time is fixed under this Act to be in advance of standard time, be held to be, and shall be determined by reference to, summer time unless the contrary is expressed, provided, or stipulated in that enactment, regulation, by-law, rule, proclamation, Order in Council, order, notice, contract, agreement, deed or instrument.

The benefits of plain English drafting can be appreciated through a comparison with a similar provision, drafted in a more modern style, in s 7 of the *Standard Time and Summer Time Act 1972* (ACT): 'The time must be worked out using (a) ACT standard time; or (b) if the time is in relation to a summer time period—ACT summer time.' Section 28(3) of the NT Act provides that the standard time stated in s 4 of the *Standard Time Act* (NT) applies. The NSW, Qld, SA, WA and Tasmanian Acts are silent on this issue but it is reasonable to assume that the legal time in each of these states is applicable.

In terms of duration or passage of time, a day means a 24-hour period commencing at midnight, and a month means a calendar month. See s 22(1)(a) of the Commonwealth Act, s 21 of the NSW Act, s 44 of the Vic Act, s 36 of the Qld Act, s 3 of the SA Act, s 62 of the WA Act, s 46 of the Tas Act and s 19 of the NT Act. So for example a month starting 20 May ends on the last second of 11.59pm on 19 June. Similarly three months starting 20 May ends on the last second of 11.59pm on 19 August.

If an Act says that something applies 'at' a certain date, this means it starts at 12.00.01am on that date. If it applies 'from' a certain date, that date is excluded. So if something applies from 15 January, it applies from 12.00.01am on 16 January. Also if the last date to do something falls on a weekend or public holiday, then it can be done on the next business day and still be compliant with the legislation.

See the new s 36(1) of the Commonwealth Act which provides:

Calculating periods of time

Item	Column 1 If the period of time:	Column 2 then the period of time:
1	is expressed to occur between 2 days	includes both days.
2	is expressed to begin at, on or with a specified day	includes that day.
3	is expressed to continue until a specified day	includes that day.
4	is expressed to end at, on or with a specified day	includes that day.
5	is expressed to begin from a specified day	does not include that day.
6	is expressed to begin after a specified day	does not include that day.
7	is expressed to end before a specified day	does not include that day.

The former provision in s 36(1) of the Commonwealth Act is still the basis for most of the state and territory provisions, so it warrants quoting (also the former s 36(2) which in essence remains the same in the new Commonwealth Act):

> (1) Where in an Act any period of time, dating from a given day, act, or event, is prescribed or allowed for any purpose, the time shall, unless the contrary intention appears, be reckoned exclusive of such day or of the day of such act or event.
>
> (2) Where the last day of any period prescribed or allowed by an Act for the doing of anything falls on a Saturday, on a Sunday or on a day which is a public holiday or a bank holiday in the place in which the thing is to be or may be done, the thing may be done on the first day following which is not a Saturday, a Sunday or a public holiday or bank holiday in that place.

See s 36 of the NSW Act, s 44 of the Vic Act, s 38 of the Qld Act, s 27 of the SA Act, s 61 of the WA Act, s 29 of the Tas Act, s 151 and s 151A of the ACT Act and s 28 of the NT Act.

Some Interpretation Acts provide that, if no time period is stated, the action should occur at 'all convenient speed'—see s 38(4) Qld, s 27(3) SA, and s 63 WA. In the ACT the phrase used in s 151B is 'as soon as possible'. Otherwise, it can be assumed that the action should occur within a reasonable time, which varies depending on the circumstances.

Meaning of 'may' and 'shall'

Historically the use of the words 'shall', 'must', 'is required to', 'may', 'can', 'could', 'will', 'it shall be lawful to', and 'if he or she thinks fit' raised statutory interpretation conundrums for courts. Were these descriptors setting out a mandatory obligation, or discretion? For example if a statute said that a person 'may not' do something, did this mean that they were not allowed to do that thing, or that they may, or may not, at their discretion? This area is known as statutory discretions and obligations, and the confusion at common law has now been resolved by the modern approach to statutory interpretation.

The Interpretation Acts provide that the word 'may' confers a discretion: see s 33(2A) of the Commonwealth Act, s 9(1) of the NSW Act, s 45(1) of the Vic Act, s 32CA(1) of the Qld Act, s 34 of the SA Act, s 56(1) of the WA Act, s 10A(1)(c) of the Tas Act and s 146(1) of the ACT Act. There is no equivalent provision in the Northern Territory Act.

Conversely the word 'shall' is mandatory: see s 9(2) of the NSW Act, s 45(2) of the Vic Act, s 32CA(2) of the Qld Act, s 34 of the SA Act, s 56(2) of the WA Act and s 146(2) of the ACT Act. Section s 10A(1)(a) of the Tasmanian Act says 'must' is mandatory and (b) provides that 'is to' and 'are to' are directory.

A provision relating to 'shall' is omitted from the Northern Territory and the Commonwealth Acts, but to a great degree it no longer matters, because the court must look at what Parliament intended rather than which word was used. In *Project Blue Sky Inc v Australian Broadcasting Authority* (1998) 194 CLR 355, the High Court said:

> a court, determining the validity of an act done in breach of a statutory provision, may easily focus on the wrong factors if it asks itself whether compliance with the provision is mandatory or directory ... A better test for determining the issue of validity is to ask whether it was a purpose of the legislation that an act done in breach of the provision should be invalid.

This reasoning may be applied to statutory discretions and obligations—whether the word 'may' or 'must' is used, the reader should ask whether it was a purpose of the legislation that the action or inaction was required or optional.

Commencement

Generic provisions as to commencement appear in all the Interpretation Acts.[5] For example s 3A of the Commonwealth Act says that an Act 'shall come into operation on the twenty-eighth day after the day on which that Act receives the Royal Assent, unless the contrary intention appears in the Act'. This saves Parliament putting a provision into every Commonwealth statute saying 'This Act commences 28 days from the date of assent'. The 28-day period is similarly provided for in the NSW Act s 23(1), and the WA Act s 20(2). In Tasmania, legislation comes into force 14 days from the date of assent (s 9(3) Tas) and in Queensland, South Australia and the Northern Territory, legislation comes into force on the actual day of assent, unless the legislation itself says otherwise: s 15A Qld, s 7 SA and s 6 NT. In the ACT, legislation commences on the day after notification in the Gazette: s 73 ACT. Although s 11 of the Victorian Act used to provide for commencement 28 days from the date of assent, the provision is now silent about a default time period. It now is necessary for a commencement provision to appear in every single Act. Of the 35 new Victorian Acts passed in 2011 by the time of writing of this book, most provided for the Act to come into force on the date of assent, or if they specified a date to be proclaimed, they also included a specific date by which the legislation would come into force if it had not been proclaimed by then.

5 A discussion of commencement of delegated legislation is included in Chapter 11.

Therefore in practice in most jurisdictions the reader must not only find the date of assent and add the requisite number of days but must also check the legislation itself to see if an alternative commencement provision has been enacted. The most common alternative provisions are (a) the specification of a particular date; (b) that the Act commences on the date of assent, or (c) that the Act commences on a date to be fixed by proclamation. Alternative (c) requires the reader to also check the Gazette to find the date of proclamation. Of course many law students simply rely on the information provided in the 'Notes' to each Act. Section 6 of the Commonwealth Act provides for judicial notice:

> The date appearing on the copy of an Act printed by the Government Printer, and purporting to be the date on which the Governor-General assented thereto, or made known the King's assent, shall be evidence that such date was the date on which the Governor-General so assented or made known the King's assent, and shall be judicially noticed.

It is common, in circumstances where the Act commences on a date to be proclaimed, for the Act to provide that the first two sections, containing the short title and the commencement clause, commence immediately. Some of the Interpretation Acts provide a generic provision to that effect. For example s 22 of the Western Australian Act provides:

> [W]here an Act provides that the Act, or portion of the Act, is to come into operation on a day to be fixed by proclamation, that provision and the provision providing for the short title of the Act, unless it is otherwise expressly provided, shall come into operation on the day on which the Act receives the Royal Assent.

Similar provisions exist in s 9(3A) of the Tasmanian Act, s 75(1) of the ACT Act and s 6(3) of the Northern Territory Act. The NSW Act provides that even though the provision has not commenced, it has effect: section 23 states in relevant part:

> (6) An Act may be referred to by its short title (or name) even though the provision that specifies the short title (or name) has not commenced.
>
> (7) If an Act provides for its commencement, whether by proclamation under the Act or otherwise:
>
> (a) that provision has effect for the purposes of subsection (1) (b), and
>
> (b) in the case of an Act that provides for its commencement by proclamation under the Act—
>
> such a proclamation may be made and shall have effect, even though that provision has not commenced.

The Commonwealth Act does not contain such a provision however it is common where commencement is to be by proclamation that a specific provision be included in the Act giving effect to that section and the short title. See for example:

FAIR WORK ACT 2009 - SECT 2

Commencement

(1) Each provision of this Act specified in column 1 of the table commences, or is taken to have commenced, in accordance with column 2 of the table. Any other statement in column 2 has effect according to its terms.

Commencement information		
Column 1	Column 2	Column 3
Provision(s)	Commencement	Date/Details
1. Sections 1 and 2 and anything in this Act not elsewhere covered by this table	The day on which this Act receives the Royal Assent.	7 April 2009

In the period before the legislation comes into force, some powers are permitted to be exercised in relation to preparatory measures such as drafting regulations or creating an administrating body. These are provided for in the Interpretation Acts—see for example s 4 of the Commonwealth Act, which states in relevant part:[6]

> (1) This section applies if an Act is enacted and at a time (the *start time*) after its enactment the Act will confer power to make an appointment, or to make an instrument of a legislative or administrative character (including rules, regulations or by-laws), because:
>
> (a) the Act will commence at the start time; or
>
> (b) the Act will be amended at the start time by an Act that has been enacted and that commences at that time.
>
> Exercise of power before start time
>
> (2) The power may be exercised before the start time as if the relevant commencement had occurred.
>
> (3) Anything may be done before the start time for the purpose of enabling the exercise of the power, or of bringing the appointment or instrument into effect, as if the relevant commencement had occurred.

6 See also s 26 of the NSW Act, s 13 of the Vic Act, s 17 of the Qld Act, s 14C of the SA Act, s 25 of the WA Act, s 81 of the ACT Act, s 11 of the Tas Act and s 8 of the NT Act.

(4) The exercise of a power under subsection (2) does not confer a power or right or impose an obligation on a person before the relevant commencement except so far as is necessary or convenient for the purpose of:
  (a) bringing the appointment or instrument into effect; or
  (b) bringing the Act conferring power into operation; or
  (c) making the Act conferring power fully effective at or after the start time.

(5) An appointment, or a provision of an instrument, made under subsection (2) takes effect at the start time or a later time specified in the appointment or instrument.

One instrument may rely on subsection (2) and existing power

(6) To avoid doubt, a single instrument may be made before the start time partly under subsection (2) and partly under a power already conferred by an Act.

On the day of commencement, the legislation commences at the very first second of that day, that is, 12.00.01 am. This is the case even where the legislation commences at the time of assent—if the Governor-General assents to the legislation at 4.00 pm, it is taken to have commenced one second after midnight that day, some 16 hours before.

Amendment

Legislation is most commonly amended through passage of an amendment Act. For example the *Native Title Act 1993* (Cth) was amended, *inter alia*, by the *Native Title Amendment Act 2007* (Cth). Alternatively, for minor amendments such as the change of a person's title or name of a relevant body, or change to penalties, an 'omnibus' Act may be used, in which one Act amends multiple Acts. Often, but not always, these will be titled 'Statutory Reform (Miscellaneous Provisions)' Acts.

Once the amendments provided for in the amending legislation have been incorporated into the primary Act(s), the amending Act is usually repealed. This can be provided for in the amending Act itself. See for example the *World Youth Day Amendment Act 2007* (Cth), s 5(1) of which provides: 'This Act is repealed on the day following the day on which this Act commences'. In other words, as soon as the amendments to the principal Act take effect, the amending Act is repealed. In some jurisdictions repeal occurs automatically when the amendments take effect.[7] See for example s 89 of the ACT Act, which provides in relevant part:

(1) An amending law is automatically repealed on the day after—
  (a) all of its provisions have commenced; or
  (b) the last of its provisions that have not commenced are omitted or cannot commence.

7 See s 30C of the NSW Act, s 22C of the Qld Act and s 89 of the ACT Act.

> ...
>
> (3) An amending provision of a law is automatically repealed immediately after all of the amendments and repeals made by it (or to which it relates) have commenced.

Commonly, once amendments are made to legislation, reprints are prepared which incorporate all amendments made since the Act was passed. As the reprinted Act has been compiled by parliamentary printers and has not been enacted in that form, it is used for convenience only. However, if Parliament chooses to pass a consolidating Act, bringing together the original legislation plus amendments made to it since, then the consolidated Act is the full official version of the legislation. It is assumed that consolidating Acts do not change the law, unless a clear parliamentary intent to do so is evident. Note, however, that consolidation is a different process from codification, where not only the legislation is consolidated but also the common law.[8]

The Interpretation Acts typically provide that where an amending Act repeals parts of an existing Act, the existing provisions remain in force until the new Act comes into force. See for example s 29 of the New South Wales Act, which provides:[9]

> If an Act or statutory rule repeals some or all of the provisions of some other Act or statutory rule and enacts new provisions in substitution for the repealed provisions, the repealed provisions continue in force until the new provisions commence.

Can amendments have retrospective effect, for example dating back to the commencement of the primary Act, or applying only from the date the amendment comes into effect? In *Maxwell v Murphy* (1957) 96 CLR 261 Fullagar J at 286 stated that the courts will make different presumptions, depending whether a procedural or substantive amendment is in issue:

> the distinction is probably best stated by saying that it is between statutes which create or modify or abolish substantive rights or liabilities on the one hand and statutes which deal with the pursuit of remedies on the other hand. In the former class of case there is a presumption against retrospective operation ... [i]n the latter class of case there is no such presumption: on the contrary, the presumption is that the enactment applies in all proceedings commenced after it became law, and it may be right to construe it as applying even in proceedings commenced before it became law.

Courts can struggle to interpret legislation which has been amended, particularly where it is unclear how a newly added provision relates to the existing provisions. This is borne out in the following case exercise.

8 Codes are interpreted slightly differently from normal legislation. This is discussed in Chapter 13.
9 See also s 29 NSW, s 21 Qld, s 16(3) SA, s 35 WA, s 15 Tas and s 14 NT.

Case exercise

'An indecent interpretation'

Swami touched the private parts of a 15-year-old girl and had sexual intercourse with her. He was charged under the *Crimes Act 1900* (NSW). Before nominating the relevant section, it is necessary to provide some contextual background.

The law regarding indecent assault used to be encapsulated in s 61E of the *Crimes Act 1900* (NSW), as follows:

> Any person who assaults another person and, at the time of, or immediately before or after, the assault, commits an act of indecency upon or in the presence of the other person, shall be liable to imprisonment for 4 years or, if the other person is under the age of 16 years, to penal servitude for 6 years.

A problem had arisen in some cases where the behaviour of the adult was indecent but was not covered by this indecent assault provision—for example where a man exposes himself to a child and gets the child to kiss his penis or stroke it with their hand. To close the gap in the law, the Act was amended to add a second part to s 61E, making the existing provision s 61E(1) and the new provision s 61E(2). This provided:

> Any person who commits an act of indecency with or towards a person under the age of 16 years, or incites a person under that age to an act of indecency with that or another person, shall be liable to imprisonment for 2 years.

Other sections of the Act which are also relevant to the case at hand are:

> (71) Whosoever unlawfully and carnally knows any girl of or above the age of ten years, and under the age of sixteen years, shall be liable to penal servitude for ten years.
>
> (72) Whosoever attempts unlawfully and carnally to know any girl of or above the age of ten years, and under the age of sixteen years, or assaults any such girl with intent carnally to know her, shall be liable to penal servitude for five years.
>
> (78) No prosecution in respect of any offence under section 61E(1), 71 or 72 ... shall, if the person upon whom the offence is alleged to have been committed was at the time of the alleged offence over the age of fourteen years and under the age of sixteen years, be commenced after the expiration of twelve months from the time of the alleged offence.

Therefore, indecent assault and carnal knowledge charges must be laid within a year. No such limitation applies to charges relating to acts of indecency. In the present case, as the year had expired, the Crown charged Swami with acts of indecency under s 61E(2), using admissions of his having had sexual intercourse with the girl to prove the case.

The question is—could he be charged under s 61E(2) when his offences were covered by s 61E(1)? Does each provision cover its own offence, or is indecent assault merely a more serious form of an act of indecency, in the same way that assault occasioning actual bodily harm is more serious than common assault? Or are acts which do not amount to indecent assault just acts of indecency, such that one excludes the other?

Please make your own decision before reading onwards.

The real case is *Saraswati v R* (1991) 172 CLR 1. If you concluded that the defendant's conduct did come under s 61E(2), you are in agreement with the trial judge and the Court of Criminal Appeal. If you concluded that it did not, you are in agreement with the majority of the High Court, which decided 3:2 to allow the appeal. Effectively the Court allowed the somewhat unsatisfactory situation that a person who has been charged with an act of indecency may be able to defend themselves by showing that the behaviour was actually indecent assault or unlawful carnal knowledge.

The majority included Gaudron, Toohey and McHugh JJ, who took into account the legislative context and background in holding that the later, general provision creating an offence of indecent dealing was designed to deal with acts of indecency not amounting to assault. Gaudron J explained the reasoning at [4] of her judgment:

> It is a basic rule of construction that, in the absence of express words, an earlier statutory provision is not repealed, altered or derogated from by a later provision unless an intention to that effect is necessarily to be implied. There must be very strong grounds to support that implication, for there is a general presumption that the legislature intended that both provisions should operate and that, to the extent that they would otherwise overlap, one should be read as subject to the other ... More particularly, an intention to affect the earlier provision will not be implied if the later is of general application.

Deane and Dawson JJ, in the minority, wanted to dismiss the appeal. Dawson J stated at [16] that he could see 'no justification for concluding that the legislature intended the offence of committing an act of indecency to exclude the offence of carnal knowledge or of indecent assault'. Deane J considered at [7] that the jury could convict an accused of the offence of indecency where it was 'established beyond reasonable doubt that he is guilty of either that offence or the offence of indecent assault'.

You might also consider, or discuss with others: if a High Court interpretation of a statute can only be reached by a slim majority, perceptions of judicial objectivity and application of the rule of law may give way to a perception that the outcome depends to some extent on which judge hears the matter. Could this cause lawyers to focus on jurimetrics (the study of judges) relating to statutory interpretation more so than on statutory interpretation itself?

Repeal

Just as Parliament has power to make and amend legislation, it may repeal provisions at will, simply by passing repealing legislation. The newer Act may as a whole repeal the older Act with the same short title. Or the newer Act may repeal aspects of the older Act, and may at times replace them with alternative provisions.[10] Repeals may be express or implied.[11]

The effect of repealing legislation is that the repealed Act no longer has force. This does not mean, however, that it is repealed 'from the beginning'—rather, it still was valid law for the time it was in force. This means that rights and liabilities accrued under the legislation while it was in force may still be the subject of litigation before the courts, whether or not litigation has commenced prior to the repeal. This is provided for in the new s 7 of the Commonwealth Act:[12]

> Where an Act repeals in the whole or in part a former Act, then unless the contrary intention appears the repeal shall not: ...
>
> (c) affect any right privilege obligation or liability acquired accrued or incurred under any Act so repealed; or
>
> (d) affect any penalty forfeiture or punishment incurred in respect of any offence committed against any Act so repealed; or
>
> (e) affect any investigation legal proceeding or remedy in respect of any such right privilege obligation liability penalty forfeiture or punishment as aforesaid;
>
> and any such investigation legal proceeding or remedy may be instituted continued or enforced, and any such penalty forfeiture or punishment may be imposed, as if the repealing Act had not been passed.

If, however, the repealing Act is itself repealed, this does not revive the former legislation. This is provided for in s 7(1) of the Commonwealth Act:[13]

> The repeal of an Act, or of a part of an Act, that repealed an Act (the *old Act*) or part (the *old part*) of an Act does not revive the old Act or old part, unless express provision is made for the revival.

---

10 It should also be noted that under s 109 of the Australian Constitution, where there is inconsistency between a state and federal act, the federal act will prevail to the extent of inconsistency. This does not repeal the state act, and if the federal act is repealed, the state act may have its full application.

11 See s 8A of the Commonwealth Act.

12 See also s 30 of the NSW Act, s 14 of the Vic Act, s 20 of the Qld Act, s 16 of the SA Act, s 37 of the WA Act, s 16 of the Tas Act, s 84 of the ACT Act and s 12 of the NT Act.

13 See also s 28 of the NSW Act, s 14 of the Vic Act, s 19 of the Qld Act, s 17 of the SA Act, s 34 of the WA Act, s 14 of the Tas Act, s 86 of the ACT Act and s 11 of the NT Act.

Where an Act has a sunset clause, the Act is treated as having been repealed on the date at which the Act expires. The same applies where a particular part or division of an Act has a sunset clause. See for example the anti-terrorism provisions in the *Criminal Code Act 1995* (Cth) which include:

> 104.32 Sunset provision
>
> (1) A control order that is in force at the end of 10 years after the day on which this Division commences ceases to be in force at that time.
>
> (2) A control order cannot be requested, made or confirmed after the end of 10 years after the day on which this Division commences.

Here the reality is obvious—the provision has no effect after 10 years. It is not *repealed*. We could draw an analogy with a fixed-term employment contract: when it expires we would not say that employment has been terminated. Instead, it has expired due to the effluxion of time, without action needing to be taken by either party. It is the same with a sunset clause. The Act is no longer in force due to the effluxion of time, without any repealing action being necessary. However, the practical effect is the same as repeal—the Act no longer applies but rights derived under it are preserved. Section 7(3)(b) of the Commonwealth Act[14] provides that repeal or amendment of an Act includes 'the expiry, lapsing or cessation of effect of the Act or part'.

What if an Act makes reference to another Act, but since the first Act was passed, the second Act has been amended or repealed? Section 10 of the Commonwealth Act provides:[15]

> Where an Act contains a reference to a short title that is or was provided by law for the citation of another Act as originally enacted, or of another Act as amended, then:
>
> (a) the reference shall be construed as a reference to that other Act as originally enacted and as amended from time to time; and
>
> (b) where that other Act has been repealed and re-enacted, with or without modifications, the reference shall be construed as including a reference to the re-enacted Act as originally enacted and as amended from time to time and, where, in connexion with that reference, particular provisions of the repealed Act are referred to, being provisions to which provisions of the re-enacted Act correspond, the reference to those particular provisions shall be construed as including a reference to those corresponding provisions.

Note that this reverses the common law presumption against giving such provisions an ambulatory operation, as seen for example in *Commissioner for Government Transport*

14 See also s 16 NT.

15 See also s 68 of the NSW Act, s 14H and 14J of the Qld Act, s 17 of the Vic Act, s 14B of the SA Act, s 16 of the WA Act, s 102 and s 50 of the NT Act.

(NSW) v Deacon (1957) 97 CLR 535 at 546, where it was held that the incorporated reference is the version of the second Act in force at the time of the Act, not including any amendments since.

In practice it can sometimes be difficult to differentiate between an amendment and a repeal, as some amendments impliedly repeal existing provisions, such as by substituting another provision or replacing words within a provision. Essentially, if the original provision and the amendment cannot sit together, the amendment is actually a repeal. In determining which is which, one should look to the substance of the change, regardless of the way it is described. If words are merely added, that is an amendment not a repeal (see Gibbs J in *Mathieson v Burton* (1971) 124 CLR 1 at 21). However, as stated by Windeyer J in the same case, at 10:

> [A]n amendment which permanently reduces the ambit of any of the provisions of an Act involves a repeal of it in part ... Provisions of a later Act which are inconsistent and irreconcilable with the provisions of a former Act dealing with the same subject matter are thus an implied repeal of them.

See also *Goodwin v Phillips* (1908) 7 CLR 1, where Griffiths J at 7 stated:

> where the provisions of a particular Act of Parliament dealing with a particular subject matter are wholly inconsistent with the provisions of an earlier Act dealing with the same subject matter, then the earlier Act is repealed by implication ... if the provisions are not wholly inconsistent, but may become inconsistent in their application to particular cases, then to that extent the provisions of the former Act are excepted or their operation is excluded with respect to cases falling within the provisions of the later Act.

The relevant maxim is *leges posteriores priores contrarias abrogant* (subsequent laws repeal those that came before, and enacted to the contrary). It should be noted, however, that courts will not imply repeal readily, but will prefer to find a construction that can allow both provisions to sit together. After all, it is presumed that Parliament does not intend to contradict itself.

Case exercise

'Does it mean what it says?'

The Clerk of the Parliaments of Western Australia has sought a declaration from the High Court as to whether he can lawfully present two bills that have been passed through both Houses of Parliament, to the Governor for assent. The first is the Electoral Distribution Repeal Bill ('the Repeal Bill') and the second is the Electoral Amendment Bill ('the Amendment Bill'). The issue arises under s 13 of the *Electoral Distribution Act 1947* (WA), which provides:

> It shall not be lawful to present to the Governor for Her Majesty's assent any Bill to amend this Act, unless the second and third readings of such Bill shall have been passed with the concurrence of an absolute majority of the whole number of the members for the time being of the Legislative Council and the Legislative Assembly respectively.

An absolute majority differs from a simple majority in requiring more than half of the total members to vote in favour of it, not merely those who are present and voting.

The Repeal Bill was the first to be passed. Clause 3 repealed the *Electoral Distribution Act 1947* (WA), including s 13. The following day the Amendment Bill was passed. Both bills achieved an absolute majority in the Legislative Assembly but only a simple majority in the Legislative Council.

Does s 13 apply to either or both bills? Can either or both bills be lawfully presented by the Clerk to the Governor for assent? In making your decision, consider whether it could be argued that the Repeal Bill was a 'repeal' not an 'amendment', such that s 13 does not apply to it. In that case, as the Repeal Bill repealed s 13, the Amendment Bill could then be passed with a simple majority. If so, both bills may be lawfully presented.

In reaching your conclusion consider some of the background to the legislation. Provisions governing electoral distribution in Western Australia were initially set out in the State Constitution of 1889, as amended in 1904. They provided a requirement for absolute majority to 'repeal or alter' the Constitution. Later, the provisions for defining electoral districts were moved to a separate Act, the *Electoral Distribution Act 1947* (WA), which contained altered wording, namely 'to amend' with no mention of repeal.

Please decide before proceeding.

The real case is *Attorney-General (WA) v Marquet* (2003) 217 CLR 545. If you decided s 13 did apply to the Repeal Bill, you are in agreement with five judges of the High Court. If you decided it did not, you are in agreement with Kirby J in dissent. How, then, did the High Court majority reason that a Bill that was expressly stated to repeal an Act was actually a Bill that amended the Act? How did the High Court decide to give such an expansive definition of 'amend' as to include any change or alteration, including repeal?

The majority judgment of Gleeson CJ, Gummow, Hayne and Heydon JJ (Callinan J agreed but wrote his own judgment) reasoned that it was no simple repeal because there would necessarily have to be replacement provisions enacted—it was impossible to continue with *no* provisions for electoral distribution. They said that, while the ordinary meaning of 'repeal' is to rescind the Act or provision, and 'amend' is to make a change short of entirely rescinding it, one must look not only at the form in which the legislation is cast but also to the substance: at [47]. They said that 'the difference in language cannot be treated as determining the issue which now arises' at [40] and that '[a] question to be decided is whether the legislation, on its true construction, distinguishes between those two concepts' at [50].

Callinan J, in his individual judgment, agreed with the majority, stating at [273]–[274]:

> [H]ow anomalous it would be if 'amend' when used in a constitution were to be read so narrowly as to exclude, or have no application to a repeal, so as to enable a legislature, without complying with the requirements of s 13, to obliterate or extinguish entirely part of the Constitution, but not to amend it even by the addition or deletion of a mere word or phrase: that although the Parliament might not tinker with, it was entitled to annihilate a constitution or a substantial provision of it. In my opinion therefore, 'amend' in s 13 of the EDA should be read to include and apply to a purported 'repeal'.

Kirby J, at [136] in dissent, concluded that although the repeal of a section or part of an Act may constitute an amendment, the repeal of an entire Act cannot be construed as an amendment. By definition a repeal leaves nothing of substance to be 'amended'. Ultimately, 'if Parliament had meant to attach procedural requirements to the total 'repeal' of the 1947 Act, it could have said so, but it did not': at [134].

Invalidity

At times courts may hold that certain statutes, or parts of them, are invalid. This occurs where the Federal Parliament acts *ultra vires*—the subject matter does not fall within one of the heads of power in s 51 of the Australian Constitution. From December 2011 there is no specific provision in the Commonwealth Act providing that where a section or part of an Act is held to be invalid, the remainder of the Act may continue to have operation.[16] The former s 15A of the Commonwealth Act provided:

> Every Act shall be read and construed subject to the Constitution, and so as not to exceed the legislative power of the Commonwealth, to the intent that where any enactment thereof would, but for this section, have been construed as being in excess of that power, it shall nevertheless be a valid enactment to the extent to which it is not in excess of that power.

The analogy here is to contract law, where the doctrine of severability provides that invalid provisions are severable from the contract, leaving the remainder of the

16 There is a similar provision with respect to regulations in s 46(2) which provides: 'If any instrument so made would … be construed as being in excess of the authority's power, it is to be taken to be a valid instrument to the extent to which it is not in excess of that power'. See the case exercise titled 'To compensate or not to compensate, that is the question' on page 245 in Chapter 13, which related to the result of a provision in delegated legislation which had in part been found invalid.

contract intact and enforceable. Dixon J in *Bank of New South Wales v Commonwealth* (1948) 76 CLR 1 stated at [84]:

> The effect of such clauses is to reverse the presumption that a statute is to operate as a whole, so that the intention of the legislature is to be taken prima facie to be that the enactment should be divisible and that any parts found constitutionally unobjectionable should be carried into effect independently of those which fail. To displace the application of this new presumption to any given situation arising under the statute by reason of the invalidation of part, it must sufficiently appear that the invalid provision forms part of an inseparable context. The general provision contained in s 15A of the *Acts Interpretation Act 1901–1941* produces this effect, as does s 46(b), which similarly deals with severance in subordinate legislation.

And at [85]:

> But in applying s 15A and s 46 (b) the courts have insisted that a provision, though in itself unobjectionable constitutionally, must share the fate of so much of the statute, regulation or order as is found to be invalid, once it appears that the rejection of the invalid part would mean that the otherwise unobjectionable provision would operate differently upon the persons, matters or things falling under it or in some other way would produce a different result. This consideration supplies a strong logical ground for holding provisions to be inseverable, whether the prima-facie presumption be in favour or against severability. It is important where there is no statutory clause like s 15A and it is important in using s 15A. For the inference in such a case is strong that provisions so associated form an entire law and that no legislative intention existed that anything less should operate as a law.

The majority High Court judgment in *Victoria v The Commonwealth* (1996) 187 CLR 416 ('Industrial Relations Case') included this statement at [81]:

> It is well settled that s 15A cannot be applied to effect a partial validation of a provision which extends beyond power unless 'the operation of the remaining parts of the law remains unchanged'. Nor can it be applied to a law expressed in general terms if it appears that 'the law was intended to operate fully and completely according to its terms, or not at all'.
>
> Where a law is expressed in general terms, it may be more difficult to determine whether Parliament intended that it should, nonetheless, have a partial operation. And there is an additional difficulty if it 'can be reduced to validity by adopting any one or more of a number of several possible limitations'. It has been said that if, in a case of that kind, 'no reason based upon the law itself can be stated for selecting one limitation rather than another, the law should be held to be invalid'.

The High Court decision in *Australian National Airways Pty Ltd v Commonwealth* (1945) 71 CLR 29 discussed s 15A in relation to legislation that purported to nationalise interstate airlines in Australia. The High Court found that the *Australian Airlines Act 1945* (Cth) was inconsistent with s 51 and 92 of the Constitution. The issue then arose as to whether the legislation was wholly invalid or only invalid with respect to the states, and could therefore still apply with respect to the territories. Latham CJ stated:

> In my opinion the Act has been carefully drafted so as to avoid difficulties in the application of s 15A of the *Acts Interpretation Act 1901–1941*. I regard this provision as a direction to the Court to treat all statutes as being valid as far as possible, and to assume, as the general intention of Parliament, that as much of an Act shall operate as can operate, even if other parts may fail. In the present case special pains have been taken, it appears to me, to make the different provisions of the Act severable. ... The invalidity of the inter-State provisions in Part IV does not, in my opinion, affect the Territorial provisions. The two sets of provisions are separately expressed and can operate quite independently of each other. ... If the inter-State provisions are struck out of Part IV the rest of the Act can operate according to its terms. Thus I am of opinion that the invalid provisions are severable and that the Act as a whole is not invalid by reason of the invalidity of portion of Part IV.

It remains to be seen whether the courts will consider an approach of partial invalidation of a provision in the absence of a legislative directive to do so, but there is no reason the same approach should not continue. The role of the courts is to give effect to legislation as far as possible, and if severing certain offending words from a provision can allow the provision to have some valid application, the courts will most likely continue to do so. Therefore, it can be considered that where the offending provisions can be severed without affecting the operation of the rest of the Act, the remainder will remain valid. Otherwise the whole Act will be invalidated.

What if the primary legislation is itself valid, but a repeal or amendment proves to be invalid? Does that revive the form of the legislation prior to amendment? Certainly if legislation that amends the common law is held to be invalid, the common law revives. Although the situation is not provided for in the interpretation legislation, there is High Court authority.

Prior to an amendment of the *Commonwealth Electoral Act 1918* (Cth) by the *Electoral and Referendum Amendment (Electoral Integrity and Other Measures) Act 2006* (Cth), prisoners serving a sentence of three years or longer were not entitled to vote. The 2006 amendment provided that prisoners serving any sentence of imprisonment were not entitled to vote. In *Roach v Electoral Commissioner* (2007) 233 CLR 162 the High Court held that the amendment was invalid, but that the pre-2006 legislation was valid and continued in force. Gummow, Kirby and Crennan JJ stated at [97]:

> The plaintiff first directs attention to the text of [the repealing provisions in amendment Act] ... The effect of the plaintiff's submission is that these Items remain effective to repeal the relevant three year provision of the 2004 Act and this is so even without its

> replacement by the regime of the 2006 Act. That submission should be rejected. There is disclosed no Parliamentary 'intention' to remove the 2004 Act provisions independently of the adoption of the new provisions, and to leave a gap in the Electoral Act. This is not a case, if one may be found, where the invalidity of new provisions leaves intact the repeal of the earlier provisions; here the efficacy of the former was a condition of the repeal of the latter. This is apparent both as a matter of form and of substance.

This authority cannot be used as an absolute precedent, because the conclusion was contingent on there being 'no Parliamentary intention' disclosed in the relevant Act. Therefore in deciding whether the previous Act is revived, one must look closely to the wording of the Act to see whether there is a separate intention that the prior legislation be repealed notwithstanding that the replacement provisions prove invalid. It is submitted that this would rarely be the case.

We now come to the most important provision in each of the Interpretation Acts, to which two separate chapters are dedicated (Chapter 4 on purpose and context, and Chapter 5 on intention and other techniques). There is also specific consideration of the use of materials within the Act (Chapters 6 and 7) and outside it (Chapter 8) in statutory interpretation.

CHAPTER 4

CONTEXT AND PURPOSE

The key task of statutory interpretation is to find the ordinary meaning of the words, not in isolation, but taking into account their context and purpose. That context or purpose may indicate that a meaning other than the ordinary meaning is to apply. Therefore in practice we read a provision to gain a sense of meaning based on our ordinary understanding of the words used, and then we must proceed directly to context and purpose (covered in this chapter) as well as intention and other interpretive techniques (covered in the next chapter) before returning in earnest to assess the meaning, and whether it is the ordinary meaning (covered in Chapter 7). The centrality of the need for purposive interpretation is the reason it is covered first in this book.

The statutory formulation for giving effect to an interpretation that promotes the purpose is s 15AA of the Commonwealth Act, as formulated since December 2011:

> In interpreting a provision of an Act, the interpretation that would best achieve the purpose or object of the Act (whether or not that purpose or object is expressly stated in the Act) is to be preferred to each other interpretation.

This form of wording was already used in s 14A of the Queensland Act and in s 139 of the ACT Act. It replaces the previous Commonwealth provision, which read:

> In the interpretation of a provision of an Act, a construction that would promote the purpose or object underlying the Act (whether that purpose or object is expressly stated in the Act or not) shall be preferred to a construction that would not promote that purpose or object.

This form of wording remains in s 33 of the NSW Act, s 35(a) Vic, s 18 WA, s 62A NT, s 8A Tas and s 22 SA. The South Australian provision includes an additional phrase, 'where a provision is reasonably open to more than one construction'. For ease of reference, the formulation used in Queensland, the ACT and at the Commonwealth level will be referred to as the 'best achievement' approach and the formulation used in NSW, Victoria, WA, NT, Tas and SA will be referred to as the 'preferred construction' approach. It must be noted that all references to s 15AA in this book are to the previous, 'preferred construction' approach, since the new s 15AA was only coming into force at the time of writing. It will take some time for the courts to wrestle with the implications of the change. Some discussion about the difference is provided below.

When the 'preferred construction' approach was legislated it posed, on its face, some difficulty. It literally instructs that if there are two potential constructions available, the interpreter should prefer the one that promotes the purpose of the Act. This was certainly the view of the Federal Court in *Trevisan v Commissioner of Taxation* (1991) 29 FCR 157, where Burchett J said at 162:

> Section 15AA requires a court to prefer one construction to another. Such a requirement can only have meaning where two constructions are otherwise open. The section is not a warrant for redrafting legislation nearer to an assumed desire of the legislature. It is not

> for the courts to legislate; a meaning, though illuminated by the statutory injunction to promote the purpose or object underlying the Act, must be found in the words of Parliament.

Other courts have not been put off by the specific wording, considering themselves obliged to consider the purpose of the Act under all circumstances, regardless. This commenced with McHugh J's statement, while still a judge of the Supreme Court of New South Wales, in *Kingston v Keprose Pty Ltd* (1987) 11 NSWLR 404. He said, at 423 of the judgment:

> A search for the grammatical meaning still constitutes the starting point. But if the grammatical meaning of a provision does not give effect to the purpose of the legislation, the grammatical meaning cannot prevail. It must give way to the construction which will promote the purpose or object of the Act. The *Acts Interpretation Act 1901* (Cth), s 15AA and the *Interpretation Act 1987* (NSW), s 33, both require this approach to statutory construction.

This statement has been cited with support in each jurisdiction that continues to use the 'preferred construction' approach. See for example in Victoria, *Director of Public Prosecutions v Siourtou* [2007] VSCA 233; in Western Australia, *Hewitt v Benale Pty Ltd* [2002] WASCA 163; and in the Northern Territory, *R v Ahwan* [2005] NTSC 47 and *Thompson v Primary Producers Improvers Pty Ltd* [2004] NTCA 12.

Even the South Australian provision, which adopts the 'preferred construction' approach with an additional limiting phrase 'where a provision of an Act is reasonably open to more than one construction', has been held to not be so limited: Cox J in *Burch v South Australia* (1998) 71 SASR 12 at 18 stated:

> [T]he section does not state that the purpose or object of an Act may only be considered where the provision being construed is reasonably open to more than one construction. It simply says what is to be done when that is the case.

Perhaps the logic was that, in order to properly apply the section, one must consider the purpose and then consider whether the construction promotes it or not, but it is undeniable that the ordinary wording of the section did direct itself to the situation where more than one construction was available.

The difference in the two approaches, in superior courts at least, may mean little, since '[b]y the time problems of statutory (still more constitutional) interpretation reach this Court, it is rare that only one outcome is available', as Kirby J stated in *Attorney-General (WA) v Marquet* (2003) 217 CLR 545 at [129]. It may indeed apply to all courts with virtually all pieces of legislation, given that in real life 'there will rarely be any one uncontroversially clear public meaning, simply because of the chronic imprecision of the general terms in which laws must be couched and the diversity of situations to which it must be applied'.[1] In well litigated sections in which there is ample court authority as to the section's scope, the task of the lower courts may not entail too much controversy. But with the predominance of legislation as a source of law in the twenty-first century, and the move to plain English drafting, the acceptable ambit of newly created or reformulated legislation will need, in many cases, to be worked out through the judicial process.

Is there really any difference between the two approaches? The High Court in *Chugg v Pacific Dunlop Ltd* (1990) 170 CLR 249 at 262 considered that there was, when applying the Victorian provision encapsulating the 'preferred construction' approach:

> The choice directed by s 35(a) of the *Interpretation of Legislation Act* is not as to the construction which 'will best achieve' the object of the Act. Rather, it is a limited choice between 'a construction that would promote the purpose or object (of the Act)' and one 'that would not promote that purpose or object'.

The Federal Court in *Brian William Skea v the Minister of Immigration, Local Government and Ethnic Affairs* [1994] FCA 1151 has reiterated this view, stating at [14] that 'the question 15AA requires a court to address is whether one construction promotes the purpose of the Act and another does not. It is not which would best achieve the objects of the Act'.

So the courts obviously saw a difference between the two formulations of the purposive approach. What about Parliament? Did the movement from the 'preferred construction 'to a 'best achievement' approach signal a new way forward, or was it merely a clarification and simplification of the existing approach?

Although reference to the amendment of s 15AA in the Explanatory Memorandum in 2011 was extremely brief, there is a clear indication that the new 'best achievement' approach is perceived to be less restrictive than the 'preferred construction' approach:

> (99) Section 15AA, which deals with interpretation of Acts, is currently expressed in absolute terms, i.e. a construction that will promote the purpose of an Act is to be preferred to one that will not. Section 15AA does not address the situation where there is a choice between two or more constructions that will promote Parliament's purpose.
>
> (100) The limited nature of section 15AA was confirmed by three High Court judges in a case on the equivalent Victorian provision (see *Chugg v Pacific Dunlop Pty Ltd* (1990) 95 ALR 481 at 489, Dawson, Toohey and Gaudron JJ).
>
> (101) Therefore section 15AA is being amended to provide that a court is to prefer the construction of an Act that will 'best achieve' the purpose or object of the Act.

1 T Campbell, 'Ethical Interpretation and Democratic Positivism' in Corcoran, S and Bottomley, S (eds) *Interpreting Statutes* (Federation Press, 2005) 83, 89.

Accordingly, it can be said that the new 'best achievement' approach is broader than the 'preferred construction' approach—it allows not only a choice between a construction that promotes the purpose and one that does not, but also a choice between two constructions that both promote the purpose. It explicitly covers what the courts have already been doing for some time, when faced with more than one construction that could promote the purpose.

This chapter focuses next on the statutory context, including what comes within the context, when context may be considered, and how it may affect the outcome. It then addresses the purpose of legislation, including where to find the purpose, and difficulties caused by latent or multiple purposes. The next chapter proceeds to the related concept of intention, together with ways in which courts 'read down' provisions or 'read in' words in order to give effect to the purpose of legislation in circumstances where the words as enacted do not readily do so. There is also consideration of the 'spirit' or 'equity' of the statute, of dynamic interpretation, analogical use of statutes, and of the inherent limits or boundaries of the courts in the interpretation task.

Context

It can be said that the shift in recent decades has been from 'text' to context'.[2] Instead of literalism, there is a contextual (and purposive) approach. Contextualism is a theory of interpretation that requires interpretation in the context of the standard public meaning of the text.[3]

That is not to say that the literal approach did not make any reference to context whatsoever; just that it merely considered the intrinsic context. This is seen in the classic formulation of the literal approach by Higgins J in the *Engineers Case*:[4]

> The fundamental rule of interpretation, to which all others are subordinate, is that a statute is to be expounded according to the intent of the Parliament that made it; and that intention has to be found by an examination of the language used in the statute as a whole.

The modern approach to context includes the immediate context—that is, reading the Act as a whole—but also the broader context. As Spigelman CJ has said, '[t]he courts no longer approach a statute with scissors in one hand and a dictionary in the other': *R v Campbell* (2008) 73 NSWLR 272 at [49].

2 J J Spigelman, 'The Intolerable Wrestle: Developments in Statutory Interpretation', Address to the Australasian Conference of Planning and Environment Courts and Tribunals, 1 September 2010, 5.

3 T Campbell, 'Ethical Interpretation and Democratic Positivism' in Corcoran, S and Bottomley, S (eds) *Interpreting Statutes* (Federation Press, 2005) 83, 88.

4 *Amalgamated Society of Engineers v Adelaide Steamship Co Ltd* (1920) 28 CLR 129.

What is included in the 'context'?

There is no comprehensive list of matters capable of coming within the broader context of an Act—it depends on what may be relevant for the particular piece of legislation. Gleeson CJ has said:[5]

> That the history of a legal text, and the circumstances in which it was written, may usefully inform an understanding of the meaning of the text is undeniable. Use of such information is a routine part of legal reasoning.

In *Singh v Commonwealth* (2004) 222 CLR 322, Gleeson CJ stated at [12]:'Meaning is always influenced, and sometimes controlled, by context. The context might include time, place, and any other circumstance that could rationally assist understanding of meaning'.

The joint judgment of the High Court in *CIC Insurance Ltd v Bankstown Football Club Ltd* (1997) 187 CLR 384 stated at 408 that context is used 'in its widest sense to include such things as the existing state of the law and the mischief which, by legitimate means ... one may discern the statute was intended to remedy'.

It may be said that the immediate context includes all intrinsic materials (see Chapters 6 and 7) and the broader context includes all extrinsic materials (see Chapter 8). The interpreter of legislation may embark on a journey encompassing historical circumstances, government policy, legislative background, parliamentary debates and documents, the constitution, international law and more.

When can or should context be considered?

It is not necessary for there to be an ambiguity in the operative provision for context to be considered. See the joint judgment of the High Court in *CIC Insurance Ltd v Bankstown Football Club Ltd* (1997) 187 CLR 384 at 408, 'the modern approach to statutory interpretation ... insists that the context be considered ... not merely at some later stage when ambiguity may be thought to arise'. See also Gleeson CJ's comment that:[6]

> Reference to context ... is not confined to circumstances where the text would otherwise be unintelligible or at least ambiguous. Utility, not necessity, is the reason for reference to context.

In the Federal Court see also *Parrett v Secretary, Department of Family & Community Services* (2002) 124 FCR 299 at [25], where Madgwick J stated:

> It is now clear, if it were ever not, that blinkered literalism has no place in the interpretation of federal statutes. Indeed, regard to context precedes any finding of ambiguity.

---

5 M Gleeson, 'The Meaning of Legislation: Context, Purpose and Respect for Fundamental Rights' Address to Victoria Law Foundation, Melbourne, 31 July 2008, 12.

6 Ibid at 10.

There have been judicial pronouncements that one should 'start' with the context (*Project Blue Sky Inc v Australian Broadcasting Authority* (1998) 194 CLR 355) and that the context should be considered 'at the first instance': see Mason J in *K & S Lake City Freighters Pty Ltd v Gordon & Gotch Ltd* (1985) 157 CLR 309 at 315:

> Problems of legal interpretation are not solved satisfactorily by ritual incantations which emphasise the clarity of meaning which words have when viewed in isolation, divorced from their context. The modern approach to interpretation insists that the context be considered in the first instance.

But surely one must start with the text of the provision itself—after all, the search is for the context of the provision, be that the immediate or the broader context discussed above. An analogy may be drawn to undertaking legal research—the research question or topic must be settled upon before the research takes place, in order to pull from research sources the salient information. It is submitted that both the context and the purpose should be explored after reading the operative provision being interpreted, starting with intrinsic materials and then proceeding to extrinsic materials as relevant.

Case exercise

'You kids get lost, you can't play here'

Wayne is employed at a sand mine at Redhead near Newcastle in New South Wales. He operates a front-end loader. The mine site is unfenced, and from time to time children make their way onto the mine site to play in the sand. Recently Wayne spotted some kids and told them to get lost. He thought he'd scare them off by driving after them in the front loader. It moved slowly, so the children would have no trouble getting away. However his vision was obscured by a bucket at the front end of the machine and he did not notice that one of the boys had tripped. He ran over the 13 year old, killing him. Wayne has been charged with criminally negligent homicide. Section 18 of the *Crimes Act 1900* (NSW) provides:

> (1) (a) Murder shall be taken to have been committed where the act of the accused, or thing by him or her omitted to be done, causing the death charged, was done or omitted with reckless indifference to human life, or with intent to kill or inflict grievous bodily harm upon some person, or done in an attempt to commit, or during or immediately after the commission, by the accused, or some accomplice with him or her, of a crime punishable by imprisonment for life or for 25 years.
>
> (b) Every other punishable homicide shall be taken to be manslaughter.
>
> (2) (a) No act or omission which was not malicious, or for which the accused had lawful cause or excuse, shall be within this section.

(b) No punishment or forfeiture shall be incurred by any person who kills another by misfortune only.

It was clear that Wayne did not intend to injure the boys—he just did not consider an obvious risk. Did that mean that, because he had no malice, he could not come within s 18? If so, did that mean that there was no such offence as manslaughter by a negligent act? What do you think?

The real case is *R v Lavender* (2005) 222 CLR 67. If you decided he was covered by s 18, you are in agreement with the trial judge, Giles JA in dissent on the Court of Criminal Appeal, and the High Court. If you decided he was not covered, you are in agreement with the majority of Court of Criminal Appeal (Hulme and Adams JJ).

The High Court held that, despite the text of the provision, the context showed that the first sentence of s 18(2)(a) does not affect the common law definition of manslaughter in s 18(1)(b). Gleeson CJ, McHugh, Gummow and Hayne JJ in their joint judgment stated at [33] that 'This case provides an example of the importance of context in resolving questions of statutory construction'. That context included the Division in which the section was placed, the Act as a whole, the common law on homicide, and the history of the legislation. The context made all the difference to the outcome of this case.

Kirby J agreed with the joint judgment, saying at [69]:

> For me, the arguments of statutory construction, legislative history and legal principle and policy, advanced by the parties for and against the disposition of the court below, are more evenly balanced than they have seemed to the other members of this Court … I ultimately come to the same result only because that outcome is less unsatisfactory than the alternative would be. In this sense, the appeal illustrates once again the highly contestable nature of statutory interpretation. It also illustrates the importance of consistency of approach to such problems, so that it cannot be said that the courts pluck out considerations of 'context', 'purpose' and 'history' arbitrarily, so as to sustain the outcomes of interpretation at which they arrive in some, but not other, cases.

He also drew attention to the sporadic use of context in statutory interpretation at [109]:

> Context … is indeed an important ingredient in the interpretation of statutes. But it is one that must be used consistently, not intermittently, selectively or idiosyncratically … If a narrow and literal approach is taken in one case, but rejected in another, in the name of 'context', those affected by the law are entitled to have the reasons for the change of approach. If context is important for statutory construction, why is it not always important?

Kirby J also referred to a statutory presumption that penal provisions are strictly construed, which is discussed in Chapter 10.

While there is judicial agreement that statutory interpretation should be not only contextual but also purposive and textual (one cannot apply the meaning from the context and purpose divorced from the actual words used), in practice these must go hand in hand—the context may reveal the purpose, the textual meaning may be adjusted by the context, and so on. See McHugh J's comments in *Saraswati v R* (1991) 172 CLR 1 at [7]:

> [I]t is always necessary in determining 'the ordinary meaning' of a provision ... to have regard to the purpose of the legislation and the context of the provision as well as the literal meaning of the provision. Sometimes the purpose of the legislation is expressly stated; sometimes it can be discerned only by inference after an examination of the legislation as a whole; and sometimes it can be discerned only by reference to the history of the legislation and the state of the law when it was enacted.

Purpose

Readers may be forgiven for thinking that there is nothing new about considering the purpose of the Act—after all wasn't that the point of the 'mischief' rule,[7] also referred to as the rule from *Heydon's Case*,[8] which has been around for half a millenium? Didn't it instruct us to look at the state of the law before the Act, the mischief the Act was intended to address, the remedy Parliament has adopted, and find an interpretation that suppresses the mischief and advances the remedy? That much is true, but there is a difference between the common law purposive approach under the mischief rule, and the modern purposive approach under the interpretation legislation. Dawson J expressed this difference in *Mills v Meeking* (1990) 169 CLR 214 at 235 when considering the Victorian interpretation legislation:

> The requirement that a court look to the purpose or object of the Act is thus more than an instruction to adopt the traditional mischief or purpose rule in preference to the literal rule of construction. The mischief or purpose rule required an ambiguity or inconsistency before a court could have regard to purpose ... The approach required by s 35 needs no ambiguity or inconsistency; it allows a court to consider the purposes of an Act in determining whether there is more than one possible construction ... [It] requires a court to construe an Act, not to rewrite it, in the light of its purposes.

Accordingly, there is no need to identify an ambiguity in a statutory provision before the purpose can be considered. In interpreting legislation, regard should always

7 It is assumed readers have a basic understanding of statutory interpretation. Readers not familiar with the mischief rule should refer to Chapter 9 page 170.

8 (1584) 76 ER 637.

be had to its purpose. Despite that, some judges still refer to 'mischief' while others use 'purpose'.[9] The purpose addresses the mischief, so both terms work together.

It may well be that the grammatical meaning of the words used promotes the purpose, in which case the task is straightforward. As McHugh J stated in *Saraswati v R* (1991) 172 CLR 1 at [7],

> In many cases, the grammatical or literal meaning of a statutory provision will give effect to the purpose of the legislation. Consequently, it will constitute the 'ordinary meaning' to be applied. If, however, the literal or grammatical meaning of a provision does not give effect to that purpose, that meaning cannot be regarded as 'the ordinary meaning' and cannot prevail. It must give way to the construction which will promote the underlying purpose or object of an Act.

In other words the grammatical or literal meaning of words will be the 'ordinary meaning' where no doubt is created by the purpose or context of the Act. The 'ordinary meaning' is further discussed in Chapter 7.

What is the purpose and how do we find it?

The purpose of legislation is to give effect to a government policy, which is typically discussed in Parliament, and should be included in the Explanatory Memorandum presented at the same time as the Bill. The Explanatory Memorandum may therefore be a useful document to consult, as will the Hansard records of parliamentary debates—noting however that the words of a minister cannot be substituted for the text of the law.[10] Explanatory Memoranda and Parliamentary Debates are further discussed in Chapter 8 on extrinsic materials.

The Act itself may expressly state the purpose in the Long Title. See for example the Long Title of the *Tradex Scheme Act 1999* (Cth):

> An Act to establish a scheme, to be known as the Tradex Scheme, for the importation, without payment of duties of customs or other taxes, of goods that are to be subsequently exported, and for related purposes.

There may also be an 'Objects' clause in the Act. See for example s 3 of the *Tobacco Advertising Prohibition Act 1992* (Cth):

> Object
>
> (1) This Act is intended to limit the exposure of the public to messages and images that may persuade them:
>
> (a) to start smoking, or to continue smoking; or
>
> (b) to use, or to continue using, tobacco products.
>
> (2) The object is to improve public health.

9 J J Spigelman, 'The Intolerable Wrestle: Developments in Statutory Interpretation', Address to the Australasian Conference of Planning and Environment Courts and Tribunals, 1 September 2010, 7.

10 *Mills v Meeking* (1990) 169 CLR 214 per Dawson J at 235.

This gives us a hint of the difference between purpose and intention, which is discussed further below. Here the overall purpose or object is to improve public health, and the intention to give effect to that purpose is to limit tobacco company advertising of products in order to stimulate demand for them.

How broadly can the purpose be stated? Assuming we are able to identify the purpose of the legislation through such consideration, at what level of generality is the court to apply it?

Case exercise

'The specificity and generality continuum'

Scott heard a knock at the door, and answered it. Immediately he was set upon and violently attacked, being punched, kicked, and stabbed in the stomach with a broken bottle. Police have apprehended the offender and he has been convicted of malicious wounding. Scott has now claimed compensation for his physical injuries and the associated shock, under the *Victims Support and Rehabilitation Act 1996* (NSW). The Act provides for compensation to be paid for 'compensable injuries', which are specified in Schedule 1, along with the standard amount payable for various types of injury. Clause 5 of Schedule 1 relates to claims for shock:

> The following applies to the compensable injury of shock:
>
> (a) Compensation is payable only if the symptoms and disability persist for more than 6 weeks.
>
> (b) The injury comprises conditions attributed to post traumatic stress disorder, depression and similar conditions.
>
> (c) The psychological symptoms include anxiety, tension, insomnia, irritability, loss of confidence, agoraphobia and pre-occupation with thoughts of self-harm or guilt.
>
> (d) The physical symptoms include alopecia, asthma, eczema, enuresis and psoriasis.
>
> (e) Relevant disabilities include impaired work or school or other educational performance, significant adverse effects on social relationships and sexual dysfunction.

The amount payable was stated as follows:

Shock	**[$]**
Lasting 6 to 13 weeks	2,400
Lasting 14 to 28 weeks	9,600
Lasting over 28 weeks (but not permanent)	18,000
Permanent symptoms and disability	48,000

Scott's shock-related symptoms persisted for more than six weeks, but it could not be said that he had a 'disability'. If he has symptoms but no disability, does that mean he cannot recover compensation related to shock?

Note that Clause 8 of Schedule 1, provides:

> An injury not specifically mentioned in Column 1 of the table to this Schedule is a compensable injury if, in the opinion of the Tribunal or compensation assessor dealing with the application for statutory compensation:
>
> (a) the injury is similar to an injury specifically mentioned in the table, and
> (b) the injury has caused symptoms or disability lasting for at least 6 weeks.
>
> The standard amount of compensation for the injury is the standard amount for that similar injury.

Further, s 3(a) of the Act states that the object of the Act is 'to give effect to a statutory scheme of compensation for victims of crimes of violence'.

Decide before proceeding.

The real case is *Victims Compensation Fund Corporation v Brown* (2003) 201 ALR 260. If you decided that he had to have 'symptoms and disability' you are in agreement with the original compensation assessor, the Victims Compensation Tribunal, Spigelman CJ in dissent in the New South Wales Court of Appeal, and the High Court. If, instead of deciding the words had to be read conjunctively, you said that the 'and' could be read as 'or' so that it was sufficient that he had symptoms if not disability, you are in agreement with Phelan DCJ in the District Court, and Mason P and McClennan J, the majority in the New South Wales Court of Appeal.

Heydon J wrote the main judgment in the High Court, concurred with by each of the other judges. He commenced by referring to the operative provision, saying that the ordinary meaning of 'and' as being conjunctive. He then considered the table, which only referred to disability in the bottom row, saying it 'shows only that the drafting has not perhaps been uniform or flawless throughout': at [14]. The word 'and' was used in the bottom row of the table to merely 'emphasise the need ... for concurrence of both symptoms and disability'.

Heydon J checked the legislative background and found no reason there to depart from the ordinary meaning of 'and'. He essentially agreed with the dissenting judgment of Spigelman CJ in the New South Wales Court of Appeal, where it was reasoned that at times injuries were only stated as requiring 'symptoms' and other times 'symptoms and disability' but never 'disability' alone. This context suggests that where 'symptoms and disability' is used, both are required.

Given the High Court's concurrence with the reasoning of Spigelman CJ, it is worthwhile referring to his judgment in *Victims Compensation Fund Corp v Brown* (2002) 54 NSWLR 668. There His Honour referred to the argument advanced by Brown that the purpose of the legislation was to 'compensate victims', saying at [10]–[13]:

> Even if I were to accept a legislative purpose stated at that level of generality, that would not entail that any ambiguity must be construed in such a way as to maximise compensation ... the very specificity of the provisions of the legislation indicate that the legislative purpose is to provide compensation in accordance with the Act and not otherwise. The issue before the Court is the determination of the circumstances in which compensation is payable. The Court is not required to give the most expansive possible interpretation of such circumstances ... The requirement of disability is, in my opinion, intended to limit compensable shock to that which is serious enough to impact on a person's lifestyle, work or study.

Clearly, then, it cannot be a matter of finding the purpose and applying the statute to give effect to that purpose, if the intention of Parliament was not to achieve that purpose at all costs. We cannot state the purpose of legislation at too high a level of generality. Yes, the purpose of the legislation in the above case exercise was to compensate victims, but it was not to compensate *any* and *all* victims. Therefore, as stated by Pearce and Geddes, 'the level of specificity with which purpose is articulated can be critical to the outcome of the case'.[11]

What if the purpose is not expressly stated?

What if the Act does not expressly state the purpose? It is not uncommon for an Act to have no express statement of legislative purpose. This is because, discussed in Chapter 2, there may need to be a degree of compromise in order to gain successful passage of a Bill through both Houses of Parliament. McHugh J referred to this in *Stevens v Kabushiki Kaisha Sony Computer Entertainment* (2005) 224 CLR 193 at [126]:

> Much modern legislation regulating an industry reflects a compromise reached between, or forced upon, powerful and competing groups in the industry whose interests are likely to be enhanced or impaired by the legislation. In such cases, what emerges from the legislative process is frequently not a law motivated solely by the public interest. It reflects wholly or partly a compromise that is the product of intensive lobbying, directly or indirectly, of Ministers and parliamentarians by groups in the industry seeking to achieve the maximum protection or advancement of their respective interests. The only purpose of the legislation or its particular provisions is to give effect to the compromise. To attempt to construe the meaning of particular provisions of such legislation not solely by reference to its text but by reference to some supposed purpose of the legislation invites error.

11 D C Pearce and R Geddes, *Statutory Interpretation in Australia* (LexisNexis, 7th ed, 2011) 37.

Gleeson CJ referred to this extra-judicially in 2008:[12]

> [T]here may be some matters about which Parliament has deliberately refrained from forming or expressing a purpose. Indeed, it may be that which has made possible the compromise achieved by the legislation. Gaps in a legislative scheme may be deliberate. Parliament might have found it expedient to leave it to the courts to fill them in. Or the gaps might be unintentional, because a potential problem has been overlooked, in which case, there may be no discernable purpose that is an aid to construction.

In some situations the real purpose behind the Act may be different from the stated purpose, or may be intentionally hidden in the obscure provisions of the Act. Spigelman CJ likes to cite *R v Wilson; Ex parte Kisch* (1934) 52 CLR 234, a case which is also a good example of how the law of statutory interpretation protects fundamental rights (discussed in Chapter 11). The legislation being interpreted in the *Kisch* case was the *Immigration Restriction Act 1901* (Cth).[13] The long title of the Act was:

> To place certain restrictions on Immigration and to provide for the removal from the Commonwealth of prohibited Immigrants.

Section 3 gave effect to the purpose through the means, *inter alia*, of a dictation test, which provided in the relevant part:

> The immigration into the Commonwealth of the persons described in any of the following paragraphs of this section (herein-after called 'prohibited immigrants') is prohibited, namely:
>
> (a) Any person who when asked to do so by an officer fails to write out at dictation and sign in the presence of the officer a passage of fifty words in length in an [*sic*] European language directed by the officer …

Thus the Long Title does not specify what sort of 'restrictions on immigration' the Act seeks to achieve, and s 3(a) suggests there is a desire for immigrants who can speak a European language. This legislation preceded the era of objects clauses and explanatory memoranda, but the true purpose was clear from the words used by Prime Minister Edmund Barton when he introduced the bill into Federal Parliament:

> We are guarding the last part of the world in which the higher races can live and increase freely for the higher civilisation. I place before the house a measure of definite and high policy.

12 M Gleeson, 'The Meaning of Legislation: Context, Purpose and Respect for Fundamental Rights' Address to Victoria Law Foundation, Melbourne, 31 July 2008, 22.

13 The text of the legislation is not available on AustLII but see http://foundingdocs.gov.au/resources/transcripts/cth4ii_doc_1901a.pdf.

And, after the law was enacted:

> [T]his ideal had not been achieved easily. In the months preceding the adoption of the legislation, the Australian political sphere was fraught with contention. The politicians were divided. How could they best achieve a White Australia?

In practice the choice of a dictation test in a 'European language' as 'directed' by the officer enabled the exclusion of coloured immigrants such as those from Asia, who were unlikely to speak a European language, but it could also be used to exclude 'undesirable' Europeans, by selecting a European language they were unlikely to know.

Kisch was a Communist journalist from Czechoslavakia who wanted to attend a communist peace conference in Australia. Another invited speaker from New Zealand was given a dictation test in Dutch and was excluded when he failed it; Kisch was given the test in Scottish Gaelic.

The issue before the High Court was whether Scottish Gaelic was a 'European language'. The High Court majority held that it was not, so the dictation test administered to Kisch was invalid. Even though Scottish Gaelic was a language used in Europe it was not a European language, namely a standard form of speech recognised as the received and ordinary means of communication among the inhabitants in a European community. Census figures showed that it was the speech of a rapidly diminishing number of people in the remote highlands of Scotland and was not the recognised speech of a community organised politically, socially or on any other basis.

Whether or not the purpose is expressly stated, and whether or not refraining from stating the true purpose was intentional, the task of the court remains the same—finding and achieving the purpose. As stated by the Federal Court in *Municipal Officers' Association of Australia v Lancaster* (1981) 54 FLR 129 at 153:

> In many cases, an Act does not contain provisions setting out in express words the policy and purpose of the legislation, but this does not prevent the court from determining the policy or purpose of the legislation by a consideration of the legislation itself, or in other words determining the object of the legislation from a consideration of the provisions of the legislation.

This means that even if the purpose is not expressed, the courts can determine it by consideration of the Act as a whole.

What if there are multiple purposes?

The statutory instruction, whether in the 'best purpose' or 'preferred promotion' formulation, uses the singular phrase 'the purpose or object' of the Act. This implies that a single purpose can be found for every Act (although perhaps we could apply the generic rule discussed in Chapter 3 on page 30—that the singular includes the plural). It is already well recognised that the notion that Parliament has a single intent or purpose for each piece of legislation is fictitious.[14] As stated extra-judicially by Gleeson CJ:

> Acts of Parliament sometimes have mixed, and even inconsistent, purposes, and even where they have a single or dominant purpose there may be uncertainty about the extent to which it has been pursued.[15]

Multiple purposes create challenges in the interpretation task. Kirby P said in *Avel Pty Ltd v Attorney-General for New South Wales* (1987) 11 NSWLR 126 at 127 that '[a] "purposive" approach founders in the shallows of a multitude of obscure, uncertain and even apparently conflicting purposes'. This weighing-up exercise has been described by Spigelman CJ as 'the intolerable wrestle' of statutory interpretation, where the general rule of purposive construction 'may be of little assistance'.[16]

Perhaps s 15AA needs further amendment, to cover not only a choice between a construction that promotes the purpose and one that does not, and a choice between two constructions that both promote the purpose, but also a choice of which purpose best applies to the operative provision, or which purpose is the dominant purpose (what we might call the 'uberpurpose' or 'grundpurpose') compared with other, lesser purposes, and how the legislation goes to achieve that purpose as compared with the other purposes. But the more value-laden the 'leeways of choice' given by the legislature to the judiciary, the more blurred the lines between law and policy become, and the politicisation of the judicial task only undermines this appointed arm of government.

What if the legislation represents a political compromise between different purposes?

The courts have already wrestled with legislation that represents a compromise between different purposes. In *Carr v Western Australia* [2007] HCA 47, in which the High Court applied the 'preferred construction' approach, Gleeson CJ said:

> That general rule of interpretation, however, may be of little assistance where a statutory provision strikes a balance between competing interests, and the problem of interpretation is that there is uncertainty as to how far the provision goes in seeking to achieve the

14 See D K Smith, 'Interpreting the Corporations Law—Purpose, Practical Reasoning and the Public Interest' (1999) 21 *Sydney Law Review* 161, 172.

15 M Gleeson, 'The Meaning of Legislation: Context, Purpose and Respect for Fundamental Rights' Address to Victoria Law Foundation, Melbourne, 31 July 2008, 22.

16 J J Spigelman, 'The Intolerable Wrestle: Developments in Statutory Interpretation', Address to the Australasian Conference of Planning and Environment Courts and Tribunals, 1 September 2010, 18 and 20.

> underlying purpose or object of the Act. Legislation rarely pursues a single purpose at all costs ... For a court to construe the legislation as though it pursued the purpose to the fullest possible extent may be contrary to the manifest intention of the legislation and a purported exercise of judicial power for a legislative purpose ... the general purpose of legislation of the kind here in issue is reasonably clear; but it reflects a political compromise. The competing interests and forces at work in achieving that compromise are well known. The question then is not: what was the purpose or object underlying the legislation? The question is: how far does the legislation go in pursuit of that purpose or object?

Gleeson CJ has made extra-judicial comments to similar effect:[17]

> Parliament is constantly striking a balance between competing considerations of policy. Issues of statutory construction often take the form of disputes as to the balance that has been struck. The question is not so much one of identifying the legislative purpose as of working out how far Parliament has gone in pursuit of that purpose.

The challenge of interpreting legislation which strikes a compromise between competing objectives is evident in the following case exercise.

Case exercise

'In the course of official questioning'

A friend of Shane's, Mick, was angry about Tony having informed on him to police about a robbery. He'd served time in prison as a result, and wanted to get Tony back. Shane and Mick talked about it and decided Shane would lure Tony to a log landing site where Shane used to work, Mick would kill him, and they'd bury him in a decent sized hole dug with an excavator. All went according to plan.

Police questioned Shane about the murder, and at one stage he asked if they could go up to the roof. Once there he admitted that he and Mick were involved and asked for indemnity. He refused to repeat what he had said on videotape, but did write out a statement and signed it. A few months later Shane was arrested for the murder. In a videotaped interview he claimed his previous confession was false. After three hours of questioning, the interview was terminated and the police completed certain formalities which lasted about half an hour, after which they left to take Shane to a hospital to obtain blood and hair samples. As they were heading to the car in the police car park Shane said to the police officers: 'Sorry about the interview—no hard feelings. I was just playing the game. I suppose I shouldn't have said that, I suppose you will make notes of that as well'.

---

17 M Gleeson, 'The Meaning of Legislation: Context, Purpose and Respect for Fundamental Rights' Address to Victoria Law Foundation, Melbourne, 31 July 2008, 20–21.

Shane is now being tried for murder. Is his statement in the car park admissible?

Section 8 of the *Criminal Law (Detention and Interrogation) Act 1995* (Tas) provides in relevant part:

> (1) In this section—
>
> 'confession or admission' means a confession or an admission—
>
> (a) that was made by an accused person who, at the time when the confession or admission was made, was or ought reasonably to have been suspected by a police officer of having committed an offence; and
>
> (b) that was made in the course of official questioning;
>
> 'official questioning' means questioning by a police officer in connection with the investigation of the commission or the possible commission of an offence;
>
> (2) On the trial of an accused person for a serious offence, evidence of any confession or admission by the accused person is not admissible unless—
>
> (a) there is available to the court a videotape of an interview with the accused person in the course of which the confession or admission was made; or
>
> (b) if the prosecution proves on the balance of probabilities that there was a reasonable explanation as to why a videotape referred to in paragraph (a) could not be made, there is available to the court a videotape of an interview with the accused person about the making and terms of the confession or admission or the substance of the confession or admission in the course of which the accused person states that he or she made a confession or an admission in those terms or confirms the substance of the admission or confession; or
>
> (c) the prosecution proves on the balance of probabilities that there was a reasonable explanation as to why the videotape referred to in paragraphs (a) and (b) could not be made; or
>
> (d) the court is satisfied that there are exceptional circumstances which, in the interests of justice, justify the admission of the evidence.

This section was introduced in 1991, following a 1990 report of the Law Reform Commissioner of Tasmania titled *Police Powers of Interrogation and Detention* which recommended that police confessional evidence must be by way of electronic recording unless there was some reasonable excuse for not making such a recording. This would avoid the risk of discrediting the justice system by unreliable or even false confessions sworn by police to have been made by the accused.

A Bill giving effect, *inter alia*, to the recommendation was presented to Parliament. The Second Reading Speech of the Minister of Justice referred to the fact that the Bill represented a compromise between, on the one hand, expanding police powers of investigation, detention and interrogation, and on the other hand, ensuring appropriate safeguards are in place to protect accused persons and ensure they are brought promptly before a justice. So the

Bill would liberalise the powers of police but require that 'police confessional evidence' be recorded for it to be admissible. The Minister spoke at length about the value of recorded interviews but did not specifically refer to the phrase 'in the course of questioning'.

Decide what you think before proceeding.

The real case is *Kelly v R* (2004) 218 CLR 216. If you decided the statement is admissible, you are in agreement with the trial judge in the Supreme Court of Tasmania, who allowed the statement for jury consideration on the basis that it was not made 'in the course of official questioning'. Likewise the Court of Criminal Appeal majority comprising Underwood and Evans JJ, and the High Court per Gleeson CJ, Hayne and Heydon JJ. If you decided the statement was not admissible, you are in agreement with Slicer J in the Court of Appeal, who said the effect of the section was that all confessions must be videotaped unless one of the four exceptions in s 8(2) applies. You are also in agreement with McHugh and Kirby JJ on the High Court. It should be said that all judges on the High Court agreed that the case should be dismissed, because even if the evidence were not admitted it was likely the remainder of the evidence would have been sufficient to convict Shane Kelly.

The High Court majority (Gleeson CJ, Hayne and Heydon JJ) stated the need to first identify the purpose or object of the Act, and then work out the construction that promotes that purpose or object: at [41]. They said at [43]:

> [T]hough it may be accepted that the purpose or object of s 8 of the Act was to overcome the 'perceived problems' identified in many earlier cases, as the range of legislative responses shows, those problems can be overcome in different ways and to different degrees. The 'purpose or object' identified does not compel any particular construction of the quite detailed language of s 8 of the Act. What the correct construction is must depend on the particular words used.

The words used do not require the statement to be said in response to a question: at [45] 'but the expression "in the course of official questioning" marks out a period of time running from when the questioning commenced to when it ceased ... it does not provide that video-recording is a condition for admissibility of all confessions' at [52]. Therefore the majority considered that the 'course of official questioning' ended when the interview was concluded, so the unrecorded statement made in the car park was admissible.

McHugh J refused to use such a narrow construction of the phrase 'in the course of official questioning', saying at [83] that was only possible if those words 'are read with a temporal connotation and in isolation, without regard to the policy or purpose of s 8(2)'. He referred to the mischief to which the Act was addressed, which was 'the attack on the integrity of the administration of justice by false or unreliable confessions or admissions allegedly made by suspects during a police investigation of a serious criminal offence': at [104]. He said at [97]:

> Given the mischief to which the Australian legislatures have directed their attention and the policy behind the enactments, it would not be defensible to make the admissibility of

> confessions or admissions made during the period of vulnerability turn upon fine verbal distinctions between the legislation of particular jurisdictions … As far as the statutory language will permit, the legislation of the various jurisdictions should be interpreted liberally and uniformly to give effect to what is a national policy behind this class of legislation.

McHugh J referred to the fact that the phrase 'in the course of official questioning' was used in a definition that had the purpose of aiding in the construction of a statute, not creating substantive law. Therefore, 'to construe the definition before its text has been inserted into the fabric of the substantive enactment invites error as to the meaning of the substantive enactment': at [103]. He concluded that the purpose of the section was to exclude all police confessions that were not recorded, and the phrase 'in the course of official questioning' had been added to ensure confessions made to other persons besides police were still admissible. It should be broadly interpreted as 'in connection with' police questioning.

Kirby J described himself as using a 'functional approach' at [171]. He considered the legislative background, and particularly the issue of 'police verbals' which 'bedevilled the administration of criminal justice in Australia' at [136]. He referred to the legislative compromise inherent in the Tasmanian Parliament at [143], and the 'opaque and ambiguous' phrase used in the section at [168]. He said that the text itself envisaged a follow-up interview in s 8(2)(b), and in the circumstances 'it would have been a small inconvenience to return the appellant to the videotape recording facility to confront him': at [161]. He decided that limiting the interpretation to words said in a room in a police station with recording equipment and excluding words before and after would undermine the statutory purpose: at [149].

In essence, the interpreter of Commonwealth legislation must consider intrinsic and extrinsic materials in considering purpose, be they express or latent, singular or multiple, aligning or conflicting, and must follow a process (described in more detail in Chapter 14):

a If there is one purpose and one possible meaning, it is a simple matter of checking that the meaning promotes the purpose, taking into account the context;

b If there is more than one possible meaning, but only one purpose, one must select the meaning that promotes or best achieves the purpose,[18] taking into account the context;

c If there is more than one possible meaning, and more than one purpose, with those multiple purposes aligning, one must select the dominant purpose, or the most applicable purpose to the section, and choose the meaning that gives effect to that purpose, taking into account the context; and

18 Depending on whether the applicable jurisdiction uses the 'best achievement' or 'preferred constructive' approach as discussed at the outset of this chapter.

d If there is more than one possible meaning, and more than one purpose, with a compromise between conflicting purposes, one must explore how the balance between the conflicting purposes has been struck and, taking into account the context, choose the meaning that best gives effect to that balance.

Needless to say, this will often be a difficult task, and there will be times where the courts reach an interpretation with which Parliament does not agree. But, as Gleeson CJ has said, 'where courts have mistaken legislative purpose, or given a construction that defeats the purpose, it is of course within the power of Parliament to amend the legislation'.[19]

This chapter has focused on context and purpose, but it has not yet considered another word frequently used in the Interpretation Acts, the 'intention' of Parliament—also often referred to judicially as the 'will' of Parliament. Nor has there been any discussion of the techniques used to stretch or shrink the ambit of a statutory provision to give effect to its purpose. These are considered in the next chapter.

19 M Gleeson, 'The Meaning of Legislation: Context, Purpose and Respect for Fundamental Rights' Address to Victoria Law Foundation, Melbourne, 31 July 2008, 22.

CHAPTER 5

INTENTION AND INTERPRETIVE TECHNIQUES

Continuing from the previous chapter, this chapter furthers discussion of the interpretive task by considering the vexed notion of 'intention' and where it fits into statutory interpretation. It also looks at interpretive techniques that constrict the meaning of a provision, otherwise referred to as 'reading down', and techniques that expand the meaning of a provision, referred to as 'strained interpretation', 'reading in', 'ambulatory interpretation', 'equity of the statute' and 'dynamic' interpretation of statutes.

Intention

The word 'intention' is frequently used in statutory interpretation legislation, and there are ample judicial references to the 'will' of Parliament. How is 'intention' used in statutory interpretation? How does it relate to 'purpose'? Are the terms synonymous, or has purpose taken over as the preferred term, with intention being discredited as being fraught with the danger of misuse? In short, these questions continue to plague courts, and the exact relationship has not yet crystallised. The following is submitted to be the appropriate connection between these two concepts.

The 'purpose' of an Act is given effect by its provisions. Parliament does not insert provisions into an Act for no reason. Parliament must be assumed to have intended each provision it has legislated, in some way and to some extent, to give effect to the purpose of the legislation. But there are many ways in which a stated purpose may be given effect. One could draw a simple analogy: if our purpose was to reach the airport, we may intend to achieve that purpose by, for example, taking a taxi, a train, a bus, a combination of train, bus and ferry, or we may be given a lift. We may intend to pay for that by cash, voucher, credit card or a kiss. And so on. The intention in relation to the aspects of carriage and payment contribute to achievement of the overall purpose. In this way, a statutory purpose can be seen to focus on the 'why' and the 'who' whereas intention focuses on the 'what' and the 'how'. That is, the purpose looks at 'why' the legislation is needed and 'who' it is directed towards, and the intention is concerned with 'what' is done to meet the purpose and 'how' it should be implemented. Therefore, giving effect to the intended meaning of a statutory provision furthers the achievement of the legislative purpose.

Similarly, what is concluded to be the intended meaning of a statutory provision may be affected by the legislative purpose itself—see for example Gummow, Hayne, Crennan and Bell JJ in *Plaintiff M70/2011 v Minister for Immigration and Citizenship* [2011] HCA 32 at [98], considering s 198(2) of the *Migration Act 1958* (Cth), which provided for removal of 'unlawful non-citizens', saying that to read that section

> as providing a power to remove from Australia to *any* country that is willing to receive the person concerned any offshore entry person who claims to be a person to whom Australia

> owes protection obligations, but whose claims have not been assessed, would deny the legislative intention evident from the Act as a whole: that its provisions are intended to facilitate Australia's compliance with the obligations undertaken in the Refugees Convention and the Refugees Protocol.

Intention has been referred to in less than flattering terms by some members of the judiciary, but that criticism has been made in terms of the difficulty of application rather than inherent problems with the concept itself. See for example McHugh J in *Singh v Commonwealth* (2004) 222 CLR 322 at [52]:

> Intention in the context of statutory interpretation is an 'obvious legal fiction'. But it is 'a useful judicial construct because the judge is required to make the choices that best express the statutory text's meaning'.

Gleeson CJ in *Wilson v Anderson* (2002) 213 CLR 401 at [8] said:

> In the construction or interpretation of a statute, the object of a court is to ascertain, and give effect to, the will of Parliament. Courts commonly refer to the 'intention of the legislature'. This has been described as a 'very slippery phrase', but it reflects the constitutional relationship between the legislature and the judiciary. ... Parliament manifests its intention by the use of language, and it is by determining the meaning of that language, in accordance with principles of construction established by the common law and statute, that courts give effect to the legislative will.

Extra-judicially he has defended the validity of using intention in statutory interpretation:[1]

> Intention is a slippery concept, but, properly employed, it is valid, and expresses the constitutional place of courts in giving effect to legislative will. The *Acts Interpretation Act 1901* (Cth) itself makes repeated reference to 'intention' in the course of laying down rules of interpretation. How, in the face of the statute, a court could declare intention to be an inadmissible concept is impossible to understand.

The reason intention gives cause for consternation is that it is easy, when talking about the intention of Parliament, to think of the actual intention of the particular Parliament that passed the legislation, however long ago that may have been.[2] That is a common error made when intention is used in statutory interpretation. What is being sought is not the actual intention of Parliament, but a metaphor for describing

1 M Gleeson, 'The Meaning of Legislation: Context, Purpose and Respect for Fundamental Rights' Address to Victoria Law Foundation, Melbourne, 31 July 2008, 13.

2 See the High Court back in 1955: 'it is the real intention of the legislature that must be ascertained ... you begin with the prima face presumption that permissive or facultative expressions operate according to their ordinary natural meaning': *Ward v Williams* (1955) 92 CLR 496 at 505.

the intention revealed through examination of the statute in the light of its context and purpose. (Ask yourself, or discuss with others: how can parliamentary intent be an objective concept?)

Judicial explanations of this distinction include:

- 'A statute is the expression of the will of Parliament. Since Parliament is an institution, the term "will", like "intention", is metaphorical, but it reflects the exercise of constitutional authority by a law-giver'.[3]
- 'The task of the courts is to interpret the words used by Parliament. It is not to divine the intent of the Parliament. The courts must determine what Parliament meant by the words it used. The courts do not determine what Parliament intended to say'.[4]
- The word 'intended' 'is not a solecism. It is a common term of judicial exposition, but not to be misunderstood as a reference to the mental processes of some individual, or individuals'.[5]
- 'It has been said that to attribute an intention to the legislature is to apply something of a fiction. However, what is involved here is not the attribution of a collective mental state to legislators. That would be a misleading use of metaphor'.[6]
- 'The legislative intention … is not an objective collective mental state. Such a state is a fiction which serves no useful purpose'.[7]
- 'What is involved is the search for an objective intention of Parliament, not the subjective intention of ministers or Parliamentarians. Subjective intention, even that of a minister expressed in a Second Reading Speech, is, as has often been held, not relevant'.[8]
- In identifying historical meaning we do not confine interpretation to 'what those who wrote it may have had in mind' and to do so 'would be to fall into the error of seeking the subjective intention of the founders'.[9]
- 'The danger to be avoided in references to legislative intention is that they might suggest an exercise in psychoanalysis of individuals involved in the legislative process … The words "intention", "contemplation", "purpose", and "design"

---

3 M Gleeson, 'The Meaning of Legislation: Context, Purpose and Respect for Fundamental Rights' Address to Victoria Law Foundation, Melbourne, 31 July 2008.

4 J J Spigelman, 'The Intolerable Wrestle: Developments in Statutory Interpretation', Address to the Australasian Conference of Planning and Environment Courts and Tribunals, 1 September 2010, 20.

5 Gleeson CJ in *Singh v Commonwealth* (2004) 222 CLR 322 at [26].

6 *Zheng v Cai* (2009) 239 CLR 446 at 455–6.

7 *Lacey v Attorney-General of Queensland* [2011] HCA 10 at [43].

8 J J Spigelman, 'The Intolerable Wrestle: Developments in Statutory Interpretation', Address to the Australasian Conference of Planning and Environment Courts and Tribunals, 1 September 2010, 21.

9 *Singh v Commonwealth* (2004) 222 CLR 322 per Gummow, Hayne and Heydon JJ at [162].

are used routinely by courts in relation to the meaning of legislation. They are orthodox and legitimate terms of legal analysis, provided their objectivity is not overlooked'.[10]

An analogy may be usefully drawn to the law of contract—when ascertaining the meaning of a contractual term, we do not look at what the parties thought when they entered the contract—we look at what a reasonable person reading that contract would think it means. See Gleeson CJ in *Wilson v Anderson* (2002) 213 CLR 401 at [8]:

> The law of contract seeks to give effect to the common intention of the parties to a contract. But the test is objective and impersonal ... If the contract is in the form of a document, then it is the meaning that the document would convey to a reasonable person that matters. ... it is only the document that can speak to the third person. In the case of a will, or a deed, or other written instrument, the object of a court is to discover, and give effect to, the intention of the testator, or parties; but it is in the meaning of the instrument, discovered according to established principles of construction, that such intention is found.

Just as a third party (such as a creditor, insurer, discounter or buyer in due course) is entitled to rely upon the terms of the contract as they are expressed in the contract, so too should third parties (such as courts, individuals and companies) be entitled to rely on the terms of a statute as they are expressed in that statute.

What if there was no actual parliamentary intent?

What happens if no intention can be found—indeed, if it is clear that there was no intention of Parliament because Parliament did not turn its mind to the question in issue, or foresee that the statute would be applied in a particular situation? Should the interpreter try to work out what, if the issue had been considered or the situation had been envisaged by Parliament, it would have done?

Evidently the interpretation task requires rectification of the defect, as far as that is possible. See Dawson J in *Mills v Meeking* (1990) 169 CLR 214 at 235:

> Reference to the purposes may reveal that the draftsman has inadvertently overlooked something which he would have dealt with had his attention been drawn to it and if it is possible as a matter of construction to repair the defect, then this must be done.

How, then, should the interpreter fill in the vacuum of intention? Give this some thought in relation to the two case exercises below.

---

10 *Singh v Commonwealth* (2004) 222 CLR 322 per Gleeson CJ at [19].

Case exercise

'When cannabis ain't cannabis'

Gloria flew into Perth from overseas, and, as drugs were found in her luggage, she has been arrested and charged with drug importation. She admits she was carrying cannabis, but denies it is a prohibited import because what she imported was not *cannabis sativa*. The relevant provision, s 233B of the *Customs Act 1901–75* (Cth) provided

(1) Any person who ...
  (b) imports, or attempts to import, into Australia any prohibited imports;
  (c) without lawful excuse (proof whereof shall lie upon him) has in his possession any prohibited imports to which this section applies which have been imported into Australia in contravention of this Act ...

shall be guilty of an offence.

(2) The prohibited imports to which this section applies are prohibited imports that are narcotic goods.

Relevant definitions, from s 4 of the Act, include:

'Cannabis'—a cannabis plant, whether living or dead, and includes, in any form, any flowering or fruiting tops, leaves, seeds, stalks or any other part of a cannabis plant or cannabis plants and any mixture of parts of a cannabis plant or cannabis plants, but does not include cannabis resin or cannabis fibre.

'Cannabis plant'—a plant of the genus *Cannabis sativa*.

Narcotic goods—'goods that consist of a narcotic substance'.

Narcotic substance—'a substance or thing the name of which is specified in column 1 of Schedule VI to this Act'.

Column 1 of Schedule VI listed cannabis, and cannabis is a prohibited import under reg 5(i) of the *Customs (Prohibited Imports) Regulations 1956* (Cth). It is noted that in plant nomenclature, the genus is 'Cannabis' and three species come within that genus, namely *Cannabis sativa*, *Cannabis indica* and *Cannabis ruderalis*. At the time of passage of the legislation it was thought there was only one species, *Cannabis sativa*. The general rule as stated in the International Code of Botanical Nomenclature is that, while a species may be written as two separate words, a genus is either a single word or is hyphenated (such as 'mahi-mahi' or 'Douglas-fir').

Decide for yourself—does the legislation cover all cannabis, or only *Cannabis sativa*?

The real case is *Yager v R* (1977) 139 CLR 28. If you decided the legislation covered all cannabis, you are in agreement with the District Court of Western Australia, the Court of Criminal Appeal and the majority of members of the High Court. If you decided it does not cover all cannabis, you are in agreement with Murphy J, in dissent on the High Court.

In essence the High Court acknowledged that Parliament had made a mistake in describing cannabis, but that the description used was correct at the time, as it was thought that there was only one kind of cannabis. That error was not enough to conclude that Parliament only prescribed one of three species to be covered by the legislation.

Barwick CJ stated at 34:

> [T]he statute was clearly and expressly referring to a genus and not to a species. It would be little to the point that the statute may have misdescribed the genus. That circumstance would not warrant the statute being read to apply only to a species when in truth it unambiguously referred to a genus.

Similarly Mason J stated at 45:

> At best the applicant's case is that Parliament was mistaken in treating cannabis sativa as a genus, but this cannot alter the circumstance that Parliament prescribed a genus; it does not allow us to say that Parliament prescribed a species. Nor does it permit us to say that the statutory definition should be ignored or treated as if it was of no effect.

The Court, therefore, took account of the subjective beliefs of Parliament at the time of making the legislation to find that they intended to cover all cannabis and not just one species of it.

In dissent, Murphy J relied upon the statutory presumption that penal provisions are strictly construed (see Chapter 10). He said that the expression in the statute was ambiguous, and as it is a criminal statute, it should be construed strictly in favour of the accused. To be fair, a civilian is entitled to expect of its government that rules be expressed in language that everyone can reasonably be expected to understand. Therefore the conviction should be quashed.

Consider the significance in the above case that consideration was in fact made of what would have been in the actual minds of the parliamentarians at the time of passing the legislation.

Case exercise

'Reviving the right or the right to act?'

Kitty and Stuart were married and had two children. Two years ago Stuart was crossing a road when he was knocked down by a car driven negligently by Lionel William Murphy. He subsequently died from his injuries.

The *Compensation to Relatives Act 1897–46* (NSW) provided a right of action for a widow, parent or child of a deceased person to claim compensation from the wrongdoer. However s 5 of the Act provided:

> Not more than one action shall lie for and in respect of the same subject-matter of complaint, and every such action shall be commenced within twelve months after the death of such deceased person.

Unfortunately Kitty did not bring an action within the required year. However, the Act was amended 2.5 years later, with the twelve month period being extended to six years. Kitty has commenced an action for compensation under the new provisions. Does she have a right to do so?

Decide whether the amendment revived Kitty's right to bring an action, in circumstances where Parliament quite clearly did not think about what would happen to cases between one and six years from death (which were statute-barred at the time of the amendment) or even what would happen to the cases which were within the twelve months (but considered to be in the past in relation to the new six-year rule).

Once you have decided, read on.

The real case is *Maxwell v Murphy* (1957) 96 CLR 261. If you decided Kitty Maxwell did not have a right to commence an action under the new provisions, you are in agreement with the Full Court of the Supreme Court of New South Wales, and the majority of the High Court (Dixon CJ, Williams, Kitto and Taylor JJ). If you decided she did have a right, you are in agreement with Fullagar J in dissent on the High Court.

The High Court held that the action ceased to be maintainable twelve months after Kitty's husband died, and the action was not revived by the subsequent amendment, even though it came into force and action was commenced within six years of the husband's death.

It was acknowledged that the interpretation difficulty lay in the inadvertence of Parliament. See Dixon CJ at 266:

> [I]t is unfortunately only too plain from the brief words substituting one period of time for the other that there was never any advertence to the effect the amendment would or might have in relation to deaths that had already occurred.

Similarly Kitto and Taylor JJ described it as 'a very special problem of statutory construction' at 291, saying at 293:

> One could not, we think, construe the amendment as applying in cases where the period of twelve months fixed by the principal Act had commenced to run and was still current when the amending Act was passed, unless one were prepared to hold that it applies also in cases in which the twelve months had then expired but the period of six years from the death had not. The distinction was plainly not adverted to at all. But to hold that the amendment applies in the latter class of cases would be to attribute to Parliament an intention of so

> unusual a kind, and one so clearly demanding a deliberate judgement as to its fairness, that it could hardly have been formed without finding expression in clear words; and there is not even a hint of it to be found.

Consideration was given to the position of the wrongdoer in this situation. It could be said that he, or his insurer, would consider at the expiry of twelve months that there was no scope to be held liable. To allow the amendment to revive the right 'would impose anew a liability that had ceased to exist. The presumptive interpretation is against such an operation': per Dixon CJ at 269. One can see the logic in this reasoning if an analogy is drawn to detrimental reliance on a representation, where there has been a change of position such as discarding evidence or other material suitable for a defence on the basis it is no longer needed as an action is statute-barred.

Fullager J, in dissent, referred to the lack of decisive indication of the intention of the legislature, except the long title says it is 'An Act to enlarge the period within which actions may be brought'. He said at 285: 'I am not able to see any inherent probability that the legislature would, if it had thought about the matter, have been zealous to avoid disappointment to a wrongdoer who might have thought himself safe, or to his insurance company'.

It could be said that this decision opted for the 'default position' of not applying an intention to revive an action where there was not discernible intention to do so. One cannot help but wonder, if the action had been brought by someone whose husband had died the day before the new legislation came in, whether the outcome would have been different. Technically, the legislation providing for the period of twelve months was repealed after the death, removing the right to claim compensation that existed at that time, and the new legislation, passed the day after the death, should only apply to deaths that occur after the legislation was passed. The 'default position' that would then be likely to apply is that the period of twelve months would be encapsulated in both the previous and the current Act (which provides for an extra five years), so the court would almost certainly hold that an action could be brought.

Can we consider whether the outcome was intended?

Although it can be difficult to ascertain a positive intention where there has been legislative inadvertence, courts may use the effect, or outcome to work out what was *not* intended. See for example Gibbs J in *Public Transport Commissioner of NSW v J Murray-More (NSW) Pty Ltd* (1975) 132 CLR 336 at 350: 'where two meanings are open … it is proper to adopt that meaning that will avoid consequences that appear irrational and unjust'.

See also the judgment of Mason and Wilson JJ in *Cooper Brookes (Wollongong) Pty Ltd v Federal Commissioner of Taxation* (1981) 147 CLR 297 at 320–321:

> There are cases in which inconvenience of result or improbability of result assists the court in concluding that an alternative construction which is reasonably open is to be preferred to the literal meaning because the alternative interpretation more closely conforms to the legislative intent discernible from other provisions in the statute …
>
> [W]hen the judge labels the operation of the statute as 'absurd', 'extraordinary', 'capricious', 'irrational' or 'obscure' he assigns a ground for concluding that the legislature could not have intended such an operation and that an alternative interpretation must be preferred … If the choice is between two strongly competing interpretations, as we have said, the advantage may lie with that which produces the fairer and more convenient operation as long as it conforms to the legislative intention. If, however, one interpretation has a powerful advantage in ordinary meaning and grammatical sense, it will only be displaced if its operation is perceived to be unintended.

This reference by the courts to the consequences of a particular interpretation is a variant on consideration of the purpose—does the outcome reached by using a particular interpretation support the purpose? If not, it cannot have been intended.

Interpretive techniques

Words are, to some extent, elastic. Courts can constrain or strain interpretation to reach an appropriate outcome. This will involve giving the words a narrower or broader ambit than they would appear on their face to have.

Reading down

Courts will often 'read down' general words to constrain their meaning. This involves giving general words a legally specific meaning rather than applying the plain meaning. Spigelman CJ has said that 'The process of reading down general words has a rich legal history. It is an acceptable, indeed essential, technique of interpretation'.[11] The case exercise provides an opportunity to consider this technique in practice.

Case exercise

'A tale of pure or adulterated edible seaweed'

A shop selling Japanese groceries, including packets of dried seaweed, has been charged by a food inspector with 17 counts of selling adulterated food. The relevant legislative provision,

11 J J Spigelman, *Statutory Interpretation and Human Rights*, The MacPherson Lecture Series, Vol 3 (2008) 128.

s 10 of the *Pure Food Act 1908* (NSW) prohibits the sale of adulterated food, defined under s 5(e) as being food containing substances in excess of the quantity or proportion provided in the regulations. The *Pure Food Regulations 1937* (NSW) provide, *inter alia*, the level of metal concentration (antimony) allowed in food as being no more than 1.5mg of metal per kilo of food. Reg 5(2)(a) provides:

> For the purposes of determining the concentration of a metal in a food pursuant to this Regulation—
>
> (a) the concentration of a metal in a food shall be determined with respect to the edible content of the good that is ordinarily consumed and, in the case of food in a dried or concentrated form, shall be determined with respect to the mass of the food after dilution or reconstitution.

The seaweed contained in the packets of dried seaweed offered for sale exceeded 1.5mg of metal per kilo. However, in diluted form the concentration of metal was below the maximum level. In other words the dried product breached the regulations and was considered adulterated food, but the diluted seaweed was not adulterated. Has the shop breached the regulations? Bear in mind that seaweed is often used in Japanese food in its dried form as well as its diluted form.

Reach your own decision before proceeding.

The real case is *Tokyo Mart Pty Ltd v Campbell* (1988) 15 NSWLR 275. If you decided there was a breach, you are in agreement with the Local Court, the Supreme Court and the Court of Appeal. If you decided there was not, you are original.

The Court considered the language of the section, its context and purpose. The purpose of the legislation is to prohibit the sale of adulterated food that would be consumed by a purchaser. The Court therefore concluded that it is the concentration of the metal in the food in whatever form it is consumed that is relevant. If the dried food was consumed in dried form, its metal concentration must be within the prescribed limit.

To achieve this result the Court had to read down general language in the provision to give effect to the purpose of the legislation. The Court considered that the legislative drafters intended to cover the situation of both dried and diluted or reconstituted foods, but did not contemplate foods which are consumed in either dried or diluted form. The Court stated, at 283:

> Legislative inadvertence may consist, *inter alia*, of either of two things. The draftsman may have failed to consider what should be provided in respect of a particular matter and so fail to provide for it. In such a case, though it may be possible to conjecture what, had he adverted to it, he would have provided, the court may not, in my opinion, supply the deficiency. In the other case, the legislative inadvertence consists, not in a failure to address the problem and determine what should be done, but in the failure to provide in the instrument express

> words appropriate to give effect to it. In the second case, it may be possible for the court, in the process of construction, to remedy the omission ... it is an omission not of purpose but of verbiage and as such appropriate to be cured.

The scope for reading down is, of course, limited by the words that are used. For example in *Wainohu v New South Wales* [2011] HCA 24 at [102] Gummow, Hayne, Crennan and Bell JJ attempted to read down s 13(2) of the *Crimes (Criminal Organisations Control) Act 2009* (NSW), otherwise known as the bikie legislation, which provided that a judge may make a declaration without providing any grounds or reasons. The provision was simple and clear: 'If an eligible judge makes a declaration or decision under this Part, the eligible judge is not required to provide any grounds or reasons ...' Accordingly the Court found itself unable to read down the provision—to do so 'would involve re-writing the sub-section'. Consequently the failure to require reasons to be given rendered the whole statutory provision invalid.

Reading in

Just as courts may wish to constrain the ordinary meaning, to confine it within appropriate parameters, there are times when the Court will wish to strain or 'read in' words. A strained construction is used where the text of the legislative provision would not otherwise stretch enough to give effect to the purpose. See similar comments by McHugh J[12] in *Kingston v Keprose Pty Ltd* (1987) 11 NSWLR 404 at 422, *Kelly v R* (2004) 218 CLR 216 at [98] and quoted here from *Newcastle City Council v GIO General Ltd* (1997) 191 CLR 85 at 113:

> If the legislature uses language which covers only one state of affairs, a court cannot legitimately construe the words of the section in a tortured and unrealistic manner to cover another set of circumstances... Nevertheless, when the purpose of a legislative provision is clear, a court may be justified in giving the provision 'a strained construction' to achieve that purpose provided that the construction is neither unreasonable nor unnatural.

This approach has its limits, as it may be that the words used in the Act simply cannot be construed to give effect to the purpose: see *Cooper Brookes (Wollongong) Pty Ltd v FCT* (1981) 147 CLR 297, per Mason and Wilson JJ.

In practice, often drafting errors or parliamentary inadvertence create gaps or uncertainties in legislation could have been avoided if additional words had been used.[13]

12 One could be forgiven for thinking that 'strained construction' in Australian statutory interpretation is largely attributable to McHugh J.

13 See *Bermingham v Corrective Services Commission of New South Wales* (1988) 15 NSWLR 292, McHugh JA at 302: 'To give effect to the purpose of the legislation, a court may read words into the legislative provision if by inadvertence Parliament has failed to deal with an eventuality required to be dealt with if the purpose of the Act is to be achieved'.

Courts will use a technique of 'reading in' words, which is a metaphor for reading the statutory provision 'as if' it contained those words. McHugh J's statement in *Newcastle City Council v GIO General Ltd* (1997) 191 CLR 85 about three preconditions to be satisfied before words can be read into legislation, drawn from English authority, has been cited with approval sufficient times for it to be established in Australian law:

> First, the court must know the mischief with which the statute was dealing. Second, the court must be satisfied that by inadvertence Parliament had overlooked an eventuality which must be dealt with if the purpose of the legislation is to be achieved. Third, the court must be able to state with certainty what words Parliament would have used to overcome the omission if its attention had been drawn to the defect.

Perhaps it was the choice of words by McHugh J which caused concern about this technique. In his judgment in *Saraswati v R* (1991) 172 CLR 1, for example, he said at [8]:

> [O]nce a court concludes that the literal or grammatical meaning of a provision does not conform to the legislative purpose as ascertained from the statute as a whole including the policy which may be discerned from its provisions, it is entitled to give effect to that purpose by addition to, omission from, or clarification of, the particular provision.

The reference to courts being 'entitled' to make 'addition to' legislation sets alarm bells ringing about the separation of powers. Spigelman CJ's more constrained formulation of the technique is contained, *inter alia*, in his judgment in *R v Young* (1999) 46 NSWLR 681 at 687:

> If a court can construe the words actually used by the parliament to carry into effect the parliamentary intention, it will do so notwithstanding that the specific construction is not the literal construction and even if it is a strained construction. The process of construction will, for example, sometimes cause the court to read down general words, or to give the words used an ambulatory operation ... The construction reached in this way will often be more clearly expressed by way of the addition of words to the words actually used in the legislation. [However], the words which actually appear in the statute must be reasonably open to such a construction. Construction must be text based.

It must be stressed, therefore, that the courts are not amending the legislation itself—they are not usurping the role of Parliament by altering the wording of the provision. They are merely using the technique to explain how they are construing the provision, reading it 'as if' it contained the additional words. Spigelman CJ further explained this in a lecture in 2008:

> In my opinion, the relevant authorities are consistent with a process of interpretation by which the court interprets the words actually used by the Parliament by giving them

effect *as if* they contained additional words which must be complied with or as if some words were deleted for a specific application ... The reformulation of a statutory provision with additional or fewer words should be understood as a means of expressing the Court's conclusion with clarity, rather than as a description of the actual reasoning process which the Court has conducted.[14]

The following case exercise provides an opportunity to read in words to a legislative provision.

Case exercise

'A farmer in financial drought'

James has a 40 per cent interest in a 455-hectare rural property in Narrabri known as 'Jays'. For some years he used the property for pig production, then for cattle raising and fattening, then cropping, and later, for breeding dogs. His tractor broke down, and he had a heart attack followed by coronary by-pass operation, then returned to the property to sow crops, which failed due to drought. Lately his only income has been from breeding dogs for sale. He has now applied for restart income support and a re-establishment grant under the *Farm Household Support Act 1992* (Cth). Section 4 provides:

Subject to this Division, a person is qualified for restart income support in respect of a period if:

(a) the period begins on or after the re-start scheme payment commencement day; and
(b) throughout the period, the person (i) is a farmer; and (ii) is at least 18; and (iii) is an Australian citizen, and (iv) is in Australia; and
(c) the person has been a farmer for a continuous period of at least 2 years immediately before the period; and
(d) a certificate of inability to obtain finance issued in respect of the person has effect throughout the period.

Section 3(2) of the Act defines farmer as a person who:

(a) has a right or interest in the land used for the purpose of a farm enterprise; and
(b) contributes a significant part of his or her labour and capital to the farm enterprise; and
(c) derives a significant part of his or her income from the farm enterprise.

14 J J Spigelman, *Statutory Interpretation and Human Rights*, The MacPherson Lecture Series, Vol 3 (2008) 132–4.

Is James a farmer? If he is earning no income, can he meet the definition in s 3(2)(c)? In reaching your decision, an excerpt from the Hon John Anderson, in his Second Reading Speech to the House of Representatives is provided:

> This bill has been carefully designed to meet the coalition's longstanding commitment to address these important welfare issues while at the same time taking account of the uniqueness of family farm business structures and the vulnerability of farming families to natural events.
>
> Just as importantly, the measures contained in this bill offer carefully targeted assistance to those who wish to adjust out of farming. Additionally, it provides income support for those farm families who find themselves suffering financial hardship as a result of exceptional circumstances which are beyond their capacity to manage. The new farm family restart scheme is the government's key program for delivering income support to the farm sector. It also provides assistance to those who wish to leave the industry.

Consider the above material and decide for yourself before reading on.

The real case is *Parrett v Secretary, Department of Family & Community Services* (2002) 124 FCR 299. Centrelink refused James Parrett's application on the basis that he is not a farmer. An Authorised Review Officer (ARO) at Centrelink affirmed the refusal. James sought review at the Social Security Appeals Tribunal (SSAT). The SSAT concluded he was a farmer, but because James had applied for review more than three months after the ARO's decision, its decision could not apply from an earlier date, and as he sold the remaining land and farm assets to pay off debt between the initial application and their decision, he was still ineligible to apply. James applied to the Administrative Appeals Tribunal for review of the decision and was back to square one when the AAT decided he did not meet the definition of farmer. He appealed to the Federal Court of Australia, which set aside the decision of the AAT.

Madgwick J considered that the policy behind the legislation was to provide an incentive for farmers whose farms were no longer financially viable to leave farming through a payment as financial encouragement. It provided 'a welfare safety net for the farming community': at [42]. He said that 'The legislation in question is beneficially intended for needy farmers and, in cases of doubt, should be liberally construed' at [42]. He said at [44]:

> The real question in the case, it seems to me, is whether the language of the Act, and in particular the phrase 'derives a significant part of his or her income' can fairly be given a construction, even if a strained one, that is nevertheless text-based and seems more consonant with the Act's stated purpose, and its other purposes more generally to be inferred.

The Court concluded that the three conditions were met for 'reading in'—it was clear what the statute was aiming to do, and it was clear that Parliament overlooked the situation of a farmer earning no money, given that 'nothing cannot in ordinary language be considered a "significant part" of nothing': at [43]. It could also be said with certainty the words Parliament would have used in s 3(2)(c) to overcome the omission of the case of the farmer receiving no farm income, if its attention had been drawn to the omission. They would have been:

> Derives *or attempts to derive* a significant part of his or her income from the farm enterprise *but is prevented from doing so by the vicissitudes of ill-health, seasonal factors or lack of means to continue farming.*

Therefore the Court 'read in' the words in italics, reading the legislation 'as if' it contained them.

It could be said that the methodology is justified but the expression 'reading in' leaves something to be desired. Perhaps 'gap filling' could be used,[15] or 'reading as if' or 'explanative reading', which would cover the situation of both reading legislation as if certain words were added or omitted. Pearce and Geddes have previously suggested the expression may give way in favour of 'implication',[16] but the process is different from *implying*, which is about making an indirect indication—that is, intending to say something indirectly rather than expressly, as opposed to failing to intend anything, which is what triggers the process of 'reading in'.

Ambulatory or dynamic interpretation

In reading cases that involve issues of statutory interpretation, it is evident that courts adapt certain expressions, and different expressions may be used to describe essentially the same reasoning process. For example 'ambulatory interpretation' and 'dynamic interpretation' both involve giving statutory provisions a meaning that can change over time.[17] The statute is considered to be 'always speaking'. [18] An effort is made to give effect to the 'spirit' of the law, which has been referred to as the 'equity of the statute'.[19] Although various expressions have been used by courts, they are all manifestations of a common approach, which is a triumph of substance over form and pragmatism over formalism.

Historically, such an approach was denounced. It was strongly considered illegitimate and outside the judicial task to make up for inadequacies and deficiencies

15 'Gap filling' may be as emotionally charged as 'reading in'. See *Marshall v Watson* (1972) 124 CLR 640, where Stephen J at 649 stated that the judicial function does not include filling gaps in legislation.

16 D Pearce and R Geddes, *Statutory Interpretation in Australia* (LexisNexis, 6th ed, 2006) 55.

17 See for example *Corporate Affairs Commission (NSW) v Yuill* (1991) 172 CLR 319 at [9] of McHugh's judgment, where the expression 'reasonable excuse' was said to have an ambulatory operation.

18 See for example *Forsyth v Deputy Commissioner of Taxation* [2007] HCA 8.

19 See for example *Comcare v Thompson* [2000] FCA 790.

in statutes.[20] For example John Austin in the nineteenth century used strong language in describing such interpretation:

> In that bastard interpretation *ex ratione legis*, which is styled *extensive*, the law is applied to a case which it clearly omits, because the omitted case falls within its principle. In that spurious interpretation *ex ratione legis*, which is styled *restrictive*, the law is *not* applied to a case which it certainly includes, because the case, which is included by its actual provisions, is not embraced by the general design of the lawgiver.

Early in the twentieth century American legal scholar Roscoe Pound weighed into the debate, saying that the concern with 'spurious interpretation' is that it brings the courts into disrepute by exposing them to political pressure and personalising judicial administration.[21] But times have changed, and perhaps it was short-sighted to consider that a statute, with a potentially indefinite life, whose meaning may 'evolve beyond original expectations of its drafters',[22] should be frozen in time despite movements in society which may not have not been addressed by Parliament through further legislative amendment or development.

Each formulation of this approach—always speaking, ambulatory, equity of the statute and dynamic interpretation—has been referred to by various courts as if it were an approach of their own.

The 'always speaking' formulation is, quite simply, that a statute continues to speak or address changing legal circumstances over time. It reflects the notion of statutes as living instruments, much in the same way as the common law is organic. In some jurisdictions the 'always speaking' approach is now enshrined in Interpretation Acts. See s 8 of the WA Act which provides:

> A written law shall be considered as always speaking and whenever a matter or thing is expressed in the present tense, it shall be applied to the circumstances as they arise, so that effect may be given to every part of the law according to its true spirit, intent, and meaning.

There is a similar provision in s 21 of the SA Act. Such an approach is more readily accepted in relation to constitutions, which are designed to last over time and are difficult to amend. Gleeson CJ has charmingly commented: 'It is one thing to say that a statute … is "always speaking". The question is: what is it saying?'.[23]

The 'ambulatory' formulation infers that very general and broad provisions were intended to be given an ambulatory meaning, that is, to take into account later changes.

---

20 J J Spigelman, *Statutory Interpretation and Human Rights*, The MacPherson Lecture Series, Vol 3 (2008) 109–110.

21 R Pound, 'Spurious Interpretation' (1907) 7(6) *Columbia Law Review* 379.

22 W N Eskridge Jnr, *Dynamic Statutory Interpretation*, Harvard University Press, Cambridge Mass, 1994, 48.

23 M Gleeson, 'The Meaning of Legislation: Context, Purpose and Respect for Fundamental Rights' Address to Victoria Law Foundation, Melbourne, 31 July 2008, 15.

See *R v Gee* (2003) 212 CLR 230, and see also *Deputy Commissioner of Taxation v Clark* [2003] NSWCA 91, where Spigelman CJ stated at [142]:

> Where, as here, Parliament has chosen a formulation which is of indeterminate scope and of a high level of generality, a court should interpret the provision on the basis that the intention of the original enactment was that the particular application of the provision may vary over time ... whether there has been any relevant change in the context which justifies a conclusion that conduct which may not have constituted a 'good reason' in 1992, should now be regarded as a 'good reason'.

Equitable interpretation developed historically from a view that a statute has both a body (the words) and a soul (the sense and reason of the law).[24] Blackstone described interpreting the will of the legislature by the 'signs' given, including not only the words used, the subject matter, the context, the effects and consequences of the law, but also its spirit or reason.[25] He considered the 'spirit and reason of the law' to be the most 'universal and effectual' way to interpret legislation.

The 'equity of the statute' was therefore used to contract (shrink) a provision so as to exclude a situation that is not within the spirit of the statute, and expand a provision so as to include a situation which is not within the language but is within the spirit. According to Corcoran, it can even be used to 'permit a statute to enter the common law as a generating legal principle'.[26] Whilst the expression 'equity of the statute' is seldom used, it has not been discredited in a superior court and is still open for use.

'Dynamic interpretation' involves interpreting statutory provisions in the light of the present context, including the common law, and the current state of societal values and political policy. The term 'dynamic' is used to differentiate this approach from the 'static' or 'originalist' treatment of a statute. It has been described by a Yale Professor in this way: 'Interpretation is not an archeological discovery, but a dialectical creation'.[27]

All of the above formulations have the same thing in common—the principle that statutes should be progressively interpreted in their context, ensuring each statute does not cover something it should not or not cover something that it should. The best way to describe it may be a 'principled dynamic approach', which houses 'always speaking', ambulatory construction, equity of the statute and dynamic interpretation within the one approach; signalling that, while interpretation should be adjusted to existing circumstances, it should do so in a principled manner, considering the true spirit or substance of the law. It is a sign of a mature system if Parliament can confidently avoid exhausting the minutiae of interpretive possibilities in any given Act, knowing that

24 Plowden, *Commentaries*, annexed to *Eyston v Studd* (1574) 75 ER 688.

25 W Blackstone, *Commentaries on the Laws of England* (9th edn, 1783) 59.

26 S Corcoran, 'Theories of Statutory Interpretation' in S Corcoran and S Bottomley (eds) *Interpreting Statutes* (Federation Press, 2005) 8, 11.

27 William N Eskridge, 'Dynamic Statutory Interpretation' (1987) 35 *University of Pennsylvania Law Review* 1482.

the courts will, in good faith, apply what they have enacted in a consistent but flexible manner to ensure that fair and just outcomes can be achieved regardless of linguistic deficiencies or unforeseen circumstances which may affect a statute's application.

As stated by Suzanne Corcoran:[28]

> Statutory interpretation cannot be divorced from general principles of justice and fairness. The use of such a principled approach to interpretation theory gives decision-makers the flexibility required to reach just and fair results when interpreting individual circumstances. It is, of course, based upon a necessary degree of trust; trust that the judicial system will exercise its discretion appropriately. But that trust is a fundamental aspect of Australian constitutional arrangements.

The approach is not radical or unprecedented, and aspects of it are already part of the furniture of statutory interpretation. For example, as is discussed in Chapter 7, we use a current dictionary when we look up words in statutes that may be a century old, and expressions such as 'vehicle' have been used to encompass planes even though they were not yet invented when the original legislation was passed.[29] See the discussion on page 120 on 'denotation' and 'connotation'. Also the legislative 'context' as discussed in Chapter 4 is not limited to the historical context, and as discussed above, 'intention' is an objective concept and is not limited to the subjective intentions of the parliamentarians who originally passed the legislation.

Could it also be called a 'pragmatic' approach? According to Corcoran, a pragmatic approach is 'particularly suited to the Australian historical and political context as it permits the integration of well developed traditions and techniques of interpretation with contemporary social and political circumstances'.[30] She refers to Kirby J's dissenting judgment in *Sheahan v Carrier Air Conditioning Pty Ltd & Campbell* (1997) 189 CLR 407 as an example of the pragmatic approach. There, Kirby J said that his conclusions 'find support when consideration is given to the way in which that legislation was intended to operate in the real world'. He considered the unintended and undesirable consequences a narrow interpretation would create, would undermine a 'long standing legislative policy'.

Formalist judges thrown into the rushing river of pragmatism continue to cling to branches along the side, refusing to be swept along. The following case exercise demonstrates the very real choice judges have in the approach they adopt. As Spigelman CJ has said, 'the basic principles do not appear to be in dispute. It is in the application of these principles that differences emerge'.[31]

---

28 S Corcoran, 'The Architecture of Interpretation: Dynamic Practice and Constitutional Principles' in S Corcoran and S Bottomley (eds) *Interpreting Statutes* (Federation Press, 2005) 31, 50.

29 *Lake Macquarie Shire Council v Aberdare County Council* (1970) 123 CLR 327.

30 S Corcoran, 'Theories of Statutory Interpretation' in S Corcoran and S Bottomley (eds) *Interpreting Statutes* (Federation Press, 2005) 8, 25.

31 J J Spigelman, 'The Intolerable Wrestle: Developments in Statutory Interpretation', Address to the Australasian Conference of Planning and Environment Courts and Tribunals, 1 September 2010, 32.

Case exercise

'Parliament needs a crystal ball'

Stephen Thompson became incapacitated while working as Assistant Director-General at the National Library of Australia. The amount of compensation he received varied over time according to what he would have earned were he still in his position. The relevant provision was s 8(6)(c) of the *Safety, Rehabilitation and Compensation Act 1988* (Cth), which provided:

> Subject to this section, if the minimum amount per week payable to an employee in respect of his or her employment by the Commonwealth or a licensed corporation at the date of the injury is increased, or would have been increased if the employee had continued in that employment, because of:
>
> (a) the attainment by the employee of a particular age;
> (b) the completion by the employee of a particular period of service; or
> (c) the receipt by the employee of an increase in salary, wages or pay by way of an increment in a range of salary, wages or pay applicable to the employee or to his or her office, position or appointment; the normal weekly earnings of the employee before the injury, as calculated under the preceding subsections, shall be increased by the same percentage as the percentage by which that minimum amount per week is increased, or would have been increased, as the case may be.

Upon the introduction of Australian Workplace Agreements, Stephen argued that his compensation should be equivalent to the salaries negotiated under the AWA system by occupants of his former position, seeing that incremental 'across the board' increases were no longer applied.

Do you agree with this argument? Is the legislative provision open to that interpretation? Consider the meaning of the words 'by way of an increment'. Decide before proceeding.

The real case is *Comcare v Thompson* [2000] FCA 790. If you decided that the statute could accommodate Stephen Thompson's argument you are in agreement with the Administrative Appeals Tribunal, and if not, you are in agreement with the Federal Court of Australia.

The Federal Court recognised the inherent challenge that the legislation was not drafted with a system of AWAs in mind, and had not been amended subsequent to the introduction of AWAs. The court acknowledged that it was difficult to accept that, as a result, compensation should become frozen in time.

The Court discussed the notion of the 'equity of the statute', which would apply the principle inherent in the legislation, that the level of compensation should be varied over time just as one's salary would have varied had the worker remained on the job, saying:

> In substance, what the Tribunal has done so as to give effect to 'the spirit of the Act', has been to add a new paragraph (d) to the sub-section that reads, in effect—

(d) the receipt by the employee of a negotiated increase in salary.

However the Court held, at [43] that:

> [T]here is no proper basis for assuming in the present case that salary increases of the type that result from AWAs would be ones that the legislature could be taken to have intended would fall within the compensatory regime … there would be no basis in any event for extending the statute to them—even if some surviving vestige of the equity of the statute doctrine allowed for extensive interpretation beyond the techniques to which I have referred above.

Consider, or discuss with others, what limits should there be to such principled dynamic or pragmatic interpretation? What is your reasoning? Does it suggest a broad or narrow approach?

Formalists shy away from giving effect to the spirit or principle underlying legislation, concerned about the ramifications for parliamentary sovereignty and the separation of powers doctrine, and confident in the power of Parliament to further legislate if the words it has used have resulted in an interpretation by courts that it finds unsatisfactory.

But the divide between formalism and dynamism, for want of a better word and avoiding the term 'activism', is not as vast as it may seem. Even the most formalist judge cannot avoid the legislative edict that interpretation of the text must take into account the context and purpose of the enactment. And even the 'dynamic principled' or 'pragmatic' approach is not without its limits, some of which have been identified by Spigelman CJ:

- 'Interpretation must always be text based … the task is to interpret the words of the legislature, not to divine the intent of the legislature'.[32]
- 'The courts must determine what Parliament meant by the words it used. The courts do not determine what Parliament intended to say'.[33]
- 'The overriding test is that the meaning must be reasonably open'.[34]
- The interpretation must be based on the intentions of Parliament and not the judge: 'It is all too easy for the identification of purpose to be driven by what the particular judge regards as the desirable result in a specific case'.[35]

32 J J Spigelman, *Statutory Interpretation and Human Rights*, The MacPherson Lecture Series, Vol 3 (2008) 134.
33 Ibid at 120.
34 Ibid at 123.
35 J J Spigelman, 'The Intolerable Wrestle: Developments in Statutory Interpretation', Address to the Australasian Conference of Planning and Environment Courts and Tribunals, 1 September 2010, 16–17.

See similar comments by Gleeson CJ:[36]

> Judicial exposition of the meaning of a statutory text is legitimate so long as it is an exercise, undertaken consistently with principles of law and logic, in discovering the will of Parliament; it is illegitimate when it is an exercise in imposing the will of the judge.

Ultimately, provided courts stay on the side of the fence that is 'interpret', and do not stray across to the other side that is 'legislate', and provided the interpretation is not merely an application of the purpose divorced from an actual statutory provision read in its context, the interpretive task remains legitimate.[37]

There remains, however, a concern about each camp. Regarding the pragmatist approach, the concern is the lack of consistency in the way judges apply the approach. The relative degree of emphasis placed upon the text, context and purpose varies from judge to judge, and that differing emphasis can lead to significantly different outcomes. Even Kirby J and Spigelman CJ, whose contribution to the way forward in statutory interpretation will become more apparent as the years go on, differ in emphasis. Spigelman CJ has said that:

> Although ... Justice Kirby also makes frequent reference to starting with the text, his approach is to treat a number of principles of statutory interpretation as operating simultaneously. These are principles which he has described as the 'textual analysis principle'; 'the contextual interpretation principle' and the 'purposive construction principle' ... these are all relevant matters but they are not of equal application. As the quote states, 'the language ... is the surest guide'. 'Context' and 'purpose' are described as matters which 'may require consideration'.

It is hoped that judges in the pragmatic camp will, with time, develop a consistent approach to the relative weighting to be given to text, context and purpose.

The concern regarding the formalists is the habit of writing judgments as if the conclusions reached were inevitable, even obvious. In order to achieve this certainty it may be necessary to sidestep important issues and consideration. Sean Brennan has recognised this in relation to native title cases:[38]

> '[F]ormalism' refers to a tendency to see a very high degree of determinacy in legal questions, including those that reach appellate courts, and a corresponding belief that judges can typically or frequently reach decisions without resort to wider normative

---

36 M Gleeson, 'The Meaning of Legislation: Context, Purpose and Respect for Fundamental Rights' Address to Victoria Law Foundation, Melbourne, 31 July 2008, 7.

37 As warned by Mason J in *State Government Insurance Commission (SA) v Trigwell* (1979) 142 CLR 617 at 633–4: 'The court is neither a legislature nor a law reform agency. The court cannot, and does not, engage in the wide-ranging inquiries and assessments which are made by governments and law reform agencies as a desirable, if not essential, preliminary to the enactment of legislation by an elected legislature'.

38 S Brennan, 'Statutory Interpretation and Indigenous Property Rights' (2010) 21 *PLR* 239 at 244.

> considerations. This can include a disinclination to deploy the techniques of statutory interpretation which imply the judicial task involves value-laden choices and issues of justice.

The concern is not so much the narrowness of the approach, but the presentation of a judicial decision as if it were a mathematical solution. The tone of some recent formalist judgments suggests that there is one right answer, that the interpretation is obvious and that the provision is not ambiguous. This is despite the often see-sawing of interpretation across the lower courts, and lack of unanimity within each appellate court including the High Court itself. As stated by Michael Kirby, '[t]hose who hanker after certainty can sometimes convince themselves that it exists more often than it does. The wish is parent to the conclusion'.[39] And later in the same article:[40]

> [J]udges may have difficulty in explaining exactly why they chose one interpretation over another. Maintenance of the rule of law suggests that there should be a discriminating reason and that judges should be obliged to identify and justify it.

He has also written more recently on the need for judges to 'explore their conscious and even subconscious minds to explain why they prefer one approach or conclusion to the meaning of contested words over another', using his own judgment in *Carr v Western Australia* (2007) 232 CLR 138 to undertake such an exploration by way of example.[41]

39 M Kirby, 'Towards a Grand Theory of Interpretation' (2003) 24(2) *Statute Law Review* 95 at 102.

40 Ibid at 110.

41 M Kirby, 'Statutory Interpretation: The Meaning of Meaning' (2011) 35 *Melbourne University Law Review* 113.

CHAPTER 6

INTRINSIC MATERIALS: STATUTE COMPONENTS

The immediate context of a provision is the Act in which it is located. Intrinsic materials include elements or components of the Act which may be used in the interpretation task. We can use other parts of an Act to interpret a specific provision because statutes are to be read as a whole. This principle was stated by the High Court in the *Gas Employees Case*:[1]

> It is a received canon of interpretation that every passage in a document must be read, not as if it were entirely divorced from its context, but as part of the whole instrument.

This common law formulation has been reinforced in the ACT with a specific provision saying that statutory provisions must be read in the context of the statute as a whole: s 140.

We cannot therefore, simply read the words of the applicable section of an Act and apply them without looking at the words of surrounding sections and indeed, the whole Act. As stated by Mason J in *K&S Lake City Freighters Pty Ltd v Gordon & Gotch Ltd* (1985) 218 CLR 216 at 514:

> [To] read a section in isolation from the enactment of which it forms a part is to offend against the cardinal rule of statutory interpretation that requires the words of a statute to be read in their context.

In order for an Act to sit together as a coherent whole, individual sections may need to be read slightly differently from their ordinary meaning, or more broadly or narrowly than their mere words would suggest.

There may, however, be instances where particular Parts of an Act have a specific focus, so the section is read in the context of the Part rather than the whole Act. Additionally some provisions may be 'leading' while others are 'subordinate'. The High Court discussed this in *Project Blue Sky Inc v Australian Broadcasting Authority* (1998) 194 CLR 355 at [70]:

> Reconciling conflicting provisions will often require the court 'to determine which is the leading provision and which the subordinate provision, and which must give way to the other'. Only by determining the hierarchy of the provisions will it be possible in many cases to give each provision the meaning which best gives effect to its purpose and language while maintaining the unity of the statutory scheme.

This chapter considers the intrinsic context of an Act, commencing first by examining the anatomy of an Act, including which aspects may be used in interpretation, and then considering how particular words, and particular forms of expression, are interpreted, including finding meaning where a suboptimal choice of words has been used.

---

1 *Metropolitan Gas Co v Federated Gas Employees Industrial Union* (1924) 35 CLR 449, 455.

As a general rule in several jurisdictions, components of an Act which have been passed by Parliament can be used in interpretation, but components which have been included by drafters but have not been subjected to parliamentary debate are not formally considered to be part of the Act (and therefore of value in interpreting the legislation). In the discussion below it cannot be stated absolutely whether a particular component will be used in a particular instance of statutory interpretation. However, with Commonwealth legislation the position has, since December 2011, been simplified by the new s 13, which provides that everything in an Act is part of the Act—meaning it *can* be used in interpretation:

> (1) All material from and including the first section of an Act to the end of:
>
> (a) if there are no Schedules to the Act—the last section of the Act; or
>
> (b) if there are one or more Schedules to the Act—the last Schedule to the Act; is part of the Act.
>
> (2) The following are also part of an Act:
>
> (a) the Long Title of the Act;
>
> (b) any Preamble to the Act;
>
> (c) the enacting words for the Act;
>
> (d) any heading to a Chapter, Part, Division or Subdivision appearing before the first section of the Act.

Long Title

The use of a Long Title as a statement of the purpose of legislation is part of the English tradition, but its use in modern legislation is decreasing. Where it is used, the Long Title appears at the commencement of the Act, and includes the rationale, topic and audience of the legislation.

For example the *Aged or Disabled Persons Care Act 1954* (Cth) has a Long Title which states 'An Act to provide for Assistance by the Commonwealth towards the provision of Care for Aged Persons or Disabled Persons, and for other purposes'.

It is common to see the general expression 'and for other purposes', as Parliament rarely wants to confine legislation to the items stated in the Long Title. Of course, it would not be appropriate if the above Act, for example, contained provisions relating to execution of criminals—they would belong in a separate Act. Therefore, 'other purposes' means other purposes in the realm of those that have been stated.[2]

Long Titles are often referred to by the High Court when identifying the object or purpose of legislation. A simple example from the time of writing (June 2011) is *Wainohu v New South Wales* [2011] HCA 24, where French CJ and Kiefel J stated at [8]: 'The object of the Act, as appears from its Long Title, is …'

---

2 See *ejusdem generis* and *noscitur a sociis* in Chapter 9.

As is clear from s 13(2)(a) of the Commonwealth Act, cited above, Long Titles may be used in statutory interpretation.

Short Title

For ease of reference and to save referring each time to the Long Title, Parliament designates a Short Title for each Act, which is typically the first section of an Act. A recent example is 'This Act may be cited as the *National Health and Hospitals Network Act 2011*'. By convention, the jurisdiction of the Act is added at the end when referring to the Act in writing, even though this is not specifically provided for in the short title provision.

In almost every case the Long Title will be more explanative than the Short Title. An exception is the *Public and Environmental Health Act 2011* (NT), with a Long Title 'An Act about public and environmental health'. The value of including a Long Title in these circumstances is unclear.

Short titles may be used in interpretation, although their brevity usually means little value can be extracted from them. See for example Kirby J in *Wurridjal v The Commonwealth of Australia* (2009) 237 CLR 309 at [301]: 'As indicated by the short title of the *Emergency Response Act*, the federal intervention in question in these proceedings involves an extensive series of initiatives'. See also *Osland v Secretary to the Department of Justice* (2008) 234 CLR 275 per Kirby J at [114]:

> As the short title of the FOI Act suggests, as its Long Title affirms, and as its stated objects demonstrate, the public purpose of the FOI Act is precisely to enhance transparency in government to the extent provided.

Occasionally the Short Title may be of more interpretive value than the Long Title. For example the *Tax Laws Amendment (Temporary Flood And Cyclone Reconstruction Levy) Act 2011* (Cth) has as its Long Title 'An Act to amend the law relating to taxation, and for related purposes'. The Short Title of this legislation, which was introduced to cover the cost of natural disaster recovery in Queensland after flooding and cyclones in 2011, tells the reader far more than the Long Title.

Preamble

Preambles are introductory statements which 'set the scene' by describing the background and motivation behind any document. Here is an example of a Preamble from the *Historic Shipwrecks Act 1976* (Cth):

> WHEREAS, by an Agreement between the Netherlands and Australia Concerning Old Dutch Shipwrecks that was signed on 6 November 1972 (being the agreement a copy of the text

> of which is set out in Schedule 1 to this Act), the Netherlands, as successor to the property and assets of the Dutch "Vereenigde Oostindische Compagnie", transferred to Australia all its right, title and interest in and to wrecked vessels of the Dutch "Vereenigde Oostindische Compagnie" lying on or off the coast of the State of Western Australia and in and to any articles thereof and Australia accepted that right, title and interest:
>
> AND WHEREAS it is desirable that Australia should protect those wrecked vessels and articles, and the remains of, and any articles associated with, other ships of historic significance, being remains or articles that are situated in, or have been removed from, Australian waters or waters above the continental shelf of Australia:
>
> BE IT THEREFORE ENACTED by the Queen, and the Senate and House of Representatives of the Commonwealth of Australia, as follows:—

Preambles are common in international treaties and resolutions of United Nations bodies. See for example the Preamble to the United Nations Security Council resolution which provided for intervention in Libya in 2011:[3]

> The Security Council ...
>
> Reiterating the responsibility of the Libyan authorities to protect the Libyan population and reaffirming that parties to armed conflicts bear the primary responsibility to take all feasible steps to ensure the protection of civilians,
>
> Condemning the gross and systematic violation of human rights, including arbitrary detentions, enforced disappearances, torture and summary executions,
>
> Further condemning acts of violence and intimidation committed by the Libyan authorities against journalists, media professionals and associated personnel ...

Preambles are also used in constitutions. In 1999 the following Preamble text was proposed for the Australian Constitution, but failed to achieve the necessary majorities at referendum:

> With hope in God, the Commonwealth of Australia is constituted as a democracy with a federal system of government to serve the common good.
>
> We the Australian people commit ourselves to this Constitution:
>
>> proud that our national unity has been forged by Australians from many ancestries; never forgetting the sacrifices of all who defended our country and our liberty in time of war;
>>
>> upholding freedom, tolerance, individual dignity and the rule of law;

3 Security Council Resolution 1973, 17 March 2011.

> honouring Aborigines and Torres Strait Islanders, the nation's first people, for their deep kinship with their lands and for their ancient and continuing cultures which enrich the life of our country;
>
> recognising the nation-building contribution of generations of immigrants;
>
> mindful of our responsibility to protect our unique natural environment;
>
> supportive of achievement as well as equality of opportunity for all;
>
> and valuing independence as dearly as the national spirit which binds us together in both adversity and success.

However, Preambles are quite unusual in modern legislation—of 150 Commonwealth Acts passed in 2010, there were no original Acts with a Preamble and only one Act amended the wording of a Preamble in an existing Act. At the time of writing in mid-2011, in total there were only 52 Commonwealth Acts in force with Preambles and only 17 of those Acts were passed in the past 25 years. Of those, five are not 'proper' Preambles but rather are stated to be a 'User's Guide' or 'Reader's Guide' and lack the common characteristic of a Preamble in setting out the background and motivations behind the Act.

Where a Preamble appears in an Act, it may be used in interpretation, see for example the Commonwealth Act s 13(2)(b). Historically the High Court has limited reference to the Preamble to situations of ambiguity—see Griffith CJ in *Bowtell v Goldsborough, Mort & Co Ltd* (1906) 3 CLR 444 at 451. However, under the modern statutory approach there is no prerequisite of ambiguity—Mason J stated, in *Wacando v the Commonwealth* (1981) 148 CLR 1 at 23:

> It has been said that where the enacting part of a statute is clear and unambiguous it cannot be cut down by the preamble. But this does not mean that a court cannot obtain assistance from the preamble in ascertaining the meaning of an operative provision. The particular section must be seen in its context; the statute must be read as a whole and recourse to the preamble may throw light on the statutory purpose and object.

Under the modern statutory approach the instruction is to prefer an interpretation that promotes the purpose of the Act, and to ascertain that purpose one must consider not only an objects clause but its overall context, of which the Preamble is a part.

Anne Winckel has written about the dual constructive and contextual role of a Preamble.[4] The *constructive role* is the use of a Preamble to resolve ambiguity in the wording of a provision through consideration of the motivations behind the act, and the mischief intended to be remedied, and the *contextual role* is the use of the Preamble as part of examining the overall context in which the legislation was made, including

---

4 A Winckel, 'The Contextual Role of a Preamble in Statutory Interpretation' (1999) 23 *Melbourne University Law Review* 184.

its intended scope. It could therefore be said that the traditional approach was to only use preambles in a constructive role, whereas nowadays it is appropriate to use them also in a contextual role.

Objects clause

To ward off any doubt about the purpose of legislation, objects clauses are commonly included in Acts. They are a more flexible, modern variant on a Long Title or Preamble, commonly being drafted with sub-sections and lists. For example s 3 of the *National Broadband Network Companies Act 2011* (Cth) which provides:

> Objects
>
> (1) The main objects of this Act, when read together with Part XIC of the *Competition and Consumer Act 2010*, are as follows:
> (a) to provide a regulatory framework for NBN corporations that promotes the long-term interests of end-users of carriage services or of services provided by means of carriage services;
> (b) to ensure that NBN Co remains in Commonwealth ownership until [listed events];
> (c) to provide a framework for restrictions on private ownership or control of NBN Co.
>
> (2) The other objects of this Act, when read together with Part XIC of the *Competition and Consumer Act 2010*, are as follows:
> (a) to ensure that the supply of an eligible service by an NBN corporation is on a wholesale basis;
> (b) to ensure that an NBN corporation does not supply a content service;
> (c) to ensure that an NBN corporation does not supply a non-communications service;
> (d) to ensure that an NBN corporation does not supply goods that are not for use in connection with the supply of an eligible service by the NBN corporation;
> (e) to restrict the investment activities of NBN corporations;
> (f) to provide a framework for the functional separation of NBN corporations;
> (g) to provide a framework for the divestiture of assets of NBN corporations;
> (h) to ensure that an NBN corporation provides open access to eligible services on a non-discriminatory basis.

When an objects clause appears in an Act, it may be used in interpretation. However, it is not exhaustive, and consideration must be given to the objects as apparent from the whole of the Act, and the way in which those objects were intended to be furthered by the legislation. See *Municipal Officers' Association of Australia v Lancaster* (1981) 54 FLR 129 where the Federal Court stated *per curiam*:

> It is necessary also to make reference to what is meant by the words 'objects of this Act' appearing in sub-section 140(1)(c) of the Act. It is not sufficient to take those words as

> referring only to the paragraphs appearing in s 2 of the Act. It is true that those paragraphs are said to be 'the chief objects of the Act', but it is necessary to consider the method by which the legislature has implemented those objects.

There is also nothing to prevent a court from referring to extrinsic materials in identifying purpose to supplement the intrinsic guidance provided by an objects clause. For example in *Forsyth v Deputy Commissioner of Taxation* (2007) 233 ALR 254 a joint judgment of six members of the High Court considered not only the objects clause but also the Second Reading Speech and the Explanatory Note accompanying the bill. Extrinsic materials are discussed further in Chapter 8.

Definition sections

It is extremely common for Acts to have a definitions section (also often headed 'Interpretation') towards the beginning of the Act. For example the *Tertiary Education Quality and Standards Agency Act 2011* (Cth) has a dictionary in s 5 which commences with the typical phrase 'In this Act' and proceeds to define no fewer than 80 terms with a specific definition for the purposes of that Act.

In lengthy Acts, there may be definition sections at the beginning of individual parts. For example s 44AB of the *Competition and Consumer Act 2010* (Cth) is the first section in Part IIIAA of the Act. It commences with the phrase 'In this Part, unless the contrary intention appears ...' and then defines four specific terms relevant to that Part.

Where a definitions section is provided in an Act, the definitions should generally be used in construing all provisions that use defined words or phrases. A statutory definition will override a dictionary definition, and a definition in one Act cannot be applied to that word or phrase where it appears in another Act unless it is similarly defined in that Act. Mason J in *Yager v R* (1977) 139 CLR 28 at 43, said that '[t]here is perhaps even stronger reason for reaching this conclusion when one statute is domestic in character and the other is a statute which gives effect to an international convention and is consequently bound to apply the definitions which the convention contains'.

A definition may be disregarded where it is evident from the context in which the defined term appears that the definition is not intended to apply. Some Interpretation Acts explicitly provide for this, while others rely implicitly on the common law. See for example s 6 of the NSW Act which provides:

> Definitions that occur in an Act or instrument apply to the construction of the Act or instrument except in so far as the context or subject-matter otherwise indicates or requires.

See also ss 32A and 32AA of the Qld Act; s 19(1) of the SA Act; s 156 of ACT Act and s 17 of the NT Act.

A definition is precisely that—an explanation of a word or phrase to assist in interpretation—it is not a substantive legislative provision in its own right. There have been occasions where definition sections have been used as if they enacted substantive law, and it is indeed tempting to give substantive effect to them where the contents are demonstrative of the legislative intent. See for example the High Court majority approach in *Kelly v R* (2004) 218 CLR 216, discussed as a case exercise on page 65. McHugh J in dissent stated at [103]:

> [T]he function of a definition is not to enact substantive law. It is to provide aid in construing the statute. Nothing is more likely to defeat the intention of the legislature than to give a definition a narrow, literal meaning and then use that meaning to negate the evident policy or purpose of a substantive enactment. There is, of course, always a question whether the definition is expressly or impliedly excluded. But once it is clear that the definition applies, the better—I think the only proper—course is to read the words of the definition into the substantive enactment and then construe the substantive enactment—in its extended or confined sense—in its context and bearing in mind its purpose and the mischief that it was designed to overcome. To construe the definition before its text has been inserted into the fabric of the substantive enactment invites error as to the meaning of the substantive enactment.

Statutory definitions may be exhaustive or non-exhaustive, depending on whether they are framed with the word 'means' or 'includes'. Where a statute says that a term 'means' something, that is an exhaustive, complete definition. But where a statute says that a term 'includes' a list of things, they are merely examples and do not limit the definition from including other things. The examples given assist the reader to understand the provision without limiting it to them. So for example s 3 of the *Witness Protection Act 1994* (Cth) uses *inter alia* the following definitions:

> 'information', in relation to the identity of a person includes, but is not limited to, information about one or more of the following in relation to the person:
>
> (a) appearance;
> (b) voice quality or accent;
> (c) mannerisms;
> (d) address or location;
> (e) particular skills and qualifications;
> (f) personal history.

'witness' means:

(a) a person who has given, or who has agreed to give, evidence on behalf of the Crown in the right of the Commonwealth or of a State or Territory in:
  (i) proceedings for an offence; or
  (ii) hearings or proceedings before an authority that is declared by the Minister by notice in the *Gazette* to be an authority to which this paragraph applies; or
(b) a person who has given, or who has agreed to give, evidence otherwise than as mentioned in paragraph (a) in relation to the commission or possible commission of an offence against a law of the Commonwealth or of a State or Territory; or
(c) a person who has made a statement to the Australian Federal Police or an approved authority in relation to an offence against a law of the Commonwealth or of a State or Territory; or
(d) a person who, for any other reason, may require protection or other assistance under the NWPP; or
(e) a person who, because of his or her relationship to, or association with, a person referred to in paragraph (a), (b), (c) or (d) may require protection or other assistance under the NWPP.

The above definition of 'witness' is exhaustive while the definition of 'information' is non-exhaustive. On occasion a definition may include both 'means' and 'includes', so that the definition is both limited and instructive of what could come within it. For example s 4 of the *Workers Compensation Act 1987* (NSW) provides:

'injury'—

(a) means personal injury arising out of or in the course of employment;
(b) includes—
  (i) a disease which is contracted by a worker in the course of employment and to which the employment was a contributing factor; and
  (ii) the aggravation, acceleration, exacerbation or deterioration of any disease, where the employment was a contributing factor to the aggravation, acceleration, exacerbation or deterioration; and
  (iii) does not include … a dust disease …

This definition was considered in *Darrin Zickar v MGH Plastic Industries Pty Ltd* (1996) 187 CLR 310, where the High Court disagreed with the approach taken by the Court of Appeal in considering paragraphs (a) and (b) as mutually exclusive. The High Court held that paragraph (b) does not contract the ambit of paragraph (a)—instead, the examples given in paragraph (b) give an extended meaning to 'injury', going beyond personal injury to also cover disease. As stated by Toohey, McHugh and Gummow JJ:

> [T]here is no rule of construction which requires inclusive words to be read as exclusive of any elements which otherwise fall within the meaning of the word or expression being defined, and no occasion with this legislation for the imposition of such a construction.

Finally, a definition may be expressed with reference to another Act or even an international instrument. In both cases the definition will apply to the current version of the other Act or instrument.

Case exercise

'Too old to fly?'

John has for many years been a Qantas B747-400 Captain. His employment came to an end when he turned 60, in accordance with a Qantas policy that pilots not continue employment beyond that age. He claims Qantas has wrongfully terminated his employment and has discriminated against him on the ground of age. Qantas says it did not terminate his employment, as his employment agreement never provided for his employment to continue past age 60.

The relevant legislative provision is the *Industrial Relations Act 1988* (Cth), s 170DE(1) of which provides:

> An employer must not terminate an employee's employment unless there is a valid reason, or valid reasons, connected with the employee's capacity or conduct or based on the operational requirements of the undertaking, establishment or service.

> Section 170DF provides:
>
> (1) An employer must not terminate an employee's employment for any one or more of the following reasons, or for reasons including any or more of the following reasons … (f) … age …
>
> (2) Subsection (2) does not prevent a matter referred to in paragraph 1(f) from being a reason for terminating employment if the reason is based on the inherent requirements of a particular position.

The Act further provides that 'termination' of employment has the same meaning as in the *Termination of Employment Convention* (1982), a product of the International Labour Organisation which entered into force in Australia in 1994. It provides in Article 3:

> For the purpose of this Convention the terms 'termination' and 'termination of employment' mean termination of employment at the initiative of the employer.

Qantas argues that many international routes preclude pilots over 60 from flying. The relevant industrial agreement provides that Qantas pilots serve Qantas 'in any part of the world where [it] may from time to time be operating'. Although John remains physically and mentally capable of continuing in his position, he cannot legally fly to many parts of the world, and therefore cannot complete a substantial part of his position. It is therefore an inherent requirement of the particular position that pilots be under 60 years of age.

The test for 'inherent requirement' was established by the Human Rights and Equal Opportunity Commission in *X v Department of Defence* [1995] EOC 92-715:

> [T]here must be a clear and definite relationship between the inherent or intrinsic characteristics of the employment and the disability in question, the very nature of which disqualifies the person from being able to perform the characteristic tasks or skills required in [the] specific employment.

John argues that he could fly shorter routes within Australia and in countries such as New Zealand, Fiji and Bali, which do not apply the 'Rule of 60', so it cannot be an inherent requirement of the position. Qantas argues in response that this would not work with its bidding system, in which pilots put in for flights and all pilots use some of the shorter flights to make up their total hours in each roster period. Also some international flights to his nominated destinations go on to other international destinations, rather than being return flights. If John were exempted from the general roster requirements he would not be a standard B747-400 captain—he would occupy a specially created position.

What do you think? Has Qantas 'terminated' John's employment, or has it naturally come to an end? If it has terminated the employment, is it with a valid reason? Is being under 60 an 'inherent requirement' of being a Qantas B747-400 captain, such that s 170DF(2) applies?

Decide before proceeding.

The real case is *Qantas Airways Ltd v Christie* (1998) 193 CLR 280. If you decided it was an inherent requirement of John Christie's position you are in agreement with the trial judge and the High Court majority comprising Brennan CJ, Gaudron and McHugh JJ. If you decided it was not, you are in agreement with the Full Court of the Industrial Relations Court and Kirby and Gummow JJ on the High Court. The High Court looked at the whole context of Christie's employment, not only his physical capacity to fly aeroplanes, and concluded that being under 60 was an inherent requirement of the job.

Headings

Headings appear in legislation at the top of parts, divisions and subdivisions, and can also appear within individual sections. As discussed above, from December 2011 the whole of any Commonwealth Act, including all headings, may be used in interpretation.[5]

5 See Cth Act s 13(2)(d).

The Explanatory Memorandum to the Acts Interpretation Amendment Bill 2011 (Cth) stated at [93] that 'New section 13 is intended to capture all headings (including the heading to the first section of the Act)' and at [94]:

> This means for example that section headings within the Act (which have been treated as not forming part of the Act because of existing subsection 13(3)) will become part of the Act from the commencement of the amendment. This is unlikely to have the effect that material that was not included in the text of a Bill presented before the Commonwealth Parliament will become part of existing Acts, given that the practice has in fact been to include this material in the text of the Bill presented to Parliament. Rather, the effect will simply be that words in Acts which were in the text of a Bill presented to Parliament will now be treated as part of the Act.

Only the Queensland Act takes a similar stance—s 14(2) has made headings in Acts part of the Act since June 1991. The remaining states and territories retain the previous position (for the time being), under which headings to Parts Divisions and Subdivisions into which any Act is divided are deemed to be part of the Act: s 35(1) of the NSW Act, s 36(1) of the Vic Act, s 14(1) of the Qld Act, s 19(1) of the SA Act, s 32(1) of the WA Act, s 6(2) of the Tas Act, s 126(1) of the ACT Act and s 55(1) of the NT Act. However, headings to individual sections are not: s 35(2) of the NSW Act, s 36(3) of the Vic Act, s 19(1) of the SA Act, s 32(2) of the WA Act, s 6(4) of the Tas Act and s 127(3) of the ACT Act.

Case exercise

'Lost in transit'

A business recently contracted a freight company to carry a consignment of magazines worth $55 000 from Sydney to Adelaide. On the way, as a result of negligent driving, the carrier's delivery vehicle was involved in a collision. The consignor wants to recover for the loss of the goods but the carrier is relying on an exclusion of liability clause in the 'Conditions of Carriage'. The conditions also provide for the application of South Australian law, and the consignor is claiming the exclusion clause is void by reason of s 133 of the *Motor Vehicles Act 1959* (SA), which provides:

> Any contract (whether under seal or not) by virtue of which a person contracts in advance out of any right to claim damages or any other remedy for the negligence of any other person in driving a motor vehicle shall to that extent be void.

Section 133 is contained within Part IV of the Act, which is headed 'THIRD PARTY INSURANCE'. The Long Title reads:

> An Act to consolidate and amend certain enactments relating to the registration of motor vehicles, drivers licenses and third party motor insurance, and for other purposes.
>
> The carrier says that s 133 only applies to bodily injury, not property loss or damage. It is housed within a scheme for third party insurance that is directed towards personal injury and so the section should be read down.

What do you think? Can the heading to Part IV limit the coverage of s 133? Decide before proceeding.

The real case is *K & S Lake City Freighters Pty Ltd v Gordon & Gotch Ltd* (1985) 157 CLR 309. If you decided the section was limited to personal injury you are in agreement with the Supreme Court of South Australia and Mason J on the High Court. If you decided it covered property damage as well as personal injury, and the heading to the Part did not limit its operation, you are in agreement with the High Court majority, comprising Gibbs CJ, Brennan, Deane and Dawson JJ.

Gibbs CJ considered the words used in s 133 in their ordinary and natural meaning, saying that applying them to cover contracting out of the right to claim damages of any kind would 'not bring about a result that could be described as inconvenient, improbable or unjust, and still less absurd or irrational': at [4]. Deane J, with whom Dawson J agreed, said the heading to Part IV was 'not inappropriate' for s 133 (at [7]) and the provision could not be read down or confined to the subject matter of other provisions in Part IV. He said at [6]:

> This is particularly the case where the proposed confinement of those plain words would exclude applications of the words actually used to circumstances to which their application would be neither unexpected nor surprising such as to preclude a person from contracting out of a right to claim for damages for injury to his clothing or personal effects sustained as a result of physical impact.

Brennan J simply reasoned that s 133 operated independently of the other sections in Part IV and so the heading did not affect it.

Mason J, in dissent, said that although the provision was expressed in general terms, the context showed that it should be limited to personal injury. He said at [4]:

> Problems of legal interpretation are not solved satisfactorily by ritual incantations which emphasise the clarity of meaning which words have when viewed in isolation, divorced from their context. The modern approach to interpretation insists that the context be considered in the first instance, especially in the case of general words, and not merely at some later stage when ambiguity might be thought to arise.

His Honour said that the context, including the Long Title and the heading to Part IV, showed that the legislation was devoted to establishing a scheme of compulsory insurance to cover death or bodily injury of owners and drivers of motor vehicles arising out of their use in any part of Australia. He stated, at [11] of his judgment:

> [T]hat context demands that the section be read more narrowly than if it had stood alone so that it does not extend to include contracts relating to claims in respect of loss of property ... a natural reading of the section requires that it be confined to rights to damages in respect of death or bodily injury, these being the benefits which the statute is concerned to provide.

See also the case exercise titled 'Ships as sisters and surrogates' in Chapter 9.

Schedules

These are used where detailed information is needed to support a provision. They are usually tables, lists, or templates. See for example the *Customs Tariff Act 1995* (Cth) which has eight Schedules:

Schedule 1: Classes of countries and places in relation to which special rates apply

Schedule 2: General rules for the interpretation of Schedule 3

Schedule 3: Classification of goods and general and special rates of duty

Schedule 4: Concessional rates of duty

Schedule 5: US originating goods

Schedule 6: Thai originating goods

Schedule 7: Chilean originating goods

Schedule 8: ASEAN-Australia-New Zealand (AANZ) originating goods

An example of a provision referring to a Schedule is in s 8 of the Act:

(1) Subject to subsection (2), an item in Schedule 4 applies to goods if the goods are described in the second column of that item.

(2) If goods are described in the second column of 2 or more items in Schedule 4, the item in that Schedule that applies to the goods is:

  (a) the item under which the least amount of duty would be payable in respect of the goods; or

  (b) if there are 2 or more such items, the last occurring such item.

This is therefore a substantive provision of the Act which gives application to a Schedule. The new section 13(1) of the Commonwealth Act, as with the previous provision, includes Schedules as part of the Act. See also s 35(1) of the NSW Act, s 36(1) of the Vic Act, s 19(1) of the SA Act, s 31(2) of the WA Act, s 126(5) of the ACT Act, s 6(3) of the Tas Act and s 55(1) of the NT Act. These provisions have the effect that Schedules are applied alongside relevant sections in statutory interpretation.

Notes

Margin notes, headnotes and footnotes are typically included when legislation is drafted, to help make the legislation more readable and easily understandable. See for example the *Atomic Energy Act 1953* (Cth):

> **34A Application of the *Criminal Code***
>
> Chapter 2 of the *Criminal Code* applies to all offences created by this Act.
>
> Note: Chapter 2 of the *Criminal Code* sets out the general principles of criminal responsibility.

Until December 2011, s 13(3) of the Commonwealth Act provided that 'No margin note, footnote or endnote to an Act … shall be taken to be part of the Act'. The former position is maintained in states and territories. See s 35(2)(c) of the NSW Act, s 36(3) of the Vic Act, s 14(7) and s 35C of the Qld Act (which says that a note in an Act, as opposed to a footnote or endnote, is part of the Act), s 19(2)(b) of the SA Act, s 32(2) of the WA Act, s 6(4) of the Tas Act, s 127(1) of the ACT Act and s 55(6) of the NT Act. In those jurisdictions, notes continue to form part of the extrinsic materials to the Acts and therefore can be considered during the interpretation task in any event.

The new s 13 of the Commonwealth Act makes no specific reference to notes. However, 'all material' from the first section to the last would include any notes. This therefore changes the position, at the Commonwealth level at least, with respect to the use of notes. This is confirmed by the Explanatory Memorandum to the Acts Interpretation Amendment Bill 2011 (Cth) which reads in relevant part:

> [93] New section 13 states that all material in an Act, from the first section to the end of the last Schedule, is part of the Act. Certain material appearing before section 1 is also part of the Act. New section 13 is intended to capture all headings (including the heading to the first section of the Act) and explanatory notes within the Act. Historically in the

United Kingdom and the Australian colonies, elements like marginal notes and section headings were added to the text of a Bill after passage through Parliament, and the current subsection 13(3) reflects this history. However, from federation, marginal notes and section headings have been included in Bills as part of the text considered by the Commonwealth Parliament. They are able to be amended by Parliament or under the supervision of Parliament. It is appropriate for this material to be treated as part of the Act, and given appropriate weight in interpreting the terms of the Act. This weight will ordinarily be less than the words of the section itself, given the function of such notes and section headings (see *Wacando v The Commonwealth* (1981) 148 CLR 1 at 16, Gibbs CJ).

(95) This change is likely to make little practical difference to the interpretation of Commonwealth Acts. Currently anything in the text of an Act can be taken into account in the interpretation of the Act, even if it does not form part of the Act under existing subsection 13(3) (see paragraph 15AB(2)(a)). New section 13 will enable section headings and explanatory notes within the Act, as set out in new section 13, to be used in interpreting the Act without the need for recourse to section 15AB.

(96) New section 13 would not prescribe how much weight (if any) should be given to particular material forming part of an Act in interpreting the Act. Of course, primacy should normally be given to the substantive provisions of an Act over headings and explanatory notes in interpreting an Act.

(97) When an Act is published (in electronic or printed form), end notes and other references or information are often added. This information is not part of the Act (though it may form part of the context for interpretation under section 15AB of the Acts Interpretation Act).

This means that 'all material' is the material that is passed, so it includes notes, headnotes and footnotes but not endnotes.

An example of a note being argued in statutory interpretation is *Breavington v Godleman* (1988) 169 CLR 41. There, an issue was raised as to whether there was a distinction between 'acts' and 'Acts'—typically 'acts' are actions taken by a person, while 'Acts' are statutes. However the Commonwealth argued that there was no effective difference, using a 1901 margin note to the section which referred to US legislation, saying that US case law supporting this proposition was thereby applicable. The High Court was not convinced that reference to the US law in a note made US case law applicable to the interpretation of the section. Toohey J stated at [40] 'I would reject this submission. Marginal notes are not to be read as part of an Act. They are not, therefore, to be taken into account for the purposes of interpretation'. How would this case be decided today? The note would be considered part of the Act, but it remains very unlikely that the effect would be to import US cases into interpretation of the Australian provision.

Punctuation

The new s 13 would also suggest that punctuation is part of 'all material' and is therefore part of the Act and to be included in its interpretation. This is already the case in some states—see s 14(5) of the Qld Act and s 19 of the SA Act. However, punctuation cannot be determinative, given the overriding instruction for courts to interpret legislation so as to give effect to its purpose. Punctuation cannot effectively defeat the purpose of a legislative provision. Dawson J commented in *Chew v R* (1992) 173 CLR 626, regarding the placement of a comma in a provision which read 'An employee ... shall not make improper use of his position ... to gain, directly or indirectly, an advantage for himself' at [4]:

> The presence of a comma immediately before the words 'to gain' may be thought to indicate that the words which follow are used disjunctively rather than conjunctively and hence to indicate result alone rather than purpose or intention ... It can scarcely be thought that the insertion of a comma ... was intended to give a different meaning to the words ... Whilst punctuation may sometimes be helpful as an aid to construction, in these circumstances it would be wrong, in my view, to allow the presence of a comma to control the meaning of the sub-section.

Examples

Simply said, examples may be used in interpreting a provision but cannot override the substantive provision.[6] The new s 15AD of the Commonwealth Act allows examples to extend the operation of the provision:

> **15AD Examples**
>
> If an Act includes an example of the operation of a provision:
>
> (a) the example is not exhaustive; and
> (b) the example may extend the operation of the provision.

An example of such an Act is in the *Autonomous Sanctions Act 2011* (Cth), s 16 of which provides:

> (1) An individual commits an offence if:
>   (a) the individual engages in conduct; and
>   (b) the conduct contravenes a sanction law.
> (2) An individual commits an offence if:
>   (a) the individual engages in conduct; and

6 For the states and territories see s 36A of the Vic Act, s 14D of the Qld Act, s 19A of the SA Act, s 132 of the ACT Act, s 62D of the NT Act.

(b) the conduct contravenes a condition of an authorisation (however described) under a sanction law.

Example: An example of an authorisation is a licence, permission, consent or approval.

In older statutes the same information may have been expressed using an *ejusdem generis* style of expression, such as 'It is an offence to engage in any conduct in contravention of an authorisation in the form of a licence, permission, consent, approval, or in any other form'. The ongoing use of Latin maxims such as *ejusdem generis* is discussed in Chapter 9.

Penalties

Commonly in criminal statutes, penalties are provided for. An example from s 82 of the *Crimes Act 1900* (NSW) is:

> Whosoever, being a woman with child,
>
> unlawfully administers to herself any drug or noxious thing, or
>
> unlawfully uses any instrument or other means,
>
> with intent in any such case to procure her miscarriage shall be liable to imprisonment for ten years.

If a penalty appears below a number of subsections it is the penalty for breach of any of them. Unless stated otherwise, all such penalties are maximums not mandatory periods. See s 4D of the *Crimes Act 1914* (Cth), s 18 of the *Crimes (Sentencing Procedure) Act 1999* (NSW), s 111 of the *Sentencing Act 1991* (Vic), ss 41 and 41A of the Qld Act, s 30 SA Act, s 72 WA Act, s 37 of the Tas Act, ss 134 and 135 ACT Act and s 38C of the NT Act. Under the modern approach, whether a penalty is fixed or maximum depends on the reading of the Act as a whole in the light of its context and purpose, which may disclose an intention that the penalty be fixed.

Having now considered the various components of an Act, the next chapter focuses on the text itself.

CHAPTER 7

INTRINSIC MATERIALS: THE TEXT

It may be tempting, with the plethora of provisions and rules on statutory interpretation, to overlook the primacy of the text itself. Spigelman CJ has stated extra-curially:[1]

> [T]here are a number of recent High Court judgments which indicate that the degree of flexibility with respect to the text that has, on occasion, been displayed by judges in intermediate courts of appeal, has gone too far. There are indications that the judiciary must, with greater force and clarity, refocus its attention on the text itself.

All words have meaning

The starting point for consideration of the text is the rule that all words have meaning. At the turn of the last century, referring to English authority, Griffith CJ stated in *Commonwealth v Baume* (1905) 2 CLR 405 that there was a:

> known rule in the interpretation of Statutes that such a sense is to be made upon the whole as that no clause, sentence, or word shall prove superfluous, void, or insignificant, if by any other construction they may all be made useful and pertinent.

More recently on the High Court, Brennan J expressed the same sentiment in *Project Blue Sky Inc v Australian Broadcasting Authority* (1998) 194 CLR 355 at [71]: 'a court construing a statutory provision must strive to give meaning to every word of the provision'. Of course it may not always be possible to give a full and active meaning to every word in a statute, but the courts are not at liberty to ignore any word or to consider any words to be insignificant. It must be presumed that if Parliament included a word or phrase in a statute it did so for a reason.

Ordinarily, the meaning is the ordinary meaning

As a default position, the meaning should be the ordinary meaning, giving consideration to the sense in which words are used. This is because many words are used in different senses—consider for example the word 'made'. In one sense, it may mean created—'we made a baby'. In another, it may mean arranged—'I made my bed', progress—'we made ground', success—'a made man', or theft—'the man made off with the woman's purse'.

1 J J Spigelman, 'The Intolerable Wrestle: Developments in Statutory Interpretation', Address to the Australasian Conference of Planning and Environment Courts and Tribunals, 1 September 2010, 20.

It is particularly important that the interpretation task does not entail disaggregating each word in a provision into their individual meaning, and then putting them back together to work out the meaning of the phrase, as this will not give effect to the words in the sense they are used, which is often contingent on the words they are used with. An often cited quote from Learned Hand J in *Cabell v Markham* (1945) 148 F 2d 737 at 739 is:

> Of course it is true that the words used, even in their literal sense, are the primary, and ordinarily the most reliable, source of interpreting the meaning of any writing: be it a statute, a contract, or anything else. But it is one of the surest indexes of a mature and developed jurisprudence not to make a fortress out of the dictionary; but to remember that statutes always have some purpose or object to accomplish, whose sympathetic and imaginative discovery is the surest guide to their meaning.

More recently Spigelman CJ has said:[2]

> By 'text' I do not intend to refer to individual words, or phrases, or sentences considered in isolation from their context. Nor do I mean to imply that the way to construe an Act of Parliament is to take the statute in one hand and a dictionary in the other and search for a literal meaning of the words of Parliament. I do not intend to suggest that it is first necessary to show ambiguity before principles of construction come into play. Happily, understanding some texts involves no more than giving clear language its plain meaning. Often, however, there is more to it than that.

Case exercise

'Hummer hummer'

DIPL is an Australian company that imports vehicles, modifies them and resells them. One of those vehicles is a Krystal Hummer H2 motor vehicle, which is 'stretched' to carry 14 passengers. The Federal Commissioner of Taxation considers the Hummer to be a limousine, upon which luxury car tax should be paid. DIPL disputes this and says no luxury tax is payable.

The relevant legislation is the *A New Tax System (Luxury Car Tax) Act 1999* (Cth), which provides in s 7-5 that luxury car tax is payable on all taxable importations of luxury cars. Section 25-1(1) defines a luxury car as a 'car whose luxury car tax value exceeds the luxury car tax threshold'. 'Car' is defined in s 27-1 as a motor vehicle that is:

(a) designed to carry a load of less than 2 tonnes or fewer than 9 passengers; or
(b) a limousine (regardless of the number of passengers it is designed to carry).

2 M Gleeson, 'The Meaning of Legislation: Context, Purpose and Respect for Fundamental Rights' Address to Victoria Law Foundation, Melbourne, 31 July 2008, 7.

The Hummer, in being stretched to carry 14 passengers, did not come under paragraph (a), so to meet the definition of a 'car' it has to be considered a limousine. 'Limousine' is not defined in the Act. The Australian Oxford Dictionary defines 'limousine' as 'a large, luxurious car'.

The Explanatory Memorandum that accompanied the introduction of s 27-1(b) of the Act stated that 'the definition of car [was] intended to include all passenger cars (including station wagons), all 4 wheel drive vehicles, light trucks, motor homes, campervans and hearses': Explanatory Memorandum, A New Tax System (Indirect Tax and Consequential Amendments) Bill (No 2) 1999, [1.70].

What do you think? Is a Hummer covered by the luxury car tax? Decide before proceeding.

The real case is *Dreamtech International v FCT* [2010] FCAFC 103. If you decided the Hummer is a limousine, you are in agreement with the Federal Commissioner of Taxation, the Administrative Appeals Tribunal, the Federal Court and the Full Court of the Federal Court. If you decided that it is not, you are original.

The Court considered that, while it is a question of law whether the Act used the word 'limousine' in a sense other than in the ordinary sense, if the word has no technical legal meaning and it is determined the ordinary meaning applies, determination of that ordinary meaning is a question of fact: at [18]. It stated at [26]: 'Parliament chose the word "limousine". If it had intended to define the word to have a meaning different from its ordinary meaning, it would have. It did not'. The Court held that there was nothing to suggest that the word 'limousine' should be given 'anything other than its ordinary meaning': at [32]. The Court held that the Tribunal's finding of fact that a limousine is 'considerably larger than a standard road vehicle, conveying a sense of luxurious motor transport driven by a chauffeur' was reasonably open.

A technical or legal meaning may be used

The plain and ordinary meaning of words may be the answer, but it may equally be varied (read 'strained', 'stretched', 'read down' etc as discussed in Chapter 5) as a result of consideration of the sense in which the words are used, in their context and in the light of the objective intent of the provision and purpose of the legislation in which they are contained. This process may result in the 'technical' or 'legal' meaning of a word or phrase being applied. The question whether a word or phrase in a statute is to be given its ordinary meaning or a technical meaning is a question of law.[3]

The technical meaning is the commercial or trade meaning of a word, used where it is clear that the audience of a statute is not the general public. For example the term 'pastry', when used in ordinary parlance, would include a pie, apple Danish or croissant, but in the trade, a 'pastry chef' is a person who makes desserts, whether or not they have pastry in them—for example icecream and chocolate mousse are both 'pastries' within the commercial or trade meaning. That meaning was applied in relation to the Act which was directed at industry not consumers.[4] The High Court has described there being a 'presumption' in favour of a trade meaning being given in revenue statutes.[5]

Is it possible, then, to give some elements of a phrase an ordinary meaning and others a technical meaning? The High Court unanimously ruled in *Collector of Customs v Agfa Gevaert Ltd* (1996) 186 CLR 389 that it was. There, to import photographic paper duty free, it had to use a 'silver dye bleach reversal process'. This was interpreted using a trade meaning for 'silver dye bleach' and an ordinary meaning for 'reversal'. Agfa argued that the expression had to be construed as a whole—once it was identified that the whole phrase had no accepted trade meaning, the ordinary meaning of the words should be used. The process did include silver, dye and bleach, and there was reversal in the process. The Court rejected this, saying it was a composite phrase directed to an audience concerned with photographic film processing, and '[t]o accept the argument of Agfa would be to deny the import of logic and common-sense in matters of statutory construction'. The Court went on to state:

> In the area of statutory interpretation and construction, courts must be wary of propounding rigid rules. Even the use of general rules carries dangers in this area because of the tendency for such rules to be given an inflexible application. Nevertheless, when construing a composite phrase which does not have a trade meaning, it will ordinarily make sense for a court or tribunal to take notice of the trade meaning of a word or words within that expression, provided such an interpretation does not lead to a result which is absurd in the sense that the result may be unworkable or impracticable, inconvenient, anomalous or illogical, futile or pointless, or artificial. Consideration of the trade meaning of individual words in such cases is more likely than not to lead to the interpretation that the makers of the instrument had in mind.

Generally speaking, where a word or phrase has an established legal meaning this will be used in interpretation (see Chapter 10 on statutory presumptions) unless it is evident from the purpose of the Act that an ordinary or other meaning was intended.

---

3 *Jedko Game Co v Collector of Customs (NSW)* (1987) 12 ALD 491. See also *Collector of Customs v Agfa Gevaert Ltd* (1996) 186 CLR 389: 'All that is required for a reviewable question of law to be raised is for a phrase to be identified as being used in a sense different from that which it has in ordinary speech'.

4 See *Herbert Adams Pty Ltd v Federal Commissioner of Taxation* (1932) 47 CLR 222.

5 *Collector of Customs v Agfa Gevaert Ltd* (1996) 186 CLR 389.

In other words the court will be concerned with finding the meaning that best promotes the purpose of the Act. Kirby J in *Palgo Holdings Pty Ltd v Gowans* (2005) 221 CLR 249 at 266 made the approach crystal clear:

> the correct question is not whether a legal or an ordinary meaning should be given to a particular statutory term. Rather, it is what is the natural and ordinary meaning of the language read in its context and with attention to the legislative purpose and available materials that disclose that purpose.

Case exercise

'A mere pawn'

Cash Counters Byron is a business in Byron Bay that lends people small sums of money, usually repayable within seven days. The loan agreement includes two parts. The first is a 'Secured Loan Agreement' recording the amount of the loan, the amount of interest and the due date for repayment. The second part is a 'Bill of Sale/Goods Mortgage' deed operating to mortgage property. The borrower transfers title in an item or items of personal property to the lender as security for the loan, and the borrower has to keep the goods in their custody, look after them and insure them.

However there is also a statement that the property is 'in storage at the mortgagor's request'. Cash Counters Byron argues that storing the property for the customer satisfies its obligation to insure them, as it means the goods will be covered by the business insurance policy. In practice, the goods are always 'stored' at Cash Counters Byron. Customers assume or are told that doing so is necessary to get the loan, that on repayment the goods will be returned to them, and if they do not make repayment, the goods will be sold.

The *Pawnbrokers and Second-hand Dealers Act 1996* (NSW) provides in s 6:

> A person must not carry on a business of lending money on the security of pawned goods except in accordance with a licence held by the person.

Cash Counters Byron argues that it does not need a licence because it is not a pawnbroker. 'Pawnbroker' is defined in s 3 of the Act as 'a person who carries on a business of lending money on the security of pawned goods'. There is no definition of 'pawned' or 'pawned goods' provided.

Section 4 states:

> (1) This Act does not apply so as to affect any activities conducted in accordance with a licence, permit or other authority under another Act (for example the Property, Stock and Business Agents Act 1941, the Firearms Act 1996, or the Motor Dealers Act 1974).

> In particular, this Act does not require a person to obtain a licence under this Act to carry on a business or any activity that is authorised by a licence, permit or other authority issued to that person under any other Act.
>
> (2) This Act does not apply:
>
> (a) to dealing in second-hand goods in the course of a fundraising appeal authorised under the Charitable Fundraising Act 1991, or
>
> (b) to the business of an auctioneer, or
>
> (c) to the extent provided by the regulations, in relation to such persons and circumstances as the regulations may prescribe.

Section 5 states:

> If a person receives goods under a contract of sale where the seller has the right to buy back the goods, then for the purposes of this Act:
>
> (a) the person receiving the goods is taken to be lending money on the security of the goods, and
>
> (b) the price at which the goods are to be sold under the contract is taken to be the amount lent, and
>
> (c) the difference between the amount lent and the price at which the goods may be bought back is taken to be the interest payable.

What do you think? Is Cash Counters Byron in the business of lending money on the security of pawned goods? Are the 'mortgaged' goods actually 'pawned' goods? Decide before proceeding.

The real case is *Palgo Holdings Pty Ltd v Gowans* (2005) 221 CLR 249.

If you decided that Cash Counters Byron is a pawnbroker, you are in agreement with the Local Court, Supreme Court, Court of Appeal and Kirby J on the High Court. If you decided it is not, you are in agreement with the majority of the High Court.

The majority, comprising McHugh, Gummow, Hayne and Heydon JJ, considered that the word 'pawn' has a long-established legal meaning as a bailment of personal property as security for a debt (with a right to detain but no actual ownership in the property). The law has differentiated this from a 'mortgage' under which the title to the property passes conditionally to the lender.

The majority considered that the Act did not indicate that 'pawned goods' included 'goods that are the subject of other forms of security transaction'. The text and the context show that it covered bailment of personal property as security for a debt, distinct from a chattel mortgage. The majority said 'the distinction is not to be elided by treating one kind of transaction as being subsumed in the other' at [25]. Further, 'there is no basis for reading the definition of pawnbrokers as extending to a business embracing all kinds of transaction in which a lender of money takes possession or custody of goods' at [28].

In dissent, Kirby J said that '[i]solating a word, such as "pawned", and affording it meaning torn from its context is a discredited approach to interpretation, given the way that language is ordinarily used and understood by human beings' at [37]. He said that the essence of the 'pawn' or 'hock' transaction is taking possession of personal property as security for a loan, with an entitlement to sell it in case of default, which is how Cash Counters Byron conducted its business: at [70]. He concluded that the word be given its ordinary meaning and not the legal or technical meaning, otherwise clever drafting could be used to circumvent the Act, stating at [99]:

> I have previously warned against the danger of the 'encrustation' of the statute which may result from the uncritical importation of the strict legal meaning of a statutory word or phrase. The danger is apparent in this case. The strict legal meaning of 'pawned goods' as excluding goods over which there also exists a chattel mortgage should not be used to assist those who use devices to circumvent the operation of the 1996 Act in frustration of the important social purposes it reveals.

Current meaning

The meaning given to words in a statute is the modern meaning, not the meaning of the words at the time the statute was enacted (unless of course the Act specifies otherwise or it is obvious from the context that it was intended so). Provisions to this effect have been included in s 21 of the SA Act and s 8 of the WA Act. This means, for example, that 'writing' may cover email or fax communications even though faxes and internet technology may not have been in existence at the time the statute was passed. On the one hand this may be considered a manifestation of the 'always speaking' approach discussed in Chapter 5, and on the other hand, it may be rationalised that if the meaning of a word changes, and Parliament does not want the new meaning to apply, it should pass amending legislation, and the failure to do so can be taken as an endorsement of the new meaning.

Kirby J discussed the importance of applying the current meaning in *Coleman v Power* (2004) 220 CLR 1 at [245]:

> The notion that Acts of Parliament in Australia are read in accordance with the subjective intentions of the legislators who voted on them is increasingly seen as doubtful. It involves an approach to statutory construction encapsulated in the maxim: *contemporanea expositio est optima et fortissima in lege*. The essential flaw in that maxim derives from

> the fact that laws, once enacted, operate thenceforth, as from time to time applicable. The words of a statute should normally be interpreted 'in accordance with their ordinary and current meaning' ... The suggestion that the meaning of the Act in question here is forever governed by the 'intention' of the legislators who sat in the Queensland Parliament in 1931 is not one that I would accept ... It does not represent the purposive approach to legislation now followed by this Court. The purpose postulated in that meaning is an objective one, derived from the living language of the law as read today. It is not derived from the subjective intentions of parliamentarians held decades earlier, assuming that such intentions could ever be accurately ascertained.

The difference may be described as that between 'denotation' and 'connotation'. The denotation is the specific, literal object, but the connotation is the sense in which it is used. The connotation encompasses the associations connected to a certain word, the aggregation of attributes demonstrating what a word signifies. In legislation, the connotation does not change but the denotation can. In *Deputy Commissioner of Taxation v Clark* [2003] NSWCA 91 Spigelman CJ stated at [139]–[141]:

> Statutes may be interpreted on the basis that the connotation of the language remains the same whereas its denotation may differ over time ... So the word 'gas' was interpreted to include the supply of liquefied petroleum gas, whereas only coal gas would have been in the contemplation of the Parliament at the time the legislation was adopted ... Nevertheless, the court will need to be satisfied that the word or words was or were intended to be used in a generic sense in the relevant statute. The words 'motion picture films' were found not to have been employed in such a generic sense, and accordingly did not extend to a video cassette, for purposes of the stamp duty legislation.

Dictionary meaning

The dictionary, definitions or interpretations provisions in an Act will be of primary application in interpreting words or phrases in that Act. For undefined words, reference may be had to a dictionary (as an extrinsic material, see Chapter 8). It stands to reason that, if the meaning to be applied is the modern meaning, a court should use the current edition of the dictionary. However, courts have not been particular about this, often referring to more than one dictionary at a time, without referencing the edition or year of publication, and to dictionaries of Australian and English origin. Evidently it all depends what the parties refer to, or what happens to be within arm's reach in the Judge's chambers.

It is disappointing that, while we have graduated from reliance on English precedents, we do not seem to have graduated from reliance on English dictionaries. Of the five most recent High Court decisions, at the time of writing, which refer to a dictionary, only one used an Australian dictionary:

- *Wainohu v New South Wales* [2011] HCA 24 per French CJ and Kiefel J at [34]: 'The term "persona designata" means "[a] person pointed out or described as an individual, as opposed to a person ascertained as a member of a class, or as filling a particular character"', referencing *Jowitt's Dictionary of English Law*, 3rd edn (2010) at 1700.
- *White v Director of Public Prosecutions (WA)* [2011] HCA 20 per French CJ, Crennan and Bell JJ at [10]: 'The ordinary meaning of the word "property" is "[t]hat which one owns; a thing or things belonging to a person or persons ..." and "[a] house or piece of land owned"', referencing the *Shorter Oxford English Dictionary*, 6th edn (2007) at 2370. Gummow J used the same dictionary in his judgment, saying at [21]: 'The relevant ordinary meaning of the verb "use" is to "[m]ake use of (a thing), esp. for a particular end or purpose; utilize, turn to account"'.
- *Commissioner of Taxation v BHP Billiton Limited* [2011] HCA 17 per French CJ, Heydon, Crennan and Bell JJ at [42]: 'The Commissioner contended that the expression "capable of", as used in relation to rights in s 243–20(2), means "susceptible to"' referencing the *Oxford English Dictionary*, 2nd edn (1989), vol 2 at 856, senses (3) and (4).
- *Jemena Gas Networks (NSW) Limited v Mine Subsidence Board* [2011] HCA 19 per French CJ, Gummow, Hayne, Heydon, Crennan and Kiefel JJ at [47]: 'In s 12A(1)(b) "anticipated" is used in the sense described as the ninth meaning of "anticipate" in the Oxford English Dictionary: "To look forward to, look for (an uncertain event) as certain"' referencing the 2nd ed (1989), vol 1 at 522.
- *Hogan v Hinch* [2011] HCA 4 per French CJ at [34]: 'The word "identify" has a number of shades of meaning. In s 42(1)(c) it bears its ordinary meaning, namely to ascertain or establish that a given person is an offender or is a person who has appeared or given evidence in a proceeding under the Act', referencing the *Oxford English Dictionary*, 2nd edn (1989), vol VII at 619 and the *Macquarie Concise Dictionary*, revised 3rd edn (2004) at 586.

Although in most instances a general dictionary is used, there have been occasions where a legal dictionary is used (see *Wainohu* above) or even a specialist technical dictionary—see *Re John Kirkpatrick v Commonwealth of Australia* [1985] FCA 440, where an issue was raised regarding use of a medical dictionary to find the definition of 'compensation neurosis'. In practice a medical dictionary may well have been the only dictionary to contain a definition of that term.

Consistent meaning across an Act

Where a word appears several times within the one Act, it is assumed that the word is used consistently. Of course, if a part of the Act provides a different definition that will apply, and under the modern approach, if a different meaning promotes the purpose of the Act, this will be used.

Where, within an Act, a different word is used in a place where the same word could have been used, it is assumed that Parliament intended a different meaning, otherwise it would have used the same word. This may be difficult to apply, however, where an Act has been amended at different times in different parts. According to Pearce and Geddes, '[t]he issue will ultimately turn on the view the court forms as to the care exercised by the drafter in the choice of words'.[6]

Variants of words

Section 18A of the Commonwealth Act provides:

> In any Act, unless the contrary intention appears, where a word or phrase is given a particular meaning, other parts of speech and grammatical forms of that word or phrase have corresponding meanings.

This means, for example, that one can draw upon the definition of 'use' when interpreting the word 'using' or 'apply' when interpreting the word 'application'. Similar provisions exist in s 7 of the NSW Act, s 39 of the Vic Act, s 32 of the Qld Act, s 4AA of the SA Act, s 9 of the WA Act, s 157 of the ACT Act and s 23 of the NT Act.

Limiting words

Limiting words, such as 'solely', 'primarily', 'exclusively' and 'only' may be used to limit the operation of the provision. Whether minor deviations are permitted depends on the intention of Parliament. They cannot be disregarded altogether, but they may not be determinative. A relevant Latin maxim is *de minimis non curat lex*—the law does not pay heed to trifling matters. In other words, if the deviation is trifling or minor it may be disregarded when determining whether a 'sole', 'only' or 'exclusive' requirement has been met. It may be considered by the court as immaterial to the determination, even

6 D Pearce and R Geddes, *Statutory Interpretation in Australia* (LexisNexis, 7th ed, 2011) 121.

if for example, a literal meaning of a requirement that a consequence must be solely attributable to an action would be to say that no deviation whatsoever is permitted. At the time of writing, the Latin maxim itself has been referred to in full only five times by the High Court, and only once in the past 30 years. That was in *Amaca Pty Ltd v Ellis* (2010) 240 CLR 111 in relation to causation for lung cancer where the sufferer was a smoker who was exposed to asbestos fibres. It was considered that any contribution that was not *de minimis* was material. In other words trifling matters could be disregarded.

Case exercise

'Convenience stores at Uni'

A university operates on a large parcel of land, with no shopping centre within a three-kilometre radius. The university has leased some buildings in the central courtyard to retail operators including a general shop, a travel agent and a bank. Although the university grounds were open to the public, in practice the shops are only used by students and staff at the university.

A dispute has arisen as to whether the university has to pay land taxes to the local council. All land is taxable but s 132(1)(fii) of the *Local Government Act 1919* (NSW) creates an exception for 'land which is vested' in the University, which is 'used or occupied by the University … solely for the purposes thereof'.

The Local Council argues that, because the leased shops operate with a view to making a profit, the land is taxable, and the University argues that the shops are there for the purposes of the university. Is that enough to meet the 'solely' requirement in the legislation? Is it sufficient that they are leased for the University's purposes, even if they also make a profit for the lessee's own purposes? What do you think? Decide before proceeding.

The real case is *Ryde Municipal Council v Macquarie University* (1978) 139 CLR 633 which was decided under the now repealed local government legislation. If you decided that the land was ratable you are in agreement with Reynolds JA in dissent on the Court of Appeal, and Jacobs and Aickin JJ on the High Court. If you decided that it was not, you are in agreement with the Supreme Court of New South Wales, the majority of the Court of Appeal, and the majority of the High Court, comprising Gibbs CJ, Stephen and Murphy JJ.

The High Court majority held that the university was still using the land solely for its purposes, even when it granted the leases which resulted in other entities occuping parts of the land. The words 'using' and 'occupying' are not synonymous, and '[a] person who owns land may be said to use it for his own purposes notwithstanding that he permits someone else to occupy it, even under a lease': Gibbs J at 639.

Hendiadys

It is not uncommon for composite phrases to appear in legislation and other documents such as contracts—take for example 'cease and desist', 'good and ready', 'sick and tired', 'heart and hardy', 'rock and roll'. Where such expressions are used in legislation the court must decide whether Parliament intended them to be read conjunctively or disjunctively. For example in *Victims Compensation Fund Corporation v Brown* (2003) 201 ALR 260, the High Court read the expression 'symptoms and disability' conjunctively—the victim had to have both symptoms and disability for compensation to be payable. Heydon J, with concurrence from the other members of the Court, stated at [34]:

> The contention that 'symptoms and disability' could be treated as being 'a composite or portmanteau phrase' is reminiscent of, though perhaps not identical with, a method of avoiding collisions between conjunctive constructions and disjunctive constructions which was raised in oral argument as a possible solution to the present problem. That method turned on construing the expression 'symptoms and disability' as a hendiadys—an expression in which a single idea is conveyed by two words connected by a conjunction, like 'law and heraldry' to mean 'heraldic law'. Thus the expression 'shall promptly co-operate with the Committee and assist to carry out its duties' has been construed to create an obligation of prompt cooperation with the Committee in the area of carrying out its duties. For the first and second respondents the advantage of that approach would be that it would not render fatal the fact that, approaching any limb independently, they had symptoms but no disability. However, sub-cll (c) and (e) of cl 5 proceed on the assumption that 'symptoms' and 'disability' are distinct entities, not linked integers or elements in a single idea more complex than each taken singly. A composite expression is one which is a compound created out of at least two elements or integers which is different from each of them. A portmanteau expression combines the meanings of two distinct words to create a new expression. The characterisation of 'symptoms and disability' as 'a composite or portmanteau phrase' did not explain how, short of bluntly reading 'and' as 'or', the two elements or integers worked together to create a new composite or portmanteau result.

Temporal expressions

Legislation will often contain expressions which carry a temporal quality, be that future tense ('will', 'could'), past tense ('did', 'was') or present tense ('is'). The court, in interpreting these words, will take into consideration the context in which they appear and the overall purpose of the legislative scheme. In *New South Wales Crime*

Commission v Kelly [2003] NSWCA 245, for example, the New South Wales Court of Appeal considered the word 'will' in s 24(1) of the *Criminal Assets Recovery Act 1990* (NSW) which provided in relevant part:

> If the Supreme Court is satisfied that an assets forfeiture order will operate to cause hardship to any dependant of the person who will forfeit an interest in property under the order, the Court:
>
> (a) may order that the dependant is entitled to be paid a specified amount out of the proceeds of sale of the interest, being an amount that the Court thinks is necessary to prevent hardship to the dependant.

Did the phrase 'will forfeit an interest in property' mean that the order for payment to a dependant had to occur before the property was forfeited? In other words if the property had already been forfeited, was a dependant suffering hardship as a result of no longer being entitled to a payout? Such a literal interpretation would not promote the purpose of the Act. Clearly, the provision was clumsily drafted. The Court held at [23]–[24]:

> To avoid repugnancy and make legislative sense this phrase should be read as 'dependant of the person who has forfeited an interest in property under this order' ... The purpose of s 24 was to relieve dependants from hardship caused by an assets forfeiture order. To my mind, it is absurd to suggest that that purpose should be defeated by a technicality, namely, that the dependant must apply for and obtain an order before the assets forfeiture order is made ... Such an arbitrary, unreasonable, pointless and ill-expressed limitation could achieve no sensible public purpose.

Case exercise

'The land is sinking'

Jemena owns a gas pipeline that runs from Moomba to Sydney, mostly underground. Expert consultants predicted that longwall mining operations by West Cliff Colliery, a subsidiary of BHP Billiton Ltd, would create land subsidence at the point at which the pipeline crosses Mallaty Creek in Campbelltown, and mitigation works would be needed. Given the significant impacts that damage to the pipeline would have, Jemena undertook work to fill in the subsidence under the pipes.

The *Mine Subsidence Compensation Act 1961* (NSW) provides for the creation of a fund, administered by a board, which is comprised from contributions by mining companies and is used to pay owners of land affected by land subsidence as a result of the mining. Section 12A of the Act provides in relevant part:

> (1) Subject to this section, claims may be made under this Act for payment from the Fund of: …
>
> (b) an amount to meet the proper and necessary expense incurred or proposed by or on behalf of the owner of improvements or household or other effects in preventing or mitigating damage to those improvements or household or other effects that, in the opinion of the Board, the owner could reasonably have anticipated would otherwise have arisen, or could reasonably anticipate would otherwise arise, from a subsidence that has taken place, other than a subsidence due to operations carried on by the owner.

Jemena has claimed against the Board for the work it had done, which came to over $2.7 million. The Board has refused the claim because the subsidence had to have taken place already at the time the work was done to prevent damage from it. Jemena had done the preventative works during a period in which the subsidence progressed from just 4 cm to 27 cm.

Are you going to conclude that the fund should reimburse Jemena, or has it not met the requirements of the legislation? It is agreed that the pipeline is an 'improvement', that Jemena is its owner, and that damage would have been caused by subsidence if preventative or mitigatory work had not been done. So the work avoided damage which would, had it not been prevented, have been far more expensive to correct. The issue all turns on the phrase 'from a subsidence that has taken place'. Did the expense have to be incurred after the subsidence had occurred or was it enough that it had commenced?

The real case is *Jemena Gas Networks (NSW) Limited v Mine Subsidence Board* [2011] HCA 19. If you decided Jemena was not entitled to claim on the Fund, you are in agreement with the Board, the Land and Environment Court, the Court of Appeal of the Supreme Court of New South Wales, and Bell J in dissent on the High Court. The ordinary meaning of the words 'has taken place' were considered to relate to a past event. If you decided it can claim, you are in agreement with the six judges in the majority on the High Court.

The High Court majority considered the words 'or could reasonably anticipate would otherwise arise' to be forward looking, and may have been added without Parliament modifying the words 'that has taken place': at [30]. They found that 'There are linguistic difficulties in the appellant's construction. But there are linguistic difficulties in all possible constructions … [i]n these circumstances it is necessary to look for the least irrational construction' at [30]. They considered the purpose of the provision as the prevention and reduction of damage before it was caused: at [40]. It was held that the mischief being addressed by s 12A(1)(b) was minimisation of damage as opposed to allowing maximum damage to be caused and then reimbursed from the Fund, saying at [41]:

> A construction which would deny the owner's claim when it took the former, sensible, option rather than the latter, riskier, one is a construction having irrational effects. On those grounds it ought to be rejected.

Bell J in dissent said that the ordinary grammatical meaning of the provision confines valid claims to improvements after subsidence has occurred but before damage has resulted. She said that the Act did not provide for reimbursement of preventative works with respect to anticipated subsidence. Defending her formalist approach, Bell J stated at [61]:

> It is not in issue that it is better to carry out preventative works than to wait until damage is done ... the question is not whether it is unreasonable to take no remedial action ... [i]t is whether the scheme introduced into the Act ... confers that power on the Board alone.

This is reminiscent of historical judgments adopting the declaratory theory. It would appear that poorly drafted provisions force a court to either engage in mental gymnastics to reach what is considered a fair outcome, or to express regret that an unreasonable result was caused by an unreasonable provision.

Common words and expressions

Some words and expressions are more prevalent in legislation than others, and it is impossible to cover them all within this chapter. Illustrative examples discussed below include 'deemed', 'have regard to', and words such as 'used', 'import' and 'publish'.

'Deemed'

The word 'deemed' is a mechanism of statutory fiction—it deems something that is *not*, to *be*—for example, possessing a certain quantity of drugs is deemed to be supply; having less than that quantity remains merely possession. Similarly, an injury that results in a certain degree of impairment is deemed to be a serious injury. Synonymous words are 'shall be taken to be' and 'as if'. In *Western Australia v Olive* [2011] WASCA 25, the Court of Appeal of the Supreme Court of Western Australia considered a deeming provision. Buss JA stated at [122]–[124], with concurrence of the other members of the Court:

> The words 'is to be taken to be' are a reasonably common drafting device in modern statutes enacted by the Parliament of this State. They are a form of deeming provision ... The words 'is to be taken to be an indictment', in s 83(5)(b) of the Criminal Procedure Act, are a deeming provision. The Parliament has created a statutory fiction by enacting, in essence, that notwithstanding the form and substance of a prosecution notice, the notice is to be taken to be an indictment. Section 83(5)(b) creates a fictitious factual circumstance by transmogrifying the prosecution notice into an indictment ... The evident purpose of this deeming provision is to facilitate, within the overlapping legislative scheme of which it is part, the sentencing of an offender who has been committed for sentence by a court of summary jurisdiction to a superior court. The offender appears before the superior court for sentencing on the basis that, notwithstanding the summary conviction, he or she is liable to the indictment penalty instead of the summary conviction penalty.

'Have regard to'

The expression 'have regard to', and the synonymous expression 'take into consideration', require a decision maker to take notice of, and take something into account, without its being determinative. For example in *R v Hunt; Ex parte Sean Investments Pty Ltd* (1979) 25 ALR 497, the High Court considered the expression 'the Permanent Head shall, in determining the scale of fees, in relation to a nursing home ... have regard to costs necessarily incurred in providing nursing home care in the nursing home'.

Mason J, with concurrence of Gibbs J, stated at 504 that this requires the Permanent Head to 'take those costs into account and to give weight to them as a fundamental element in making his determination'. Murphy J similarly commented at 508 that the requirement 'tends in itself to show that his duty in respect of those costs is limited to having regard to them. He must take them into account and consider them and give due weight to them, but he has an ultimate discretion'.

'Used'

Some words are said to have a 'protean' quality—'used' is one of them.[7] It is a versatile word which can easily mean different things in different contexts, and may be construed broadly or narrowly. It can be challenging in statutory interpretation contexts to establish the parliamentary intent behind its use.

7 M Gleeson, 'The Meaning of Legislation: Context, Purpose and Respect for Fundamental Rights' Address to Victoria Law Foundation, Melbourne, 31 July 2008, 4.

Case exercise

'It's ramshackle and derelict but we're still using it'

There is a piece of land in Wagga Wagga in New South Wales on which is a two-storey building. In the past it was used for a motor registry, and then for government storage, but since then it has lain empty. There was some effort to convert the site for use as a lab, but that did not come about. So a decision was made to sell the land, and for that purpose a surveyor and a real estate agent both briefly entered the land.

The Wagga Wagga Land Council has claimed the land but has been refused on the basis it was still in use by the Department of Lands. A court action has been brought by the New South Wales Aboriginal Land Council on behalf of the Wagga Wagga Land Council. The relevant statutory provision is s 36(1) of the *Aboriginal Land Rights Act 1983* (NSW), which defines 'claimable land' as:

> lands vested in Her Majesty that, when a claim is made for the lands under this Division—
> (a) are able to be lawfully sold or leased, or are reserved or dedicated for any purpose, under the Crown Lands Consolidation Act, 1913, or the Western Lands Act, 1901;
> (b) are not lawfully used or occupied; and
> (c) are not needed, nor likely to be needed, for an essential public purpose.

It is not in contention that the land is vested in the Crown, is able to be lawfully sold or leased, and, given it was to be sold, is not needed for an essential public purpose. So the key issue is whether the land is 'lawfully used or occupied'. What do you think? Make your decision before reading on.

The real case is *Minister Administering the Crown Lands Act v NSW Aboriginal Land Council* [2008] HCA 48. If you decided the land was still being used, you are in agreement with the Minister for Lands and the Land and Environment Court of New South Wales. If you decided the land was not being used, you are in agreement with the Court of Appeal and the High Court.

The joint judgment of Hayne, Heydon, Crennan and Kiefel JJ considered the land to be clearly unoccupied, with transitory visits being insufficient to constitute 'use' of the land. In his separate judgment Kirby J at [30] identified the word 'use' as ambiguous, and said it was necessary to look to the context, including the beneficial and remedial purposes of the Act, which is addressed to the physical use of land and not a 'purely notional, potential, contingent or future "use"'.

'Import'

Another word with a 'protean' quality is 'import'. The challenge for the courts has been the use of an act (of importing) for what is actually a process (of importation). They have had to determine whether particular goods have been 'imported' or not. Is a good that has not been 'imported' still an 'import'? Two case exercises are provided here, one concerning when importing is considered to have commenced, and the other concerning when it is completed.

Case exercise

'Quick! Throw the drugs overboard!'

Barry and his friends recently travelled from Bali to Australia on the vessel Mariana. They had nearly made it to Darwin—indeed they had crossed the notional three-mile boundary which separates Australian territorial sea from the high seas, when an Army helicopter carrying Customs officers hovered above the vessel. They rushed to grab several suitcases containing in total 31 kg of cannabis, threw them overboard and washed down the decks, so by the time Customs officers boarded the vessel no cannabis was found. Needless to say it was retrieved from the sea by the authorities.

Barry was charged relevantly with both importing into Australia a prohibited import, under s 233B(1) of the *Customs Act 1901* (Cth), which made it an offence to import into Australia prohibited imports, of which cannabis was one. Neither 'import' nor 'importation' is defined in the Act.

The question is whether the drugs have been imported. At what point did importation occur? Was the act of bringing the suitcases on the vessel within three nautical miles from the coastline an act of importation? Or did the vessel actually have to enter the port? Or did the drugs actually have to be unloaded from the vessel and cleared by Customs? What do you think? Decide before proceeding.

The real case is *The Queen v Bull* (1974) 131 CLR 203. The Supreme Court referred certain questions of law to the High Court, which held that importation had not yet occurred—it did not cover any goods on a boat that had come within the three nautical mile limit of Australian territorial waters. The issue, said Barwick CJ at 212, was not as simple as looking up the word 'import' in the dictionary, because the focus was on 'when goods are imported into Australia *within the meaning of the Act*' (emphasis added):

> The question is not what constitutes importation in an abstract or universal sense: the question is when, according to the provisions of the Act, are goods imported into Australia.

> However, in general, importation of goods, in my opinion, according to the natural meaning of the words, involves landing them, or bringing them within a port for the purpose of landing them in the country or place in relation to which importation is regulated.

He went on to say, at 224:

> The process of importation as distinct from the act of importation is not confined to what occurs at the actual time or place when and where the goods are imported ... a ship ... may be used in the process of the importation of the goods though because of official intervention they are not, in the result, imported.

McTiernan J said that Parliament no doubt had the power to legislate in relation to prohibited imports brought within the three-mile limit, but the statute as it presently stood did not cover such power: at 248. A prohibited import was still a prohibited import, 'notwithstanding that it has not been imported' at 249.

Case exercise

'More than just furniture'

Belinda Campbell was once a pharmacist but now has a shop in Leichardt in Sydney, selling furniture that she imports from Indonesia by the container load. The containers are packed by her business associate in Indonesia, and delivered to her Leichardt store. On occasion he has included additional packages in with the furniture, which have not been declared for customs purposes. On these occasions, once the container arrives at Belinda's business premises and is unpacked, the business associate, or someone sent by him, collects the packages.

In the past Belinda has looked to see what was in the packages. On one occasion she found cigarettes and on another, cold tablets. At that time cold tablets still contained pseudoephedrine, which is a border-controlled precursor because it can be used to manufacture drugs. Another container was due to arrive and Belinda was notified that it had been selected for random inspection by Australian Quarantine and Inspection Services (AQIS). Officers found a large quantity of cold tablets with brand names Sudafed and Actifed. The cold tablets contained sufficient pseudoephedrine to manufacture 50–70 kg of 'ice', a prohibited drug, with a street value of $20–56 million. AQIS replaced some of the packages and notified Campbell that the inspection had been cancelled. The container was transported to the shop, and when the packages were collected, she was arrested along with the two men collecting the packages.

When Belinda had first heard that the inspection had been cancelled, she called her husband and said 'There is a God'; 'I just feel like going running around the street screaming hooray'; 'I feel like crying, you don't know how emotional I am it's just been killing me' and 'we're very, very lucky, and um we have to sort something else to do'. These conversations were intercepted with listening devices.

Campbell has been charged under s 307.11 of the *Criminal Code Act 1995* (Cth), which provides:

> A person commits an offence if:
> (a) the person imports or exports a substance; and
> (b) either or both of the following apply:
> (i) the person intends to use any of the substance to manufacture a controlled drug;
> (ii) the person believes that another person intends to use any of the substance to manufacture a controlled drug; and
> (c) the substance is a border controlled precursor; and
> (d) the quantity imported or exported is a commercial quantity.

Section 3.1 of the Code requires the physical and fault or intent elements to coincide in time. The physical element is the conduct or act, which in this Act is where the person 'imports' (or exports, as the case may be).

Has Campbell committed an offence under the Code? Before reading on, make your own judgement. If you are unsure, ask yourself:

- The act: did she import a commercial quantity of a border controlled precursor?
- The intent: did she believe that the business associate intended to use it to manufacture a controlled drug?
- Coincidence: did she have the requisite intent at the time the act of importing took place? When does importation take place? Is it when the container clears customs, or when it arrives in her shop in Leichardt and is unpacked?

The real case is *Campbell v R* [2008] NSWCCA 214. If you decided she had committed an offence, you are in agreement with the Supreme Court. If you decided she had not, you are in agreement with the Court of Criminal Appeal. The Court reasoned that the word 'imports' as used in the provision must be considered in its context, and the context of s 307.11 of the *Criminal Code Act 1995* (Cth) 'suggests that a precise, rather than expansive, sense of the word "imports" has been adopted': Spigelman CJ at [126]. Goods have been imported when they pass the point at which they can remain in Australia. Therefore there was held to be no coincidence of act as intent.

'Publish'

With the rise of internet communications, companies publish more and more information on their websites. Recently the question arose as to whether 'publish' can include blog (weblog) postings by individuals to a company's site, where those individuals comment about the company's products or services.

Case exercise

'Guilt written all over your Facebook'[8]

Allergy Pathway Pty Ltd ('the company') operates clinics for allergy diagnosis and treatment, using a 'muscle strength indicator' technique. In its marketing the company uses its website, Facebook and Twitter pages, as well as radio advertising and YouTube. It gave an undertaking that it would not publish statements about being able to test for, and cure, allergies.

Clients posted testimonials about the company's services on the company's Facebook 'wall', including:

> 'My asthma and eye symptoms no longer happen after my treatment'

> 'Allergy Pathway is amazing. It has worked wonders for me in so many ways. I had food allergies for as long as I can remember, avoiding seafood and shellfish and even bread! After one treatment I could eat seafood with no noticeable reaction'

> 'thank you for curing my daughter of all her allergies … she has gone from having red skin, puffy eyes, watery eyes and nose, coughing, etc to being a healthy 4 year old that can now eat anything'

> 'I can now wear gloves at work without my hands suffering from painful itchy cracked bleeding skin and rash which I had for 8 years and NO other conventional treatment could cure … I am glad to say it has cleared up now after Allergy Pathway treatments'

> 'As a practicing naturopath, I have found this technique to be the most effective method of treating allergic reactions and intolerances'

The Australian Competition and Consumer Commission claims that the company is in contempt of its undertaking as a result. Do you think the company has 'published' the statements posted by members of the public on the company's Facebook page?

8 This title has been taken from A Macinnis, 'Guilt written all over your Facebook: Liability for publication in social media', *Law Society Journal,* June 2011, 30.

How would you go about resolving this? How would you find out what 'publish' means in its ordinary and natural sense? Does it cover only positive acts, or also omissions? If there is no statutory definition of the term, where would you go to find one, and what would be your authority for doing so? Can a dictionary definition give the final answer, or do you still need to consider the Act as a whole?

Decide before proceeding.

The real case is *Australian Competition and Consumer Commission v Allergy Pathway Pty Ltd (No 2)* [2011] FCA 74 where Finkelstein J held that, because the company was aware of the statements posted on its Facebook page, but failed to remove them, it has effectively published them. He stated at [33] that although the initial publication was by a member of the public, the company:

> accepted responsibility for the publications when it knew of the publications and decided not to remove them. Hence it became the publisher of the testimonials. In any event it is clear that it caused them to continue to be published from the time it became aware of their existence.

In reading, most blog readers assume comments made by the public are not endorsed by the company whose site they are posted on.

Having considered the intrinsic materials in an Act, both in their component parts (Chapter 6) and in the words that are used (this chapter) the next chapter focuses on the use of extrinsic materials in statutory interpretation.

CHAPTER 8

EXTRINSIC MATERIALS

It is commonplace, when reading documents such as books, to refer to other documents, such as dictionaries. The dictionary is an 'extrinsic' material being used in the interpretation of the book's contents. Similarly, it is common in modern statutory interpretation to make reference to extrinsic materials. Indeed, a contextual interpretation will usually oblige a court to do so.

Reference to extrinsic materials is provided for in the Interpretation Acts. The Commonwealth provision in the *Acts Interpretation Act 1901* (Cth) is s 15AB, which has been in force since 1984 but applies to all Commonwealth legislation, including Acts passed before its inception. It covers when and how extrinsic materials may be referred to, the kinds of materials to which regard may be had, and other considerations to take into account. Each of these aspects is covered below. Similar (and sometimes identical) provisions exist in the states and territories—see s 35(b) of the Vic Act, s 14B of the Qld Act, s 19 of the WA Act, s 8B of the Tas Act, ss 141 to 143 of the ACT Act (referring to 'non-legislative context' instead of 'extrinsic materials') and s 62B of the NT Act. There is no provision in the South Australian interpretation legislation, so reliance is placed on the common law approach to extrinsic materials (see below).

Using extrinsic materials to interpret text

The express provisions of the Interpretation Acts focus on the use of extrinsic materials to interpret text—s 15AB(1) of the Cth Act provides:

> Subject to subsection (3), in the interpretation of a provision of an Act, if any material not forming part of the Act is capable of assisting in the ascertainment of the meaning of the provision, consideration may be given to that material:
>
> (a) to confirm that the meaning of the provision is the ordinary meaning conveyed by the text of the provision taking into account its context in the Act and the purpose or object underlying the Act; or
>
> (b) to determine the meaning of the provision when:
>
> (i) the provision is ambiguous or obscure; or
>
> (ii) the ordinary meaning conveyed by the text of the provision taking into account its context in the Act and the purpose or object underlying the Act leads to a result that is manifestly absurd or is unreasonable.

This is an awkward provision. First, the chapeau (introductory text) only allows for consideration of extrinsic material which is 'capable of assisting in the ascertainment of the meaning of the provision'. In practice, one cannot reach a conclusion as to whether extrinsic material is capable of assisting without considering it, so this provision is somewhat circular.

Second, the use of 'confirm' in paragraph (a) is unfortunate. This word is not defined in the Interpretation Acts, and, using them to interpret themselves (reminiscent of the 'chicken and the egg' cliché) we should look to the ordinary meaning of the word unless the context suggests an alternative meaning should be used. 'Confirm' is used in normal parlance to mean reinforce, strengthen, support, corroborate, and establish more firmly. It has a different meaning from, for example, the expression 'identify whether' or 'determine if'. In order to *confirm* that a meaning is the ordinary meaning, we must first have some idea of what the ordinary meaning is, so that we can confirm it. What if we find we are wrong, and are unable to confirm that the meaning is the ordinary meaning? Paragraph (a) says nothing about changing our minds. Matthew Stubbs has written on the uncertainty created by the use of the word 'confirm' where use of extrinsic material to 'confirm' the ordinary meaning reveals some uncertainty:[1]

> The approach suggested by s 15AB(1) itself, at this point, is that reference to the extrinsic material is no longer permitted and the ambiguity just revealed must now be 'forgotten' in favour of the more simplistic unambiguous reading without reference to the extrinsic material. Surely, it is not appropriate for the Parliament to require such an instance of judicial amnesia and oversimplification in the face of potentially relevant extrinsic materials.

However, the better view is that the interpreter retreats from their inquiry under paragraph (a) and comes back within paragraph (b), because the use of 'may' in the chapeau is directed to the use of extrinsic materials; it is not an indication that paras (a) and (b) are non-exhaustive. Paragraph (b) allows for the use of extrinsic material to 'determine' the meaning, but that requires establishment of ambiguity, obscurity, absurdity or unreasonableness.[2] Perhaps it could be said that if the enquiry under paragraph (a) fails to confirm the meaning to be the ordinary meaning, there must be some ambiguity. This issue was raised in *Re Australian Federation of Construction Contractors; Ex Parte Billing* (1986) 68 ALR 416, where the High Court had to decide whether a second reading speech could be relied upon. The High Court stated:

> Section 15AB of the *Acts Interpretation Act 1901* (Cth), as amended, does not permit recourse to that speech for the purpose of departing from the ordinary meaning of the text unless either the meaning of the provision to be construed is ambiguous or obscure or in its

1 M T Stubbs, 'From Foreign Circumstances to First Instance Considerations: Extrinsic Material and the Law of Statutory Interpretation' (2006) 34(1) *Federal Law Review* 103.

2 McHugh J in *Saraswati v R* (1991) 172 CLR 1 at [9] has commented that 'surprisingly' the Interpretation Act 'contemplates that the ordinary meaning (i.e. the literal meaning modified by context and purpose) may be manifestly absurd or unreasonable and authorises resort to extrinsic material to give the provision a different meaning'.

> ordinary meaning leads to a result that is manifestly absurd or is unreasonable. In our view neither of those conditions is satisfied in the present case.

Compare this with the discussion by Madgwick J in *Parrett v Secretary, Department of Family & Community Services* (2002) 124 FCR 299 at [32]:

> Section 15AB(1)(a) has sometimes been considered as being of limited utility ... [t]he view seems to have been taken that one cannot look to extrinsic material under para (1)(a) of s 15AB if the effect of such resort would be to depart from the ordinary meaning of the statutory text. However, with respect, para (1)(a) permits resort to extraneous material for the purpose of confirming ('to confirm') that the real meaning of the text is its ordinary meaning. Para (1)(a) does not prohibit sensible use of a contrary indication resulting from a lack of such confirmation after looking at the non-statutory material, nor would it seem logical or profitable that such a prohibition should be implied, having regard to the far-reaching effect, which I take now to be settled, of s 15AA.

Why, then, was the word 'confirm' adopted? According to Patrick Brazil, the rationale was that extrinsic material may further strengthen one's conviction as to the ordinary meaning of a provision—'[i]t can set the mind, and argument, to rest'.[3] That being the case, the provision could have read 'confirm the meaning is the ordinary meaning or, if not, determine the meaning to be given in the light of the Act's context and purpose'. Unfortunately the amendments to the Commonwealth Act made in 2011 did not encompass a reconsideration of the wording of s 15AB.

The use of the word 'may' in the chapeau demonstrates the discretionary nature of reference to extrinsic materials. If, as in *Mills v Meeking* (1990) 169 CLR 214, the language is clear and the purpose expressly stated in the Act, there may be no cause to refer to extrinsic materials. See Mason CJ and Toohey J at [18]:

> [T]here is no need to have resort to extrinsic material; the provisions may be given their ordinary grammatical meaning. If the language of a statute is ambiguous or uncertain, a risk of injustice will bear upon the construction to be given to words used. But, if the language is not ambiguous or uncertain, a court will apply its ordinary and grammatical meaning unless to do so will give the statute an operation which obviously was not intended ... This legislation is not relevantly ambiguous or uncertain.

One could expect such occasions to be rare in cases before superior courts. Even where the purpose is expressly stated in the Act, this may not be determinative (see Chapter 6) and in any event, the context includes not only intrinsic but extrinsic context of the Act.

---

3 P Brazil, 'Reform of Statutory Interpretation—the Australian Experience of Use of Extrinsic Materials: With a Postscript on Simpler Drafting', Address to Law Commission Legislation Seminar, National Library Auditorium, Wellington, 18–19 March 1988, published in (1988) 62 ALJ 503, 504.

Using extrinsic materials for context and purpose

Section 15AB makes no reference to the use of extrinsic materials to identify the context and purpose. Yet, as context includes not only the intrinsic context (the surrounding provisions) but also the extrinsic context (in which the legislation sits), and as the purpose of the Act may be revealed not only by consideration of intrinsic materials (such as the Long Title or objects clause) but also extrinsic materials (such as parliamentary debates), there is a very high probability that courts will need to use extrinsic materials when considering context and purpose. As stated by High Court majority in *CIC Insurance Ltd v Bankstown Football Club Ltd* (1997) 187 CLR 384 at 408: 'the modern approach to statutory interpretation (a) insists that the context be considered in the first instance, not merely at some later stage when ambiguity might be thought to arise, and (b) uses "context" in its widest sense to include such things as the existing state of the law'.

It is therefore circular, in paragraph (a), to say that extrinsic materials may be used to confirm a meaning 'taking into account' its context and purpose, when it has already been necessary to consider the context and purpose in arriving at a meaning that one wishes to confirm. A better wording may be found in s 25 of the Victorian Act, which simply provides that 'consideration may be given to any matter or document that is relevant'. This gives the Court freedom to decide what is relevant in any given case.

Despite its wording, s 15AB has been treated as authorising use of extrinsic materials to examine context and purpose. See the judgment of Mason CJ, Deane, Dawson, Toohey, Gaudron and McHugh JJ in *Bropho v Western Australia* (1990) 171 CLR 1 at [16]:

> [T]he contemporary approach to statutory construction, with its added emphasis on legislative purpose ... and permitted reference to a range of extrinsic materials for the ascertainment of that purpose (see, e.g., Acts Interpretation Act 1901 (Cth), s.15AB ...)

See also Patrick Brazil's claim, four years after the introduction of s 15AB, that it was introduced to address 'the extent to which extrinsic material could be used for the purpose of ascertaining object or purpose, or for otherwise interpreting legislation'.[4] If that were the case, surely some specific reference would have been made in s 15AB to the use of extrinsic materials to examine statutory purpose.

4 Ibid at 503.

Common law approach to use of extrinsic materials

The non-exhaustive treatment of extrinsic materials in the Interpretation Acts suggests that common law approaches to the use of extrinsic materials coexist with statutory approaches, rather than having been subsumed within them. In South Australia, where there is no statutory provision regarding use of extrinsic materials, the common law approach continues.

Historically, courts made little or no reference to extrinsic materials—where one was taking the words in an Act literally, there was little need to go beyond the text of the Act.[5] However, the mischief rule expanded the court's vision to the state of law prior to enacting the legislation and the gap that needed to be addressed by legislative action. It came to be accepted at common law that where a provision is ambiguous, reference may be made to extrinsic materials. The common law approach considered using extrinsic materials as something of a last resort after exhausting the application of ordinary rules of statutory construction.

The common law has crept beyond the position of statutory provisions on the use of extrinsic materials, even in jurisdictions where parliaments have given a broad scope to their use. For example *Catlow v Accident Compensation Commission* (1989) 167 CLR 543 involved the application of Victorian legislation, which is broader than the Commonwealth provision. Brennan and Gaudron JJ stated, at [6]:

> Whether or not extrinsic material is considered in interpreting a statutory provision, it is clear that the meaning attributed to the statute must be consistent with the statutory text. If the meaning which would otherwise be attributed to the statutory text is plain, extrinsic material cannot alter it. It is only when the meaning of the text is doubtful (to use a neutral term rather than those to be found in s 15AB(1) of the *Acts Interpretation Act*), that consideration of extrinsic material might be of assistance. It follows that it would be erroneous to look to the extrinsic material before exhausting the application of the ordinary rules of statutory construction. If, when that is done, the meaning of the statutory text is not doubtful, there is no occasion to look to the extrinsic material. In our opinion, that is the present case.

Spigelman CJ has commented that *Catlow* 'suggests a restrictive approach to the use of extrinsic materials of a character which is not consistent with much judicial practice'.[6] In other words, regardless of the problems in using extrinsic materials under the Interpretation Acts, there remains a justified option at common law for using them.

---

5 It is assumed here that readers have a basic background in statutory interpretation. Those unfamiliar with traditional common law approaches should refer to Chapter 9.

6 J J Spigelman, 'The Intolerable Wrestle: Developments in Statutory Interpretation', Address to the Australasian Conference of Planning and Environment Courts and Tribunals, 1 September 2010, 27.

Which extrinsic materials can be used?

Section 15AB(2) of the Commonwealth Act provides:

> Without limiting the generality of subsection (1), the material that may be considered in accordance with that subsection in the interpretation of a provision of an Act includes:
>
> (a) all matters not forming part of the Act that are set out in the document containing the text of the Act as printed by the Government Printer;
>
> (b) any relevant report of a Royal Commission, Law Reform Commission, committee of inquiry or other similar body that was laid before either House of the Parliament before the time when the provision was enacted;
>
> (c) any relevant report of a committee of the Parliament or of either House of the Parliament that was made to the Parliament or that House of the Parliament before the time when the provision was enacted;
>
> (d) any treaty or other international agreement that is referred to in the Act;
>
> (e) any explanatory memorandum relating to the Bill containing the provision, or any other relevant document, that was laid before, or furnished to the members of, either House of the Parliament by a Minister before the time when the provision was enacted;
>
> (f) the speech made to a House of the Parliament by a Minister on the occasion of the moving by that Minister of a motion that the Bill containing the provision be read a second time in that House;
>
> (g) any document (whether or not a document to which a preceding paragraph applies) that is declared by the Act to be a relevant document for the purposes of this section; and
>
> (h) any relevant material in the Journals of the Senate, in the Votes and Proceedings of the House of Representatives or in any official record of debates in the Parliament or either House of the Parliament.

Similar inclusive lists appear in the states and territories (except South Australia): see s 34(2) of the NSW Act; s 35(b) of the Vic Act, s 14B(3) of the Qld Act, s 19(2) of the WA Act, s 8B(3) of the Tas Act, s 142 of the ACT Act and s 62B(2) of the NT Act.

While the listed materials are considered in turn below, the important initial point is the use of 'includes' in the chapeau, showing that the list is not exhaustive. Common extrinsic materials are not listed, for example dictionaries and other cases. The essential test is one of relevance and value—after all, the extrinsic material is being used to assist in the interpretation task. Overall the approach to the use of extrinsic material mimics the civil law system approach to evidence, wherein most types of evidence are admissible, but weighting depends on their veracity.

Further, while there does not appear to be a particular hierarchy of extrinsic materials, some are used more frequently than others, with second reading speeches and explanatory memoranda featuring the most prominently. In some instances a plethora of extrinsic materials are used in the one case.

Some extrinsic materials are excluded from use in statutory interpretation. This includes the use of delegated legislation to interpret primary legislation, except in circumstances of an 'as enacted' clause providing that regulations made under the Act can be treated as part of the Act.[7] Additionally, extrinsic materials created after the legislation which express a view as to its meaning are not generally applicable. For example in *Parrett v Secretary, Department of Family & Community Services* (2002) 124 FCR 299 Madgwick J refused to consider a Centrelink policy document which provided instruction to staff in assessing applications made under an Act. Even though it could not be dismissed as 'merely the expression of a self-serving view of the departmental authority', it had been promulgated at a time when it could not have influenced Parliament: at [36].

Law Reform Commission reports

Law Reform Commissions are government agencies which are responsible to Parliament and come within the Attorney-General's portfolio. Although in one sense 'independent' of government, Law Reform Commissions do not have power to investigate any area of law which may be in need of reform—they are limited to conducting inquiries on topics requested by the Attorney-General. The primary task is to undertake research on the law, including comparative approaches in other common law jurisdictions, and engage in consultations with stakeholders and the general public. The aim is to consider the topic as broadly as possible and recommend whether reform is appropriate and if so, what form it may take. In some instances, the Law Reform Commission will go so far as to draft recommended legislation.

As agencies of government, Law Reform Commissions produce reports that are well regarded and considered highly persuasive, so their recommendations are often implemented. For example the Australian Law Reform Commission boasts that over 85 per cent of its reports have been either substantially or partially implemented.[8] Some reports, however, explore an issue but are never implemented—an example is the *Recognition of Aboriginal Customary Laws Final Report* (ALRC Report 31) from 1986, which recommended functional recognition of Aboriginal customary law.

A recent example of judicial use of a Law Reform Commission Report in statutory interpretation may be seen in *Spencer v Commonwealth of Australia* (2010) 241 CLR 118, per French CJ and Gummow J at [18]–[19]:

> Section 31A was introduced into the *Federal Court Act* by the *Migration Litigation Reform Act 2005* (Cth) ... The adoption of the provision for summary judgment reflected in s 31A was

---

7 An 'as enacted' clause provides that the regulations should be treated as if they were enacted by the parliament, putting them on the same level.

8 See www.alrc.gov.au/about (accessed 30 June 2011).

> recommended in 2000 by the Australian Law Reform Commission. Although not initially accepted by the Government the recommendation was revisited in a Departmental Strategy Paper in December 2003, inspired in part by 'the growth in the volume of unmeritorious litigation in the Federal Court and the [Federal Magistrates Court] over the last few years, particularly in migration cases'. The Strategy Paper ultimately recommended the adoption of the ALRC's recommendation and was referred to in the Second Reading Speech for the Migration Litigation Reform Bill 2005.

Law Reform Commission Reports are easily found online.[9] The exception is South Australia, which only had a law reform committee for a brief time.[10]

Explanatory memoranda

As discussed in Chapter 2, a Bill must contain all and only the material that, if passed, will become the Act. The Explanatory Memorandum (referred to in some jurisdictions as Explanatory Notes or Statements) is the document in which the responsible Minister places an explanation of the provisions, why they are included and what they are intended to cover. Clearly, these documents may be helpful to shed light on intention. According to Brazil, the Explanatory Memoranda must have been circulated to the Members of Parliament before the Bill to which it relates was enacted.[11]

Take for example the amendment to s 15AA of the Commonwealth Act, discussed in Chapter 4. The change was from a phrasing where 'an interpretation that promotes the purpose of the Act is preferred to one that does not' to an interpretation that 'best promotes the purpose'. The part of the Explanatory Memorandum relating to this change provided:

> [99] Section 15AA, which deals with interpretation of Acts, is currently expressed in absolute terms, ie. a construction that will promote the purpose of an Act is to be preferred to one that will not. Section 15AA does not address the situation where there is a choice between two or more constructions that will promote Parliament's purpose.
>
> [100] The limited nature of section 15AA was confirmed by three High Court judges in a case on the equivalent Victorian provision (see *Chugg v Pacific Dunlop Pty Ltd* (1990) 170 CLR 249 at 489, Dawson, Toohey and Gaudron JJ).
>
> [101] Therefore section 15AA is being amended to provide that a court is to prefer the construction of an Act that will 'best achieve' the purpose or object of the Act.

9 See www.austlii.edu.au/au/special/lawreform/.
10 See an index at http://library.flinders.edu.au/resources/collection/special/lawreform/draft_reports.html.
11 P Brazil, 'Reform of Statutory Interpretation—the Australian Experience of Use of Extrinsic Materials: With a Postscript on Simpler Drafting', Address to Law Commission Legislation Seminar, National Library Auditorium, Wellington, 18–19 March 1988, published in (1988) 62 ALJ 503, 510.

A recent example of judicial use explanatory memoranda is *Edwards v Santos Ltd* [2011] HCA 8, where Heydon J stated at [22]–[24]:

> The plaintiffs, on behalf of the Wongkumara People, have for some time been pursuing but have not yet succeeded in a native title claim ... [t]he petroleum defendants are the holders of Authority to Prospect ... On 16 January 2001 six representatives of the Wongkumara People (four of whom are among the plaintiffs) and the petroleum defendants (amongst others) entered an Indigenous Land Use Agreement ('the ILUA') under the [Native Title Act]. The ILUA was not registered. It was to expire on 16 January 2006 ... The function of the ILUA was to deal with problems arising from the fact that native title can be difficult to prove, and the processing of native title claims can take a long time. To use the words of the Explanatory Memorandum to the Native Title Amendment Bill 1997:
>
>> [O]ver most of mainland Australia, governments and others seeking to use land do not know if native title exists, and if it does, who holds it. It is difficult in such circumstances to have agreements which provide the necessary level of legal certainty. These provisions [including what is now Pt 2 Div 3 subdiv C of the NTA] are designed to give security for agreements with native title holders, whether there has been an approved determination of native title or not, provided certain requirements are met.
>>
>> Not only did the ILUA give security to the petroleum defendants in dealing with native title claimants who may become native title holders, but it gave the plaintiffs, as native title claimants, the opportunity to obtain immediate advantages which would otherwise be postponed until a perhaps distant day when their native title claim succeeds.

Explanatory memoranda/notes/statements for recent years in each jurisdiction except South Australia are available online at AustLII.[12]

Note however that not all courts support the proposition that Explanatory Memoranda are useful in the interpretation task. See for example the Full Court of the Federal Court in *Telstra Corp Ltd v Hurstville City Council* (2002) 118 FCR 198 at 216–7: 'It is a rare day when an explanatory memorandum provides much assistance in the construction of a statute'.

Second reading speeches/Parliamentary debates

These are considered together, even though second reading speeches are listed separately from parliamentary debates in the Interpretation Acts. The reality is that the second reading speech, as with all parliamentary reference to, and debate on, a Bill, is

12 At www.austlii.edu.au. Click on the jurisdiction and then the link to explanatory memoranda.

located in the Hansard, and the only reason for referring to the second reading speech separately is that it is of most use as an extrinsic material, as it is when the Minister explains the reason for the legislation and what it is attempting to achieve. It cannot, however, be assumed that the Minister's views on the legislation are synonymous with the views of Parliament as a whole. The nature of the legislative process and the often inherent political compromise that is involved militate against the assumption that all members of Parliament sing from the same songsheet.

Case exercise

'American soldier goes AWOL'

Doug is an American-born permanent resident who has been living in Australia for the past 30 years. Recently he was arrested by New South Wales police, who handed him over to the Royal Australian Naval Police at HMAS Penguin. He remains in custody. Police say they acted under a warrant issued by a naval officer. They say Doug is a deserter having gone absent without leave (AWOL) from the United States Marine Corps. He has admitted that he was injured in 1970 during the Vietnam War and left the naval hospital in Danang without permission, travelling directly to Australia and remaining ever since. Was he rightfully arrested?

The relevant legislation is the *Defence (Visiting Forces) Act 1963* (Cth). The Long Title of the Act is:

> An Act to make provision with respect to Naval, Military and Air Forces of other countries visiting Australia, and for other purposes.

Part III of the Act is headed 'Deserters and Absentees Without Leave'. Within that Part, s 19(1) provides for the issue of a warrant, on a written request by a designated authority of particular countries (including the US) to arrest 'a member of the forces of that country who is a deserter or an absentee'. The following two sections then cover detention and delivery into the custody of the designated authority.

Section 5(1) defines 'Visiting forces' as 'any body, contingent or detachment of the forces of a country that is for the time being present in Australia by arrangement with the Minister'. Section 5(2) provides that a reference to a member of a visiting force is to be read 'as a reference to a person who, in accordance with the law of the country to which the visiting force belongs, is serving as a member of the visiting force'.

Section 8(2) provides that the Act has jurisdiction over:

(a) members of any visiting force of that country; and

(b) all other persons who, being neither Australian citizens nor persons ordinarily resident in Australia, are for the time being subject to the service law of that country otherwise than as members of that country's forces.

The second reading speeches of the Minister, Sir Garfield Barwick, included:

> Part III—Deserters and Absentees Without Leave, and Part IV—Attachment of Personnel and Mutual Powers of Command, are not limited to visiting forces. Their provisions will automatically apply to Commonwealth countries, and they can, by regulation, be applied to other countries whether the countries have visiting forces in Australia or not ...
>
> Mr. Deputy Speaker, Part III of the bill relates to deserters and absentees without leave from the forces of countries within the Commonwealth of Nations, and other countries to which the part may be applied by regulation. They need not be deserters or absentees from a visiting force.
>
> At some future date it may be that the provisions will find their place in general defence legislation where they may more properly belong, but for convenience now we copy the plan of the 1939 act and include them in the visiting forces legislation.

Does the legislation cover Doug? Does it include any deserting member of any defence force who happens to be in Australia? Does the title of the Act limit the content to visiting forces? Does it only cover deserters who, at the time of going AWOL, are attached to a visiting force that is in Australia? Does it make any difference that Doug has permanent residency?

Decide before proceeding.

The real case is *Re Bolton; Ex parte Beane* (1987) 162 CLR 514. If you decided Douglas Beane was rightfully arrested, you are in agreement with Toohey J on the High Court. If you decided he was not, you are in agreement with the remainder of the High Court—Mason CJ, Wilson, Dawson, Brennan, Deane and Gaudron JJ, who all restricted application of the legislation to visiting forces.

The joint judgment of Mason CJ, Wilson and Dawson JJ stated at the outset that 'The process of construction is in this case a difficult one and it is not surprising that reasonable minds may differ in the conclusions to which they come, as indeed has happened here' at [2]. They said that s 19 is ambiguous, and referred to the second reading speech but cautioned at [4] that, while it is an aid to interpretation, it cannot be determinative:

> The words of a Minister must not be substituted for the text of the law. Particularly is this so when the intention stated by the Minister but unexpressed in the law is restrictive of the liberty of the individual. It is always possible that through oversight or inadvertence the clear intention of the Parliament fails to be translated into the text of the law. However unfortunate it may be when that happens, the task of the Court remains clear. The function of the Court is to give effect to the will of Parliament as expressed in the law.

Brennan, Deane and Gaudron JJ in their separate judgments focused on the fact Beane had not committed any (extraditable) offence, failing which he has the right to be free. It would be impermissible for the Executive government to permit a foreign military force to extradite an Australian resident in circumstances where it would not have such a power itself.

Toohey J in dissent considered the parts of the Act to be independent, such that Part III is not confined to visiting forces. He considered the legislative history to support that interpretation, and '[i]f there is any doubt about the matter, that doubt is put to rest by reference to the second reading speeches' at [11].

Patrick Brazil has commented that this case 'stands as a warning ... that extrinsic materials will not necessarily redeem a failure to translate the intent of Parliament into the text of the law'.[13]

Resort to second reading speeches is highly prevalent today. Take for example the comment by Kirby J in *Vanit v R* (1997) 190 CLR 378 at 399–400: 'As is usual nowadays, the court was taken to the second reading speech of the minister and the explanatory memorandum circulated by the Attorney-General'. Not all judges are in favour of this use despite its prevalence—see for example Meagher JA in *Monier Lrd v Szabo* (1992) 28 NSWLR 53 at 67, referring to second reading speeches not only failing to resolve an ambiguity, but raising 'fresh ambiguities'. He said, quite simply: 'The habit should cease'. Following suit, Heydon J stated in *Lacey v Attorney-General of Queensland* [2011] HCA 10 at [86]:

> Excessive recourse to second reading speeches is one of the blights of modern litigation. Modern legislation permits it, or is often assumed to permit it, to a much greater extent than the common law rules of statutory construction did. Experience is tending to raise grave doubts about the good sense of that legislation ... But the fact remains that the courts can investigate what Ministers say. There are rare occasions when that investigation has value. This is one of the rare occasions.

There can be instances where draft legislation is intentionally passed in an imperfect state knowing that courts will make use of the second reading speech. Keith Mason has referred to one such occasion:[14]

13 P Brazil, 'Reform of Statutory Interpretation—the Australian Experience of Use of Extrinsic Materials: With a Postscript on Simpler Drafting', Address to Law Commission Legislation Seminar, National Library Auditorium, Wellington, 18–19 March 1988, published in (1988) 62 ALJ 503, 512.

14 K Mason, 'The Intent of Legislators: How Judges Discern It and What They Do if They Find It', in *Statutory Interpretation: Principles and Pragmatism for a New Age* (Judicial Commission of New South Wales, 2007) 33 at 37.

> I remember well the response of Mr Dennis Rose QC, then Chief General Counsel in the Commonwealth Attorney-General's Department, in relation to a sensible suggestion for amendment to the 'final draft' of the Bill that was being settled by the Committee:
> 'Your point is a good one, but it is just too late to take the Bill back to Parliamentary Counsel. But let me promise this: I will have a statement put into the Minister's Second Reading speech saying that the legislation is intended to operate in the way you have proposed'.

Perhaps a hierarchy in extrinsic materials which favours explanatory memoranda over second reading speeches could reduce reliance on the latter. In any event the second reading speech could rarely be considered in isolation, as pointed out by the High Court in *Re Australian Federation of Construction Contractors; Ex parte Billing* (1986) 68 ALR 416 at [4]:

> [T]he Minister's speech does not purport to be an exhaustive description of the legislation and must be read in the context of the Bill itself and the explanatory memorandum.

In practical terms, it is counsel for the parties who bring second reading speeches in, but it is submitted that it remains the task of the court to determine their admissibility and value. It is difficult to support the unanimous High Court decision in *Hoare v R* (1989) 167 CLR 348, where it was stated at [16], in relation to the use of a second reading speech in one party's submissions without objection by the other party: 'In the absence of any such objection, we are prepared to assume for the purposes of the present case that the Court is entitled to refer to those ministerial statements'. While the Court was construing legislation from South Australia which lacked a provision on extrinsic materials, the Court did not identify its reliance on common law rules, and if it had, it would have been hard pressed to find a test that extrinsic materials may be considered if the parties do not object.

Parliamentary Committee reports

The process by which Bills are considered by Parliamentary Committees was discussed in Chapter 2. It is not uncommon for Parliament to delegate detailed scrutiny of Bills to a Parliamentary Committee. For example the Scrutiny of Bills Committee of the Senate examines Bills before they are debated by the Senate, identifying issues with the Bills such as over-delegation of power under regulations, or impact on individual liberties. As with other extrinsic materials, Parliamentary Committee reports may be of value in the interpretation task, depending on the relevance of what was said, but they will of course not be determinative.

A fairly recent example where a Parliamentary Committee report was used is *Minister for Immigration and Multicultural and Indigenous Affairs v Nystrom* (2006) 230

ALR 370. Gummow and Hayne JJ at [60] stated, in relation to legislation providing for the cancellation of visas on the grounds of failing a character test due to a substantial criminal record:

> Even prior to the enactment of the 1998 Strengthening Amendment Act, a report of the Joint Standing Committee on Migration stated:
>
> > [T]he power of cancellation under s 501 also extends to permanent residents, and may be exercised even where a person becomes liable to deportation. It is, therefore, possible to cancel the permanent visas of non-citizens convicted of crimes in Australia and to have such persons removed, rather than deported, from the country. Furthermore, as the cancellation power is not limited by the time a non-citizen has spent in Australia, criminals who can no longer be deported because of the ten year rule remain subject to visa cancellation and removal unless they obtain citizenship.
>
> The Committee noted that the Bill which became the 1998 Strengthening Amendment Act was intended to strengthen those powers in s 501[61].

Commonwealth Parliamentary Committee reports are available online.[15]

International treaties and agreements

Where legislation gives effect to an international treaty, a court may look at that treaty to resolve ambiguities.[16]

The equivalent to the Interpretation Acts in international law is the Vienna Convention on the Law of Treaties (1974), which provides in relevant part:

> Article 31
>
> General rule of interpretation
>
> (1) A treaty shall be interpreted in good faith in accordance with the ordinary meaning to be given to the terms of the treaty in their context and in the light of its object and purpose.
>
> (2) The context for the purpose of the interpretation of a treaty shall comprise, in addition to the text, including its Preamble and annexes:
>
> (a) any agreement relating to the treaty which was made between all the parties in connection with the conclusion of the treaty;

---

15 At www.aph.gov.au/house/committee/report_register/index.htm for the House of Representatives, and www.aph.gov.au/Senate/committee/register/report/index.htm for the Senate.

16 According to Pearce and Geddes, 'More recently, the courts have also taken international agreements into consideration in the process of interpreting legislation with which those agreements have no explicit connection': D Pearce and R Geddes, *Statutory Interpretation in Australia* (LexisNexis, 7th ed, 2011) 80.

(b) any instrument which was made by one or more parties in connection with the conclusion of the treaty and accepted by the other parties as an instrument related to the treaty.

(3) There shall be taken into account, together with the context:

(a) any subsequent agreement between the parties regarding the interpretation of the treaty or the application of its provisions;

(b) any subsequent practice in the application of the treaty which establishes the agreement of the parties regarding its interpretation;

(c) any relevant rules of international law applicable in the relations between the parties.

(4) A special meaning shall be given to a term if it is established that the parties so intended.

Article 32

Supplementary means of interpretation

Recourse may be had to supplementary means of interpretation, including the preparatory work of the treaty[17] and the circumstances of its conclusion, in order to confirm the meaning resulting from the application of article 31, or to determine the meaning when the interpretation according to article 31:

(a) leaves the meaning ambiguous or obscure; or

(b) leads to a result which is manifestly absurd or unreasonable.

These provisions may be useful where interpreting treaty provisions annexed in Schedules to an Australian Act.

Case exercise

'Accidental service of in-flight food and beverages'

Brian decided to fly Qantas to London via Bangkok. During the flight he was seated in the economy cabin and was served the usual refreshments. Some time during the flights he suffered deep venous thrombosis ('DVT'). He claims the cause was cramped seating, discouragement of passengers from moving about the cabin, offering alcohol, tea and coffee during the flights, and failure to generally warn of the dangers of DVT and ways to prevent or reduce its incidence. He is claiming compensation for his injury.

17 Those looking for preparatory work of a treaty are advised to search for the French term *travaux préparatoires*, which is regularly used by English-speaking lawyers.

The relevant legislation is the *Civil Aviation (Carriers' Liability) Act 1959* (Cth), which provides that the international treaties on carriage by air, the Warsaw Convention and its various protocols, have the force of law in Australia. The instruments are themselves reproduced in Schedules to the Act. Brian's argument is framed in terms of Article 17 of Montreal Protocol No. 4 to the Warsaw Convention which provides:

> The carrier is liable for damage sustained in the event of the death or wounding of a passenger or any other bodily injury suffered by a passenger, if the accident which caused the damage so sustained took place on board the aircraft or in the course of any of the operations of embarking or disembarking.

Brian claims that he suffered 'bodily injury' and the term 'accident' should be broadly interpreted to include omissions such as failing to provide suitable flight conditions and failing to warn passengers of precautions they could take to minimise or eliminate the risk of DVT.

What do you think? Is Brian's situation covered by Article 17? Decide before proceeding.

The real case is *Povey v Qantas Airways Limited* (2005) 216 ALR 427. If you decided Brian Povey's situation was not covered you are in agreement with the High Court. If you decided it was covered, you are alone in dissent.

Gleeson CJ, Gummow, Hayne and Heydon JJ, with Callinan J concurring, emphasised at [12] that:

> Because the entry into the international agreement can create no rights in Australian domestic law without there being legislation giving effect to those rights, the source of the right which the appellant seeks to enforce must be found in the Carriers' Liability Act.

The embedding of an international instrument in domestic legislation called for the application not of domestic rules on statutory interpretation, but of principles of treaty interpretation using the Vienna Convention of the Law of Treaties.

Additionally, the importance of interpreting international treaties uniformly across municipal (domestic) jurisdictions was recognised. The majority stated that, as the Convention was drafted by French jurists, common law concepts such as 'failure to warn' are 'irrelevant and unhelpful' at [41]. Reference was made to French and Anglo-American interpretation of the word 'accident' and it was concluded that to be an accident, something unusual or unexpected had to have occurred.

Kirby J agreed with the main judgment but made useful further comments on the interpretation of treaties embedded in domestic legislation, for example at [141]–[143]:

> [D]eference to international comity will sometimes appear to be in conflict with the ultimate judicial duty to give meaning to the words of the treaty ... The price exacted for the building of the international rule of law is a proper attempt on the part of municipal judges, who thereby exercise a kind of international jurisdiction, to perform tasks of interpretation,

> so far as possible, in ways that are compatible with the decisions of respected courts of high authority in other lands, struggling with the same or similar problems ... What is impermissible is an attempt to manipulate the language of the international treaty to avoid an outcome that seems harsh by contemporary domestic perspectives. Few developments would so undermine the growing development of international law as this.

McHugh J, although recognising the need for consistent interpretation of treaties, relied heavily on common law reasoning. He said at [48] that there can be an accident when airline employees engage in conduct causing injury that is not intended or reasonably foreseeable, such as discouraging passengers from moving around or encouraging them to remain seated, and supplying alcoholic or caffeinated beverages. He said at [77]–[78]:

> No one should doubt the importance of the domestic courts of parties to an International Convention achieving uniformity in interpreting and applying the Convention's provisions. But this does not mean that a domestic court of a contracting party must mechanically apply statements made by a court of another contracting party when the precise issue before that court was significantly different from that which confronts the domestic court. To require the courts of other contracting parties to do so would mean that the first curial statement on the subject would be controlling. Where, as here, the statement of the court of another contracting party was made in circumstances vastly different from those that confront this Court, we should not automatically apply it.

Key aspects of statutory interpretation relevant to this context, as demonstrated from the above case, include:

- The importance of recognising that it is the domestic provision that brings the international treaty that is applied, and not the treaty itself that is directly applied;
- The importance of a uniform interpretation of an international treaty by domestic courts in convention countries;
- Use of the international equivalent to the Interpretation Acts, the Vienna Convention on the Law of Treaties (1974), to interpret treaty provisions; and
- That there may be limited value in reasoning by analogy to domestic meanings and common law concepts.

Legislative history

It can be useful, particularly where an Act has been amended several times over a number of years, to interpret the Act as a whole in the light of its various permutations. For example if one was interpreting a word or phrase which has been used in other sections within an Act, and established that the section was added 40 years after the surrounding provisions, it would raise an issue as to whether it was intended for the word or phrase to be consistently applied across the provisions, as there may have been a parliamentary oversight.

Case exercise

'The Low Loader'

Ash is a crane driver who was recently asked by his employer to go with a crane from Perth to a remote area and use it to do two jobs before returning. His employer contracted Container Handlers to transport the crane. The truck that carried the crane was a prime mover with attached 'low loader' and was driven by Jason, an employee of Container Handlers. En route a routine inspection was carried out and smoke and fumes were noticed coming off a rear-wheel hub of the low loader. Jason decided, as the wheels affected were the third set from the rear, that they should be removed. Both men worked together to achieve this with Jason giving instructions. They used a chain and hooks, but the chain was not long enough and the axle slipped off the jack, crushing Ash's hand against the chassis of the low loader.

Ash was awarded more than $900 000 in damages for the injury caused by Jason's negligence, which fell within the responsibility of Jason's employer, Container Handlers. Container Handlers has claimed under their third party insurance policy with the Insurance Commission of Western Australia (ICWA) but ICWA is refusing to pay the claim. The insurance policy was issued subject to a statutory requirement which appears in the *Motor Vehicle (Third Party Insurance) Act 1943* (WA). Section 4(1) of the Act provides:

> When any motor vehicle is on a road there is required to be in force in relation to the motor vehicle a contract of insurance entered into by the owner of the motor vehicle under which the owner has insured subject to and in accordance with this Act against any liability which may be incurred by the owner or any person who drives the motor vehicle in respect of the death of or bodily injury to any person directly caused by, or by the driving of, the motor vehicle.

Section 3(7) of the Act provides:

> For the purposes of this Act, the death of or bodily injury to any person shall not be taken to have been caused by a vehicle if it is not a consequence of the driving of that vehicle or of the vehicle running out of control.

Section 6(1) of the Act contains requirements in respect of policies. It provides:

> In order to comply with this Act a policy of insurance must:
>
> (a) be issued by the Commission;
>
> (b) except as provided in this section insure the owner of the vehicle mentioned in the policy and any other person who at the time drives that vehicle, whether with or

> without the consent of the owner, in respect of all liability for negligence which may be incurred by that owner or other person in respect of the death of or bodily injury to any person directly caused by, or by the driving of, the vehicle in any part of the Commonwealth; and
>
> (c) be in a form substantially similar to that contained in the Schedule.

The Schedule provides, relevantly:

> The Insurance Commission of Western Australia, subject to the warranties and conditions contained in this Policy and to the provisions of the *Motor Vehicle (Third Party Insurance) Act 1943,* in this Policy referred to as 'the Act', agrees to insure the owner of the motor vehicle described in the Traffic Licence issued herewith and any other person who drives that motor vehicle, whether with or without the consent of the owner, in respect of all liability for negligence which may be incurred by the owner or other person in respect of the death of or bodily injury to any person directly caused by, or by the driving of, that motor vehicle in any part of the Commonwealth during the period from the date of the issue of this Policy to the date of expiry of the said Traffic Licence....
>
> CONDITIONS ...
>
> (3) The Commission is entitled to all rights remedies and benefits which may accrue to it by virtue of the Act.
>
> (4) This contract of insurance is subject to the provisions of the Act.

The relevant policy issued by the ICWA to Container Handlers was in accordance with the Schedule, and specifically stated that it was issued pursuant to the Act.

The Act had been the subject of recent prior amendment, under the *Motor Vehicle (Third Party Insurance) Amendment Act 1987* (WA).

The wording of s 4(1) of the Act before amendment, in relevant part, was:

> When any motor vehicle is on a road there is required to be in force in relation to the motor vehicle a contract of insurance entered into by the owner of the motor vehicle under which the owner has insured subject to and in accordance with this Act against any liability which may be incurred by the owner or any person who drives the motor vehicle in respect of the death of or bodily injury to any person caused by or arising out of the use of such motor vehicle.

A court decision under the Act was what prompted amendment. It was *Dickinson v Motor Vehicle Insurance Trust* (1987) 163 CLR 500, which involved a child who was left in a stationary vehicle by her father, who had gone shopping. The child was injured as a result of playing with a box of matches left by her father, causing the vehicle to catch fire. The High

Court held that the injury arose out of the use of the motor vehicle, and therefore came within the policy. The Court stated that at 505:

> The test posited by the words 'arising out of' is wider than that posited by the words 'caused by' and the former, although it involves some causal or consequential relationship between the use of the vehicle and the injuries, does not require the direct or proximate relationship which would be necessary to conclude that the injuries were caused by the use of the vehicle.

That case was specifically referred to in the second reading speech by the Deputy Premier, Mr Malcolm Bryce:

> The decision in the Dickinson case is generally considered to have opened the floodgates for the entitlement of persons injured in stationary motor vehicles to recover damages ... Parliament thus intended that the liability of the Motor Vehicle Insurance Trust was to be limited to the payment of damages for injury or death sustained by persons in consequence of the negligent driving of motor vehicles ... The full implications of Dickinson are still largely unknown. Unless the Act is suitably amended, it is anyone's guess as to the scope of claims which may ultimately be found to fall within the meaning of the words 'in the use of a motor vehicle.[18]

What do you think? Does Ash's injury come within the insurance policy? Decide before proceeding, or if you are having difficulty, consider the following pointers.

1. Notice that Condition 4 says the policy is subject to the Act, thereby bringing the Act into the policy. Notice that s 4(1), s 6(1) and the Schedule all use the same phrase, 'death of or bodily injury to any person directly caused by, or by the driving of, the motor vehicle'. Was the low loader part of the motor vehicle? If yes, was Ash's injury directly caused by the motor vehicle? Was it directly caused by the driving of the motor vehicle?
2. As the Act needs to be interpreted as a whole, check the other relevant provisions. What do you make of s 3(7)? Can a definitions section be used to limit the scope of the Act? If so, was Ash's injury a consequence of the driving of the vehicle? Was it the consequence of the vehicle running out of control? Notice the omission of the word 'directly' from s 3(7)—is this of any significance?
3. Give some thought to the purpose of the Act. You have not been given an objects clause, so you need to decide whether you can identify the purpose of the Act from extrinsic materials, and if so, whether they clearly guide you.

18 Western Australia, Legislative Assembly, *Parliamentary Debates* (Hansard), 12 November 1987 at 5759–60.

The real case is *Insurance Commission of Western Australia v Container Handlers Pty Ltd* (2004) 218 CLR 89. If you decided Ashley Sutton's injury was covered, you are in agreement with the Full Court of the Supreme Court of Western Australia.[19] If you decided it was not covered, you are in agreement with the trial judge[20] and the High Court.

Although the Full Court of the Supreme Court of Western Australia unanimously agreed that driving the vehicle in extreme heat caused the problem, and that the work on the roadside was sufficiently connected to the driving as to come within the 'driving' of the vehicle, the High Court unanimously agreed otherwise. It held that while his injury was directly caused by the motor vehicle, it was not a consequence of the driving of the vehicle, and therefore the policy did not cover it. Each judge prepared a separate judgment, and aspects relevant to the use of extrinsic materials are outlined here.

Callinan J referred to the second reading of the Amendment Bill, stating that it revealed the legislative intent to 'arrest the judicial trend' of 'regarding the merest connexion of a motor vehicle with the infliction of personal injury' as being an injury arising from the use of the motor vehicle. He agreed that 'driving' and 'running out of control' used in 3(7) are 'confined to the notion of a vehicle in motion'.

McHugh J also referred to the second reading speech to the Amendment Bill but cautioned at [33] that 'while statements in second reading speeches concerning legislative intent are a guide—often useful and sometimes a definitive guide—as to the meaning of the legislation, they do not replace the words of the Act'. He reasoned at [27] that s 3(7) states by double negative what is excluded, and:

> to treat s 3(7) as a true definitional provision has the result that the first limb—'directly caused by ... a vehicle'—is completely covered by the second limb—'directly caused by ... the driving of ... a vehicle'—except for those cases where the vehicle runs out of control. In other words, it renders redundant the first limb ... I cannot believe that any parliamentary drafter would go to such trouble to achieve the effect ... s 3(7) limits rather than defines or excludes the operation of s 6(1)(b) and the statutory policy ... by imposing an additional requirement [of 'driving'].

Gummow J reasoned that the requirement that the injury be directly caused by the vehicle is not removed by s 3(7). Similarly, Heydon J stated that it is clear the Schedule and s 3(7) reflect the intention to narrow the scope of indemnity and exclude events taking place after the vehicle has stopped and the engine has been turned off. Kirby J also referred at [115] to the intentional purpose of the legislation in reducing the ambit of coverage, and therefore insurance premiums, saying that 'Courts must give effect to, and not frustrate, such a purpose when it is clear from the language of the legislation'. The word 'directly' cannot be disregarded 'simply because courts disapprove of such words'.

19 *Container Handlers Pty Ltd v Insurance Commission of Western Australia* (2001) 25 WAR 42.
20 *Sutton v Container Handlers Pty Ltd* [2000] WADC 254.

Other documents

The categories of extrinsic materials are not closed, so potentially any extrinsic material may be of use. Two types of materials which are not mentioned, perhaps because their use is so automatic, are dictionaries and cases. There is also the potential to refer to other legislation. Delegated legislation cannot be referred to unless power is given in the Act for regulations to amend the Act—see *Ward v Commissioner of Police* (1997) 151 ALR 604 at 614.

Dictionaries are a commonly used extrinsic material. They are useful in identifying the ordinary meaning of a word, recognising however that words may have several meanings; that it is necessary to select the most applicable meaning in context; and that it is important not to disaggregate a phrase into individual words, look them up in the dictionary, and piece them back together to establish the meaning of the phrase. Although the task involves identifying the current meaning, and arguably in the modern Australian context should be a definition in an Australian dictionary, in practice courts have used dictionaries from any year of publication, and there has been substantial reliance on English dictionaries. This was discussed in Chapter 7.

Cases, being outside the statute, are a form of extrinsic material in interpreting legislation. It must be remembered that while there is a body of law found inside cases (the 'common law') there are also particular cases that interpret legislation ('case law') and as these are external to the legislation itself, they can rightly be referred to as a form of extrinsic material. Previous cases involving the application of the same provision under consideration, or considering the overall purpose of the same Act under consideration, may be of use. However, caution should be exercised, as it is not acceptable to simply find a case that interprets the same word or phrase and apply that. Words and phrases used in different Acts or at common law may not bear the same meaning in the context of the Act under consideration.

The *in pari material* (in analogous case) principle allows us to look to analogous legislation to work out the meaning of words. In practice, however, this approach will usually be of little weight. Let's say for example we are looking for the meaning of 'significant'. Assume it is not defined in the Act we are considering, but we find a definition of it in another Act. What authority do we have to argue that the definition of 'significant' in the other Act can be applied where it is used in the present Act? None, unless the Act expressly states that the definition from the other Act is to apply. This was the case, for example, in the *Crimes (Criminal Organisations Control) Act 2009* (NSW) which, *inter alia*, made it an offence for certain persons to engaged in a 'security activity within the meaning of the *Security Industry Act 1997*'. That Act contains in s 4 a definition of 'security activity' that runs to over 650 words.

Otherwise, our task is to find the ordinary meaning of the word, which, in the absence of an intrinsic definition, may require resort to a dictionary. We must then consider whether there are circumstances arising from consideration of the context and purpose that would warrant departing from that ordinary meaning. Whether the word is defined in other legislation or not is of little relevance unless the Acts sit together as part of an overall legislative scheme. This may occur within a jurisdiction where a number of Acts are passed relating to a tax, or it may occur across jurisdictions where an Act is part of 'national scheme' or 'mirror scheme' legislation. This comes about where the Attorney-Generals have coordinated to develop a single approach to a topic of law, usually outside a constitutional head of power—in other words, the Federal Parliament does not have power to bring in a single national law. Each jurisdiction enacts the same legislation, and typically s 17 of the Victorian Act, for example, will be identical to s 17 of the Queensland Act. To support the maintenance of a desired national approach, which is evident from the larger legislative context, courts will attempt to interpret the Act in their jurisdiction in a manner that preserves uniformity of interpretation across mirror jurisdictions.[21] See for example *Australian Securities Commissioner v Marlborough Gold Mines Ltd* (1993) 177 CLR 485, where the High Court majority stated at 492:

> [U]niformity of decision in the interpretation of uniform national legislation ... is a sufficiently important consideration to require that an intermediate appellate court ... should not depart from an interpretation placed on such legislation by another Australian intermediate appellate court unless convinced that that interpretation is plainly wrong.

Proliferation and limits

Over the past two decades there has been a massive proliferation in the use of extrinsic materials. This is likely to be the result of increased, instant, free online availability of materials as much as it is the result of enacting provisions like s 15AB of the Cth Act. Section 15AB(3) contains an express limitation on their use:

> In determining whether consideration should be given to any material in accordance with subsection (1), or in considering the weight to be given to any such material, regard shall be had, in addition to any other relevant matters, to:
>
> (a) the desirability of persons being able to rely on the ordinary meaning conveyed by the text of the provision taking into account its context in the Act and the purpose or object underlying the Act; and
>
> (b) the need to avoid prolonging legal or other proceedings without compensating advantage.

21 An analogy may be drawn to the interpretation of international treaties by domestic courts, discussed above.

See also s 34(3) of the NSW Act, s 14B(2) of the Qld Act, s 19(3) of the WA Act, s 141(2) of the ACT Act and s 8B(2) of the Tas Act. As stated by Heydon J in *Insurance Commission of Western Australia v Container Handlers Pty Ltd* (2004) 218 CLR 89 at [35]:

> The safeguards against litigation becoming delayed in a flood of extraneous material of doubtful value, appear to lie not in narrowing the kinds of material to which reference can be made but by keeping a close and sensible eye on whether, as a practical and discretionary matter, one should look at such material.

Perhaps judicial reluctance to refuse admission of certain material is based on concern about appeals, although, according to Pearce and Geddes, 'if a court properly exercised its discretion under s 15AB and decided against consideration of extrinsic material, that would not be a basis for an appeal, even if the appeal court would have exercised the discretion differently'.[22] Perhaps the better course would be for courts to make adverse costs orders where lawyers waste court time with lengthy recourse to extrinsic materials that contribute little to their case.

22 D Pearce and R Geddes, *Statutory Interpretation in Australia* (LexisNexis, 6th ed, 2006) 89.

CHAPTER 9

TRADITIONAL COMMON LAW APPROACHES

As the Interpretation Acts do not codify the rules of statutory interpretation, traditional common law approaches to statutory interpretation, developed and refined across centuries, continue to have some use. This chapter considers the relationship between common law and statutes, and the degree to which there is ongoing applicability of the literal, golden and mischief rules and common law maxims. Common law statutory presumptions are considered separately in Chapter 10.

Common law and statutes

Historically there were few statutes, and the large majority of law was derived from judicial decisions. That was the case until last century, when we experienced a massive proliferation of legislation as a source of law. The doctrine of parliamentary sovereignty makes statutes prevail over the common law, with the exception of High Court decisions on constitutional validity. We have 'well and truly entered the age of statutes',[1] and '[n]o area of the law has escaped statutory modification'.[2]

Regardless of the centrality of legislation as a source of law, the task of its interpretation remains with the judiciary. Judgments as to whether particular conduct comes within legislation can give legislation broad or narrow interpretation, and thereby expand or contract the area of law governed by the statute. There is some effort, where more than one interpretation is open, to choose the one that is consistent with the common law: see *Balog v Independent Commissioner Against Corruption* (1990) 169 CLR 625. The same applies where an interpretation may be more consonant with the principles of equity: see *Minister for Lands and Forests v McPherson* (1991) 22 NSWLR 687.

As to the use of decisions involving statutory interpretation in later cases, a common law precedent-style approach is not warranted. As Gummow J stated in *Brennan v Comcare* (1994) 50 FCR 555 at 572–3, applying the rules of statutory interpretation is different from applying the doctrine of precedent. The exception would be where the same Act has previously been interpreted by a superior court in directly aligned factual circumstances—a rare occurrence indeed, and in reality such matters are unlikely to run to trial. In the remainder of cases, courts are not bound by the interpretation placed on particular words by other courts—it all depends on context. As Spigelman CJ stated in *Deputy Commissioner of Taxation v Clark* [2003] NSWCA 91 at [132]: 'What

1 M Kirby 'ALJ @ 80: Past, Present and Future', Address at a conference to celebrate the 80th anniversary of the *Australian Law Journal*, Sydney, 16 March 2007, www.hcourt.gov.au/speeches/kirbyj/kirbyj_16mar07.pdf.

2 J J Spigelman, 'Statutory Interpretation and Human Rights', Address to the Pacific Judicial Conference, Vanuatu, 26 July 2005, www.lawlink.nsw.gov.au/lawlink/Supreme_Court/ll_sc.nsf/pages/SCO_speech_spigelman260705.

can be regarded as "good reason" in one statute will not necessarily be acceptable as "good reason" in another statute. The context provides the relevant limitation'.

Legal disputes may raise issues of statutory interpretation that were simply not envisaged or considered by Parliament. Legislative omissions may be due to inadvertence or there may simply be confidence that the statutory formulation is sufficiently clear. Take for example *Chugg v Pacific Dunlop Ltd* (1990) 170 CLR 249, which concerned the death of an employee while servicing a machine in a factory. The relevant statutory provision, s 21 of the *Occupational Health and Safety Act 1985* (Vic), provided that the employer must 'provide and maintain *so far as is practicable* for employees a working environment that is safe and without risks to health' (emphasis added). This provision appears quite clear on its face, but what is missing is an indication of onus of proof—is it the employer who must justify their workplace practices, or is it the employee who is pleading a failure to maintain a safe work environment? The general rule that 'he who pleads must prove' works only if it is clear whether the provision constitutes a primary obligation (to be proved by the plaintiff) or an exception or qualification (to be proved by the defendant).

Dawson, Toohey and Gaudron JJ reasoned that what is practicable depends on the severity of the risk, ways it can be managed, whether they are available and suitable in the circumstances, and the cost involved in implementing them. These matters could be expected to be in the knowledge of the company rather than the informant in workplace safety matters (usually either a Minister of the State or an inspector). However, if the employer were to bear the onus of proof, it would have the 'burden of anticipating and negating the practicability of every possible means of avoiding or mitigating a risk or accident that might be raised in the course of cross-examination': at [24]. Therefore the expression would have to be treated as an exception.

However, Brennan J, in his separate judgment, stated that '[t]o treat those words in that clause as words of exception would be to place a forced and unnatural construction on the clause' at [2]. Deane J also struggled with settling on the legislative intent, and concluded that 'it would seem desirable that there be prompt legislative action, in places where such provisions are made to perform that dual function, to clarify whether it was in fact the legislative intent that the onus of proving what was or was not practicable in an employer's business should be cast upon an injured employee' at [4].

In other cases vagueness in statutory expression is intentional. It may be considered a necessary by-product of legislating in an arena of divided political conditions. Legislation may need to be drafted in extremely broad terms to enable it to pass through both Houses, and this ultimately places far greater responsibility in the hands of the courts. Gleeson CJ has said extra-judicially:

> The meaning of the word 'policy' is protean, and its unexplained use is often a source of confusion, but in one of its senses judges nowadays are commonly required, by Acts

> of Parliament, to make what could fairly be described as policy choices about a wide range of matters. They cannot avoid this responsibility when it is conferred by statute. Even a black-letter lawyer is compelled to respond when Parliament legislates in technicolour.[3]

How can courts in a democracy make policy decisions? How can they give effect to the intent of Parliament when factions within Parliament vary markedly in their views? How can they give primacy to the text in situations where the text is left deliberately vague? How can they respond to the statutory recipe of 'ordinary meaning' mixed with context and seasoned with a generous dose of purpose, when there may be multiple purposes, competing purposes, or inherent/unspoken purposes? A methodology that attempts to grapple with these issues is provided in Chapter 14.

Some judges do not hide from the fact that specific legislative provisions may be interpreted quite differently by different judges, depending on the approach they take to the interpretation task. See for example the comment of Heydon J (with concurrence of all judges) in *Victims Compensation Fund Corporation v Brown* (2003) 201 ALR 260 at [10]: 'It is, of course, common for seemingly small points of construction to generate such sharp and evenly held differences of opinion in this manner'. See also Kirby J in *Kelly v R* (2004) 218 CLR 216 at [144]: 'As in most cases of statutory construction reaching this Court, there are arguments both ways'.

Can parties appeal on the basis of errors in statutory interpretation? Most certainly. As Mason J recognised in *Yager v R* (1977) 139 CLR 28 at 45, construction of statutes has been recognised as a question of law. Therefore, for example, where issues of statutory interpretation arise in the context of a jury trial, it is up to the judge to decide what connotation a word should be given: Barwick CJ at 34. As appeals may be lodged on the basis of errors in statutory interpretation, judges labour to explain their approach to the interpretation task, what they have made of the various applicable words and phrases, what they see to be the statutory purpose and context, and what extrinsic materials they have used to so inform themselves. Much attention is given to the High Court's reasoning on issues of statutory interpretation, although Spigelman CJ has cautioned practitioners not to 'pore over the entrails of High Court judgments as if one was interpreting the Delphic Oracle'.[4] But where courts exercise a choice between alternative interpretations, provided they show that their process of reasoning and the outcome is open, such discretion cannot be overridden, even if the appellate court would have exercised the discretion differently.

---

3 M Gleeson, 'The Meaning of Legislation: Context, Purpose and Respect for Fundamental Rights' Address to Victoria Law Foundation, Melbourne, 31 July 2008, 4.

4 J J Spigelman, 'The Intolerable Wrestle: Developments in Statutory Interpretation', Address to the Australasian Conference of Planning and Environment Courts and Tribunals, 1 September 2010, 21.

The relationship between legislation and the common law should be one of complementarity. As Gleeson CJ stated in *Brodie v Singleton Shire Council* (2001) 206 CLR 512 at [31]:

> Legislation and the common law are not separate and independent sources of law; the one the concern of parliaments, and the other the concern of courts. They exist in a symbiotic relationship.

To truly be symbiotic, both sources of law must dovetail into a common understanding, forming the basis for a coherent and aligned corpus of law. To achieve this, it is necessary to reason by analogy from common law to statutes and vice versa. As Roscoe Pound, legal scholar and former Dean of Harvard Law School, said over a century ago, 'Statute and common law should be construed together, just as statute and statute must be'.[5] Pound cautioned against the assumption that statutes should be restricted to direct and narrow application, seeing them as a potential source of principle from which we may reason by analogy.[6] This 'analogical development of statutes',[7] therefore, involves drawing upon the common law in interpreting statutes, and, arguably, drawing upon statutes in developing the common law.

Examples of reasoning to the common law in interpreting statutes is commonplace, given that many statutes add to or vary the common law. The most recent example at the time of writing is *Byrnes v Kendle* [2011] HCA 26, per French CJ at [10]:

> The *Trustee Act 1936* (SA) ... confers power on a trustee to invest trust funds in any form of investment. When the trustee, who exercises that power, is not a person engaged in the profession, business or employment of being a trustee or investing on behalf of others, he or she has a duty, imposed by s 7 of the Trustee Act, to 'exercise the care, diligence and skill that a prudent person of business would exercise in managing the affairs of other persons'. It was submitted for the Byrnes, that while the statutory duty relates to investment, its existence as a presumptive duty under the statute requires a conclusion that analogous principles at general law continue to apply ... None of ss 6, 7 or 8 however, is directed to the power of a trustee to lease a house held on trust nor to the duties of the trustee in relation to such leasing. Under the general law, a trustee with power to manage trust property has power to lease it for a short term.

Examples of reasoning from statutes to develop the common law, which were frequent hundreds of years ago, are now quite rare. It was raised by Professor Atiyah in 1984 in this manner:

---

5 R Pound, 'Common Law and Legislation' (1908) 21(6) *Harvard Law Review* 383 at 400.
6 Ibid at 385–6.
7 P Finn, 'Statutes and the Common Law: The Continuing Story' in S Corcoran and S Bottomley (eds) *Interpreting Statutes* (Federation Press, 2005) 52, 54.

> If, as I have suggested, statute law and common law do, at least in many areas, work together in some kind of legal partnership, creating sometimes amalgams of law of various kinds, [is it] possible for the courts to take account of statute law, in the very development of the common law itself? Can the courts, for instance, use statutes as analogies for the purpose of developing the common law? Can they justify jettisoning obsolete cases, not because they have been actually reversed by some statutory provision, but because a statute suggests that they are based on outdated values? Could the courts legitimately draw some general principle from a limited statutory provision, and apply that principle as a matter of common law? It must be clear that using statutes in this way is fundamentally different from any process of construction, however benevolent or liberal that might be. Construction, as a matter of theory at least, requires the court to give effect to what it thinks the legislation actually enacts. Using statutes by way of analogy quite clearly involves using them to produce results which the legislation does not enact.[8]

In *R v L* (1991) 174 CLR 379, the High Court was faced with an argument by a husband, charged with raping his wife, that there was a common law obligation for a wife to have sexual intercourse with her husband.

There was a state legislative provision, in s 73(3) of the *Criminal Law Consolidation Act 1935* (SA), which provided that 'No person shall, by reason only of the fact that he is married to some other person, be presumed to have consented to sexual intercourse with that other person'. However, the husband referred to a federal provision, s 114(2) of the *Family Law Act 1975* (Cth), which provided that a court 'may make an order relieving a party to a marriage from any obligation to perform marital services or render conjugal rights'. He argued that it was inherent in the Commonwealth provision that a spouse has an obligation 'to perform marital duties' and 'render conjugal rights' and pursuant to s 109 of the Constitution, the Commonwealth provision should prevail to the extent of inconsistency.

The High Court held unanimously that the State Act was not invalid by reason of inconsistency with a Commonwealth Act. In their joint judgment Mason CJ, Deane and Toohey JJ at [19] reasoned:

> [E]ven if the respondent could, by reference to compelling early authority, support the proposition that … by reason of marriage there is an irrevocable consent to sexual intercourse, this Court would be justified in refusing to accept a notion that is so out of keeping with the view society now takes of the relationship between the parties to a marriage. The notion is out of keeping also with recent changes in the criminal law of this country made by statute, which draw no distinction between a wife and other women in defining the offence of rape. The Criminal Code (Q), s 347 as enacted by Act No. 17 of 1989;

8 Professor Atiyah, 'Common Law and Statute Law' (1985) 48 *Modern Law Review* 1 at 6.

> The Criminal Code (WA), s 325 was repealed by Act No. 74 of 1985 and see now Ch. XXXIA-Sexual Assaults; The Criminal Code (Tas), s185(1), enacted by Act No. 71 of 1987; Crimes Act (NSW), s 61T; Crimes Act (Vic), s40 read with s 62. It is unnecessary for the Court to do more than to say that, if it was ever the common law that by marriage a wife gave irrevocable consent to sexual intercourse by her husband, it is no longer the common law.

According to Spigelman CJ, the way the relationship between a statute and the common law should operate depends on how the statute sits with the existing common law. If it aligns with or builds on the common law, then it should be interpreted liberally and used by analogy to develop the common law. If it is inconsistent or incompatible with the common law, it should be interpreted strictly, without being used to develop the common law by analogy, and common law presumptions should apply.[9]

The ongoing challenge is that, while there is said to be a single common law for Australia, there are nine separate legislatures each with power to enact statutes that may differ markedly. See for example *Esso Australia Resources Ltd v FCT* (1999) 201 CLR 49, a case concerning legal professional privilege. The common law test is whether the confidential communication was made for the sole purpose of obtaining or giving legal advice, as discussed in *Grant v Downs* (1976) 135 CLR 674. The test under the *Evidence Act 1995* (Cth), as applied to what may be adduced as evidence in court, is a dominant-purpose test, not a sole-purpose test. That test applies in Commonwealth, ACT and New South Wales jurisdictions. In their joint judgment Gleeson CJ, Gaudron and Gummow JJ refused to reason by analogy from the statute to apply the dominant-purpose test at common law. They referred to authorities in which an analogy from a statute had been used to develop the common law, but said that in each situation the analogy was 'drawn from federal statute law, or from a consistent pattern of State legislation' at [27].

Accordingly, the only real scope for reasoning by analogy to a statute in developing the common law may lie with Commonwealth legislation, and such common law as developed will not be applicable in states and territories whose legislation does not align with that of the Commonwealth.

Traditional common law approaches

In response to the rise of statutes as a form of law following the fourteenth-century development of Parliament in England, courts gradually developed guidelines for their interpretation. Generations of lawyers in Australia have been taught about the literal,

9 P Finn, 'Statutes and the Common Law' (1992) 22 *University of Western Australia Law Review* 7 at 23–24.

golden and mischief rules. These common law approaches laid the foundation for the modern statutory approach, which involves finding the ordinary meaning of words (as in the literal rule) and taking into account the purpose of the legislation (as in the mischief rule) to ensure, for example, that drafting errors do not prevent Parliament's intentions being applied (as in the golden rule).

In the 1980s, when the modern statutory approach to purpose in the Interpretation Acts came into effect, judges were unsure how they related to the traditional common law approaches. For example McHugh J said in *Cole v Director-General of Department of Youth and Community Services* (1987) 7 NSWLR 541 at 549 that the Interpretation Act was really setting aside the literal and golden rules. Dawson J in *Mills v Meeking* (1990) 169 CLR 214 said that the modern approach was *not* merely the mischief rule prevailing:

> [T]he requirement that a court look to the purpose or object of the Act is thus more than an instruction to adopt the traditional mischief or purpose rule in preference to the literal rule of construction. The mischief or purpose rule required an ambiguity or inconsistency before a court could have regard to purpose.

Today, the mention of these rules is a rarity, because the modern statutory approach can achieve the same result as the literal, golden and mischief rules but with more flexibility. Deviation from a literal reading of legislative provisions may occur as a result of consideration of the words in their context and purpose, and this consideration occurs when interpreting any provision of any Act, without there needing to be any ambiguity or absurdity. The modern statutory approach is broader and more flexible than the traditional common law approaches and, applied correctly, is more likely to create a result that is feasible and intended.

According to Spigelman CJ, 'Statutory interpretation is not merely a collection of maxims or canons. It is a distinct body of law'.[10] He considers that:

> The literal rule is now called textualism, the golden rule is now called contextualism and the mischief rule is now called purposive interpretation. In Australia, contextualism and purposivism have come to dominate over recent decades.[11]

Spigelman CJ quotes Manning in saying that textualists give precedence to the words in the statute, purposivists use the purpose to clarify ambiguous text, and strong purposivists use the purpose to depart from a clear statutory text.[12]

---

10 J J Spigelman, *Statutory Interpretation and Human Rights*, The MacPherson Lecture Series, Vol 3 (2008) 22.

11 J J Spigelman, 'Statutory Interpretation and Human Rights', The MacPherson Lecture Series, Vol 3 (2008) 12.

12 J F Manning, referred to in J J Spigelman, *Statutory Interpretation and Human Rights*, The MacPherson Lecture Series, Vol 3 (2008) 108.

Literal rule

The literal rule was the cornerstone of the common law approach to statutory interpretation, giving effect quite literally to the words Parliament has used. The best known formulation is by Justice Higgins in *Amalgamated Society of Engineers v Adelaide Steamship Co Ltd* (1920) 28 CLR 129 ('the Engineers case'):

> The fundamental rule of interpretation, to which all others are subordinate, is that a statute is to be expounded according to the intent of the Parliament that made it; and that intention has to be found by an examination of the language used in the statute as a whole. The question is, what does the language mean; and when we find what the language means, in its ordinary and natural sense, it is our duty to obey that meaning, even if we think the result to be inconvenient or impolitic or improbable.

The literal rule could on the one hand be seen as a form of respect by the judiciary for the separation of powers, or on the other hand a form of support for the common law—the narrower and more literal the reading of statutes, the less incursion into the territory of the common law.

While blanket application of the literal rule would create, at times, ridiculous outcomes,[13] the literal rule told us that courts should apply the ordinary meaning of words, and courts still seek to do that. Take for example *Cheng v R* (2000) 203 CLR 248. Cheng had been convicted, in a trial by a judge sitting alone, of importing heroin from Thailand to Australia inside marble pedestals. Cheng argued that, although he did not request trial by jury, he was entitled to it under s 80 of the Constitution, and any legislation providing for indictable offences to be heard summarily was invalid. McHugh J stated at [126]:

> The literal meaning of s 80 is very clear: trial by jury is required only where the trial is on indictment. Because this meaning results in the section being a mere procedural provision, it is natural to look to its purpose to see if the literal meaning accords with the purpose of the section. It is always legitimate to give a constitutional or statutory provision a meaning which will give effect to its purpose even if that requires a departure from the literal meaning. It is legitimate even if it requires giving the provision a strained meaning. But an examination of the purpose of s 80 leads to the conclusion, unlikely as it may have seemed, that the literal meaning of the section in fact gives effect to its purpose and intent.

Thus the literal rule gives some guidance to present-day courts looking for the meaning of words in their ordinary and natural sense. As stated by Spigelman CJ in *Deputy Commissioner of Taxation v Clark* [2003] NSWCA 91 at [115]:

> The contemporary approach to statutory interpretation is literal but not literalistic and requires words to be construed in their total context.

---

13 See for example *Higgon v O'Dea* [1962] WAR 140.

Golden rule

The golden rule developed as an exception to the literal rule, allowing courts to modify the ordinary meaning of words where the literal approach caused an absurd result. The leading formulation of this rule comes from *Grey v Pearson* (1857) 6 HL Cas 61, in which Lord Wensleydale stated:

> the grammatical and ordinary sense of the words is to be adhered to, unless that would lead to some absurdity or inconsistency with the rest of the instrument, in which case the grammatical and ordinary sense of the words may be modified, so as to avoid that absurdity or inconsistency, but not farther.

The golden rule was often used to correct errors in legislation, and other circumstances where parties attempted to avoid the obvious intended meaning of a statutory provision. A typical example of the golden rule is the reading of 'and' as 'or' and vice versa. Also in *Adler v George* [1964] 2 QB 7 an Act that made it an offence to create an obstruction 'in the vicinity of a prohibited place' was read as 'in, or in the vicinity of' to cover a person who created an obstruction *in* a prohibited place. Similarly in *R v Allen* (1872) LR 1 CCR 367 an Act provided for an offence of bigamy, defined as being married more than once. To avoid argument that nobody could be married more than once because the second attempt would be void, the definition was read as going through the marriage ceremony more than once.

Another example, from *Hall v Jones* (1942) 42 SR (NSW) 203, was reading 'all' as 'any'. In that case, s 14(6) of the *Stock Diseases Act 1923* (SA) provided that the Minister might by notification direct that all stock within a quarantine area or some part of the area should be treated for quarantine disease. At the relevant time, the Minister directed that all cattle, horses, sheep and goats within a defined quarantine area should be treated. The magistrate held that, because the statutory provision referred to 'all stock' the specification of only some stock made the notification invalid. On appeal the court read 'all' as being 'all or any', saying at 279:

> It is well established that the fact that the language of a Statute, when given its natural grammatical meaning, produces a result which appears to a Court to be unjust, unreasonable or even absurd, supplies no justification for placing a forced construction upon it, if the language is plain and unambiguous and there is nothing in the nature or subject matter of the Act which makes it manifest that the Legislature could not have meant what it appears to have said ... It is, however, a very serious matter to hold that when the main object of a Statute is clear, it shall be reduced to a nullity by the draughtsman's unskilfulness or ignorance of the law ... if words in a Statute when read in their primary or natural sense would produce a result which, in relation to the provisions of the Statute itself, are fantastic or absurd, a Court is entitled to pay the Legislature the not excessive compliment of assuming that it intended to enact sense and not nonsense.

Under the modern approach, without needing to resort to the golden rule, similar variations in the plain meaning of words are achieved through the process of 'reading down' or 'reading in' (discussed in Chapter 5). The main focus is on whether the literal, ordinary meaning of words should be varied in light of their context and the purpose of the Act in which they appear. As stated by Mason and Wilson JJ in *Cooper Brookes (Wollongong) Pty Ltd v Federal Commissioner of Taxation* (1981) 147 CLR 297 at [25]:

> When he considers that the statute admits of no reasonable alternative construction it is because (a) the language is intractable or (b) although the language is not intractable, the operation of the statute, read literally, is not such as to indicate that it could not have been intended by the Legislature. On the other hand, when the judge labels the operation of the statute as 'absurd', 'extraordinary', 'capricious', 'irrational' or 'obscure' he assigns a ground for concluding that the Legislature could not have intended such an operation and that an alternative interpretation must be preferred. But the propriety of departing from the literal interpretation is not confined to situations described by these labels. It extends to any situation in which for good reason the operation of the statute on a literal reading does not conform to the legislative intent as ascertained from the provisions of the statute, including the policy which may be discerned from those provisions.

Mischief rule

The mischief rule was based on the idea that statutes were to be interpreted by determining the purpose of Parliament in passing the legislation, and adopting an interpretation of the words of the statute that is consistent with that purpose. Its original formulation of the rule in *Heydon's Case* (1584) 76 ER 637 included four useful questions the court should ask:

> (1) What was the law before the making of the act?
> (2) What was the mischief and defect that the law did not provide for?
> (3) What remedy did Parliament establish under the act to correct that mischief or defect?
> (4) How can the court interpret the legislation so as to correct the mischief or defect according to the true intent of Parliament?

Although this approach sounds like what we do under the Interpretation Acts, the key difference is that the mischief rule was only used where the literal rule created an ambiguity or absurdity. See the quote on page 167 from Dawson J in *Mills v Meeking* (1990) 169 CLR 214. The modern statutory approach includes reference to the 'mischief' as part of identifying the purpose of the legislation. That term is still used in judicial reasoning—see for example Bell J in *Jemena Gas Networks (NSW) Limited v Mine Subsidence Board* [2011] HCA 19 at [63]:

> The Minister referred in the course of his speech to an instance in which the Board had carried out works to a residential property to avoid the damage that was likely to result from a subsidence. The mischief that the 1969 amendments were intended to redress was the lack of statutory authority for the Board to carry out such works.

Latin maxims

Having considered the traditional common law rules, attention is now turned to the Latin maxims, which are syntactical presumptions used by courts to assist in statutory interpretation. It is useful to reiterate that, as the modern statutory approach does not codify the law on statutory interpretation, these common law rules may still have some application. However, they are not determinative, and overall carry less weight than in the past. As stated by Kirby J in *Conway v R* (2002) 209 CLR 203 at 230, it is:

> an elementary mistake to approach the construction of applicable legislation as if it expresses long-standing and familiar principles. Unless the language and obvious purpose of the legislative text clearly require that approach to be adopted, it should be avoided.

Accordingly, the court will focus its attention on the overall meaning of a provision in the light of context and purpose, and if this sheds a different light on a provision than a Latin maxim would, the maxim will not be applied. To some extent the symbiotic relationship between Parliament and the courts would be furthered where parliamentary drafters can have confidence that courts will apply the standard rules, and the Latin maxims may, ironically, provide a more direct route to an outcome that serves the legislative intention than examination of context and purpose.

Noscitur a sociis

Pronounced 'noskiter-a-sock-i-ey-s', this maxim translates to 'it is known by its associates'. The meaning of a word or phrase can be determined by consideration of the words surrounding it. In some ways the thrust of the modern approach to statutory interpretation is a magnification of the *noscitur a sociis* rule—that the meaning or a word or expression may be established through a consideration of its context. It is based on the general philosophy of reading a statute as a whole. In practice, explicit reference to this maxim in modern judgments is usually unnecessary, except perhaps where a party has so referred in making their argument.

Case exercise

'Ships as sisters and surrogates'

LIL recently entered a voyage charterparty with BPSS for the carriage of a cargo of bagged rice from Asia to Africa. The cargo was not fumigated before the vessel set sail, and on arrival the cargo has been found to be infested with beetles. The cost to BPSS of arrest and detention of the vessel has totalled close to $2 million. BPSS wishes to recover this money from LIL on the basis that there was an implied term that LIL properly fumigate the cargo. It has arrested a separate vessel berthed in Darwin which is owned by LIL.

Before explaining the applicable legislative provisions it is necessary to understand some relevant elements of international shipping law.

Rights in shipping law differ from other areas of law in that there is a right, where a debt has accrued, to act '*in rem*' as opposed to '*in personam*'—acting against a vessel owned by the debtor and not just the person of the debtor. Typically the vessel is arrested by order of a court, upon request by a company that can show the vessel's owner owes money to it. The arrest prevents the vessel from leaving the port, and to save costs the debtor usually puts up security for the claim so that the vessel may be released. If the debtor cannot post security the vessel may have to be sold and crew repatriated, so that the debt can be discharged. In the present case, BPSS has proceeded *in rem* against a vessel owned by LIL to recover a debt it considers is owed by LIL.

Vessels are commonly chartered. A vessel's owner charters the vessel to another company, which may in turn sub-charter it to another company, who may in turn sub-sub-charter it. A charterparty may provide that the charterer not only obtains the right to use the vessel but also mans it and sails it, thereby making the charterer a 'disponent owner'. The disponent owner may base sub-charters to other companies on time (use of the vessel for a certain period) or voyage (use of the vessel to sail on a single trip from point A to point B). Under a voyage charter, the disponent owner continues to man and sail the ship but the cargo is the province of the voyage charterer. In the present case, BPSS is a disponent owner and LIL is a voyage charterer.

The applicable legislation is the *Admiralty Act 1988* (Cth) which provides in relevant part:

Right to proceed in rem against surrogate ship

(19) A proceeding on a general maritime claim concerning a ship may be commenced as an action in rem against some other ship if:

(a) a relevant person in relation to the claim was, when the cause of action arose, the owner or charterer of, or in possession or control of, the first-mentioned ship; and

(b) that person is, when the proceeding is commenced, the owner of the second-mentioned ship.

To succeed, BPSS must show it has a 'general maritime claim', which 'concerns a ship', that LIL is a 'relevant person', that it was 'owner or charterer of, or in possession or control of' the ship with beetle infested cargo, and that LIL is the owner of the ship that has been arrested in Darwin. It may be said that the 'second-mentioned ship' that is referred to in s 19(b) is the 'surrogate ship' referred to in the heading to s 19, although the term 'surrogate ship' appears only in the heading.

Section 3(6) of the Act defines a 'surrogate ship'. It provides:

> For the purposes of this Act, where:
>
> (a) a proceeding on a maritime claim may be commenced against a ship under a provision of this Act (other than section 19); and
> (b) under section 19, a proceeding on the claim may be commenced against some other ship;
>
> the other ship is, in relation to the claim, a surrogate ship.

LIL says it was not covered by s 19(a) because it was not 'owner or charterer of, or in possession or control of' the vessel with infested cargo. Using *noscitur a sociis*, it argues, s 19 covers only charterers who are disponent owners, with control of the ship. It was only a voyage charterer, with no real control or ownership of the vessel, having hired it for only one journey using the ship's existing crew, and was therefore not a 'charterer' under the section.

Is LIL covered by s 19, such that its vessel could be arrested in Darwin? Or can *noscitur a sociis* be applied so that LIL is not covered by the statute? In deciding, consider the following extrinsic material relating to s 19.

Australian Law Reform Commission Report No. 33, *Civil Admiralty Jurisdiction* (1986) at [205]:

> The appropriate rule is one which, as an alternative to allowing an action in rem to be commenced against the wrongdoing ship, allows such an action against a ship owned by the relevant person even though this person is not the owner of the wrongdoing ship. This will occasionally allow an action against a surrogate ship even where there could be no action against the wrongdoing ship. The most obvious examples are where the wrongdoing ship has sunk or been sold. But another case would be where the claim is by an owner against someone using the owner's ship on a time or voyage charter. In such a case the owner has already got possession of his own ship, but he could, under the recommended provision, proceed against any other ship owned by the defendant.

What do you think? Decide before proceeding.

The real case is *Laemthong International Lines Co Ltd v BPS Shipping* (1997) 190 CLR 181. If you decided LIL was covered, you are in agreement with the trial judge, the Court of Appeal of the Northern Territory, and the High Court. If you decided it was not, you are alone in dissent. Toohey J said in relation to *noscitur a sociis* that '[a]ny such approach must be applied with care' and indeed the narrow context to which *noscitur a sociis* was directed was overridden by the extrinsic context provided by the ALRC report, upon which the legislation was based.

Ejusdem generis

Pronounced 'e-use-dem-generous' this maxim translates to 'of the same kind'. If there are specific words in a statute followed by a general, catch-all phrase, the general words are limited by the specific words that come before it. Listing a number of specifics followed by a general phrase is very common in legislation—Parliament wants to expressly include certain things but doesn't want to be limited to them. When an Act says 'or any other thing' it does not literally mean any other thing, it means any other thing 'like the ones that come before'.

For example the mention of 'linoleum, carpets, floating floors and any other thing' would include 'tiles' but would not include 'curtains'. It can be seen as an example of 'reading down' words, discussed in Chapter 5. The process for applying the maxim is straightforward—identify the commonality between the specific words in the phrase (known as the 'class' or 'genus'), and then decide whether the word you have comes within the identified class.

It may, however, be difficult to identify the genus, or more than one genus may be open. Take for example a hypothetical provision, 'It is an offence for a person to use a mobile telephone, laptop computer, palm pilot or any other thing on board any flight within Australia' and we have a situation where someone uses a DTi game on a flight from Sydney to Melbourne. If the genus is electronic devices, using the DTi would be an offence, but if it is *communicative* electronic devices, it would not. Clearly in such a situation it would be the overall purpose of the Act, which may be to prevent the use of devices that interfere with satellite navigation, which would be determinative.[14]

14 This was certainly the view taken by Mahoney JA in *Mattinson v Multiplow Incubators Pty Ltd* (1977) 1 NSWLR 368 at 375: 'There are frequently ... several competing formulations of the genus. Which one is to be selected as the intended genus will, as it has been said, require that there first be ascertained what is the purpose of the statutory provision ... whether and in what manner the rule is to be applied is to be determined after the legislative intention has first been assessed'.

Case exercise

'Playing with fire'

Tanya and John have had a good afternoon, with both of their families enjoying a woodfire barbecue in John's family backyard. As the sun goes down and the temperature drops, the parents head into the house. John and Tanya remain playing in the backyard, and decide to try and rekindle the fire by dipping sticks in a can of lawnmower fuel and throwing them onto the coals. It is taking too long to run to and from the petrol can, so they tip some petrol into a cup and take it with them to the fire. Instead of dipping sticks in it, John throws petrol from the cup on the fire. The ensuing explosion of fire catches Tanya, causing severe burns.

Tanya's family is seeking victim's compensation. To do this, she must show she was the victim of an 'offence'. Section 51 of the *Summary Offences Act 1953* (SA) provides:

> Use of firearms
>
> 51(1) A person who discharges a firearm or throws a stone or other missile without reasonable cause and so as to injure, annoy or frighten, or be likely to injure, annoy or frighten, any person, or so as to damage, or be likely to damage, any property, is guilty of an offence.
>
> (2) In this section -
>
> 'firearm' means a gun or device, including an airgun, from or by which any kind of shot, bullet or missile can be discharged;
>
> 'throw' includes to discharge or project by means of any mechanism or device.

Tanya's legal team alleges that the petrol that John threw, while obviously not a stone, comes within 'or other missile'. The word 'missile' is not defined in the Act but a dictionary definition is 'an object capable of being thrown, hurled or shot'. Can it, therefore, include a liquid thrown from a container? Can you use *ejusdem generis* here?

Decide before proceeding.

The real case is *Field v Gent* (1996) 67 SASR 122. If you decided it was a missile, you are in agreement with the District Court and the majority of the Full Court of the Supreme Court of South Australia, who reasoned that a liquid is still an object, and that liquids are capable of being thrown from or in a container. If you decided it was not, you are in agreement with Debelle J in dissent, who said missiles had to be hard objects, not liquids. The Supreme Court agreed. The view of the trial judge was that the provision could not be construed *ejusdem generis* because only one word ('stone') appeared before the general phrase.

Case exercise

'The silent director'

Robert Clark and his wife Carole were directors of Southern Cross Interiors until the company was wound up. The company's liquidator obtained an order to recover from the Deputy Commissioner of Taxation a sum paid by way of group tax, which was found to be an unfair preference (favouring the Deputy Commissioner over other creditors). The Deputy Commissioner sought indemnity from the directors pursuant to s 588 FGA of the Act, which provides in relevant part:

> (1) This section applies if the Court makes an order ... against the Commissioner of Taxation because of the payment of an amount in respect of a liability under [listed provisions of the *Income Tax Assessment Act 1936* (Cth)].
>
> (2) Each person who was a director of the company when the payment was made is liable to indemnify the Commissioner in respect of any loss or damage resulting from the order.

Carole has raised a defence under s 588FGB(5) of the *Corporations Act 2001* (Cth), which provides:

> It is a defence if it is proved that, because of illness or for some other good reason, the person did not take part in the management of the company at the payment time.

Carole is arguing that she is a silent director and this is a 'good reason' for not taking part in the management of the company. Can she succeed in her defence? What meaning should be given to the expression 'illness or for some other good reason'? Can *ejusdem generis* be applied? Decide before proceeding.

The real case is *Deputy Commissioner of Taxation v Clark* [2003] NSWCA 91. If you decided the defence could apply, you are in agreement with Palmer J in the Supreme Court of New South Wales, and if you decided it could not, you are in agreement with the Full Court of the Court of Appeal. There, Spigelman CJ wrote the leading judgment, with which Handley JA and Hodgson JA concurred.

Spigelman CJ discussed the challenge in the *Corporations Law* for sole traders who are expected to have at least two company directors, and usually name their spouse or close friend as a silent director. The problem is that the silent director carries all the duties and responsibilities of an active director, and can be liable for company debt in circumstances of insolvent trading. This has been referred to as 'sexually transmitted debt'.[15] He discussed the potential application of the *ejusdem generis* rule at [126]–[127]:

> It is essential for the application of the *ejusdem generis* rule that some common characteristic capable of being described as a genus is able to be identified ... unless at least two different species are identified it is not possible to determine a relevant genus ... The process of reading down general words in a statute is a frequently recurring issue ... [a]pplication of the *ejusdem generis* rule is a specific example of this process. The application of this rule, in substance, gives the immediate verbal context determinative weight in the process of construing general words. In my opinion, this is rarely justified. Whether or not general words ought to be read down is to be determined by the whole of the relevant context, including other provisions of the statute and the scope and purpose of the statute.

In this case, the intrinsic and extrinsic context showed that abdication, avoidance or other non-participation of directors is impermissible, such that 'reasons which cause a director never to participate in management are not capable of constituting "good reason" for not participating at a particular point of time' at [133].

Situations where there is only one word before a general phrase may be reasoned in the negative, in the sense that the general phrase must cover something different from the specific word, otherwise it would have no 'work' to do. For example in *DPP v Williams* (1998) 104 A Crim R 65, which considered the administration of breath testing by taking a driver 'to a police station or other place', the Supreme Court of Victoria reasoned that, for 'other place' to have any operation, it still had to have some similarity to a police station—for example a 'booze bus' is akin to a mobile police station, but a police car is not, as that would mean interpreting the expression as literally any place, making reference to 'police station' superfluous: at [75]. All words are to be given meaning, so 'any other place' had to have some restrictive force, and in that case, the Court considered extension to a booze bus, which was like a police station on wheels, was acceptable, but the back of a police car was not. This is a de facto application of *ejusdem generis* in a situation with only one specific word before a general word.

15 B Fehlberg, *Sexually Transmitted Debt* (Oxford University Press, 1997).

Case exercise

'The risky business of aircraft noise'

Artline is in the process of selling Jason its warehouse in Botany near Sydney airport. The sale documentation, as with all such contracts, includes a 'section 149 certificate'. This refers to s 149 of the *Environmental Planning and Assessment Act 1979* (NSW), which provides that a local council will, upon application, issue a certificate providing information about planning controls or property affectations relating to any piece of land within the council area. It is often used by intending purchasers to identify any restrictions to development that may apply to the property. The s 149 certificate attached to the relevant contract of sale warranted that:

> the Council had not by resolution adopted any policy to restrict the development of the land because of the likelihood of land slip, bushfire, flooding, tidal inundation, subsidence or any other risk.

Jason is seeking to rescind the contract, arguing that the s 149 certificate failed to disclose a Council policy on aircraft noise. Artline is arguing that such a policy would not come within the warranty in any event. What would you rule in this case? Can you apply *ejusdem generis*?

Decide before proceeding.

The real case is *Mandalidis v Artline* [1999] NSWSC 909. If you decided that the expression could be read *ejusdem generis*, such that 'any other risk' should be limited to risks relating to natural features of the land and therefore would exclude a policy on aircraft noise, you would be quite right, but the Court refused to apply *ejusdem generis*, with Austin J stating at [55] and [58]:

> I accept that the *noscitur a sociis* and *ejusdem generis* rules of interpretation are available weapons in the armoury of statutory interpretation. But they are not always determinative, and it is arguable that they are less important now than once they were … the task of a modern court, where the grammatical meaning of the legislation is open to doubt, is to adopt the construction which will promote the purpose or object of the Act … After one has had regard to the objects or purposes of legislation of the kind presently under consideration, it is unlikely that much room will be left for the application of the old rules of statutory interpretation …
>
> I conclude that the word 'risk' is wide enough on its literal construction to include the risk to which the Council's policy on aircraft noise relates, and that in view of the remedial purpose of the legislation, there is no basis for reading down the word by reference to the *noscitur a sociis* or *ejusdem generis* rules of interpretation.

Here, although it is unlikely the parliamentary drafters envisaged that aircraft noise would be held to be covered by the provision, the Court's assessment of purpose was sufficient to override use of *ejusdem generis*. The context can have a similar result, as seen in *Australian Broadcasting Tribunal v Bond* (1990) 170 CLR 321 ('Bond Media Case'). The case concerned whether a decision by the Australian Broadcasting Tribunal, that Bond Media's commercial broadcasting licence be revoked because the licensee was no longer a fit and proper person, was a 'decision' of an administrative character so as to attract the review provisions under the *Administrative Decisions (Judicial Review) Act 1977* (Cth). Section 3(2) of the Act provides:

> In this Act, a reference to the making of a decision includes a reference to—
>
> (a) making, suspending, revoking or refusing to make an order, award or determination ...
> (g) doing or refusing to do any other act or thing
>
> and a reference to a failure to make a decision shall be construed accordingly.

It was argued that 'any other act or thing' should be limited to what came before it, which was six paragraphs all relating to the exercise or refusal to exercise a substantive power. Toohey and Gaudron JJ stated at [21]:

> The principles of construction embodied in the Latin expressions *ejusdem generis* and *noscitur a sociis* favour the construction of general words by reference to more particular matters dealt with in the same provision. On this approach, s 3(2)(g) of the ADJR Act might well be construed as confined to the exercise of or refusal to exercise a substantive power. On the other hand, if it had been the intention of the legislature to so limit the decisions which are reviewable under s 5 of the Act that could have been simply stated.

They read the Act as a whole and concluded s 3(2)(g) was not so confined. The context prevailed over the maxim.

Case exercise

'Cocaine, it goes straight to your brain'

Gilbert Gedeon purchased over 2.5kg of cocaine from 'Tom', who turned out to be an informer acting in a controlled operation by drug enforcement officers. The legislation that validates such operations, which would otherwise be unlawful as they involve selling drugs, is the *Law Enforcement (Controlled Operations) Act 1997* (NSW). The Act provides for authority to conduct controlled operations to be granted by the Commissioner of the New South Wales Crime Commission.

Section 7(1) of the Act provided:

> An authority to conduct a controlled operation must not be granted in relation to a proposed operation that involves any participant in the operation …
>
> (b) engaging in conduct that is likely to seriously endanger the health or safety of that or any other participant, or any other person, or to result in serious loss or damage to property; or …

A briefing was given to the Commissioner and senior law enforcement officers, during which it was disclosed that it was unlikely the cocaine would be recovered. It would, therefore, be sold on to end users in 70 000–100 000 packets.

Was the authority to conduct the controlled operation in relation to Gilbert valid? Did 'any other person' include literally any other person who might use the cocaine, or was it limited to those persons involved in the sting operation? Decide before proceeding.

The real case is *Gedeon v Commissioner of the New South Wales Crime Commission* [2008] HCA 43. If you decided that the provision did not cover end users in 'any other person' such that the authority was valid, you are in agreement with both the Common Law Division of the Supreme Court and the Court of Appeal. However, if you decided that 'any other person' literally means what it says, you are in agreement with all six sitting judges of the High Court.

The Court of Appeal had reasoned that 'any other person' had to be determined in the light of the specific words which can before it, which were relating to those in close proximity to the controlled operation. The High Court disagreed, stating 'The question of construction of par (b) of s 7(1) is not resolved by the application of any particular maxim or canon of statutory construction selected from among those which may jostle for acceptance' at [51]. The focus was on exposure to damage or peril, and as there was a foreseeable risk of seriously endangering at least some of the end purchasers of the cocaine, there was no power to issue the authority for the sting operation.

Therefore, in practice, *ejusdem generis* may still be considered, but will not apply unless its outcome is in alignment with the legislative context and purpose, such that the court is convinced of an intention that a general expression be 'read down' in the light of the specific preceding expressions.

Expressio unius est exclusio alterius

Pronounced 'express-eyo-uni-es-iks-cloo-zio-ol-teer-eus', this maxim translates to 'the express mention of one thing is the exclusion of another'. For example if a statute stated that persons over the age of 18 years may serve as a member of the armed forces, this excludes persons under the age of 18 years.

In *FAI Properties Pty Limited v John & Evangelia Apostolopoulos* [2002] ACTSC 58 the *Tenancy Tribunal Act 1994* (ACT) conferred a right to appeal from the tribunal to a court on questions of law. Justice Spender used *expressio unius est exclusio alterius* to find that the express conferral of a right of appeal on questions of law excluded the right of appeal on questions of fact or mixed fact and law.

A restatement of the *expressio* maxim is *expressum facit cessare tacitum*—if a procedure has been designated that procedure should be followed to the exclusion of other procedures. In *Minister for Immigration and Multicultural and Indigenous Affairs v Nystrom* (2006) 230 ALR 370 Gummow and Hayne JJ referred to this maxim at [54] and [61]:[16]

> Counsel for the Minister, in oral argument, invoked the maxim *expressum facit cessare tacitum* ... whilst 'rules' or principles of construction may offer reassurance, they are no substitute for consideration of the whole of the particular text, the construction of which is disputed, and of its subject, scope and purpose ... the two powers [visa cancellation and deportation] do not deal with the same subject-matter so as to attract the operation of the maxim *expressum facit cessare tacitum*.

They also said at [51]:

> [T]o read one statute as abrogated by other than express words in a later statute is a large step, different in character from the construction of parts of a subsisting whole. It is one thing to treat an earlier statutory provision as repealed by a subsequent enactment, and another to say that, as a matter of construction, whilst both provisions remain in force the power conferred by one of them is insusceptible of exercise in certain factual circumstances.

In *Ainsworth v Criminal Justice Commission* (1992) 175 CLR 564 it was argued that a provision which required the Criminal Justice Commission to observe procedural fairness in proceedings excluded the requirement that it do so with respect to its researching and reporting. The High Court joint judgment by Mason CJ, Dawson, Toohey and Gaudron JJ, stated at [19]:

> The principles of construction embodied in the maxims *expressio unius est exclusio alterius* and *expressum facit cessare tacitum*, if applied in this case, would lead to the conclusion that s.3.21(2)(a) excludes any wider duty of fairness than that there specified ... They are not to be applied if they would bring about a result which the legislature is unlikely to have intended ... it is highly unlikely that the Parliament intended that the Commission should act unfairly ... the nature of the Commission and its powers, functions and responsibilities are such that, to the extent that the Act does not provide, a duty of fairness is necessarily to be implied in all areas involving its functions and responsibilities.

---

16 They also erroneously referred to Dixon J's statement on the *generalia* maxim in *Perpetual Executors and Trustees Association of Australia Ltd v Federal Commissioner of Taxation* (1948) 77 CLR 1 at 29 as if it applied to the *expressio* maxim.

This is of course the correct result—the common law obligation of procedural fairness in reporting is not excluded by its mention as an express requirement in an Act for hearings.

A key problem with the *expressio* maxim is establishing that it was intended to apply—particularly where a statute has been amended at various times. The question for the courts is not whether the maxim applies but whether Parliament intended the maxim to apply, or better still, whether is intended the same effect as if the maxim did apply. Superior courts have repeatedly called for care and caution in its exercise. See for example Kirby J in *Rich v Australian Securities and Investments Commission* (2004) 220 CLR 129 at [122]:

> [T]his Court has warned many times that care must be exercised in the use of the *expressio unius* rule of construction ... [e]specially in an Act as large and cumbersome as that under consideration (with its history of patchwork accretions).

See also the unanimous High Court judgment in *Houssein v Under Secretary, Department of Industrial Relations and Technology (NSW)* (1982) 148 CLR 88 at [10]:

> That maxim must always be applied with care, for it is not of universal application and applies only when the intention it expresses is discoverable upon the face of the instrument ... It is 'a valuable servant, but a dangerous master'.

In some instances the maxim has been further diminished by specific provisions—see s 33(3B) of the Commonwealth Act:

> Where an Act confers a power to make, grant or issue any instrument (including rules, regulations or by-laws), the power shall not be taken, by implication, not to include the power to make provision for or in relation to a particular aspect of a matter by reason only that provision is made by the Act in relation to another aspect of that matter or in relation to another matter.

Generalia specialibus non derogant

Pronounced 'gener-arl-eea, spesh-ee-arl-ee-bus-non-dero-gant', this maxim means that general things do not derogate from special things. Therefore, if two provisions are in conflict with one another, the more specific one will prevail over the general one. For example if one provision made it an offence to bring animals on public transport, and another provided that visually impaired persons may bring guide dogs on public transport, the specific provision would be applied as an exception to the general provision such that a pet labrador would not be allowed but a trained labrador assistance dog would. In *Sue v Hill* (1999) 199 CLR 462 Gaudron J said at [128] that the *generalia* maxim 'applies only when the general provision would otherwise encompass the matter dealt with by the special or more limited provision'. If the two provisions deal with separate topics, the maxim cannot be applied.

In *Federal Commissioner of Taxation v Gulland* (1985) 160 CLR 55 the High Court considered the arrangement by a group of medical practitioners in shifting from a partnership to a company, with money going into unit trust funds which minimised their taxable income. Section 260 of the *Income Tax Assessment Act 1936* (Cth) rendered void against the Commissioner what could colloquially be described as 'tax dodges'. Gibbs CJ referred to a line of cases applying the *generalia* maxim and establishing that s 260 was a general provision which applied except where specific provisions allowed for advantage to be taken to reduce tax. Brennan J also applied the *generalia* maxim, referring to the 'choice' principle under which taxpayers can choose to organise their affairs to take advantage of tax benefits under the Act. He said at [2] of his judgment:

> One of the limitations to be placed on s 260 is justified by a familiar rule of statutory construction: *generalia specialibus non derogant* ... The Act contains a great number of specific and particular provisions ... a taxpayer who brings himself within a specific and particular provision which purports to confer a tax benefit should be entitiled to have that benefit. That intention would fail if s 260 were to operate according to its literal terms, for s 260 would avoid any arrangement which brought the taxpayer within a specific and particular provision of the Act which conferred a tax benefit ... It is necessary therefore to read down s 260.

CHAPTER 10

STATUTORY PRESUMPTIONS

Statutory presumptions are another component of the common law approach to statutory interpretation.[1] Courts will apply certain presumptions unless the statute they are interpreting uses clear words to reject or rebut that presumption. These presumptions are organic in the sense that they have developed over time. They vary in strength, and some presumptions fall out of use while others are 'discovered'.

Parliamentary drafters are well aware of statutory presumptions used by courts,[2] and they use clear words to instruct courts not to apply the presumption. This has been referred to by Spigelman CJ as the 'clear statement principle'.[3] There is High Court authority to suggest that presumptions may, in limited circumstances, be displaced by 'clear implication', a seeming oxymoron applicable where the presumption must be displaced so as to avoid rendering a provision meaningless. See *Coco v R* (1994) 179 CLR 427 at [8] of the judgment of Mason CJ, Brennan, Gaudron and McHugh JJ:

> Statutory authority to engage in what otherwise would be tortious conduct must be clearly expressed in unmistakable and unambiguous language. Indeed, it has been said that the presumption is that, in the absence of express provision to the contrary, the legislature did not intend to authorize what would otherwise have been tortious conduct ... But the presumption is rebuttable and will be displaced if there is a clear implication that authority to enter or remain upon private property was intended. Such an implication may be made, in some circumstances, if it is necessary to prevent the statutory provisions from becoming inoperative or meaningless.

Statutory presumptions are one of several tools in an interpreter's toolkit. Mostly courts use them to help resolve uncertainty, as stated by Gleeson CJ in *Wilson v Anderson* (2002) 213 CLR 401 at [9]:

> [C]ommon law and statutory principles of construction frequently demand consideration of background, purpose and object, surrounding circumstances, and other matters which may throw light on the meaning of unclear language. And there are presumptions which may be called in aid to resolve uncertainty.

Similarly, Dixon J in *Cody v J H Nelson Pty Ltd* (1947) 74 CLR 629:

> In the modern search for a real intention covering each particular situation litigated, however much help and guidance may be obtained from the principles and rules of construction, their controlling force in determining the conclusion is likely to be confined to cases where the real meaning is undiscoverable or where the court of construction, sceptical of the

1 Note however that the ACT Act provides legislative backing for statutory presumptions by providing, in s 137(3), that it is to be read in conjunction with statutory presumptions, including those that come into existence after its passage: s 137(4).

2 J J Spigelman, *Statutory Interpretation and Human Rights*, The MacPherson Lecture Series, Vol 3 (2008) 37.

3 Ibid at 88.

> foresight of the draftsman or of his appreciation of the situation presented, is better content to supply the meaning by a legal presumption than subjectively.

Specific statutory presumptions are considered below. Because of their importance and complexity, presumptions concerning fundamental rights and consistency with international law (usually human rights provisions) are considered separately in the next chapter.

Legislation does not operate retrospectively

Courts will presume, in the absence of express words to the contrary, that legislation prospectively applies from the time it enters into force. It is reasoned that, in the usual case, people who comply in good faith with the law should not later have their legal actions rendered illegal. The presumption therefore has its strongest application with respect to criminal offences: see *R v Kidman* (1915) 20 CLR 425.

Parliament does, however, have the power to make legislation operate retrospectively (properly it should be described as 'retroactively' not 'retrospectively'). An example is the *Crimes (Appeal and Review) Act 2001* (NSW) which entered into force on 15 December 2006. Section 99(2) provides that 'This section extends to a person acquitted before the commencement of this Division'.

Retrospective legislation is sometimes necessary, for example following the High Court decision in *Re Wakim; Ex parte McNally* (1999) 198 CLR 511, which determined the cross-vesting of state jurisdiction in federal courts, pursuant to s 9 of the *Jurisdiction of Courts (Cross-vesting) Act 1987* (Cth), was constitutionally invalid. Parliament passed legislation retrospectively validating decisions over the twelve years since the Act's inception.

A controversial example of retrospective legislation concerned the '*Tampa* incident' in 2001, with a Bill being put before Parliament within days of actions by the Australian government which violated the *United Nations Convention on the Law of the Sea* (1982), the *United Nations Convention Relating to the Status of Refugees* (1951), the *International Convention of the Safety of Life at Sea* (1974), and the *International Convention on Maritime Search and Rescue* (1979). The events giving rise to these violations involved a radio instruction by the Australian Coastwatch on 27 August 2001 for merchant ships in the area to render assistance to a sinking fishing boat loaded with passengers. The MV *Tampa*, a Norwegian freighter, was in the area and responded, letting the passengers board. To avoid processing the passengers as asylum seekers upon entering Australia, the government ordered the *Tampa* not to come into Australian waters. SAS troops boarded the *Tampa* and made it sail to Christmas Island. The Federal Parliament passed the *Border Protection (Validation and Enforcement of Powers) Act* 2001 (Cth), which entered into force on 27 September 2001. The Long Title of the Act provides that it is 'An Act to validate the actions of the Commonwealth and others in relation to the MV Tampa'. The Act applies to action taken by the Commonwealth in the period 27 August to 27 September 2011, and s 5(1) states that it applies to any action by the Commonwealth or its agents or officers in relation to the MV *Tampa*. Section 6 baldly states 'All action to which this Part applies is taken for all purposes to have been lawful when it occurred'.

The presumption only applies to substantive rights, not procedural rights. Laws which affect procedure are assumed to apply to all cases, arising presently and from past events. This means, for example, if someone is arrested this year for a crime committed in 2007, the law as it applied in 2007 will apply (assuming no retrospective legislation has been enacted) and the procedure by which the person will be charged and tried will be the procedure as it presently applies.

In the unanimous joint judgment of the High Court in *Rodway v R* (1990) 169 CLR 515, Rodway unsuccessfully appealed against convictions relating to the indecent assault of a girl under 17 years of age in the period 1982 to 1986, saying that the applicable law at the time, under s 136(1) of the *Criminal Code* (Tas), was that conviction could not be based on uncorroborated victim's evidence. By the time Rodway was tried, s 136 of the Code had been amended such that a judge could allow such evidence but warn a jury that it is unsafe to convict someone on uncorroborated evidence. Rodway argued that, both under the relevant Interpretation Act and the presumption against retrospectivity, the old s 136 should apply. The trial court, Court of Appeal and the High Court all agreed that the new s 136 applied. The High Court stated at [4] and [8]:

> [T]here is no presumption against retrospectivity in the case of statutes which affect mere matters of procedure ... A statute which prescribes the manner in which the trial of a past offence is to be conducted is one instance. But the difference between substantive law and procedure is often difficult to draw and statutes which are commonly classified as procedural—statutes of limitation, for example—may operate in such a way as to affect existing rights or obligations. When they operate in that way they are not merely procedural and they fall within the presumption against retrospective operation ... But ordinarily an amendment to the practice or procedure of a court, including the admissibility of evidence and the effect to be given to evidence, will not operate retrospectively so as to impair any existing right. It may govern the way in which the right is to be enforced or vindicated, but that does not bring it within the presumption against retrospectivity. A person who commits a crime does not have a right to be tried in any particular way; merely a right to be tried according to the practice and procedure prevailing at the time of trial.

An example is *Maxwell v Murphy* (1957) 96 CLR 261—see the case exercise in Chapter 5 titled 'Reviving the right or the right to act?'. There, the Court considered that the limitation period, while related to procedure, was a substantive matter, and as such the presumption against retrospectivity did not apply. Fullagar J stated at 286:

> [T]he distinction is probably best stated by saying that it is between statutes which create or modify or abolish substantive rights or liabilities on the one hand and statutes which deal with the pursuit of remedies on the other hand. In the former class of case there is a presumption against retrospective operation in the sense explained above. In the latter class of case there is no such presumption: on the contrary, the presumption is that the enactment applies in all proceedings commenced after it became law, and it may be right to construe it as applying even in proceedings commenced before it became law.

He went on to say at 291:

> The rule is, of course, like all rules of construction, only a prima facie rule. It must yield to any sufficient indication of a contrary intention ... [t]he appropriate presumption and the long title both point in the same direction ... the plaintiff's action is not statute-barred.

Although many rules of statutory interpretation apply equally to primary and delegated legislation, this presumption has little application to delegated legislation. This is because some States prohibit or otherwise limit the ability for delegated legislation to be retrospective—see s 12 and 48 of the *Legislative Instruments Act 2003* (Cth), s 39 of the NSW Act, s 32 and 34 of the *Statutory Instruments Act 1987* (Qld), s 10AA of the *Subordinate Legislation Act 1978* (SA), s 16 of the *Subordinate Legislation Act 1994* (Vic) and s 76 of the *Legislation Act 2001* (ACT). The exception is where there is an 'as enacted' provision, where Parliament allows the delegated legislation to have the same force of law as if it were enacted as an Act of Parliament. This puts delegated legislation on par with the Act.

Legislation does not have extraterritorial effect

It is common for legislation not to specify where it applies, such that it could potentially apply anywhere in the world. It is presumed, however, that legislation only applies in its jurisdiction—a state or territory Act applies only within that state or territory, and a Commonwealth Act applies only within Australia. It can cover persons and property within the jurisdiction even if they are the subject of foreign ownership or citizenship but it typically would not cover persons and property outside the jurisdiction. The presumption can be rebutted with express words or where the operation of the legislation would be rendered ineffective otherwise. An example where the presumption is rebutted is s 10A of the *Crimes Act 1900* (NSW), which provides in the relevant part:

> (2) This Part extends, beyond the territorial limits of the State, the application of a law of the State that creates an offence if there is the nexus required by this Part between the State and the offence.
>
> (3) If the law that creates an offence makes provision with respect to any geographical consideration concerning the offence, that provision prevails over any inconsistent provision of this Part.

Section 10C provides:

> (1) If:
>
> (a) all elements necessary to constitute an offence against a law of the State exist (disregarding geographical considerations), and
>
> (b) a geographical nexus exists between the State and the offence, the person alleged to have committed the offence is guilty of an offence against that law.
>
> (2) A geographical nexus exists between the State and an offence if:
>
> (a) the offence is committed wholly or partly in the State (whether or not the offence has any effect in the State), or
>
> (b) the offence is committed wholly outside the State, but the offence has an effect in the State.

This presumption has been enacted in some of the Interpretation Acts. For example s 21(1)(b) of the Commonwealth Act provides that 'references to localities jurisdictions and other matters and things shall be construed as references to such localities jurisdictions and other matters and things in and of the Commonwealth'. See also s 12(2) of the NSW Act.

In *Polites v Commonwealth* (1945) 70 CLR 60 the High Court considered that the *National Security Act 1939* (Cth), which provided for conscription to fight, 'does not refer to all persons in the world' yet there was a clear intention by Parliament that the Act authorised the Executive to require compulsory service of any person in Australia, including Mr Polites, a Greek national.

In *Re Maritime Union of Australia* (2003) 214 CLR 397 the High Court held that s 21(1)(b) of the Commonwealth Act did not apply because the relevant statutory provision, s 5(3) of the *Workplace Relations Act 1996* (Cth), expressly defined industrial issues as covering maritime employee and employer relationships relating not only to interstate trade and commerce but also between Australia and places outside of Australia.[4] Therefore, it was not in excess of the power of the Australian Industrial Relations

4 For a discussion of this case see J Gleeson, 'Extraterritorial application of Australian statutes proscribing misleading conduct' (2005) 79 *Australian Law Journal* 296.

Commission to assume jurisdiction in circumstances where the relevant employees were employed overseas by an employer incorporated in Barbados, to work on a vessel registered in the Bahamas, being paid under the terms of the International Transport Federation (which differed from the equivalent Australian Award).

Case exercise

'A part of an apartment'

Gretchen and Bruce are married and enjoy a luxurious lifestyle. Bruce has recently died and it has come to light that, although he behaved as a wealthy man, he owed approximately $26 million. The trustee in bankruptcy is trying to gather all of Bruce's assets to apply against his debts. He has identified a residential apartment in Hamburg which is in Gretchen's name. When the couple purchased the property a few years ago, it was in both of their names, but after arguments and to encourage reconciliation, Bruce had signed over his share of the property to Gretchen as a deed of gift, and Gretchen took over the mortgage.

The trustee is seeking a declaration than the transfer is void, so that one half of the apartment value reverts to the estate in bankruptcy. He is relying on s 120(1) of the *Bankruptcy Act 1966* (Cth) which provides:

> A settlement of property, whether made before or after the commencement of this Act, not being:
>
> (a) a settlement made before and in consideration of marriage, or made in favour of a purchaser or encumbrancer in good faith and for valuable consideration; or
> (b) a settlement made on or for the spouse or children of the settlor of property that has accrued to the settlor after marriage in right of the spouse of the settlor;
>
> is, if the settlor becomes a bankrupt and the settlement came into operation after, or within 2 years before, the commencement of the bankruptcy, void as against the trustee in the bankruptcy.

The legislation does not limit the definition of 'property' in the Act to property in Australia. Can you apply the presumption? Or can the court make such an order? Decide before proceeding.

The real case is *Re Doyle (Deceased) Ex parte: Brien and Doyle* (1993) 41 FCR 40. Burchett J stated at [6] that 'The seeking of a declaration in this form raises starkly the difficult question which lies at the root of this case—whether the claim the trustee wishes to raise can be determined under the Act by an Australian court'. He reasoned at [34] to [37]:

> [I]t would be a very long step into the area under the control of that country's laws for the Australian Parliament to provide that the Australian trustee in bankruptcy might avoid the title of a third party upon whom foreign land had been settled at some earlier date by a person who subsequently became bankrupt. Such a third party may have obtained a title valid under the *lex situs* [law of the place in which the property is located]. The rule of our private international law is that it is for the *lex situs* to determine the capacity of a person to deal with real estate, and the effectiveness of any conveyance … [principles such as the presumption against extra-territoriality] require that the universality which s 120 would have, if the definition of 'property' were read into it without qualification, must be limited to exclude a settlement of a foreign immovable made under foreign law.

The High Court case of *Wanganui-Rangitikei Electric Power Board v Australian Mutual Provident Society* (1934) 50 CLR 581 considered a loan agreement entered into in New Zealand under the laws of New Zealand, with repayments occurring in Sydney. During the term of the loan, the *Interest Reduction Act 1931* (NSW) was passed, applying to loans made before the Act came into force. Section 5 of the Act provided that an obligation to pay interest on a loan 'shall be deemed to be satisfied by payment of a sum equal to the amount which would have been payable as interest if this Act had not been enacted, less nine-fortieths of such amount'. The words did not indicate the territorial ambit of applicable loans, but it was held that s 5 was limited to obligations to pay interest that arise under the law of New South Wales. Evatt J stated that, in the absence of a legislative indication of the connection between New South Wales and the interest payment obligation, s 17 of the Interpretation Act NSW should apply so as to limit coverage to matters and things within New South Wales. Dixon J at 601 referred to the 'well settled rule of construction', saying:

> The rule is that an enactment describing acts, matters or things in general words, so that, if restrained by no consideration lying outside its expressed meaning, its intended application would be universal, is to be read as confined to what, according to the rules of international law administered or recognized in our Courts, it is within the province of our law to affect or control. The rule is one of construction only, and it may have little or no place where some other restriction is supplied by context or subject matter. But, in the absence of any countervailing consideration, the principle is, I think, that general words should not be understood as extending to cases which, according to the rules of private international law administered in our Courts, are governed by foreign law … The circumstances of the present case illustrate the soundness of the presumption by which, unless a contrary intention appears, statutory provisions are understood as having no application to matters governed by foreign law.

Legislation does not take jurisdiction away from the courts

It is presumed that courts of law have jurisdiction to hear legal disputes—that legislation does not take jurisdiction away from the courts. After all, in a society under the rule of law, the use of legal avenues for dispute settlement is a fundamental function of government. While each court's jurisdiction is established by the relevant court Act and other Acts conferring jurisdiction upon it, there are sufficient courts of general jurisdiction that it can be presumed that an individual with a legal problem can access a court to have it resolved.

To rebut the presumption, Parliament must expressly provide for a different forum to exercise jurisdiction over disputes coming before it. In doing so, Parliament is charging the nominated body with the responsibility of applying the legislation in specific case situations. This can only occur where Parliament has the power to confer such a responsibility, and in practice it is only intermediate in the sense there are avenues for appeal back to the courts.

For example a person whose visa is refused or cancelled does not, under the *Migration Act 1958* (Cth), have a right to appeal the decision directly in a court. The legislation expressly provides for a system of merits review, under which an independent body reviews the decision and, if necessary, alters it. In the case of visa refusal or cancellation, it is the Migration Review Tribunal (MRT), and in the case of a refusal to accord an asylum seeker refugee status, it is the Refugee Review Tribunal (RRT). Specific provisions make decisions under the Act final, but a matter may proceed to judicial review in the Federal Court, directed not to the merits of the decision but the lawfulness of the process by which the decision was made.

In contractual disputes, parties to a contract containing an arbitration clause may be referred by a court to arbitration under s 8(1) of the *Commercial Arbitration Act 2010* (NSW) which provides:

> A court before which an action is brought in a matter which is the subject of an arbitration agreement must, if a party so requests not later than when submitting the party's first statement on the substance of the dispute, refer the parties to arbitration unless it finds that the agreement is null and void, inoperative or incapable of being performed.

Similarly, s 7(2) of the *International Arbitration Act 1974* (Cth) provides that where court proceedings are instituted by a party to a valid arbitration agreement, the court must order a stay of the proceedings and refer the matter to arbitration. In either case, the court's jurisdiction to hear and determine the substantive matter is taken away by these legislative provisions. However, the court continues to have jurisdiction over matters beyond the arbitral tribunal, such as orders with respect to third parties and enforcement of an arbitral award. Courts may, for example, set aside an arbitral award in circumstances of arbitrator bias or breach of procedural fairness.

Case exercise

'Putting the commission out of commission'

The *Industrial Arbitration (Amendment) Act 1926* (Cth) created an Industrial Commission and gave it the status of a superior court of record with power to issue industrial awards and make determinations with respect to industrial disputes. The Act provided that the Industrial Commission was constituted upon the appointment of three Commissioners by the Governor-General. All three members of the Industrial Commission had be present during all sittings, and they decided by majority. An exception existed where the Industrial Commission delegated a power or function to a single member. If a member was unable to attend to his duties, the Act provided for the Governor-General to appoint someone on a temporary basis to so act.

Section 6(4) of the Act provided for the appointment by the Governor-General of a Deputy Commissioner. The Deputy Commissioner was able to exercise the powers and jurisdiction of the Commission on matters referred to it by the Commission, within limits—the Deputy Commissioner was required to remit a matter to the Commission if a party requested it, could remit any question arising in a matter to the Commission for opinion and direction, and the Commission could vary the Deputy Commissioner's decisions. Therefore the Deputy Commissioner had a role subordinate to the Commission, with jurisdiction limited to matters referred by the Commission.

Assume the Industrial Commission still exists and a member has resigned but the Governor-General has not yet appointed anyone to fill the role. Prior to the member's resignation, a matter was referred to the Deputy Commissioner pursuant to s 6(4). It was an application by the Federated Storemen and Packers Union to vary their award. During the vacancy, the Deputy Commissioner has continued in his role and has commenced a hearing. Although a party objected, the Deputy Commissioner ruled that he had jurisdiction to continue with the hearing.

What do you think? Did the Deputy Commissioner maintain power under the reference, to proceed and continue? Or had his power been suspended from the moment the Commissioner resigned until such time as another Commissioner was appointed?

Decide before proceeding.

The real case is *Magrath v Goldsborough Mort & Co Ltd* (1932) 47 CLR 121. If you decided the Deputy Commissioner could proceed with the hearing, you are in agreement with the Deputy Commissioner (Magrath), the President of the Industrial Commission (Piddington J) and two judges of the High Court, Starke and Evatt JJ. If you decided he could not, you are in agreement with the Full Court of the Supreme Court of New South Wales (Harvey CJ in Eq, Davidson and Milner Stephen JJ) and the majority of the High Court, comprising Rich, Dixon and McTiernan JJ.

Each of the majority prepared an individual judgment, containing similar reasoning. They considered the power of the Deputy Commissioner to be subordinate to, and supervised by, the Commission. The Commission was 'constituted' by three members, and while it did not cease to exist because one member had retired, its powers had fallen into abeyance. As the power was derivative from the Commission, any suspension of the Commission likewise suspended the power of the Deputy Commissioner. To find otherwise would be to convert the Deputy Commissioner's role into one of independence, absolute jurisdiction and final authority. As the Deputy Commissioner's power was suspended, he had no power to determine that he could proceed. Dixon J stated:

> It is, I think, undeniable that the material provisions of the statute proceed upon the assumption that any exercise by the Deputy Commissioner of his jurisdiction in a reference will be subject to the effective control of the Commission by way of appeal and by the remission of questions at the instance of a party for the direction of the Commission. The critical question appears to me to be whether this assumption, which is itself clearly enough exhibited, involves a legislative intention that if the control went into abeyance so should the Deputy's jurisdiction. It may be said that the assumption is sufficiently explained by attributing to the Legislature a belief that the Executive Government would not allow the powers of the Commission to be suspended for any considerable time, and that thus the assumption involves no intention whatever upon the subject. Unfortunately we are required to discover in the provisions of the statute either an intention that the jurisdiction of the Deputy Commissioner should continue notwithstanding the suspension of the Commission's control or an intention that it should not so continue. The form and expression of the provision relating to the Deputy Commissioner as well as the reason of the matter, appear to me altogether in favour of the latter intention ... The grant of a limited and qualified power in derogation of private right necessarily implies an intention that the power shall not be exercisable free of the qualifications and limitations imposed. This must be especially true of a coercive jurisdiction given to a subordinate office subject to the control and revision of a superior tribunal ... The general rule is that statutes are not to be interpreted as depriving superior Courts of power to prevent an unauthorized assumption of jurisdiction unless an intention to do so appears clearly and unmistakably.

Both judges in dissent also wrote individual judgments, applying similar reasoning. They considered that, because the reference was validly made while the Commission comprised three members, the Deputy Commissioner was free to proceed with the matter until such time as a party requested remission to the Commission, the Deputy Commissioner decided to remit a question to the Commission, or a circumstance occurred where the Commission members would sit as assessors. At that point the matter would be resumed once a replacement Commissioner was appointed. Starke J considered it 'so unreasonable and so unnecessary' to suspend the Deputy Commissioner's powers, and Evatt J said that the remission did not have to be to the Commission as originally constituted, so it was quite acceptable for the Deputy Commissioner to proceed as far as was possible, and could validly remit a question to the Commission which could not be disposed of until the vacancy was filled.

Legislation does not bind the Crown

The presumption that legislation does not bind the Crown is based on the separation of powers doctrine. If Parliament wishes legislation to bind the Crown it must usually adopt specific words, such as 'This Act shall bind the Crown', and in assenting to the Act, the Governor is agreeing to the legislation binding the Crown. The presumption evolved at a time when the Crown was far more self-contained than it presently is, and since the government now carries out its role with multitudes of entities, some of them commercial, courts are more willing to displace the presumption by necessary implication as well as where express words appear.

The presumption has been embedded in some Interpretation Acts, such as s 13 of the Queensland Act and s 6(6) of the Tasmanian Act, and reversed in others, such as s 20(1) of the South Australian Act, which has a presumption in favour of legislation binding the Crown. There has also been judicial comment to the effect that the presumption should be reworded. In *Commonwealth v Western Australia* (1999) 196 CLR 392, Gleeson CJ and Gaudron J said at [33]:

> It would be preferable, in our view, and more consonant with our constitutional arrangements, if the presumption that a statute 'does not bind the Crown' were expressed as a presumption that a statute which regulates the conduct or rights of individuals does not apply to members of the executive government ... we shall refer to that presumption as the presumption that legislation does not apply to members of the executive government.

Case exercise

'A frustrating turn of events'

A developer has 19 acres of land in Brisbane that it wants to subdivide for residential lots. After lengthy negotiation with Council, an agreement was reached whereby Council would apply for the land to be rezoned for residential development, and the developer would pave roads, plant trees, install kerbs, channels, footpaths, a bridge, electricity reticulation and sewerage and water mains. Council has applied and obtained rezoning of the land as in the agreement. However, the developer has received notice of resumption of the land by the Crown for the purpose of constructing a school.

The Council considers that it has done its part of the bargain, and the developer must do likewise. The developer is seeking a declaration from the court that the agreement is not binding due to frustration as a result of the Crown's compulsory acquisition of the land. The developer argues that, as the Crown is not bound by legislation, the rezoning has no effect on it, and therefore the Council has not, and cannot, complete its part of the agreement.

Section 13 of the *Acts Interpretation Act 1954–1977* (Qld) restates the common law presumption: 'No Act hereafter passed shall be binding on the Crown or derogate from any prerogative right of the Crown unless express words are included therein for that purpose'.

The *City of Brisbane Town Planning Act, 1964–76* (Qld) does not have a provision saying the Act binds the Crown, but s 4(1) of the Act states that the Town Plan 'shall have the force of law and be binding upon and be obeyed by Brisbane City Council and all persons whomsoever accordingly'. Council argues that the Crown comes within the definition of 'all persons' and is thereby bound by the legislation.

What do you think? Is the Act binding on the Crown? Decide before proceeding.

The real case is *Brisbane City Council v Group Projects Pty Ltd* (1979) 145 CLR 143. Group Projects obtained a declaration from the Supreme Court of Queensland that the agreement was not binding due to frustration. The Council's appeal to the Full Court was unanimously dismissed, as was the High Court appeal. Wilson J stated at [13]:

> The common law principle is not in doubt. It is that, as a matter of construction, a statute does not bind the Crown unless an intention that the Crown be bound appears either expressly or by necessary implication from the words of the statute. The test of necessary implication is not easily satisfied. It must be manifest, from the very terms of the statute, that it was the intention of the legislature that the Crown should be bound.

The reference to 'all persons' was insufficient to bind the Crown. In any event, subordinate legislation is *ultra vires* if it attempts to extend beyond the scope of the Act, such as to extend the operation of an Act to the Crown. As the Crown owned the land at the time of rezoning, and the Plan did not apply to the Crown, the rezoning did not so apply.

Conversely, in *Bropho v Western Australia* (1990) 171 CLR 1 an Act was held to bind the Crown even though there was no expression provision to that effect in the

Aboriginal Heritage Act 1972 (WA). In that case Robert Bropho sought a declaration that land on which the Swan Brewery was situated was an Aboriginal site and no excavating or erecting buildings could be done. The trial judge struck out the statement of claim on the basis that the Act did not bind the Crown. An appeal to the Full Court of the Supreme Court was likewise dismissed. The High Court allowed the appeal. The majority stated at [15]–[19]:

> [H]istorical considerations which gave rise to a presumption that the legislature would not have intended that a statute bind the Crown are largely inapplicable to conditions in this country where the activities of the executive government reach into almost all aspects of commercial, industrial and developmental endeavour and ... compete and have commercial dealings on the same basis as private enterprise.
>
> [O]nce it is accepted that a legislative intention to bind the Crown may be disclosed notwithstanding that it could not be said that that intention was 'manifest from the very terms' of the statute or that the purpose of the statute would otherwise be 'wholly frustrated', fundamental principle precludes confinement of the general words which the legislature has used in a way which will defeat that intention. Such a legislative intent must, of course, be found in the provisions of the statute—including its subject matter and disclosed purpose and policy—when construed in a context which includes permissible extrinsic aids. If such a legislative intent does appear from the provisions of a statute when so construed, it must necessarily prevail over any judge-made rule of statutory construction including the rule relating to statutes binding the Crown.
>
> The effect of the foregoing is not to overturn the settled construction ... Nor is it to reverse or abolish the presumption ... It is simply to recognise that a stringent and rigid test ... is unacceptable.

Brennan J stated at [5]–[6] of his judgment:

> To read down s 17 to exclude Crown lands would enviscerate the Act, for 93% of the State is Crown land and 50% of the State is vacant Crown land ... it would be a legal fiction to impute to the legislatures of this country or to their parliamentary counsel an intention fluctuating with the changing formulations of the presumption by the courts of this country and of England. The question whether the Crown is bound by a statute arises ordinarily in reference to statutes enacted without conscious animadversion to the strength of the presumption.

In essence, the statutory mandate to interpret provisions in the light of their context and purpose will override this presumption, where an intention can be discerned to do so, regardless of whether there is an express provision to bind the Crown.

Legislation enacting a word or phrase approves of its common law interpretation

Certain words and phrases have, across a progression of common law decisions, developed an agreed, common law meaning, or an agreed test to establish whether acts reach a threshold or satisfy a condition. Take for example expressions such as 'reasonableness', 'actual or ostensible', 'substantial', 'significant', and 'necessary implication'. Where such words or phrases, which have accepted meanings at common law, are used in legislation without being expressly defined, courts will presume Parliament intended the common law meaning or methodology for interpretation to be applied.

In South Australia this presumption has been abrogated expressly by s 18 of the *Acts Interpretation Act 1915* (SA) which provides:

> The enactment or re-enactment of a provision that has been construed in a particular manner (judicially or otherwise) in this State or elsewhere creates no presumption that Parliament has sanctioned or approved of that construction.

The High Court unanimously applied the presumption in *Re Alcan Australia Ltd; Ex parte Federation of Industrial, Manufacturing & Engineering Employees* (1994) 181 CLR 96. There, a Federation representing aluminium employees demanded that Alcan deduct union dues from employee wages upon request of the employee. A similar action had previously been brought in *R v Portus; Ex parte ANZ Banking Group Ltd* (1972) 127 CLR 353, where the High Court held that it was not an 'industrial dispute' as it was not 'a matter pertaining to the relations of employers and employees'. Some years after this decision, the *Industrial Relations Act 1988* (Cth) was passed defining 'industrial dispute' in s 4(1) as a dispute 'that is about matters pertaining to the relationship between employers and employees'. The High Court stated in *Alcan* at [20]:

> Parliament re-enacted, in s 4(1) of the Act, words which are almost identical with those considered in *Reg. v Portus*. There is abundant authority for the proposition that where the Parliament repeats words which have been judicially construed, it is taken to have intended the words to bear the meaning already 'judicially attributed to (them)' ... although the validity of that proposition has been questioned ... the presumption is considerably strengthened in the present case by the legislative history of the Act ... [which serves to] reinforce the presumption that Parliament did not intend to overturn *Reg. v. Portus*.

In practice, the same result can be achieved through the standard application of the modern statutory approach—the court can, having considered the context and purpose (including prior judicial decisions as part of the extrinsic context), determine whether it was intended that the common law meaning or another meaning was to apply.

Penal provisions are strictly construed

Legislation creating a penalty will, in circumstances of ambiguity, be construed strictly in favour of the accused person. The rationale is that, given the imbalance of resources and power between the individual and the state, a person should not be subject to deprivation of personal liberty or the payment of a significant fine on the basis of an unclear legislative requirement to that effect. The focus here is not necessarily on the statute as a whole, which may have various provisions relating to rights, obligations and penalties—the question is whether a particular provision has a penal effect. Some provisions will do both simultaneously, such as creating a right for disabled people not to be discriminated against in the workforce at the same time as creating a penalty for employers that breach the provision.

There has been some criticism of the presumption, with Gibbs J in *Beckwith v R* (1976) 135 CLR 569 saying:

> The rule formerly accepted, that statutes creating offences are to be strictly construed, has lost much of its importance in modern times. In determining the meaning of a penal statute the ordinary rules of construction must be applied, but if the language of the statute remains ambiguous or doubtful the ambiguity or doubt may be resolved in favour of the subject by refusing to extend the category of criminal offences ... the rule is perhaps one of last resort.

This was prior to the enactment of the Commonwealth Act, which has further reduced reliance on the presumption. The modern statutory approach allows consideration of whether it was intended, given the context and purpose, and often this will align with the application of the presumption. Take for example *George v Rockett* (1990) 170 CLR 104 at 487: 'To insist on strict compliance with the statutory conditions governing the issue of search warrants is simply to give effect to the purpose of the legislation'.

In *R v Lavender* (2005) 222 CLR 67 at [94] Kirby J stated:

> [T] he legislature would normally be obliged to spell out with sufficient clarity the conduct that attracts criminal liability ... Courts have now relinquished the power to create new categories of criminal offences. Interpreting penal statutes narrowly preserves this power exclusively for the legislature ... the principle suggesting a stricter approach to

> the interpretation of penal legislation may sometimes prove useful when ambiguity seems intractable.

Spigelman CJ believes we should not use the language 'strict construction' because '[i]t breaches ... constitutional courtesies ... It suggests that courts give a restricted interpretation to the language of Parliament, and do so irrespective of the intention of Parliament'.[5]

Remedial or beneficial provisions are broadly construed

Just as the presumption regarding penal provisions tends, in circumstances of ambiguity at least, towards the lesser impact on the individual, the presumption regarding remedial or beneficial statutes tends towards the greater benefit to the individual.[6] Examples include statutes providing for social welfare benefits or pension entitlements, covering occupational health and safety and workers' compensation. This presumption has no work to do if the provision is clear—it is only where there is an ambiguity, or where there is more than one interpretation that is open given the context and purpose, that an interpretation promoting the liberty of the individual is favoured.

The discussion of this presumption by Kirby J in *Minister Administering the Crown Lands Act v NSW Aboriginal Land Council* [2008] HCA 48 is illustrative:

> A sub-species of this context and purpose rule is a principle of interpretation that arises where a contested text appears in a statute that has an apparently beneficial or remedial purpose. Where different literal interpretations of such a text appear to be available to the decision-maker, it is valid, and sometimes helpful, to identify the beneficial or remedial purpose discerned. The decision-maker should then endeavour (so far as the text allows) to adopt a construction that advances that purpose in preference to one that would frustrate or diminish the attainment of the apparently intended benefits and reforms ... This beneficial or remedial reading principle is by no means new. It simply re-expresses, in the current age of enlarged legislation, a very old canon of interpretation that enjoins decision-makers to address the 'mischief' perceived in the legislation.

The case exercise on page 129 titled 'It's ramshackle and derelict but we're still using it' is on this case. Kirby J referred to the beneficial purpose of the *Aboriginal Land*

---

5 J J Spigelman, 'The Principles of Legality and Clear Statement', in *Statutory Interpretation: Principles and Pragmatism for a New Age* (Judicial Commission of New South Wales, 2007, 13 at 27.

6 Pearce and Geddes have identified a list of areas in which beneficial legislation exists, see D Pearce and R Geddes, *Statutory Interpretation in Australia* (LexisNexis, 7th ed, 2011) 292–4.

Rights Act 1983 (NSW). The word 'use' is ambiguous, as it could cover any use (such as preparing it for sale) or physical use. Given the beneficial and remedial purposes of the Act, Kirby J found that substantive use was required: at [30].

Taxation provisions construed to the taxpayer's benefit

As with the penal and beneficial provisions, it has been considered that ambiguities in taxation legislation should be construed in the taxpayer's favour. A person should only be required to pay tax where the provision creating the obligation does so clearly.

This presumption has diminished importance under the modern statutory approach, where the overriding consideration is to achieve the intention of the legislature through an examination of the text in the light of its context and purpose. It may be clear from the context what a particular provision was expecting to cover, even if on its face there is ambiguity, in which case there is no need to resort to the presumption. As stated by Brazil, 'no court has suggested that reliance on extrinsic materials to resolve ambiguities is ruled out by the view that taxing Acts should be construed strictly in favour of the taxpayer'.[7]

Section 14A(3) of the Queensland Act, which enacts the 'best achievement' formulation of the purposive approach, expressly overrides this presumption:

> To remove any doubt, it is declared that this section applies to an Act passed after 30 June 1991 despite any presumption or rule of interpretation.
>
> Example—
>
> There is judicial authority for a rule of interpretation that taxing legislation is to be interpreted strictly and in a taxpayer's favour (for example, see *Partington v AG* (1869) LR 4 HL 100 at 122). Despite such a possible rule, this section requires a provision imposing taxation to be interpreted in the way that best achieves the Act's purpose, whether or not to do so would be in a taxpayer's favour.

In *Cooper Brookes (Wollongong) Pty Ltd v Federal Commissioner of Taxation* (1981) 147 CLR 297 at 323, Mason and Wilson JJ stated that 'The fact that the Act is a taxing statute does not make it immune to the general principles governing the interpretation

7 P Brazil, 'Reform of Statutory Interpretation—the Australian Experience of Use of Extrinsic Materials: With a Postscript on Simpler Drafting', Address to Law Commission Legislation Seminar, National Library Auditorium, Wellington, 18–19 March 1988, published in (1988) 62 ALJ 503, 507.

of statutes'. Gleeson CJ has gone further, saying that 'there was a time, now gone' when a strict and narrow interpretation was given to taxing Acts.[8] This overstates the true position, which is that, while the presumption has diminished importance and the key approach is to apply the normal principles of textual, contextual and purposive interpretation, if an ambiguity remains, courts may fall back on the presumption. Of course this will not apply if there is a statutory formulation that the presumption not apply—see for example McHugh J in *Commissioner of Taxation v Linter Textiles Australia Ltd (In Liq)* (2005) 220 CLR 592 at [159]:

> Two important amendments were effected by the 1973 Act. First, s 80A(3)(a) could be applied to the advantage of the Commissioner while its predecessor section applied only to the advantage of the taxpayer. The significance of this amendment is that a court should not approach the construction of the section with any presumption against a construction that favours the Commissioner.

Legislation does not remove property rights

There is a presumption that Parliament does not intend to interfere with vested property rights, and may do so only by the use of 'unequivocal terms incapable of any other meaning'.[9] This has been described by Kirby J in *Wilson v Anderson* (2002) 213 CLR 401 at [140]:

> It is an old, wise and beneficial presumption, long obeyed, that to take away people's rights, Parliament must use clear language. The basic human right to own property and to be immune from arbitrary dispossession of property is one generally respected by Australian lawmakers.

A recent example is *Mandurah Enterprises Pty Ltd v Western Australian Planning Commission* (2010) 240 CLR 409, which concerned the compulsory acquisition of private land adjacent to the construction of the Perth to Mandurah railway. Part 9 of the *Land Administration Act 1997* (WA) provides the acquisition of land for the 'purposes of the public work'. Not all of the land was used for the public work of constructing a railway. The majority, comprising French CJ, Gummow, Crennan and Bell JJ, stated that the legislative provisions 'raise questions of statutory interpretation to be assessed

8 M Gleeson, 'The Meaning of Legislation: Context, Purpose and Respect for Fundamental Rights' Address to Victoria Law Foundation, Melbourne, 31 July 2008, 20.

9 *Commonwealth v Hazeldell Ltd* (1918) 25 CLR 552 per Griffith CJ and Rich J at 563.

by reference to the statutory presumption against an intention to interfere with vested property rights'. They held that the acquisition was invalid in relation to those portions of land which were not used for the public purpose of railway construction.

Similarly, in *R & R Fazzolari Pty Limited v Parramatta City Council* (2009) 237 CLR 603 an effort by the Crown to resume two parcels of private land was invalidated by the High Court on the basis that, while part of the overall planned construction was for Council offices, the plan involved the transfer of the land to a developer, Grocon, which would make a profit from the development. The applicable legislation, the *Local Government Act 1993* (NSW), provided that a Council could acquire land 'for the purpose of exercising any of its functions' but s 188(1) stated that it could not acquire land by compulsory process if the land was 'acquired for the purpose of re-sale'. French CJ referred to the presumption at [42]–[43]:

> The presumption has been restated on more than one occasion in this Court ... As a practical matter it means that, where a statute is capable of more than one construction, that construction will be chosen which interferes least with private property rights. That approach resembles and may even be seen as an aspect of the general principle that statutes are construed, where constructional choices are open, so that they do not encroach upon fundamental rights and freedoms at common law.

A full discussion of the statutory presumption against interference with fundamental rights is found in the next chapter.

The statutory presumption has also been applied in the area of native title—native title is taken not to have been extinguished by legislation unless there is a clear and plain intent that it should have that effect.[10] It is specifically embedded in s 13A of the WA Act, which provides that Acts will not affect native title except by express provision. This presumption applies to legislation which pre-dates the recognition of native title in *Mabo v Queensland (No. 2)* (1992) 175 CLR 1. Sean Brennan has said that 'the approach of the High Court to statutory interpretation has become a focal point in defining the relationship between indigenous peoples and the wider Australian community'.[11]

Other statutory presumptions

Presumptions are organic, in the sense that new presumptions may be recognised by the courts, just as old presumptions fall into disuse. Some old presumptions go from

10 R French, 'The Constitution and the Protection of Human Rights', Speech given at Australian National University, 20 November 2009, www.ecu.edu.au/about-ecu/vice-chancellor/distinguished-orator/the-constitution-and-the-protection-of-human-rights (13 June 2011).

11 S Brennan, 'Statutory Interpretation and Indigenous Property Rights' (2010) 21PLR 239 at 239.

strength to strength, and some new presumptions, while being identified by one court, are not taken up by others. Other statutory presumptions include:

- A legislature would not alter a statute that forms part of a collaborative and uniform national scheme, save in express terms: *R v Porter* (2001) 53 NSWLR 354 at [59];
- The Crown does not have a right of appeal, such that where a State loses a case against a private person it should not have the right to appeal that decision: *Bond v R* (2000) 201 CLR 213;
- Parliament does not intend to interfere with equality of religion: *Canterbury Municipal Council v Moslem Alawy Society Ltd* [1985] 1 NSWLR 525 per McHugh J at 544;
- Parliament does not intend to interfere with other fundamental rights: see Chapter 11;
- Every offence must contain *mens rea*, which is imputed even where it is not specifically stated: *Hogan v Hinch* [2011] HCA 4 (discussed in Chapter 11); and
- Parliament intends to legislate in conformity with international law (see Chapter 12).

It must be remembered that all statutory presumptions are rebuttable, so if the operation of a presumption would be incompatible with the purpose and context of an Act, the presumption cannot prevail.

CHAPTER 11

FUNDAMENTAL AND HUMAN RIGHTS

This chapter covers a statutory presumption regarding fundamental rights, and a statutory embedding of human rights (in Victoria and the ACT). There are significant connections to international law, but, given their importance, these are covered separately in the next chapter.

Non-interference with fundamental rights

The strongest statutory presumption is that legislation cannot, in the absence of clear words, abrogate fundamental rights. The judiciary will protect individual rights against legislative incursion in all cases except where the legislature makes express use of their power to do so. Spigelman CJ has gone so far as to say that 'The protection which the common law affords to the preservation of fundamental rights and liberties is, to a large extent, secreted within the law of statutory interpretation'.[1]

This has been referred to as a manifestation of the 'principle of legality'[2]—individuals are bound by the law but are otherwise free to determine how they live their lives and to enjoy fundamental rights and freedoms.[3] Government action against an individual should be according to law, and follow the procedures laid down by the law. So the principle of legality is in turn a manifestation of the rule of law and is based on notions of justice and fairness. To be fair, laws should not generally be retroactive, should not apply only to certain groups within society, and should only be made by those democratically elected by the people. In that sense many of the principles under the umbrella principle of legality are quasi-constitutional—they 'reflect fundamental assumptions about the relationship between the citizen and the state'.[4] According to Sean Brennan, in applying the principle of legality 'the judiciary nudges the legal system and the elected branches of government in the direction of rights protection'.[5]

The principle of legality has recently been used to limit the scope of a court's discretion, such that 'unfettered' does not actually mean without limits. The case is *Lacey v Attorney-General of Queensland* [2011] HCA 10, which concerned the power of a court under s 669A(1)(b) of the *Criminal Code* (Qld), on appeal from a criminal

---

1 J J Spigelman, 'The Principle of Legality and the Clear Statement Principle' (2005) 79 *Australian Law Journal* 769, 769; J J Spigelman, 'Statutory Interpretation: Identifying the Linguistic Register', Sir Ninian Stephen Lecture, 23 March 1999, 2.

2 J J Spigelman, 'The Principle of Legality and the Clear Statement Principle' (2005) 79 *Australian Law Journal* 769.

3 J J Spigelman, *Statutory Interpretation and Human Rights*, The MacPherson Lecture Series, Vol 3 (2008) 87.

4 Ibid at 56.

5 S Brennan, 'Statutory Interpretation and Indigenous Property Rights' (2010) 21 *PLR* 239 at 240.

sentence, to 'in its unfettered discretion vary the sentence and impose such sentence as the Court seems proper'. It was held in a majority joint judgment of members of the High Court that 'unfettered discretion' did not literally mean fully unrestricted; it was limited by the principle of legality which, so applied, 'required demonstration of an error of principle or the imposition of a manifestly excessive or inadequate sentence by the sentencing judge': at [24]. It could not be inferred that Parliament intended 'simply to plant a wilderness of single instances with more instances of its own choosing' at [55]. Therefore, before the 'unfettered discretion' arises in the hands of the appeal court, there must first be a demonstrable error on the part of the sentencing judge.

Application of the presumption to common law rights

An important distinction must be made here. Historically, there was a presumption that statutes do not interfere with the common law in totality, not just with fundamental rights. The main source of law was common law, and statutes were greeted by courts as intrusions to the common law.[6] Such a presumption holds no sway today, where a large proportion of our law is based in statute. So the important distinction is between common law rights generally (such as contract or tort), and fundamental rights. It is only the latter to which the presumption against abrogation applies. In *Malika Holdings Pty Ltd v Stretton* (2001) 204 CLR 290 at 298–9 McHugh J cautioned that 'care needs to be taken in declaring a principle to be fundamental'. The High Court said in *Bropho v Western Australia* (1990) 171 CLR 1 per Mason CJ, Deane, Dawson, Toohey, Gaudron and McHugh JJ at [13] that 'if what was previously accepted as a fundamental principle or fundamental right ceases to be so regarded, the presumption that the legislature would have have intended to depart from that principle or to abolish or modify that right will necessarily be undermined and may well disappear'.

In *Gifford v Strang Patrick Stevedoring Pty Ltd* (2003) 214 CLR 269, where the children of a father killed in a workplace accident sued the employer for their psychiatric injury, Mc Hugh J held at [36]–[37] that the right to bring an action for psychiatric injury is not a fundamental right so it does not attract the presumption:

> The presumption of non-interference is strong when the right is a fundamental right of our legal system; it is weak when the right is merely one to take or not take a particular course of action. Courts should not cut down the natural and ordinary meaning of legislation evincing an intention to interfere with these lesser rights by relying on a presumption that the legislature did not intend to interfere with them. Given the frequency with which legislatures now abolish or amend 'ordinary' common law rights, the 'presumption' of

6 See *R v Janceski* (2005) 64 NSWLR 10 per Spigelman CJ at [62].

> non-interference with those rights is inconsistent with modern experience and borders on fiction ... The right to bring an action for psychiatric injury is an ordinary legal right. It is not a fundamental right of our society or legal system similar to the right to have a fair trial or to have a criminal charge proved beyond a reasonable doubt.

The challenge is that some common law rights may be significant enough to warrant being considered fundamental. Therefore one must, before seeking to apply the presumption, look to see whether a court has declared a relevant right to be a fundamental right. Also, as pointed out by Spigelman CJ, the focus is less on the nature of the right or freedom that is violated, but on the 'extent of the intrusion'.[7] He quotes the Full Federal Court in *Minister for Immigration and Multicultural and Indigenous Affairs v Al Masri* (2003) 197 ALR 241 at [92]:

> In considering the application of the principle of construction it is appropriate to take into account not only the fundamental nature of the right that may be abrogated or curtailed, but also the extent to which, depending upon the construction adopted, that may occur. Although all interferences with personal liberty are serious in the eyes of the common law, it may be said that the more serious the interference with liberty, the clearer the expression of intention to bring about that interference must be.

Case exercise

'This is a corrupt police officer'

Patrick headed to Flinders Street mall in Townsville, Queensland and commenced heckling and distributing pamphlets headed 'GET TO KNOW YOUR LOCAL CORRUPT TYPE COPS', listing charges of corruption against several police officers. He said the following, concerning on particular officer:

> Ah ha! Constable Brendan Power and his mates, this one was a beauty—sitting outside the mall police beat in protest at an unlawful arrest—with simple placards saying TOWNSVILLE COPS—A GOOD ARGUMENT FOR A BILL OF RIGHTS—AND DEAR MAYOR—BITE ME—AND TOWNSVILLE CITY COUNCIL THE ENEMY OF FREE SPEECH—the person was saying nothing just sitting there talking to an old lady then BAMMM arrested dragged inside and detained ... boys boys boys, I got witnesses so KISS MY ARSE YOU SLIMY LYING BASTARDS.

When Constable Power approached Patrick he sang out 'This is Constable Brendan Power a corrupt police officer'. Patrick was charged with a public order offence pursuant to

7 J J Spigelman, 'The Principles of Legality and Clear Statement', in *Statutory Interpretation: Principles and Pragmatism for a New Age*, Judicial Commission of New South Wales, 2007, 13 at 30.

s 7(1)(d) of the *Vagrants, Gambling and Other Offences Act 1931* (Qld) which provided in relevant part:

> Any person who, in any public place or so near to any public place that any person who might be therein, and whether any person is therein or not, could view or hear—…
>
> (d) uses any threatening, abusive, or insulting words to any person …
>
> shall be liable to a penalty of $100 or to imprisonment for 6 months.

Patrick argued that the statute was invalid in its application to his actions because that would breach his rights to freedom of speech on political matters. What do you think? Has Patrick used 'insulting words'? Were they 'to a person' in a 'public place'? Does it make any difference that Patrick said 'This is Constable Brendan Power a corrupt police officer' rather than 'You are a corrupt police officer'? Public order offences are based on concern that they may provoke a response which may breach the peace. Can a public order offence be constituted where there is no realistic possibility that the person insulted might respond in a manner that would breach the peace (assuming that a police officer would not retaliate)? Is Patrick guilty under s 7(1)(d)?

Decide before proceeding.

The real case is *Coleman v Power* (2004) 220 CLR 1. If you decided Patrick Coleman was in breach of the provision, you were in agreement with the Townsville Magistrates Court and the High Court majority comprising McHugh, Gummow, Hayne and Kirby JJ. If you decided he was not, you are in agreement with the Court of Appeal of the Supreme Court of Queensland and Gleeson CJ, Callinan and Heydon JJ.

Each judge in the majority used the presumption, identifying free speech as a fundamental right. This meant that the provision had to be read as 'narrowly limited' (at [188]). The purpose of the legislation is to keep public places free from violence, and as police officers, as a result of their 'training and temperament' (Gummow and Hayne JJ at [188]) 'are expected to be thick skinned and broad shouldered' (Kirby J at [258]), the police officer will not physically retaliate, so there could not be a threatened breach of the peace resulting from Patrick's conduct, and his right to free speech should not be restricted by the Act. Kirby J predicted at [249]:

> The use of the interpretive principle that I have explained will become more common in the future than it has been in the past … Reading contemporary law by reference to a presumed compliance with the principles of human rights and fundamental freedoms, stated in international law binding upon Australia, will be viewed as orthodox. In statutory construction, as in much else in the law, orthodoxies are constantly being altered. This Court must keep pace with such changes in doctrine, not rest on its legal laurels.

Case exercise

'Hush now, people are listening'

Since Santo allowed access to his office to persons impersonating Telecom officers in attendance to investigate a fault, Santo's conversations have been 'bugged'. He was charged with an offence of offering a bribe to a Commonwealth officer, and recordings were used to convict him. He has appealed claiming that the evidence was inadmissible.

Section 43 of the *Invasion of Privacy Act 1971* (Qld) provides, in relevant part:

> (1) A person is guilty of an offence against this Act if he uses a listening device to overhear, record, monitor or listen to a private conversation and is liable on conviction on indictment to a penalty not exceeding $2000 or to imprisonment for not more than two years or to both such penalty and imprisonment.
>
> (2) Subsection (1) of this section does not apply ... (c) to or in relation to the use of any listening device by (i) a member of the police force acting in the performance of his duty if he has been authorized in writing to use a listening device by (a) the Commissioner of Police ... under and in accordance with an approval in writing given by a judge of the Supreme Court in relation to any particular matter specified in the approval ...

Section 46 of the Act provides that a private conversation recorded in breach of s 43 may not be used as evidence in any court proceedings.

A month before the listening devices were installed, a judge of the Supreme Court approved the use of listening devices in relation to the investigation. It also authorised trespass onto premises for installation, maintenance and retrieval of the devices.

Did the judge have power, under the legislation, to authorise trespass onto Santo's property? Has he exceeded his jurisdiction, or can it be said by necessary implication that the power to authorise the use of listening devices must include authorising their installation? Note that the listening devices used over 200 hours of Santo's electricity to record his conversations.

Decide before proceeding.

The real case is *Coco v R* (1994) 179 CLR 427. If you decided Santo Coco was correctly convicted and the installation and use of the bugs was legal, then you are in agreement with the trial judge and the Court of Appeal of Queensland. If you decided the conviction should be quashed and a new trial ordered, without the evidence being admitted, you are in agreement with the entire High Court.

The High Court held that the judge misconstrued the statute and acted *ultra vires*. They noted the absence in s 43 of express words conferring power on a court to authorise trespass, as distinct from breach of privacy. Given the fundamental nature of trespass, an intention to interfere with the right against trespass could not be implied: 'Statutory authority to engage in what otherwise would be tortious conduct must be clearly expressed in unmistakable and unambiguous language': per Mason CJ, Brennan, Gaudron and McHugh JJ at [8]. They went on to state at [10]–[12]:

> The insistence on express authorization of an abrogation or curtailment of a fundamental right, freedom or immunity must be understood as a requirement for some manifestation or indication that the legislature has not only directed its attention to the question of the abrogation or curtailment of such basic rights, freedoms or immunities but has also determined upon abrogation or curtailment of them ... General words will rarely be sufficient for that purpose if they do not specifically deal with the question because, in the context in which they appear, they will often be ambiguous on the aspect of interference with fundamental rights ... curial insistence on a clear expression of an unmistakable and unambiguous intention to abrogate or curtail a fundamental freedom will enhance the parliamentary process by securing a greater measure of attention to the impact of legislative proposals on fundamental rights.

They left open that the presumption may be displaced by necessary implication 'if it is necessary to prevent the statutory provision from becoming inoperative or meaningless': at [13]. Toohey J concurred with the main judgment, adding that 'it is difficult to conceive that the abstraction of electricity over a period of almost 200 hours could amount to anything other than a substantial trespass' at [34].

The above two case exercises demonstrate that fundamental rights include free speech (*Coleman v Power* (2004) 220 CLR 1) and rights against trespass (*Coco v R* (1994) 179 CLR 427). Other fundamental rights have been recognised by the courts—see for example *Malika Holdings Pty Ltd v Stretton* (2001) 204 CLR 290 per McHugh J at [28]:

> No doubt there are fundamental legal principles—a civil or criminal trial is to be a fair trial, a criminal charge is to be proved beyond reasonable doubt, people are not to be arrested or searched arbitrarily, laws, especially criminal laws, do not operate retrospectively, superior courts have jurisdiction to prevent unauthorised assumptions of jurisdiction by inferior courts and tribunals are examples.

Other fundamental rights include:[8]

- The right to personal liberty (see the case exercise in Chapter 8 titled 'American soldier goes AWOL', regarding *Re Bolton; Ex parte Beane* (1987) 162 CLR 514);

8 Several of these have been taken from a list provided in J J Spigelman, *Statutory Interpretation and Human Rights*, The MacPherson Lecture Series, Vol 3 (2008) 29, and J J Spigelman, 'The Principle of Legality and the Clear Statement Principle' (2005) 79 *Australian Law Journal* 769, 775.

- The right against interference with freedom of movement (see for example *Commonwealth v Progress Advertising & Press Agency Co Pty Ltd* (1910) 10 CLR 457);
- The right against retrospective application of substantive (but not procedural) laws (see for example *Rodway v R* (1990) 169 CLR 515, discussed on page 187);
- The right to a fair trial (see *Malika Holdings Pty Ltd v Stretton* (2001) 204 CLR 290 per McHugh J at [28]) including procedural fairness: (see *Gypsy Jokers Motorcycle Club Inc v Commissioner of Police* (2008) 234 CLR 532);
- The right to silence to avoid self-incrimination (see for example *Corporate Affairs Commission (NSW) v Yuill* (1991) 172 CLR 319, and see an example of rebuttal by necessary implication in *Pyneboard Pty Ltd v Trade Practices Commission* (1983) 152 CLR 328);
- The right to keep lawyer–client communications private (see *Daniels Corp International Pty Ltd v Australian Competition and Consumer Commission* (2002) 213 CLR 543, but note that displacing the privilege against self-incrimination does not necessarily rebut legal professional privilege: see also s 171 of the ACT Act);
- The right of both individuals and companies to own and control property (see *R & R Fazzolari Pty Limited v Parramatta City Council* (2009) 237 CLR 603 on page 203, and in relation to companies see *DPP v Logan Park Investments Pty Ltd* (1995) 37 NSWLR 118 per Kirby ACJ at 125, describing it as 'an important civic right', and 'an attribute of economic liberty').

According to Sean Brennan, 'the application of these protective principles has been fitful rather than consistent'.[9] One of the key problems is that the notion of ambiguity is itself ambiguous—where one person sees doubt, another sees certainty.[10]

Case exercise

'Stateless and placeless'

Ahmed has been held in executive detention as a 'boat person' for over three years. He was born in Kuwait to Palestinian parents, and came to Australia at the age of 26 without a visa or passport. He was refused a protection visa and his applications for review were unsuccessful. Two years into his detention he applied in writing to be removed from Australia. The problem is

9 S Brennan, 'Statutory Interpretation and Indigenous Property Rights' (2010) 21 *PLR* 239 at 253.

10 J J Spigleman 'Statutory Interpretation: Identifying the Linguistic Register' (1999) 4(1) *Newcastle Law Review* 1 at 2: 'The word ambiguity is often used in the more general sense to indicate any situation in which the scope and applicability of a particular statute is, for whatever reason, doubtful'.

that, given Iraqi developments in Kuwait and Israeli developments in Gaza, he is not accepted in either place, rendering him stateless—without nationality—so there is nowhere to send him.

What should be done in this situation? Can he be held in detention for the rest of his life? The applicable law, in the *Migration Act 1958* (Cth) does not appear to contemplate the situation—the legislature appears to have assumed that everyone has somewhere to be sent. It provides in relevant parts:

> (189) (1) If an officer knows or reasonably suspects that a person in the migration zone (other than an excised offshore place) is an unlawful non-citizen, the officer must detain the person.
>
> (196) (1) An unlawful non-citizen detained under section 189 must be kept in immigration detention until he or she is:
> (a) removed from Australia under section 198 or 199; or
> (b) deported under section 200; or
> (c) granted a visa ...
>
> (198) (1) An officer must remove as soon as reasonably practicable an unlawful non-citizen who asks the Minister, in writing, to be so removed....
> (6) An officer must remove as soon as reasonably practicable an unlawful non-citizen if:
> (a) the non-citizen is a detainee; and
> (b) the non-citizen made a valid application for a substantive visa that can be granted when the applicant is in the migration zone; and...
> (c) (i) the grant of the visa has been refused and the application has been finally determined;... and
> (d) the non-citizen has not made any other valid application ...

Decide before proceeding.

The real case is *Al-Kateb v Godwin* (2004) 219 CLR 562. If you decided he could be detained indefinitely you are in agreement with McHugh, Hayne, Callinan and Heydon JJ. If you decided he could not, you are in agreement with Gleeson CJ, Gummow and Kirby JJ.

The majority essentially acknowledged the presumption that Parliament did not intend to interfere with the fundamental right to freedom but said that the legislation abrogated that right using terminology which was clear, unambiguous and retractable, so detention must continue until deportation, however unlikely that may be.

The minority prepared three individual judgments. It was considered that the purpose of s 196 was removal, and once it was clear a person could not be deported, he could not be held 'for the purpose' of deportation. Ongoing detention was therefore not 'lawful detention'. Gleeson CJ was not convinced that the language was clear, as there was no indication that the legislature had directed its attention to the rights or freedoms in question and decided on abrogation or curtailment. Kirby J invoked the presumption in favour of liberty and against indefinite detention.

Broader discussion: to what extent do you consider differing attitudes towards the judicial task can affect the outcome in cases such as this?

It has been suggested that statutory presumptions, and particularly the presumption against interference with fundamental rights, have the practical effect of a common law bill of rights.[11] Spigelman CJ has stated extra-judicially:[12]

> I use the terminology of 'bill of rights' because it has acquired a level of acceptance by wide usage, and is not yet replaced by 'charter of rights', but it may be ... It may be more accurate to refer to a 'common law bill of principles', but that would not convey the sense of a systematic protection of human rights which is the result, as a matter of practical reality, of those aspects of the law of statutory interpretation which constitute common law protections of human rights.

It is difficult to accept this proposition. A 'bill of rights' is a list of rights and freedoms, housed in a constitution or an Act, by which individuals are protected against government infringement. The strongest bills of rights are entrenched in constitutions, which are more difficult to amend than Acts of Parliament. Fundamental rights recognised at common law are in the same position as a statutory bill of rights—they can be changed through simple legislative action, albeit legislation expressed in clear words. Saying that statutory presumptions amount to a common law bill of rights is akin to saying that palliative care removes the justification for euthanasia. In both instances, there is a risk of clouding much-needed action by a potentially ephemeral substitute.

Human rights

Key international instruments on human rights include:

- Universal Declaration of Human Rights (UDHR);
- International Covenant on Civil and Political Rights (ICCPR);
- International Covenant on Economic, Social and Cultural Rights (ICESCR);
- International Convention for the Elimination of All Forms of Racial Discrimination (CERD);

11 J J Spigelman, *Statutory Interpretation and Human Rights*, The MacPherson Lecture Series, Vol 3 (2008) 23; P Finn, 'Statutes and the Common Law' (1992) 22 University of Western Australia Law Review 7 at 27; D Pearce and R Geddes, *Statutory Interpretation in Australia* (LexisNexis, 7th ed, 2011) 168.

12 J J Spigelman, 'The Common Law Bill of Rights', McPherson Lecture, 2008, University of Queensland, 10 March 2008, http://papers.ssrn.com/sol3/papers.cfm?abstract_id=1806775 (16 October 2011).

- Convention on the Rights of the Child (CROC, or CRC);
- Convention on the Elimination of All Forms of Discrimination Against Women (CEDAW);
- Convention against Torture and Other Cruel, Inhuman or Degrading Treatment or Punishment ('Torture Convention' or CAT); and
- Convention on the Rights of Persons with Disabilities (CRPD).

A challenge is that not all of these instruments contain 'hard' law—some provisions are largely aspirational when they are first settled, and 'crystallise' over a number of years. Many of the rights described in the Universal Declaration of Human Rights fell within this description when the instrument was resolved in the United Nations General Assembly. Some of those rights are now considered fully enforceable.

Human rights have been implemented in Australian law across a number of Acts, including the *Racial Discrimination Act 1975* (Cth), *Age Discrimination Act 2004* (Cth), *Disability Discrimination Act 1992* (Cth), and the *Sex Discrimination Act 1984* (Cth). These Acts are interpreted according to the usual rules as discussed in this book, with the international instrument usually being appended to the Act or at least considered as extrinsic material (see Chapter 12 for a discussion on the use of international law in statutory interpretation). Their importance has been commented on by Kirby J: 'It is essential that judicial officers at every level of the hierarchy, and lawyers of every rank, should familiarise themselves with the advancing international jurisprudence of human rights'.[13] The contra view has been expressed by McHugh J in the *Al Kateb* case at [74]:

> It is not for courts, exercising federal jurisdiction, to determine whether the course taken by Parliament is unjust or contrary to basic human rights. The function of the courts in this context is simply to determine whether the law of the Parliament is within the powers conferred on it by the Constitution. The doctrine of separation of powers does more than prohibit the Parliament and the Executive from exercising the judicial power of the Commonwealth. It prohibits the Ch III courts from amending the Constitution under the guise of interpretation.

Unlike many jurisdictions around the world, Australia does not have a bill of rights. Two Australian jurisdictions have, however, passed their own bills of rights Acts. They are the *Human Rights Act 2004* (ACT) and the *Charter of Human Rights and Responsibilities Act 2006* (Vic).[14] According to Spigelman CJ:[15]

> The most significant statutory change to the law of statutory interpretation is the introduction of the special interpretation provisions in human rights acts, which impose an obligation upon courts to interpret *other* legislation so as to be consistent with the rights set

13 M Kirby, 'The Australian Use of International Human Rights Norms: From Bangalore to Balliol—A View From the Antipodes', (1993) 16(2) *UNSW Law Journal* 363 at 393.

14 There have been moves towards a bill of rights in Western Australia with the Human Rights Bill 2007 but at the time of writing it had not been passed.

15 J J Spigelman, *Statutory Interpretation and Human Rights*, The MacPherson Lecture Series, Vol 3 (2008) 62.

> out in the human rights act. Those rights can be more extensive, or less extensive, than the common law bill of rights ... there is, however, a substantial overlap.

The Acts require a delicate balancing act between what can be legitimate but contradictory human rights—my right to privacy against your right to information, my right to avoid being harassed against your right to freedom of expression, and so on.

The ACT approach

Section 30 of the *Human Rights Act 2004* (ACT) provides:

> So far as it is possible to do so consistently with its purpose, a Territory law must be interpreted in a way that is compatible with human rights.

Section 28 of the Act states that human rights may be subject to reasonable limits that are 'demonstrably justified in a free and democratic society'. The way these provisions apply is still being settled. In the Supreme Court of the ACT, Penfold J stated in *In the matter of an application for bail by Islam* [2010] ACTSC 147 at [2]:

> [Section] 30 of the *Human Rights Act 2004* is an 'ordinary' interpretation provision rather than a 'special' provision or one providing for remedial interpretation ... the ordinary processes of statutory interpretation, including s 30, should be applied in the interpretation of a provision of ACT legislation, with the aim of finding a meaning for a provision that is both human rights-compatible and consistent with purpose, before any attempt is made under s 28 of the *Human Rights Act* to justify a meaning for the provision that is incompatible with human rights.

Case exercise

'Who says I'm not fit to drive?'

Lindsay lives in the ACT and is a licensed driver. Recently he received a letter from the Road Transport Authority (RTA) indicating that he 'may no longer comply with the required medical standards to hold a driver licence'. He had to fill in a Driver Licence Medical Form and attend the Health For Industry office for a medical examination, for which he had to pay $95.00. He completed the formalities and was medically cleared as fit to drive.

Lindsay has found out that the RTA was acting on an email it received, and he wants to know who sent it and what was in it. He was inconvenienced, and is concerned someone is defaming him. His Freedom of Information request was denied by the RTA, relying on s 230(4) of the *Road Transport (General) Act 1999* (ACT), which provides an indemnity to a person who reports to the RTA 'in good faith' that someone is or may be unfit to drive.

Can you use s 30 of the *Human Rights Act 2004* (ACT) to gain access to the email? Does a right to information override s 230(4) of the Act? Decide before proceeding.

The real case is *Barton v Australian Capital Territory (Territory and Municipal Services)* [2011] ACTSC 94. The Court held that a balance must be struck between the informant's right to privacy and the public interest in discouraging vexatious and malicious reporting. The Court examined the email and determined there was no evidence of bad faith, so it declined to order release of the email to Lindsay Barton.

It is more common for s 30 to be applied in the criminal law context. For example the Supreme Court of the Australian Capital Territory has held that the threshold tests in s 19(5) of the *Bail Act 1992* (ACT) are to be given a liberal interpretation because of s 30 of the *Human Rights Act 2004* (ACT): see *In the matter of an application for bail by Massey* [2010] ACTSC 163; *R v Kristiansen* [2008] ACTSC 83; and *In the matter of an application for bail by Rodrigues* [2008] ACTSC 50. In relation to parole orders, Refshauge J in *Blundell v Sentence Administration Board of the Australian Capital Territory* [2010] ACTSC 151 considered an ambiguous provision in the *Crimes (Sentence Administration) Act 2005* (ACT):

> 150 Cancellation of parole order for non-ACT offence
>
> (1) This section applies if, while an offender's parole order is in force, the board decides that the offender has been convicted or found guilty of—
>
> (a) an offence against a law of the Commonwealth, a State or another Territory that is punishable by imprisonment; or
>
> (b) an offence outside Australia against a law of a place outside Australia that, if it had been committed in Australia, would be punishable by imprisonment.
>
> (2) Without limiting section 148 (Board powers—breach of parole obligations), the board must cancel the offender's parole order as soon as practicable under that section.

It was open for this section to cover any conviction which is entered while a person is on parole, whether or not the offence occurred during the parole period. The Court, considering the purpose of the Act in the light of s 30 of the *Human Rights Act 2004* (ACT), held that it should be limited only to those offences which occurred during the parole period, given that the aim was to discourage offenders from committing further offences while on parole.

In *R v AM* [2010] ACTSC 149 Refshauge J considered a claim by AM, who was in breach of a domestic violence order issued in favour of her parents. AM asserted that s 14 of the *Human Rights Act 2004* (ACT) permitted her to defend the charges she was facing on the grounds that her civil disobedience was part of her right to freedom of conscience and belief in non-violence. Specifically, she argued it was her conscientious obligation to confront, in a non-violent manner, people she believes have inflicted harm on her. The Court balanced the rights of the parents to privacy and protection from harm and concluded that she could not use her conscience as a defence.

The Victorian approach

The *Charter of Human Rights and Responsibilities Act 2006* (Vic) includes, *inter alia*, the following key provisions:

> Section 7(2):
>
> A human right may be subject under law only to such reasonable limits as can be demonstrably justified in a free and democratic society based on human dignity, equality and freedom, and taking into account all relevant factors including—
>
> (a) the nature of the right; and
> (b) the importance of the purpose of the limitation; and
> (c) the nature and extent of the limitation; and
> (d) the relationship between the limitation and its purpose; and
> (e) any less restrictive means reasonably available to achieve the purpose that the limitation seeks to achieve.
>
> Section 32:
>
> (1) So far as it is possible to do so consistently with their purpose, all statutory provisions must be interpreted in a way that is compatible with human rights.
> (2) International law and the judgments of domestic, foreign and international courts and tribunals relevant to a human right may be considered in interpreting a statutory provision.
> (3) This section does not affect the validity of—
>
> (a) an Act or provision of an Act that is incompatible with a human right;
> or
> (b) a subordinate instrument or provision of a subordinate instrument that is incompatible with a human right and is empowered to be so by the Act under which it is made.

Gleeson CJ has referred to these provisions extra-judicially, saying:

> [I]t will be interesting to see the kinds of case in which the courts, in due course, hold that s 32(1) mandates an abnormal interpretation of legislation ... The concept of compatibility with human rights will also inspire legal ingenuity ... The direction to courts to interpret statutory provisions in a way that is compatible with human rights is to be understood in the light of the human rights referred to. There is much room for dispute about the content of some of those rights, about the way they intersect, and about the margin of appreciation within which compatibility is to be decided. In giving courts the power, and the responsibility, to make such judgments in the process of interpretation Parliament has changed some of the rules of engagement between the legislative and judicial branches of government. It will take time for the practical effect of the change to become clear.[16]

An example of the implementation of the *Charter of Human Rights and Responsibilities Act 2006* (Vic) is *Kracke v Mental Health Review Board* [2009] VCAT 646. In that case Gary Kracke, a 37 year old man with a mental illness, had been placed under a course of involuntary medical treatment pursuant to orders issued under the *Mental Health Act 1986* (Vic). He was required to take psychotropic medication which had adverse side effects and he wanted to stop taking it. Although the Act provides for regular reviews of such orders by the Mental Health Review Board, two years passed without review. The Court held that the Board breached Gary Kracke's human right to a fair hearing under s 24(1) of the *Charter of Human Rights and Responsibilities Act 2006* (Vic) by failing to conduct the reviews in a reasonable time. In relation to the approach to interpreting the legislation, Bell P used the usual principles of statutory interpretation, which may themselves result in an interpretation which is consistent with human rights, without the need to resort to the special interpretative obligation. He proposed a detailed methodology and stated at [33] and [45]:

> The interpretation of the provisions of human rights instruments and legislation is ... evolutionary, dynamic and responsive to changing social and economic conditions. Such provisions are not interpreted according to the originalist notion that their meaning is confined to the intention of those who made them ... The principle of legality flows in the river of principle running underneath the Human Rights Act and the Charter.

The High Court had the opportunity to comment on the implementation of the Victorian statutory bill of rights recently in *Hogan v Hinch* [2011] HCA 4. The case considered the *Serious Sex Offenders Monitoring Act 2005* (Vic), which provided for the ongoing supervision of sex offenders after release from custody if it is likely they will re-offend. To further their rehabilitation, s 42 of the Act allowed the Court to make

16 M Gleeson, 'The Meaning of Legislation: Context, Purpose and Respect for Fundamental Rights' Address to Victoria Law Foundation, Melbourne, 31 July 2008, 27–9.

a suppression order preventing publication of the offender's identity where it was in the public interest to do so. An action was brought by Detective Senior Constable Hogan against Derryn Hinch for publicising the name of sex offenders via his website and during a public rally in Melbourne. French CJ referred at [5] to the fact that the ordinary approach to statutory interpretation may well achieve an interpretation that is consistent with human rights:

> Construction begins with the words of the section. It requires reference to their ordinary meaning, their context, the purpose of the Act and the purpose of the section. The principle of legality will favour a construction which, consistently with the statutory scheme, has the least adverse impact upon the open justice principle and common law freedom of speech. The *Charter of Human Rights and Responsibilities Act 2006* (Vic) also imposes an interpretive requirement that, so far as it is possible to do so consistently with their purpose, all statutory provisions must be interpreted in a way that is compatible with human rights.

French CJ considered at [39] that a compatible interpretation is one that requires the person publishing the information to know that a suppression order was in place:

> [T]here is no provision in the Act requiring that the terms of a suppression order be brought to public notice. There is a presumption that knowledge of the wrongfulness of an act is an essential ingredient in every offence ... Members of the public ... should not be expected, absent a clear indication from the language of the statute, to watch what they say because of the possibility that a suppression order may apply to the subject matter of their speech ... the words ... 'must not publish or cause to be published any material in contravention of an order' do not displace the presumption that the alleged contravenor must know of the existence of the suppression order which he or she is said to be contravening.

Most recently at the time of printing was the High Court decision in *Momcilovic v R* [2011] HCA 34, which was an appeal from the Victorian Court of Appeal. The Court of Appeal had indicated that s 32(1) should be treated as just one of many rules on statutory interpretation, rather than a 'special' rule of interpretation, saying that the process involves applying the normal principles of statutory interpretation in conjunction with s 32(1); considering whether, so interpreted, the provision breaches a human right; and if so, applying s 7(2) of the Charter to determine whether the limit is justified and if not, amend the interpretation: at [35]. The validity of s 32(1) was, *inter alia,* at issue before the High Court, which held that it was a valid rule of statutory interpretation, which is a function that may be conferred upon courts.

When using the problem-solving approach outline on page 270, readers from Victoria and the ACT should use the usual approach but, before finalising the application phrase, should check their interpretation is compatible with human rights and if not, seek to vary the interpretation unless it can be determined, on balance, that the human rights breach can be justified given the nature of the right and the way in which the legislation creates a limitation of it.

CHAPTER 12

INTERNATIONAL LAW IN STATUTORY INTERPRETATION

There is no doubt in a globalised world that international activities, including laws, have an increased domestic impact. Many of the fundamental rights discussed in Chapter 11 are based on international legal principles. This chapter commences with consideration of the basic presumption that Parliament intends to legislate in conformity with international law, and then considers in some depth the sources of international law, when and how they are, and could be, encompassed by Australian courts in the statutory interpretation task.

Legislative conformity with international law

The presumption that legislation is enacted in compliance with international legal obligations has been made by courts for more than 100 years—see *Jumbunna Coal Mine NL v Victorian Coal Miners Association* (1908) 6 CLR 309 per O'Connor J: 'every statute is to be so interpreted and applied as far as its language admits as not to be inconsistent with the comity of nations or with the established rules of international law'.[1] More recently in *Chu Kheng Lim v The Minister for Immigration, Local Government and Ethnic Affairs* (1992) 176 CLR 1 ('Cambodian "Boat People" Case') Brennan, Deane and Dawson JJ stated at [41]:

> We accept the proposition that the courts should, in the case of ambiguity, favour a construction of a Commonwealth statute which accords with the obligations of Australia under an international treaty.

In the same year, the Mason CJ and McHugh J stated in *Dietrich v R* (1992) 177 CLR 292 that international law can be used to 'resolve ambiguity or uncertainty' but not to 'effect a fundamental change': at [24].

That is not to say that Parliament cannot legislate in breach of international law—it clearly has the power to do so, and if it does, courts are bound to uphold it.[2] In *Polites v Commonwealth* (1945) 70 CLR 60, Latham CJ stated:

> The Commonwealth Parliament can legislate on these matters in breach of international law, taking the risk of international complications ... It must be held that legislation otherwise

1 See a statement from Roscoe Pound around the same time: 'The view which has prevailed ... is that the courts are to prevent interference of legislation with international law by interpretation; that to avoid a conflict between international law and a statute, the courts will resort, if need be, to strained and forced constructions': R Pound, 'Common Law and Legislation' (1907–8) 21(6) *Harvard Law Review* 383 at 395.

2 An exception in relation to obligations *erga omnes* and *jus cogens* is discussed below under customary international law.

> within the power of the Commonwealth Parliament does not become invalid because it conflicts with a rule of international law, though every effort should be made to construe Commonwealth statutes so as to avoid breaches of international law and of international comity.

In *Horta v Commonwealth* (1994) 181 CLR 183 at [10] the High Court unanimously held that Parliament does have power to pass legislation that is in breach of international law, and doing so does not render it constitutionally invalid.

Sources of international law

If courts are able to take international law into account when interpreting statutes, the questions are: what is applicable international law, what is the source of that legal obligation, and how is it applicable in Australia? This area remains unsettled, perhaps because few international lawyers (those with specific expertise in public international law) enter the judiciary. It is apparent from examination of judgments that judges tend to equate international law with treaties and conventions, while international lawyers recognise those as only one source of international law.

The accepted statement of sources of international law is in Article 38(1) of the *Statute of the International Court of Justice*, which provides:

> (1) The Court, whose function is to decide in accordance with international law such disputes as are submitted to it, shall apply:
>
> (a) international conventions, whether general or particular, establishing rules expressly recognized by the contesting states;
>
> (b) international custom, as evidence of a general practice accepted as law;
>
> (c) the general principles of law recognized by civilized nations;
>
> (d) subject to the provisions of Article 59, judicial decisions and the teachings of the most highly qualified publicists of the various nations, as subsidiary means for the determination of rules of law.

The first three paragraphs are the primary sources of international law—conventions, custom and general principles. Paragraph (d) is subsidiary, covering cases and commentary.

Consider, or discuss with others: can an analogy be drawn between treaties in international law and statutes in domestic law, and between custom and general principles in international law and common law/equity?

International treaties

There are two ways in which international treaties and conventions (these terms are used synonymously) can apply in domestic systems—the monist and dualist approach. Australia uses a dualist approach, whereby members of the executive government negotiate treaties, sign and ratify them, and then the legislature passes domestic legislation giving effect to them. Other countries, such as the United States, have a monist system, so that once the government ratifies a treaty it is automatically incorporated into domestic law.

Treaties are incorporated into domestic law in Australia by taking the substance of a treaty and enacting it in one Act, or in various provisions across a number of Acts, by annexing the treaty itself in a Schedule to an Act, or providing a executive discretion to give effect to the international legal obligation.

An example of the first method is the *Disability Discrimination Act 1992* (Cth), which gives effect to Australia's obligations under the *Convention on the Rights of Persons with Disabilities* (2007), ratified by Australia on 26 September 2008. The *Disability Discrimination and Other Human Rights Legislation Amendment Act 2009* (Cth) amended various provisions of the *Disability Discrimination Act 1992* (Cth) to bring it into line with Australia's obligations under the Convention.

Under this method, it can be more difficult to identify where the domestic provision is intending to give effect to an international treaty obligation. Assume for example there is an Act which provides that persons obtaining unemployment benefits can only be required to show they are looking for work, but cannot be expected to undertake work for the government while on the dole (such as cleaning rubbish from streets). It will not be readily apparent that this may have been implemented to give effect to Australia's obligations in relation to slavery. It will only be by examination of Hansard, or cases interpreting the legislation in which the legislative history is discussed, that the international law backdrop to the provision may become apparent.

It is also common for international treaties to be annexed in a Schedule to an Act. See for example the *Chemical Weapons (Prohibition) Act 1994* (Cth), which annexes the *Convention on the Prohibition of the Development, Production, Stockpiling and Use of Chemical Weapons and on their Destruction* (1992).[3] Section 3 states:

> The object of this Act is to give effect to certain obligations that Australia has as a party to the Convention on the Prohibition of the Development, Production, Stockpiling and Use of Chemical Weapons and on their Destruction.

Although the fundamental rule has been that mere annexation of a treaty in a Schedule will not make it part of Australian law: see Toohey J in *Dietrich v R* (1992) 177 CLR 292 at [23], the new Commonwealth provisions which make Schedules part of

3 Passed as a General Assembly Resolution on 30 November 1992 (A/RES/47/39).

the Act (s 13(1)(b) of the Commonwealth Act) have the effect of bringing an annexed treaty into Australian law. This is a comprehensive but somewhat sloppy method of bringing an international instrument into domestic law, because treaties always contain substantive provisions (as to the use of chemical weapons, for example) plus general provisions for signature, ratification, accession, and reservations, and the language of authentic texts. The latter provisions have no utility in a domestic statute.

An example of the third method, whereby legislation provides a general Executive discretion to take actions to give effect to relevant international instruments, is s 166 of the *Environment Protection and Biodiversity Conservation Act 1999* (Cth) which provides in relevant part:

> (1) This Subdivision applies if the Minister and a Minister of a State or self-governing Territory agree that it should apply in relation to an action that: ...
>
> (d) is to be taken in the State or Territory and is an action whose assessment under this Subdivision is an appropriate means of giving effect to Australia's obligations under an agreement with one or more other countries.

The orthodox view is that only treaties that have been implemented in domestic law are capable of being applied in Australia—it is the section of the domestic Act under which litigation takes place, not the article of the international instrument to which the Act gives force. Additional challenges exist in a federal system with nine legislatures. While it is a simple matter for the Commonwealth Parliament to enact laws giving national effect to international treaty obligations, the power of Commonwealth Parliament is of course limited to the heads of power under s 51 of the Australian Constitution. If the topic is not within federal jurisdiction—an example is the external affairs power in s 51(xxix)—it may fall to the states and territories to enact the international legal obligations, and in the absence of concerted effort in the Council of Australian Governments (COAG) and Standing Committee of Attorneys-General, the result may be myriad legislative provisions giving inconsistent force to Australia's international obligations.

However, the external affairs power is expansive. In *Polyukhovich v Commonwealth* (1991) 172 CLR 501 at [18] ('War Crimes Act case') Mason CJ considered the external affairs power capable of covering internal affairs:

> The very recent cases on the external affairs power ... concerned the impact on the States of Commonwealth legislation implementing Australia's obligations under international conventions designed to protect human rights and the domestic environment. These cases vindicated the regulation by the Parliament of conduct within Australia pursuant to the external affairs power when that regulation is undertaken by way of implementation of an international convention. The cases serve to illustrate the proposition that legislation enacted pursuant to the power, though necessarily concerned with some aspect of externality, will have a domestic or internal operation.

Despite the orthodox view there have been instances where international treaties and other instruments have been used in statutory interpretation even though there is no domestic legislation giving effect to them. Arguably the most reknown instance of this is *Minister for Immigration and Ethnic Affairs v Teoh* (1995) 183 CLR 273,[4] where the High Court made use of the Convention on the Rights of the Child (1991) even though Australia had not yet enacted domestic legislation giving it force of law in Australia.[5] Mason CJ and Deane J stated at [27] and [34]:

> If the language of the legislation is susceptible of a construction which is consistent with the terms of the international instrument and the obligations which it imposes on Australia, then that construction should prevail. So expressed the principle is no more than a canon of construction and does not import the terms of the treaty or Convention into our municipal law as a source of individual rights or obligations.
>
> [R]atification of a convention is a positive statement by the executive government of this country to the world and to the Australian people that the executive government and its agencies will act in accordance with the Convention. That positive statement is an adequate foundation for a legitimate expectation, absent statutory or executive indications to the contrary, that administrative decision-makers will act in conformity with the Convention and treat the best interests of the children as 'a primary consideration'. It is not necessary that a person seeking to set up such a legitimate expectation should be aware of the Convention or should personally entertain the expectation; it is enough that the expectation is reasonable in the sense that there are adequate materials to support it.

Consider, or discuss with others, whether you agree with this decision. Or do you believe only international laws enacted domestically should be used?

Kirby J in *Coleman v Power* (2004) 220 CLR 1 at [244] referred to the fact that the International Covenant on Civil and Political Rights (ICCPR) has not been enacted as part of Australian municipal law, saying '[b]ut that does not prevent courts using the statement of human rights and fundamental freedoms set forth in the ICCPR'.[6] This differed from the view of Gleeson CJ, who said at [19]:

---

4 See also *Yager v R* (1977) 139 CLR 28 per Mason CJ at 43–44 and *Kruger v The Commonwealth* (1997) 190 CLR 1 per Dawson J at 71.

5 For further discussion see Piotrowicz, RW, 'Unincorporated Treaties in Australian Law: the Official Response to the *Teoh* Decision' (1997) 71(7) *Australian Law Journal* 503.

6 Similarly in *Dietrich v R* (1992) 177 CLR 292 Brennan J said at 15: 'Although this provision of the [ICCPR] is not part of our municipal law, it is a legitimate influence on the development of the common law'. Likewise Richard Wilson stated, in an address to the Australian Academy of Forensic Sciences: '[I]t is increasingly recognised that in appropriate cases international law may be of assistance notwithstanding that it has not been incorporated into municipal law': R D Wilson, 'The Domestic Impact of International Human Rights Law' (1992) 66 *ALJR* 551 at 552.

> The ICCPR was made in 1966, signed by Australia in 1972, and ratified in 1980. The First Optional Protocol came into force in Australia in 1991. The proposition that the ICCPR can control or influence the meaning of an Act of the Queensland Parliament of 1931 is difficult to reconcile with the above statements. In particular, it is difficult to reconcile with the theory that the reason for construing a statute in the light of Australia's international obligations, as stated in *Teoh*, is that Parliament, prima facie, intends to give effect to Australia's obligations under international law. Of one thing we can be sure: the Queensland Parliament, in 1931, did not intend to give effect to Australia's obligations under the ICCPR.

This statement is problematic because it is inconsistent with the notion of legislation as 'always speaking' (discussed in Chapter 5). It is immaterial that the Act pre-dated the international instrument and it does not matter what the Parliament in 1931 intended—the intention is not the subjective intention of members of the Queensland Parliament at the time; it is an objective intent to be discovered from the words used in the Act, taking into account the purpose and the context (including the international context).

Does reference to international instruments in circumstances where the international instrument has not been enacted into domestic legislation circumvent the separation of powers? Is it a form of judicial legislation? As the question is posed by Kirby J, may courts 'thereby obscure the respective lawmaking competence of the federal and state authorities?'[7] There is of course a need to 'attend carefully to the dangers which may exist in indiscriminately picking up a provision of an international instrument and applying it as if it had the authority of local law'.[8] One must consider whether there was a reason why the legislature chose not to implement the international treaty in domestic law, particularly where a year or more has passed since the instrument was ratified by the executive.

When are international treaties used?

Assuming that what can be used in statutory interpretation is mainly international law that is implemented in domestic legislation, with some expansion to international laws which are ratified but not yet so implemented, the question is *when* the courts will do so. Mason J has stated in *Yager v R* (1977) 139 CLR 28 at [10]:

> There is no basis on which the provisions of an international convention can control or influence the meaning of words or expressions used in a statute, unless it appears that the statute was intended to give effect to the convention, in which event it is legitimate

7 M Kirby, 'The Australian Use of International Human Rights Norms: From Bangalore to Balliol—A View From the Antipodes', (1993) 16(2) *UNSW Law Journal* 363 at 371.

8 Ibid at 372.

> to resort to the convention to resolve an ambiguity in the statute ... Still less is there any foundation for resorting to the provisions of such a convention for the purpose of qualifying or modifying an express definition contained in a statute.

It is arguable that international law may be referred to where there is some ambiguity in interpreting the domestic Act giving it force of law in Australia,[9] as under the modern statutory approach as provided in s 15AB of the Commonwealth Act, an international treaty is an extrinsic material that forms part of the context and may shed light on the purpose of the Act. According to Kirby J, speaking extra-judicially:

> [T]he common law provides a perfectly appropriate vehicle for introducing such basic rights, and the jurisprudence which collects around them, into the municipal legal system. It can be done, where it is appropriate, with perfect propriety, by the technique of judicial decision-making: construing an ambiguous statute or filling a gap in the common law by reference to developing international principles. There will be occasion where this technique will not be available. The common law will be perfectly plain. The statute will be relevantly unambiguous. The international norm may seem too controversial. It may seem more appropriate to require domestic legislation on the particular subject. But in many other cases, falling short of these exceptions, it will be useful to the judge to have access to international human rights jurisprudence.[10]

Where an international treaty is applied in domestic legislation, and expressions are taken directly from the treaty as opposed to the basic sentiment, there is a collective interest that such phrases be interpreted uniformly across the various domestic jurisdictions in which the international treaty is applied. After all, the whole purpose of negotiating an international treaty on a particular topic is to achieve some international uniformity in standards applied or principles adopted. In *Rocklea Spinning Mills Pty Ltd v Anti-Dumping Authority* (1995) 129 ALR 401, Spender, Einfeld and Tamberlin JJ stated at 415:

> [A]n important consideration in examining legislation intended to implement international agreements is to give weight to the construction which the international community would attribute to the relevant instrument or concept ... it is obviously desirable that expressions used in international agreements should be construed, as far as possible, in a uniform and consistent manner by both municipal courts and international courts and panels to avoid a multitude of divergent approaches in the territories of the contracting parties on the same subject matter.

9 Kirby J has referred to the Bangalore Principles which provide that, in circumstances of ambiguity, courts may make reference to international law. Ibid at 374.

10 Ibid at 391–2.

Do treaty or statutory interpretation principles apply?

Just as there are domestic statutes on the interpretation of domestic statutes, there are international laws on the interpretation of treaties. The *Vienna Convention on the Law of Treaties* (1969), drafted by the International Law Commission, is recognised as a restatement of customary international law on treaty interpretation. It was ratified by Australia in 1974 and entered into force in 1980. In *Minister for Immigration and Multicultural and Indigenous Affairs v QAAH of 2004* (2006) 231 CLR 1 at [34] Gummow ACJ, Callinan, Heydon and Crennan JJ stated:

> Australian courts will endeavour to adopt a construction of the Act and the Regulations, if that construction is available, which conforms to the Convention ... construed by reference to the principles stated in the *Vienna Convention on the Law of Treaties* ('the Vienna Convention'), even though the Vienna Convention has not been enacted as part of the law of Australia. One of the principles stated in Art 31 of the Vienna Convention requires that regard be had to the context, object and purpose of the Convention. Another, stated in Art 32, permits recourse to the preparatory work of the Convention in the circumstances of its conclusion. But despite these respects in which the Convention may be used in construing the Act, it is the words of the Act which govern.

Articles 31 and 32 of the Vienna Convention are the key provisions—they are set out in full in Chapter 8 on pages 149–50. Article 31 familiarly provides for the good faith interpretation of treaties using their ordinary meaning in their context and in light of their purpose. Article 32 allows for recourse to 'supplementary means' to resolve ambiguities and absurdities. A ready analogy can be drawn between Article 31 of the Vienna Convention and s 15AA of the Commonwealth Act, and between Article 32 and s 15AB. In the international context the closest equivalent to explanatory memoranda and second reading speeches is the *travaux preparatoires* ('preparatory works') of an international treaty.

Which international treaties can be used?

There is no limit on which international treaties can be referred to, but obviously the strongest argument will relate to treaties that have been expressly incorporated into domestic legislation. Reference should be made to the Australian Treaty Series.[11]

Examples of treaties that have been used by Australian courts include:

1 The International Covenant on Civil and Political Rights, which appears as Schedule 2 to the *Human Rights and Equal Opportunity Commission Act 1986* (Cth),

11 At www.austlii.edu.au/au/other/dfat/treaties.

the Optional Protocol to which was referred in *Mabo v Queensland (No.2)* (1992) 175 CLR 1. The Optional Protocol gives individuals the right to bring a complaint against Australia where it is alleged human rights have been violated. Brennan J stated at 42: 'The opening up of international remedies to individuals pursuant to Australia's accession to the Optional Protocol of the ICCPR brings to bear on the common law the powerful influence of the Covenant and the international standards it imports'.

2 The Convention on the Rights of the Child was used in the *Teoh* case discussed above.

3 The Geneva Conventions, which encompass the laws of war, otherwise known as international humanitarian law, were referred to in *Polyukhovich v Commonwealth* (1991) 172 CLR 501 ('War Crimes Act case') per Mason CJ at [24]–[26].

4 The Convention Relating to the Status of Refugees (1951) and the Protocol Relating to the Status of Refugees (1967).

5 The Racial Discrimination Convention, which appears as a Schedule to the *Racial Discrimination Act 1975* (Cth).

6 The Convention Concerning the Protection of the World Cultural and Natural Heritage (1972), otherwise known as the UNESCO World Heritage Convention, provides for the declaration by UNESCO of places of special cultural or physical significance to be World Heritage sites. The High Court in *Commonwealth of Australia v Tasmania* (1983) 158 CLR 1 ('the Tasmanian Dam Case'), which ensued from a dispute over the proposed damming of the Franklin River, part of a World Heritage site, considered that, although such a designation does not bind governments, ratification of the Convention signalled an acceptance of obligations under it.

7 The Convention for the Unification of Certain Rules Relating to International Carriage by Air as amended at The Hague 1955 ('Warsaw Convention'), which provides for limitations of liability for damage caused in the international carriage of goods by air, was referred to in *Siemens Ltd v Schenker International (Australia) Pty Ltd* (2004) 216 CLR 418 in relation to whether the Convention covered damage to goods occurring outside an airport.

8 The World Intellectual Property Organization (WIPO) Copyright Treaty (1996) was referred to in *Stevens v Kabushiki Kaisha Sony Computer Entertainment* (2005) 224 CLR 193 by Gleeson CJ, Gummow, Hayne and Heydon JJ at [12], who said that the *Copyright Amendment (Digital Agenda) Act 2000* (Cth) was enacted to comply with obligations under it.

9 The General Agreement on Tariffs and Trade (GATT), the founding document in the international trade in goods since the Second World War, remains a key legal document in the World Trade Organisation. Australia's membership means its laws should conform to the requirements of WTO law. The GATT was referred to in *Rocklea Spinning Mills Pty Ltd v Anti-Dumping Authority* (1995) 129 ALR 401.

10 The Organisation for Economic Cooperation and Development (OECD) Guidelines on the Protection of Privacy and Transborder Flows of Personal Data (1980) set out core principles and guidelines for governments and business entities in collecting and managing personal information.The Guidelines, which have been endorsed by Australia, were used by Kirby P when President of the New South Wales Court of Appeal in *Ainsworth v Hanrahan* (1991) 25 NSWLR 155 in holding that use of information produced to a court under compulsion, which had not been tendered as evidence in open court, was a breach of basic privacy principles.

Customary international law

The second primary source of international law is customary international law, formed through the collective practice of states (referred to as 'state practice') and based on their belief that there is a legal obligation to engage in that practice (referred to as '*opinio juris*'). Legal principles become, over time, widely used and 'crystallise' into customary international law, often recognised through decisions of the International Court of Justice, or through resolutions of the United Nations General Assembly.

If Australian judges were not already unsettled by the discussion on using, in statutory interpretation, international instruments that have not been embedded in domestic legislation, they certainly are unsettled by such a 'vague' source of law as customary international law. McHugh J is something of an opposition leader on the use of international law in statutory (and constitutional) implementation. See for example in the *Al-Kateb v Godwin* (2004) 219 CLR 562 decision, at [65]:

> Given the widespread nature of the sources of international law under modern conditions, it is impossible to believe that, when the Parliament now legislates, it has in mind or is even aware of all the rules of international law ... Australia was 'a party to about 900 treaties'. When one adds to the rules contained in those treaties, the general principles of law recognised by civilised nations and the rules derived from international custom, it becomes obvious that the rationale for the rule that a statute contains an implication that it should be construed to conform with international law bears no relationship to the reality of the modern legislative process. Be that as it may, the rule of construction ... is too well established to be repealed now by judicial decision.

In a number of judgments Kirby J has locked horns with McHugh J on matters relating to statutory interpretation, but even he remembers a time before he became confident in grappling international law:[12]

> For me, as for most judges and lawyers of this century, brought up in the common law, international law was a vague mélange of political statements and motherhood principles—

12 M Kirby, 'The Australian Use of International Human Rights Norms: From Bangalore to Balliol—A View From the Antipodes', (1993) 16(2) *UNSW Law Journal* 363 at 364.

> not to be compared with the precise, renewable and generally just rules of municipal law made by legislatures answerable to the people and judges accountable in the courts.

Lawyers with expertise in public international law are not concerned by customary international law—it is a more stable body of law than, for instance, common law. Rarely does custom arise spontaneously (pre-emptive self defence following September 11 would be an outlying exception). Statements on customary international law by the International Court of Justice are treated as authoritative, and would be uncontroversial to apply.

An international lawyer would say that customary international law applies regardless of domestic legislation, and is an automatic part of our common law. This particularly is the case for principles of customary international law that have an elevated status—*jus cogens* and obligations *erga omnes*. *Jus cogens* ('the compelling law') are crimes which no State can legalise through legislation—war crimes, crimes against humanity, apartheid, genocide, aggression, torture, slavery, and piracy. *Erga omnes* ('flowing to all') are the obligations and implications that flow from *jus cogens*, namely the obligation to outlaw the conduct, to prosecute breaches, and extradite persons in their jurisdiction who are wanted for such crimes.

As stated by the International Court of Justice:[13]

> In view of the importance of the rights involved, all States can be held to have a legal interest in their protection; they are obligations erga omnes. Such obligations derive, for example, in contemporary international law, from the outlawing of acts of aggression, and of genocide, as also from the principles and rules concerning the basic rights of the human person, including protection from slavery and racial discrimination. Some of the corresponding rights of protection have entered into the body of general international law … others are conferred by international instruments of a universal or quasi-universal character.

Case exercise

'Modern-day sexual slavery: a tale of Fitzroy'

Wei runs a licensed brothel in Brunswick Street, Fitzroy in Victoria, known as Club 417. Five women of Thai nationality, who were previously employed in the sex industry in Thailand, have been working at Club 417 under an oral contract. The women were flown from Bangkok to Sydney and collected by an elderly couple and taken to a hotel. The person who organised their journey organised with a syndicate for purchase a 70 per cent stake in each of the women for $20 000 each, with the organiser retaining 30 per cent. For every $110 paid for a

13 *Case Concerning the Barcelona Traction, Light and Power Company (Belgium v Spain)* [1970] ICJ Rep 44 at [33].

sexual service, $43 was retained by the brothel owner and the remaining $67 was divided in 70/30 shares to the syndicate and the organiser. For the women themselves, each service deducted $50 from a notional 'debt' of $45 000, comprising the $20 000 she was purchased for, plus costs of flights and living expenses. On average each woman serviced six clients a day, six days a week, and a total of 900 acts were required, usually taking six months. At the end of this time, the woman's passport and return ticket were returned, and the woman was free to leave or to continue working independently as a prostitute.

The applicable legislation is the *Criminal Code* (Cth) which provides in relevant parts:

> 270.1 Definition of slavery
>
> For the purposes of this Division, slavery is the condition of a person over whom any or all of the powers attaching to the right of ownership are exercised, including where such a condition results from a debt or contract made by the person.
>
> 270.2 Slavery is unlawful
>
> Slavery remains unlawful and its abolition is maintained, despite the repeal by the *Criminal Code Amendment (Slavery and Sexual Servitude) Act* 1999 of Imperial Acts relating to slavery.
>
> 270.3 Slavery offences
>
> (1) A person who, whether within or outside Australia, intentionally:
>
> (a) possesses a slave or exercises over a slave any of the other powers attaching to the right of ownership ...
>
> is guilty of an offence.
>
> Penalty: Imprisonment for 25 years.

The question is whether the respondent 'intentionally possesses a slave or exercises over a slave any of the other powers attaching to the right of ownership' under s 270.3(1)(a). What do you think? Decide before proceeding.

The real case is *R v Tang* (2008) 237 CLR 1. If you decided Wei Tang's actions came within s 270.3(1)(a) you are in agreement with the jury in the County Court of Victoria and the High Court of Australia. Otherwise the Court of Appeal of the Supreme Court of Victoria upheld an appeal and ordered a retrial, so they did not conclude she was not guilty but that the directions to the jury were, *inter alia*, inadequate.

Of relevance to the present discussion, Kirby J referred to *jus cogens* at [110]–[111]:

> The present task is to construe and apply the Code, an Australian statute. However, the ostensible purpose of the relevant provisions was to introduce into Australian municipal law offences derived substantially from the 1926 Slavery Convention ... As stated in the

Code, slavery, like piracy, is a crime against humanity ... As a rule *jus cogens*, slavery is prohibited as a peremptory norm from which no derogation is permitted. This further reinforces the seriousness of slavery and hence the need to define it very carefully and precisely.

That was a case where slavery as a rule *jus cogens* had been legislated in Australia. What about the application of rules *jus cogens* where there is no applicable domestic legislation? For them to apply, an 'incorporation' theory would need to be applied (whereby international law is directly applicable) rather than the usual 'transformation' theory, whereby domestic legislation is necessary to transform an international legal obligation to a domestic one. Could a court decision 'transform' the customary international law into Australian common law? Two years into his retirement from the High Court, Anthony Mason published a paper submitting that this is not a settled point of law but, on balance, the transformation theory continues to apply in Australia.[14]

According to Amelia Simpson and George Williams, 'A particular rule's "fit" with existing domestic law, and the culture in which that law operates, can provide a yardstick by which international norms, which are too vague or contested for use in constitutional interpretation, can be excluded'.[15] They refer to the fact that, while some international law principles are readily accepted in Australia, such as laws regarding racial discrimination, others 'have a less certain operation in some contexts'.[16]

In *Nulyarimma v Thompson* (1999) 165 ALR 621 (FCFCA) actions were brought by members of the Aboriginal community alleging genocide on the part of members of government ministers and members of Parliament. Genocide was not, at that time, part of Australian law (it has since been enacted in the *International Criminal Court Act 2002* (Cth)). The argument that genocide, as a *jus cogens* norm of customary international law was part of Australian law, was rejected by the majority, Wilcox and Whitlam JJ. They reasoned that while genocide is a peremptory norm of customary international law, it is an obligation by Australia to the international community, and legislation is necessary to make it a domestic legal obligation. Wilcox J stated at [26]–[27]:

In the case of serious criminal conduct, ground rules are needed. Which courts are to have jurisdiction to try the accused person? What procedures will govern the trial? What punishment may be imposed? These matters need to be resolved before a person is put

14 A Mason, 'International Law as a Source of Domestic Law', *International Law and Australian Federalism*, 1997, 210. He stated at 218 that 'the difficulties associated with the incorporation theory and proof of customary international law suggest that, in Australia, the transformation theory holds sway'. See also Crawford and Edeson, 'International Law and Australian Law' in Ryan (ed) *International Law in Australia* (2nd edn, 1984) 78.

15 A Simpson and G Williams, 'International Law and Constitutional Interpretation' (2000) 11 *Public Law Review* 205 at 217.

16 Ibid at 227.

> on trial for an offence as horrendous as genocide ... I am unable to point to much authority for my conclusion.

With all due respect, if those concerns were valid we would have no common law at all. Lord Atkin, when faced with the curious case of a snail in a bottle,[17] did not hesitate to attach consequences for breach, so why should an Australian court, faced with a convincing case of genocide (and it is not argued that was made out in this particular case), not be capable of rendering a suitable punishment, taking into account the severity of the crime as compared to other serious (albeit domestic) crimes such as murder?

Merkel J's reasoning in dissent is more sound. His view, expressed at [132], is that customary international law is received into the common law of Australia except in cases of inconsistency, in which case legislation is necessary (although one might say that if it is a superior court the prevailing common law could be reconsidered so as to bring it into conformity with the principle of customary international law). He concluded that genocide is part of our common law, but that genocide was not made out in this case.

It is submitted that a preferred methodology for interpreting legislation in the light of customary international law where the customary international law has not expressly been legislated is as follows:

1. Is the proposed law a settled part of customary international law? Can it be said to have 'crystallised', and is there convincing evidence of this, such as a decision of the International Court of Justice or a Security Council resolution?
2. If yes, does that customary international law have application with respect to individuals, as opposed to a law that purely applies as between sovereigns?
3. If yes, is that customary international law consistent with Australian common law as it has been developed to date?
4. If yes, it can be applied directly. If not, an inferior court is bound by precedent, and it is necessary for the matter to go on appeal to a superior court which can reconsider the common law in the light of the customary international law.
5. If Parliament is dissatisfied with the approach taken by the courts it can enact legislation excluding the customary international law from application in Australia. This overrides the presumption that it would legislate in accordance with international law, and it is up to the Australian government to face the international ramifications of that breach.

Any other approach fails to give proper regard to legal obligations that apply not only to States, but to each and every person. The whole point of obligations *erga omnes* is that there is a positive obligation within States for rules *jus cogens* to be prohibited and for breaches to be prosecuted. Parliaments cannot hide behind legislative power

17 *Donoghue v Stevenson* (1932) AC 562.

in relation to these norms any more than Nazis in Nuremburg could hide behind German domestic laws authorising their behaviour. One can only hope that these matters come before the High Court at some stage in the future, preferably when there is a less formalist bench.

General principles of law

General principles recognised by 'civilised nations' are those domestic legal principles which are recognised and applied across a number of jurisdictions. Usually they are fundamental or inherent principles of law. They include, for example, the principle of good faith, self defence, necessity, the requirement that laws be certain, persons arrested should be brought to trial in a reasonable time, requirement for claims to be supported by evidence, *res judicata*,[18] *nemo iudex in re sua*,[19] *compétence de la competence*,[20] estoppel and some doctrines deriving in equity.

In *DPP v Logan Park Investments Pty Ltd* (1995) 37 NSWLR 118 Kirby ACJ referred to the *Universal Declaration of Human Rights*, Article 17 of which provides for the right to property. He stated at 125:

> Although these provisions are not, as such, part of Australian municipal law, they reflect fundamental principles of the law of civilised countries, including principles upheld by the common law in Australia. To the extent that they state applicable principles of international law, they are available to assist in the construction of ambiguous Federal legislation.

There has been no reference to Article 38(1)(c) in High Court jurisprudence. The closest is reference by Kirby J in *Re Colonel Aird* (2004) 220 CLR 308 at [117]. Although Article 38(1)(d) is referenced, which is the use of cases as a subsidiary means of interpreting international law, the sentiment expressed relates to general principles of law under Article 38(1)(c):

> The decisions of national courts, in so far as they affect the operation of universal principles of international law, contribute to the content of public international law, as the Statute of the International Court of Justice recognises. In making such decisions, including in respect of their national constitutions, municipal courts exercise a form of international jurisdiction. They should do so alert to any applicable rules of international law and so as to avoid, as far as they lawfully can, conflict with such rules.

---

18 A court will decline to hear a matter if it has already been decided before another court or other similar body such as an arbitral tribunal.

19 No one can be the judge in their own action.

20 A court may determine its own jurisdiction.

Can it, then, be inferred that the High Court does not accept that general principles of law, as a third primary source of international law, can have use in domestic statutory interpretation? It is likely that the same attitude would apply as has applied to customary international law.

The reluctance of some Australian judges to engage with international law is typified in Heydon J's dissenting judgment in *Roach v Electoral Commissioner* (2007) 233 CLR 162. The case concerned the exclusion of prisoners from voting in Australian elections, which initially covered prisoners with sentences of a year or more and in more recent times was varied to five years and then three years.[21] In 2006 the Federal Parliament passed s 93(8AA) of the *Commonwealth Electoral Act 1918* (Cth), which provided that no prisoner may vote. Vickie Roach, a prisoner, challenged the validity of the legislation. The High Court held that the legislation was invalid because no attempt was made, as it had been previously, to identify prisoners who have committed serious crimes such as to warrant being excluded from the political right of citizens to vote. Heydon J noted the reference by the Plaintiff to various instruments of civil and political rights, saying at [181]:

> [T]hese instruments can have nothing whatever to do with the construction of the Australian Constitution ... One of the instruments is a treaty to which Australia is not and could not be a party ... [T]he fact is that our law does not permit recourse to these materials. The proposition that the legislative power of the Commonwealth is affected or limited by developments in international law since 1900 is denied by most, though not all, of the relevant authorities—that is, denied by 21 of the Justices of this Court who have considered the matter, and affirmed by only one.

21 The requirement has varied over the years, from one year minimum sentence to three and five years. See Gleeson CJ at [9].

CHAPTER 13

INTERPRETING SPECIFIC INSTRUMENTS

This chapter focuses on specific types of legislation, including delegated legislation and codes, plus quasi-legislation such as rulings and guidelines issued by administrative agencies. It also considers the difference between interpretation of statutes and the Constitution, and instruments such as contracts and deeds.

Delegated or subordinate legislation

Delegated legislation, also referred to in some jurisdictions as subordinate legislation, statutory rules, statutory instruments and legislative instruments, is made by the Executive Government under the authority of Parliament as provided for in each principal Act. Following the general principle that Parliament makes law and the Executive applies it, Acts typically create the substance of a law and delegated legislation, such as regulations, provide further rules that give effect to the substance of the law as expressed in the Act.

Take for example the *Judges' Pensions Act 1968* (Cth) which provides in s 21:

> Regulations
>
> (1) The Governor-General may make regulations prescribing matters:
>
> (a) required or permitted by this Act to be prescribed; or
>
> (b) necessary or convenient to be prescribed for carrying out or giving effect to this Act.
>
> (2) The regulations may also prescribe accrued benefit multiples for the purposes of Part VIIIB of the Family Law Act 1975 or regulations made under that Act.

One of the provisions of the Act concerns the calculation of judicial pensions, with a formula which includes an 'age factor'. Section 6C(4) provides 'The regulations may prescribe the age factor, or the method for working out the age factor, for the purposes of step 1 of the method statement in subsection (3)'.

The *Judges' Pensions Regulations 1998* (Cth) provide in the relevant part:

> **3A Age factor**
>
> (1) For subsection 6C (4) of the Act, the age factor is worked out using the following formula:
>
> $$\frac{a_y \times (365 - d) + a_{y+1} \times d}{365}$$
>
> where:
>
> "a_y" is the factor mentioned in Schedule 1A that applies to the Judge's gender and age on retirement.
>
> a_{y+1} is the factor mentioned in Schedule 1A that applies to the Judge's gender and age, as if the judge were 1 year older on retirement.
>
> "*d*" is the number of days starting at the start of the day after the Judge's last birthday and ending at the end of the day he or she retires.
>
> *Note d* is equal to zero if the Judge retires on his or her birthday.
>
> (2) In this regulation:
>
> "*age*" is taken to be the Judge's age at his or her last birthday before or on retirement.

The rationale for delegated legislation is that it takes pressure off a busy Parliament and allows detailed rules to give effect to the Act to be made by persons closer to and with more expertise in the relevant subject matter. However the power of the Executive in creating delegated legislation is far more limited than that of Parliament—it cannot, for example, make delegated legislation with retrospective effect and coverage must strictly fall within the power delegated. That authority may be withdrawn at any time, and legislation passed to vary or cancel instruments made under delegated authority.

Types of delegated legislation

The title of the delegated instrument is not important—it is that it has been made pursuant to a delegation of authority from Parliament. Examples of delegated legislation include:

- *Regulations:* the most common form of delegated legislation, this is typically produced by the Minister responsible for the portfolio to which the subject matter of the legislation relates (see for example the *Judges' Pensions Regulations 1998* (Cth) discussed above);
- *Rules:* these are procedural matters, such as the rules of court (see for example the *High Court Rules 2004* (Cth));
- *By-laws:* these are most commonly used by local government authorities such as Councils (see for example the *Alice Springs (Shopping Trolley) By-Laws 2008* (NT) to 'deter the abandonment of shopping trolleys so as to provide for the safety of road users and pedestrians and preserve the visual amenity of the municipality');[1]
- *Orders:* referred to as an Order-in-Council,[2] these are decrees drafted by government and read out by the Governor (or Governor-General in the case of the Commonwealth) often in circumstances of urgency (see for example s 5.10.3 of the *Education and Training Reform Act 2006* (Vic) which provides that the Governor in Council may make any Orders giving effect to the Act);
- *Ordinances:*[3] typically issued by local government authorities, regulating specific activities such as building ordinances (see also ordinances issued under s 35 of the *Anglican Church of Australia Trust Property Act 1917* (Cth) in relation to evidence of trust property);

---

1 See http://notes.nt.gov.au/dcm/legislat/legislat.nsf/64117dddb0f0b89f482561cf0017e56f/8bdd120b1ab319f3692574d5001c4d86?OpenDocument (accessed 12 July 2011).

2 Note that an Order-in-Council made under the Royal Prerogative is primary legislation until such time as Parliament overrides it with an Act covering the same subject matter.

3 Note that this is different from 'ordinance' which is a form of primary legislation that, before self-governance, was used in the Northern Territory and the ACT, and continues to be used in non-self governing territories such as Christmas Island and Jervis Bay Territory.

- *Proclamations:* made by the Governors (or Governor-General for the Commonwealth), proclaiming legislation to commence and other matters (see for example the *Oaths (Appointments) Proclamation 2011* (SA), published in the Gazette on 28 July 2011 on p 3162, listing police officers appointed to take declarations and attest the execution of instruments;
- *Notices:* giving notice of specific requirements from time to time, such as a particular period and location in which a restriction applies (see for example the *Nature Conservation (Protected Plants Harvest Period) Notice 2011* (Qld) giving notice of the harvest period for protected plants such as sandalwood);
- *Policies:* setting out matters to be taken into account in making various decisions (take for example the *Environment Protection (Waste to Resources) Policy 2010* (SA), relating *inter alia* to the treatment of waste before it is dumped in landfill);
- *Declarations:* made by a relevant government Minister, usually declaring or deeming certain lists of things to come within a particular legislative provision (see for example a declared list of marine species by the Minister for the Environment and Heritage, under s 248 of the *Environment Protection and Biodiversity Conservation Act 1999* (Cth),[4] and see also the *Witness Protection (Complementary witness protection laws) Declaration 2011* (Cth) made under s 3AA of the *Witness Protection Act 1994* (Cth) which declares certain State and Territory laws to be complementary witness protection laws);
- *Principles:* made by a Minister or a body such as a Commission established under legislation (see for example the *MRCA Treatment Principles (Allied Mental Health Care Provider) Instrument 2011* (Cth) made under s 286(2) of the *Military Rehabilitation and Compensation Act 2004* (Cth) to extend statutory registration to cover allied mental health care providers);
- *Determinations, directions and decisions:* similar to policies and principles, these are usually made by a Minister (see for example *Defence Determination 2011/13* made under the *Defence Act 1903* (Cth) concerning the eligibility requirements for members of the Australian Defence Force with dependants including access to overseas housing, and the *Direction Not to Engage in Fishing* made under ss 41A(2) and 22(5) of the *Fisheries Management Act 1991* (Cth) to close off specified areas of the Northern Prawn Fishery).
- *Plans of management:* these are prepared by public entities such as Local Councils and National Parks and Wildlife, relating to the use of public land, and are approved by the relevant Minister (see for example the *Blue Mountains National Park Plan of Management 2001* (NSW) which includes plans for use of the park and conservation of its natural and cultural heritage); and

---

4 See www.environment.gov.au/coasts/species/marine-species-list.html (accessed 12 June 2011).

- *Public rulings:* declaring the methodology used to make various determinations (see for example public rulings of the Australian Taxation Office under the *Taxation Administration Act 1953* (Cth) such as TR 2011/2, applicable from 1 July 2011, which sets out how the effective life of a depreciating asset may be determined).

At the Commonwealth level the expression 'legislative instruments' is used to cover all instruments that are (1) of a legislative character (i.e. that determine the law and affect legal rights) and (2) made under a power delegated by Parliament.[5] Section 15AE of the *Acts Interpretation Act 1901* (Cth) states what is a legislative instrument and what not, and provides that the *Legislative Instruments Act 2003* (Cth) applies to legislative instruments, while ss 46, 46AA and 46B cover non-legislative instruments. Legislative instruments are required to be in writing, and are unenforceable until they are entered in the Register of Legislative Instruments.

In New South Wales, Victoria, and South Australia delegated legislation commences on the day it is made unless the delegated legislation itself provides otherwise.[6] Commonwealth and ACT delegated legislation commences on the day after registration of the legislative instrument in the legislative instruments register, unless another day is specified.[7] In Western Australia and the Northern Territory it commences on the date of publication in the *Gazette* unless the subsidiary legislation says otherwise.[8] In Queensland the instrument commences on the date on which it is made, or published in the *Gazette*, or other date specified.[9] In Tasmania the same commencement provisions apply to delegated legislation as to primary legislation.[10]

Delegated legislation has historically been criticised for being passed in secret and difficult to find. That is not the case today, with delegated legislation being readily available online:

- Commonwealth—www.comlaw.gov.au has a link from the homepage to legislative instruments, including current and historical compilations
- Australian Capital Territory—www.legislation.act.gov.au provides all subordinate laws, disallowable instruments, approved forms, notifiable instruments and commencement notices, both currently in force and repealed
- New South Wales—www.legislation.nsw.gov.au allows searching of regulations and environmental planning instruments

---

5 *Legislative Instruments Act 2003* (Cth) s 5.

6 See s 39 of the NSW Act, s 16 of the *Subordinate Legislation Act 1994* (Vic) and s 10A of the SA Act.

7 *Legislative Instruments Act 2003* (Cth) s 12; *Legislation Act 2001* (ACT) s 73(2).

8 See s 41 of the WA Act and s 63 of the NT Act.

9 *Statutory Instruments Act 1992* (Qld) s 32.

10 Section 5 of the Tasmanian Act provides that the definition of an Act includes delegated legislation. Section 9 provides for commencement 14 days after Royal Assent unless the instrument specifies a day, in which case it commences on that day.

- Northern Territory—www.nt.gov.au/dcm/legislation/current.html includes a link to viewing legislation by type, which includes separate alphabetical lists of regulations, rules, by-laws, and fishery management plans
- Queensland—www.legislation.qld.gov.au/OQPChome.htm allows searching of current subordinate legislation in force, or by year in which the subordinate legislation was made
- South Australia—www.legislation.sa.gov.au/ includes current and historical regulations
- Tasmania—www.thelaw.tas.gov.au/index.w3p includes statutory rules, including a drop down menu for recent rules and a list of rules that have not yet commenced
- Victoria—www.legislation.vic.gov.au/ links to statutory rules, listed by title and number with a search facility also included
- Western Australia—www.slp.wa.gov.au/legislation/statutes.nsf/default.html includes subsidiary legislation in force

Parliamentary safeguards

Parliament exercises oversight of delegated legislation. A similar procedure exists in each of the nine Australian jurisdictions, which includes publication and/or registration, parliamentary tabling and scrutiny, and a procedure for disallowance. Once made by the Executive Government (usually drafted by the Office of Parliamentary Counsel in liaison with the relevant government Ministry), delegated legislation is tabled in each House of Parliament. Typically scrutiny takes place by a parliamentary committee, such as the Senate Regulations and Ordinances Committee. These committees check legislative instruments to ensure they are within the power delegated by Parliament and do not unduly impact upon personal rights and liberties. Members of Parliament may give notice of a motion to disallow delegated legislation, and a resolution for disallowance may take place within a set number of days of the regulations being laid before it (15 days in the case of the Commonwealth).

If delegated legislation is disallowed by Parliament, it has the same effect as repeal: s 45(1) of the *Legislative Instruments Act 2003* (Cth), s 41(3) of the NSW Act, s 24(1) of the *Subordinate Legislation Act 1994* (Vic), s 50(3) of the *Statutory Instruments Act 1992* (Qld), s 14A of the SA Act, s 42(2) of the WA Act, s 65(1) of the *Legislation Act 2001* (ACT) and s 63(9) of the NT Act. If there is no disallowance but later a court declares part or all of a legislative instrument to be invalid for reason of being *ultra vires* (discussed below), whether the legislative instrument in existence beforehand can be revived will depend on the provisions. Further discussion on delegated legislation is limited to its interpretation, which is the primary focus of this book.[11]

11 For a detailed coverage on delegated legislation see D Pearce and S Argument, *Delegated Legislation in Australia* (Butterworths, 1999) 1.

Interpretation of delegated legislation

Generally speaking, the rules for interpreting primary legislation apply equally to the interpretation of delegated legislation. Section 13 of the *Legislative Instruments Act 2003* (Cth) provides in the relevant part:

> (1) If enabling legislation confers on a rule-maker the power to make a legislative instrument, then, unless the contrary intention appears:
>
> (a) the *Acts Interpretation Act 1901* applies to any legislative instrument so made as if it were an Act and as if each provision of the legislative instrument were a section of an Act; and
>
> (b) expressions used in any legislative instrument so made have the same meaning as in the enabling legislation; and
>
> (c) any legislative instrument so made is to be read and construed subject to the enabling legislation, and so as not to exceed the power of the rule-maker.
>
> (2) If any legislative instrument would, but for subsection (1), be construed as being in excess of the rule-maker's power, it is to be taken to be a valid instrument to the extent to which it is not in excess of that power.

Similar provisions exist in the States and Territories. In relation to paragraph (1) above, the application of interpretation legislation equally to delegated legislation, see s 5 of the NSW Act, s 4(1)(a) of the Vic Act, s 14 of the *Statutory Instruments Act 1992* (Qld), s 3A of the SA Act, s 3 of the WA Act, s 4(1A) of the Tas Act, s 4(1) of the ACT Act and s 4 of the NT Act. In relation to paragraph (2) above, whereby words and phrases in regulations are to have the same meaning as in the principal Act unless stated otherwise, see s 11 of the NSW Act, s 23 of the Vic Act, s 37 of the *Statutory Instruments Act 1992* (Qld), s 14 of the SA Act, s 44 of the WA Act, s 19 of the Tas Act, s 148 of the ACT Act and s 20 of the NT Act.

Courts will, in interpreting delegated legislation, attempt to give as full effect to them as possible, taking into account that they are practical oriented, may have evolved over time, and are routinely used by individuals in day-to-day activities. As with primary legislation, techniques for straining the meaning of words may be used but, unlike legislation in which courts will have to settle upon a construction, courts may if a provision is so ambiguous that courts cannot ascertain exactly what was intended, or so broad that it exceeds the delegated power, hold the provision to be *ultra vires*. The same goes for a situation where what is contained in delegated legislation is not reasonably proportionate to the ends to which the power was granted, or where the delegated legislation is uncertain to such a point that a person bound by it may not be adequately informed as to what is necessary to do or refrain from doing to comply with it.

If there is any inconsistency between the primary and the delegated legislation, the primary legislation will prevail.

Case exercise

'To compensate or not to compensate, that is the question'

Karen has suffered a work-related injury to her lumbar spine. She has applied for compensation through Comcare, a body established by Parliament. Comcare says she does not meet the criteria for compensation to be payable.

The relevant legislation is the *Safety, Rehabilitation and Compensation Act 1988* (Cth), s 24 of which provides that Comcare is liable to pay compensation for employee injuries which result in a permanent impairment of at least 10 per cent. The provision further provides that calculation of percentage impairment is determined by Comcare 'under the provisions of the approved Guide'.

The approved guide is the Comcare Guide, titled *Guide to the Assessment of the Degree of Permanent Impairment*. It is a legislative instrument which is drafted by Comcare and approved by the Minister. Clause 12 of the Comcare Guide provides:

> In the event that an employee's impairment is of a kind that cannot be assessed in accordance with the provisions of Part 1 of this Guide, the assessment is to be made under the edition of the American Medical Association's *Guides to the Evaluation of Permanent Impairment* current at the time of assessment.

The AMA Guide edition in operation at the relevant time for Karen was the 6th edition which, if applied, would entitle Karen to compensation. However Comcare argues that Clause 12 was in excess of power, so the current edition was inapplicable. Comcare's argument is based on s 14(2) of the *Legislative Instruments Act 2003* (Cth) which provides:

> Unless the contrary intention appears, the legislative instrument may not make provision in relation to a matter by applying, adopting or incorporating any matter contained in an instrument or other writing as in force or existing from time to time.

Clause 12 of the Comcare Guide, which refers to the 'current' edition of the Guide, is a provision incorporating something as existing from time to time. Comcare argues that this has rendered Clause 12 invalid. (One may question the issue of Comcare arguing against the application of its own Guide—it was Comcare, after all, who wrongly used the 'from time to time' provision in the Guide, and now it seeks to benefit from its own error.)

Decide whether in your opinion the whole provision is invalidated. If so, what will be the consequence? Should the offending words 'the edition of' and 'current at the time of assessment' be severed from the section, so that it could be read as referring to the edition applying at the time the legislative instrument was made? If yes, the 5th edition would apply and Karen would not be within the 10 per cent minimum requirement and therefore would not be entitled to compensation. What do you think? Please decide before proceeding.

The real case is *Comcare v Broadhurst* [2011] FCAFC 39. Before coming to the Full Court of the Federal Court, Karen Broadhurt had first raised the matter in the Administrative Appeals Tribunal which affirmed Comcare's denial of the claim. Her appeal to the Federal Court was allowed, and the matter was remitted to the Tribunal. However Comcare appealed the Federal Court decision to the Full Court of the Federal Court. It was held that the offending clause in the Comcare Guide could be read down, severing reference to the current edition and using the 5th edition instead.

Downes J stated at 12–13:

> It is not easy to attribute to the legislative instrument an intention that if its expressed purpose should fail a regime should continue which had been expressly rejected ... [However], the legislation and the legislative instrument should not readily be construed so that the primary purpose of providing for a standard wholly fails ... the very purpose of provisions seeking to preserve the effect of invalid legislative instruments, to the extent to which they are not in excess of power, must be to preserve the application of legislative instruments whose authors have not anticipated their invalidity. It is in that circumstance that the intention of the legislative instrument is to be considered and not in the circumstance that would have confronted the author if the problem had been appreciated in time to correct it.

Tracey and Flick JJ pointed out that, as the Comcare Guide could be varied or revoked from time to time, there was no need for it to have referred to the current edition of the American Guide in the first place. If a new edition were published, the Comcare Guide could simply be amended: at [66]. They attempted to preserve the validity of the Comcare Guide and held that they could read down the offending parts of Clause 12. However, they said that 'perhaps a different approach is warranted when consideration is being given to attempting to preserve the validity of legislation as opposed to attempting to preserve the validity of a legislative instrument, such as the present *Comcare Guide*' at [63]. This suggests that it was less important to preserve the validity of a legislative instrument than primary legislation.

Note that the restriction in incorporating other instruments 'from time to time' only applies to legislative instruments, not primary legislation.

Codes

Codifying acts, which create a code bringing together common law and legislation on a particular topic, attempt to 'cover the field' on that topic. Although Codes are far less prevalent than ordinary statutes, several jurisdictions, such as the Commonwealth,

Queensland, ACT, Western Australia, Tasmania and the Northern Territory have criminal Codes.[12]

The general rule is that codes are interpreted differently to ordinary statutes. As Weinberg AJA stated in *Campbell v R* [2008] NSWCCA 214 at [141]:

> [W]hat is being interpreted is a code and not an Act of Parliament. This means that special rules of interpretation are applicable. The language of the Code should be construed according to its natural meaning and without any presumption that it was intended to do no more than restate the existing law.

This means that the law in force before the code should not usually be considered. This was stated clearly by Dixon and Evatt JJ in *Brennan v R* (1936) 55 CLR 253:

> It is not the proper course to begin by finding how the law stood before the Code, and then to see if the Code will bear an interpretation which will leave the law unaltered.

Ostensibly we should not need to refer to cases in interpreting codes, but the mind of a common lawyer has difficulty resisting resort to cases, and certainly reference will be made to relevant cases that have been handed down interpreting the code. We simply cannot treat a Code as an island—the preceding law is not entirely irrelevant. In *Vallance v R* (1961) 108 CLR 56 Windeyer J stated at 76:

> The Code is to be read ... as an enactment of the Tasmanian Parliament ... it was enacted when it could be said of the criminal law that it was 'governed by established principles of criminal responsibility'. And for that reason we cannot interpret its general provisions concerning such basic principles as if they were written on a *tabula rasa* [blank slate], with all that used to be there removed and forgotten. Rather is ch. iv of the Code written on a *palimpsest* [reusable parchment], with the old writing still discernible behind.

Therefore, if a word or phrase that has previously been given a special or technical meaning at common law is used in a Code without a new definition being given, courts may reasonably apply the usual statutory presumption on restatement, discussed in Chapter 10 on page 198. It may also be useful to refer to common law or a prior enactment where a provision in a Code is ambiguous. As stated by Gibbs J in *Stuart v R* (1974) 134 CLR 426:

> [I]it may be justifiable to turn back to the common law where the Code contains provisions of doubtful import, or uses language which had previously acquired a technical meaning, or on some such special ground.

12 For further discussion see M Goode, 'Codification of the Criminal Law' (2004) 28 *Criminal Law Journal* 226.

In *R v Barlow* (1997) 188 CLR 1, Kirby J at 31–33 usefully summarised three rules to interpreting Codes, which apply in addition to the usual rules of statutory interpretation:

1 Meaning is determined without reference to the pre-existing law, except where it is clear the Code is codifying common law (the 'paramount rule');
2 If ambiguity in the Code means alternative meanings are arguable, an interpretation consistent with the Codes in other Australian jurisdictions will be applied; and
3 Words and phrases are to be read in the context of the Code as a whole.

Case exercise

'Meth psychosis can drive you crazy'

Colin has a psychotic disorder and a history of drug abuse. Recently, after consuming methamphetamine over a number of days, he formed the psychotic delusion that his wife Leanne was going to murder and torture him and his mother, so he stabbed her 11 times, killing her. He has been arrested and brought to trial, where he is pleading not guilty on the grounds of insanity. He says that he lacked capacity to know that he ought not do the act. The relevant provisions in the Criminal Code (Qld) are as follows:

27 Insanity

(1) A person is not criminally responsible for an act or omission if at the time of doing the act or making the omission the person is in such a state of mental disease or natural mental infirmity as to deprive the person of capacity to understand what the person is doing, or of capacity to control the person's actions, or of capacity to know that the person ought not to do the act or make the omission.

(2) A person whose mind, at the time of the person's doing or omitting to do an act, is affected by delusions on some specific matter or matters, but who is not otherwise entitled to the benefit of subsection (1), is criminally responsible for the act or omission to the same extent as if the real state of things had been such as the person was induced by the delusions to believe to exist.

28 Intoxication

(1) The provisions of section 27 apply to the case of a person whose mind is disordered by intoxication or stupefaction caused without intention on his or her part by drugs or intoxicating liquor or by any other means.

(2) They do not apply to the case of a person who has, to any extent intentionally caused himself or herself to become intoxicated or stupefied, whether in order to afford excuse for the commission of an offence or not and whether his or her mind is disordered by the intoxication alone or in combination with some other agent.

(3) When an intention to cause a specific result is an element of an offence, intoxication, whether complete or partial, and whether intentional or unintentional, may be regarded for the purpose of ascertaining whether such an intention in fact existed.

There is no definition of 'intoxication' in the Code. Do you consider that 'intoxication' includes amphetamine intoxication? Does it include the effects on the mind that occur after the drugs had worn off? Is his voluntary ingesting of methamphetamine, stated by experts to be the cause of triggering his underlying psychosis, sufficient to bring s 28(2) of the Code into application? Does 'some other agent' include an underlying mental condition?

Decide before proceeding whether the defence can be made out.

The real case is *R v Clough* [2010] QCA 120. If you decided he was unable to rely on s 27 to absolve himself of criminal responsibility for the killing, you are in agreement with the trial judge and all three judges in the Court of Appeal. If you decided he was, you are alone in your view.

The Court of Appeal unanimously held that 'intoxication' includes not only the high, but also any effect on the mind, and that 'some other agent' includes not only toxic agents introduced to the body externally, but any state or condition which operates to produce an effect.

In reaching this conclusion the Court of Appeal referred to law documents outside the Code. This included no less than ten cases, an English Act, second reading speech and a dictionary. It was clear that the absence of a definition of 'intoxication' in the Code resulted in extensive reference to the common law principle.

Quasi-legislative bodies

It is easy, as lawyers, to assume that statutory interpretation is the province of the courts. But the reality is that the main interpreters of statutes are not courts—it is only when that interpretation is challenged that the courts come into play. For example in the area of health legislation, the main entities to interpret the legal requirements are doctors and hospitals. As stated by Faunce regarding interpretations of legislation by non-law entities such as bureaucrats and professionals:

> The considerable academic reluctance to investigate and analyse them alongside judicial interpretation may have created a major obstacle to the development of a coherent theory of statutory interpretation in this area [health legislation].[13]

13 T Faunce, 'Health Legislation: Interpretation Coherent with Conscience and International Human Rights', in S Corcoran and S Bottomley (eds) *Interpreting Statutes* (Federation Press, 2005) 299, 302.

The area of corporate, market and financial services raises particular issues of statutory interpretation. Australian corporate law is heavily dominated by statute.[14] Because the *Corporations Act* has been amended so many times, it 'presents us with a heterogeneous mix of drafting styles and, therefore, a range of interpretive challenges'.[15] In addition to the *Corporations Act* there are Regulations, Listing Rules, Accounting Standards, licence conditions and policy statements. So there are several key interpreters of corporations law who are not judges—the Australian Securities and Investments Commission (ASIC), the Australian Stock Exchange (ASX), the Takeovers Panel, and the Company Auditors and Liquidators Disciplinary Board, to name a few.[16] ASIC issues 'administrative quasi-legislation'[17] in the form of Policy Statements and Practice Notes, indicating how they will administer provisions of the *Corporations Act*, and the ASX issues non-statutory rules, non-compliance with which can result in a court ordering compliance.[18] The fact that the ASX is itself a company engaging, *inter alia*, in compliance and enforcement decisions, is some cause for concern. There is certainly need for future research into the topic of statutory interpretation which extends beyond court interpretation.

Constitution

It goes without saying that federal statutes are interpreted in the light of the constitutional head of power relied upon which, when enacting legislation, Parliament may state in the objects clause—see *Leask v Commonwealth* (1996) 187 CLR 579. The High Court has the power to find federal legislation invalid where it is not properly enacted pursuant to a constitutional head of power.

But the focus here is on interpretation of the Constitution itself. The meaning and the scope of the Constitution is a substantive body of law and a Priestley 11 requirement for legal education, so the purpose here is merely to consider the Constitution in light of the rules of statutory interpretation. The High Court recognised in *Tasmania v Commonwealth* (1904) 1 CLR 329 at 338 that ordinary rules of interpretation apply to the interpretation of the Constitution.[19] Yet a Constitution, which is made to last a significant period of time and which may not be readily

14 I Ramsay, 'Corporate Law in the Age of Statutes' (1992) 14 *Sydney Law Review* 474, 474.

15 S Bottomley, 'A Framework for Understanding the Interpretation of Corporate Law in Australia', in S Corcoran and S Bottomley (eds) *Interpreting Statutes* (Federation Press, 2005) 147, 149.

16 Ibid at 148.

17 Ibid at 153.

18 Ibid at 155.

19 *Tasmania v Commonwealth* (1904) 1 CLR 329 at 338.

amended, cannot simply be interpreted as another statute. Gleeson CJ has stated extra-judicially:

> Although the Constitution is not to be treated as an ordinary statute, because of its age and enduring quality it provides some good examples both of the importance of context in interpretation, and of some conceptual problems that need to be faced.[20]

Essentially, the Constitution must be given an ambulatory interpretation or preferably, as suggested in Chapter 5, a 'principled dynamic approach'. The words must be interpreted in the light of present circumstances. This has been recognised by Kirby J in *Grain Pool of WA v Commonwealth* (2000) 202 CLR 479, stating at [16] to [23] that it is inconsistent to give the Constitution the same meaning and intent as when it was first drafted and adopted. Similarly McHugh J in *Singh v Commonwealth* (2004) 222 CLR 322 stated at [52]–[53] that 'it is no ordinary statute'. It has been designed to last over time and so it 'must be interpreted flexibly and purposively and, subject to the text and structure, in the manner best fitted to the contemporary needs of a federal system'. Gleeson CJ has said that an error 'is to treat history either as irrelevant to constitutional interpretation, or as a rhetorical weapon, to be employed when it is a support and ignored when it is an embarrassment.'[21]

Over 50 years ago, in *R v Commonwealth Conciliation and Arbitration; Ex parte Association of Professional Engineers* (1959) 107 CLR 208 at 267, Windeyer J properly distinguished between the 'connotation' and the 'denotation' of the words used in the Constitution—the connotation should not change but the denotation can:

> The denotation of words becomes enlarged as new things falling within their connotations come into existence or become known. But in the interpretation of the Constitution the connotation or connotations of its words should remain constant.

Therefore, as Zines points out, 'banking' can include electronic transfer even though this was unknown in 1900 because it is only a method, as opposed to the essence, of banking.[22] That is, the connotation is banking but the denotation can cover various ways in which banking may be conducted.

It is now common, in interpreting the heads of power in the Constitution, to make reference to extrinsic materials. For example in *Cole v Whitfield* (1988) 165 CLR 360 ('Tasmanian Lobster Case'), the High Court made significant use of Convention

---

20 M Gleeson, 'The Meaning of Legislation: Context, Purpose and Respect for Fundamental Rights' Address to Victoria Law Foundation, Melbourne, 31 July 2008, 13.

21 Ibid.

22 L Zines, 'The Interpretation of the Constitution' in S Corcoran and S Bottomley (eds) *Interpreting Statutes* (Federation Press, 2005) 64, 68.

debates despite prior refusal to do so. In *Singh v Commonwealth* (2004) 222 CLR 322 Gleeson CJ stated at [20]:

> A non-exhaustive list of potentially available extrinsic materials, including parliamentary records, is set out in s 15AB(2). That brings me to the Convention Debates, there being no reason to doubt that interpretative principles of the same kind as those set out in s 15AB are also relevant to the Constitution, making due allowance for the nature of the Constitution as an instrument of government and not an ordinary statute.

That decision concerned an argument raised by Tania Singh, a girl born in Mildura in Victoria, challenging the validity of s 198 of the *Migration Act 1958* (Cth), under which she may be removed from Australia as an unlawful non-citizen. Tania was born of Indian parents, who are 'aliens' within the meaning of s 51(xix) of the Australian Constitution, having entered Australia without visas. The question was whether she was also an alien within the meaning of s 51(xix) of the Constitution, which provides that the Commonwealth Parliament has power to make laws with respect to 'naturalisation and aliens'. She argued that, notwithstanding her Indian citizenship, and her lack of Australian citizenship, by virtue of the fact that she was born (albeit to non-citizens) in Australia, she is not an alien, and it is beyond the legislative competence of the Parliament to treat her as such. The High Court held that she came within the meaning of the constitutional term 'alien'. Relevantly, Gummow, Hayne and Heydon JJ stated at [153]: 'A power to make laws with respect to aliens does not authorise the making of a law with respect to any person who, in the opinion of the Parliament, is an alien'. McHugh J stated at [131]–[132]:

> [T]he meaning of the constitutional term 'aliens' has not changed since federation, although persons who were once outside its application are now within it ... the meaning (or connotation) of 'aliens' has remained constant, the classes of persons falling within that meaning have changed.

The focus in using extrinsic materials is not on identifying the subjective intentions of the drafters but to identify the subject matter and overall circumstances in which the constitution was passed. The High Court referred to this in *Cole v Whitfield* (1988) 165 CLR 360 at [9]:

> Reference to the history of s.92 may be made, not for the purpose of substituting for the meaning of the words used the scope and effect—if such could be established—which the founding fathers subjectively intended the section to have, but for the purpose of identifying the contemporary meaning of language used, the subject to which that language was directed and the nature and objectives of the movement towards federation from which the compact of the Constitution finally emerged.

Other documents

What of other documents, such as contracts, wills and deeds? Are they interpreted using the same principles as statutory interpretation? To a large extent, yes—the aim is to use the text of the document to discover its meaning, preferring their ordinary meaning unless there is an ambiguity or absurdity or, given the context, a different meaning should be applied.

Contracts

On the one hand it may be reasoned that a typical contract, being between two parties, should be interpreted in the light of their actual intentions at the time of entering the contract. On the other hand there is a market for contractual rights—through assignment, a contractual debt may be packaged as a derivative and sold, the contractual property may be subject to a mortgage, and in some instances goods may be sold on back-to-back terms through several parties. Those parties have a right to expect a contract to be interpreted based on an objective understanding of its text. The parol (oral) evidence rule excludes the use of statements and other documents to vary the terms of the written contract and indeed, most contracts will include a 'whole of agreement' clause in any event.[23] Those extrinsic materials may, however, be considered part of the overall context in which the contract was drafted.

A regularly used restatement of principles of contractual interpretation was by Lord Hoffman in *Investors Compensation Scheme Ltd v West Bromwich Building Society* [1998] 1 WLR 896 at 912–13:

> Interpretation is the ascertainment of the meaning which the document would convey to a reasonable person having all the background knowledge which would reasonably have been available to the parties in the situation in which they were at the time of the contract.

Essentially, the court will consider what the contract conveys to a reasonable person, taking into account the circumstances in which the contract was made (and the aim of the parties in entering it), excluding prior negotiations, and applying a meaning that is reasonable in the context, ensuring it accords with common sense. This aligns with the notion of objective intention in statutory interpretation, of textual and purposive interpretation. However, as pointed out by Spigelman CJ, 'A significant concern is whether the change in the general style of contractual interpretation—from text to context—has undermined the desirable objective of ensuring commercial certainty'.[24]

---

23 This has been described by Catherine Mitchell as 'contracting out of contextualism': C Mitchell, 'Entire Agreement Clauses: Contracting Out of Contextualism' (2006) 22 *Journal of Contract Law* 222.

24 J J Spigelman, 'From Text to Context: Contemporary Contractual Interpretation' (2007) 81 *Australian Law Journal* 322 at 323.

Commercial contracts[25] are said to be interpreted in a 'business-like' manner,[26] given a 'commercial construction'.[27] However, as Gleeson CJ, Gummow and Hayne JJ in *Maggbury Pty Ltd v Hafele Australia Pty Ltd* (2001) 210 CLR 181 stated at [43]:

> [W]hat in respect of a particular contract comprises 'business commonsense', as an apparently objectively ascertained matter, may itself be a topic upon which minds may differ and in respect of which an imputed consensus is impossible.

A challenge, of course, is that contractual disputes often arise where the circumstance was simply not in the contemplation of the parties at the time of the agreement. The agreement between the Council and the developer in the case exercise titled 'A frustrating turn of events' in Chapter 10 is a good example—neither party contemplated that the Commonwealth would compulsorily acquire the subject land. In circumstances where the parties had no intention, the focus is on what reasonable people in the position of the parties would have intended, had they thought of it. This notion of 'presumed intention' has been well accepted: see *Codelfa Construction Pty Ltd v State Rail Authority of New South Wales* (1982) 149 CLR 337.

With time the Australian approach to contractual interpretation may need to align with the accepted approach to international commercial contracts. The Convention for the International Sale of Goods (1980) ('CISG') has 77 State parties, and has been embedded in Australian legislation—see *Sale of Goods (Vienna Convention) Act 1986* (NSW), *Sale of Goods (Vienna Convention) Act 1987* (Vic), *Sale of Goods (Vienna Convention) Act 1986* (Qld), *Sale of Goods (Vienna Convention) Act 1986* (SA), *Sale of Goods (Vienna Convention) Act 1986* (WA), *Sale of Goods (Vienna Convention) Act 1987* (Tas), *Sale of Goods (Vienna Convention) Act 1987* (ACT) and *Sale of Goods (Vienna Convention) Act 1987* (NT). Article 8 of the CISG provides:

1 For the purposes of this Convention statements made by and other conduct of a party are to be interpreted according to his intent where the other party knew or could not have been unaware what that intent was.
2 If the preceding paragraph is not applicable, statements made by and other conduct of a party are to be interpreted according to the understanding that a reasonable person of the same kind as the other party would have had in the same circumstances.
3 In determining the intent of a party or the understanding a reasonable person would have had, due consideration is to be given to all relevant circumstances of

25 This includes not only sale of goods and supply of services but also for example, insurance policies. See Gleeson CJ in *McCann v Switzerland Insurance* (2000) 203 CLR 579 at [22].
26 Above n 24, 330.
27 Ibid at 322.

the case including the negotiations, any practices which the parties have established between themselves, usages and any subsequent conduct of the parties.

The internationally accepted approach, then, is to firstly apply the intention of the parties based on evidence of their knowledge at the time, and otherwise to find an objective intention. The approach is far broader than the present Australian approach to domestic contractual interpretation—it even allows consideration of subsequent conduct of the parties in determining the intent at the time the contract was entered. In an era of globalisation it is likely that, with time, domestic approaches will align more with international approaches.

Wills

The aim in interpreting a will is to give effect to the intention of the testator, as expressed in the will as a whole (mirroring the interpretation of a statute by giving effect to the intention of Parliament as expressed in the text of the Act). Indeed most of the general principles governing interpretation of statutes and contracts apply to the interpretation of wills.

Contextual interpretation is provided for in the 'armchair principle'—construing a will in the light of the relevant circumstances at the time the will was made. Efforts will be made to give a sensible meaning to the provisions in the will in order to avoid intestacy—the maxim is *ut res magis valeat quam pereat*. Extrinsic materials may be used in the interpretation of wills to prove the circumstances in which the testator made the will, but not to establish the testator's actual intention except where it is unclear which of two persons the testator was referring to.

The alignment between the interpretation of various instruments was expressed by Gleeson CJ in *Wilson v Anderson* (2002) 213 CLR 401 at [8]:

> The law of contract seeks to give effect to the common intention of the parties to a contract. But the test is objective and impersonal ... If the contract is in the form of a document, then it is the meaning that the document would convey to a reasonable person that matters. ... it is only the document that can speak to the third person. In the case of a will, or a deed, or other written instrument, the object of a court is to discover, and give effect to, the intention of the testator, or parties; but it is in the meaning of the instrument, discovered according to established principles of construction, that such intention is found.

CHAPTER 14

A SYNTHESIS: PRACTICAL SKILLS AND EXERCISES

This chapter brings together the law on statutory interpretation and proposes a problem-solving methodology that takes into account the nuances of textual, contextual and purposive interpretation. It links closely with the four practical exercises that follow (Practical Exercises A, B, C and D), which provide a series of detailed scenarios to which the rules may be applied. An effort has been made to provide practical material on core areas of law,[1] to cater to those contexts in which education regarding statutory interpretation is embedded across a course.[2] No answers are provided, not only because the scenarios are fictitious and may never come before the courts, but also to ensure they can be fully explored without the temptation to refer to a ready-made solution. They may form the foundation of assessable tasks. Consideration should be given, beyond regular essays and problem-solving exercises, to setting authentic assessment tasks[3] such as drafting a brief to counsel, written submissions, giving oral submissions, acting as a judge or submitting a mock written judgment.

Statutory Interpretation Index 1 ('SII1')

The index is a synthesis of the rules of statutory interpretation discussed in this book. It is titled Index '1' because the rules of statutory interpretation are organic and will change and develop over time, necessitating a second iteration. SII1 reflects the current law as at 2011. The general rule is that where a provision in a specific Act provides differently to this index, the Act will prevail.

No.	Rule	Chapter and page reference
1	The terms 'construction' and 'interpretation' may be used interchangeably	Ch 1, p 3
2	Statutes that have been rewritten in plain English drafting should not be taken to be different merely because different words have been used	Ch 2, p 17

1 For introductory law courses, please refer to exercises in Chapter 11 of M Sanson, T Anthony, and D Worswick *Connecting With Law* (Oxford University Press, 2nd edn, 2010).

2 For discussion on statutory interpretation in particular areas of law, see the following chapters in S Corcoran and S Bottomley (eds) *Interpreting Statutes* (Federation Press, 2005): P Weeks, 'Employment Law: A Test of Coherence Between Statute and Common Law' 166; Miriam Gani, 'Codifying the Criminal Law: Issues of Interpretation' 197; S Bronitt, 'Interpreting Law Enforcement Immunities: The Relationship Between Judicial, Legislative and Administrative Models', 223; P Bailey, R Callinan and A Dziedzic, 'Interpretive Approaches of the Tribunals and Courts in Discrimination Law' 250; Juliet Behrens, 'Interpreting Family Law: A Case for Legislative Principles and Presumptions Regulating the Making of Parenting Orders' 278; T Faunce, 'Health Legislation: Interpretation Coherent with Conscience and International Human Rights' 299.

3 See M Heath, 'Assessment Strategies' in S Kift et al, *Excellence and Innovation in Legal Education* (LexisNexis, 2011) 269, 282.

No.	Rule	Chapter and page reference
3	The Court's role is to interpret the statute, not merely to choose between the interpretations proposed by the parties	Ch 2, p 26
4	Where provisions in the Interpretation Acts and the common law conflict, the Interpretation Act provisions will prevail	Ch 3, p 29
5	The Interpretation Acts apply to the interpretation both of statutes and of all forms of delegated and subordinate legislation	Chs 3 and 13, pp 28 and 244
6	Interpretation Acts provide useful generic provisions that apply in all statutes unless an Act says otherwise	Ch 3, p 29
7	Where a statute refers to a gender, it includes the other gender: he includes she, she includes he	Ch 3, p 30
8	Where a statute refers to an age, it applies from the first moment of the day of the anniversary of a person's birth	Ch 3, p 30
9	The singular includes the plural and the plural includes the singular: (e.g. 'person' includes 'persons')	Ch 3, p 30
10	Where a statute refers to a distance, it is measured in a straight line	Ch 3, p 31
11	References to time are references to the standard or legal time, including where relevant, adjustment for daylight saving	Ch 3, p 31
12	A *day* means a 24-hour period commencing at midnight, and a *month* means a calendar month	Ch 3, p 32
13	If something starts 'at' or 'on' a certain date, it starts from the first moment of that day	Ch 3, p 32
14	If legislation commences at the time of assent, it is taken to have commenced from the first moment of that day even if the assent took place later in the day	Ch 3, p 37
15	If something starts 'from' or 'after' a certain date, it excludes that day	Ch 3, p 32
16	If something must end *before* a certain date, it does not include that day	Ch 3, p 32
17	If an obligation falls due on a weekend or public holiday it is deemed to be due on the next business day	Ch 3, p 32
18	If no time period is stated, an obligation or action must occur within a reasonable time, at all convenient speed, as soon as possible	Ch 3, p 33
19	'May' confers a discretion	Ch 3, p 33
20	'Must' and 'shall' confer a mandatory or directory obligation	Ch 3, p 33

No.	Rule	Chapter and page reference
21	'May' may be read as 'must' and vice versa if the context and purpose shows that this was intended	Ch 3, p 34
22	Unless an Act says otherwise, Commonwealth, NSW and WA Acts commence 28 days from the date of assent	Ch 3, p 34
23	Unless an Act says otherwise, Tasmanian Acts and delegated legislation commence 14 days from the date of assent	Chs 3 and 13, pp 34 and 242
24	Unless an Act says otherwise, Queensland, SA and NT acts commence on the date of assent	Ch 3, p 34
25	Acts in the ACT commence on the day after notification in the Gazette	Ch 3, p 34
26	Acts in Victoria commence on the day specified in each Act	Ch 3, p 34
27	If an Act provides that it commences on the date of Proclamation it is necessary to consult the Gazette to see if the Act has been proclaimed	Ch 3, p 34
28	Acts with 'sunset' clauses expire at the end of the stated period, and are treated as if they were repealed at that date	Ch 3, p 41
29	In the period before a new Act comes into force, some preparatory powers may be exercised and preparatory actions taken	Ch 3, p 36
30	Acts may be amended through amending legislation or by passing later, inconsistent legislation	Ch 3, p 37
31	In many cases an amending law will be automatically repealed the day after its provisions take effect	Ch 3, p 37
32	Where an amending Act repeals parts of an existing Act the existing provisions continue to apply until the new Act comes into force	Ch 3, p 38
33	Whether an Act amends or repeals a law depends on its effect and not the label that is used in the relevant Act	Ch 3, p 43
34	Repeals may be express or implied	Ch 3, p 41
35	Repealed legislation does not affect rights and obligations accrued under it while it was in force	Ch 3, p 41
36	Where a repealing Act is itself repealed, this does not revive the repealed provisions	Ch 3, p 41
37	If an Act refers to another Act, the version of that Act at the time of the relevant event is applied	Ch 3, p 42
38	Reprinted Acts do not replace the original Act and amendments passed since	Ch 3, p 38

No.	Rule	Chapter and page reference
39	Consolidated Acts replace the original Act and amendments passed since	Ch 3, p 38
40	Codifying Acts replace previous legislation and common law on the subject area	Ch 3, p 38
41	In interpreting a Code, reference may be had to common law where the Code is silent or contains an ambiguity	Ch 13, p 248
42	If part of an Act is held to be invalid, if that part can be severed without affecting the operation of the rest of the Act, the rest of the Act continues to apply	Ch 3, p 45
43	If an amending or repealing provision is held to be invalid, the common law or prior statutory provision is revived	Ch 3, p 47
44	The ordinary meaning of words should be applied unless this is inappropriate in the light of the context and purpose	Ch 4, p 50
45	For Commonwealth, Queensland and ACT Acts, the interpretation that would best achieve the purpose is to be preferred	Ch 4, p 50
46	For NSW, Vic, SA, WA, Tas and NT Acts, an interpretation that promotes the purpose is preferred to one that does not	Ch 4, p 50
47	The 'best achievement' formulation is broader and more flexible than the 'preferred purpose' formulation	Ch 4, p 53
48	In interpreting a provision, regard should be had to both the intrinsic and extrinsic context of the provision	Ch 4, p 54
49	The intrinsic context includes the Act as a whole, including relevant headings and any definitions clauses	Ch 4, p 57
50	The extrinsic context includes the historical circumstances, legislative background, government policy and so on	Ch 4, p 57
51	It is not necessary for a provision to be ambiguous in order to refer to its context	Ch 4, p 54
52	Consideration of the context should go hand in hand with consideration of the purpose	Ch 4, p 57
53	The modern purposive approach is different from the mischief rule in that there does not need to be an absurdity or ambiguity before the purpose of the Act may be considered	Chs 4 and 9, pp 57 and 170
54	The grammatical or literal meaning of a provision may apply if there is no doubt that was the intention, having considered the context and purpose	Ch 4, p 58
55	In identifying the purpose of an Act, reference may be had both to intrinsic and to extrinsic materials	Ch 4, p 58

No.	Rule	Chapter and page reference
56	If the purpose is (intentionally or otherwise) not expressly stated within the Act, extrinsic materials may be used to establish the purpose	Ch 4, p 61
57	Intrinsic materials which may assist in identifying the purpose include the Long Title, Preamble and objects clause	Ch 4, p 58
58	Extrinsic materials which may assist in identifying the purpose include but are not limited to Explanatory Memoranda, Hansard records of parliamentary debates, Law Reform Commission reports, international treaties, dictionaries, and judicial decisions	Ch 8, p 141
59	Care must be taken in determining the appropriate level of generality at which the purpose may be stated, as Parliament does not intend to achieve the purpose at all costs	Ch 4, p 61
60	If there are multiple purposes, it is necessary to choose the dominant purpose—the purpose most applicable to the relevant provision	Ch 4, p 64
61	If there are conflicting purposes, it is necessary to consider how the balance between the conflicting purposes was struck and choose the meaning that best gives effect to that balance	Ch 4, p 65
62	Parliament must be assumed to have intended that each provision it legislated somehow gives effect to the purpose of the Act	Ch 5, p 71
63	Legislative intention does not refer to the subjective intent of the Parliament that enacted the legislation—it is an objective intent to be ascertained using the text of the Act in the light of its context and purpose	Ch 5, pp 72–73
64	If no intention can be found because the circumstance was not contemplated, regard can be had to the outcome, as irrational or unjust consequences could not have been intended	Ch 5, p 78
65	Courts may 'read down' general words to constrain their meaning	Ch 5, p 81
66	Courts may give a provision a 'strained' construction to achieve the purpose, provided the construction is reasonably open	Ch 5, p 81
67	Courts may respond to drafting errors or gaps by 'reading in' words, that is, reading a provision as if it contained additional words	Ch 5, p 81
68	An 'ambulatory', 'always speaking', 'dynamic' approach may be used to allow the meaning of words to change over time in order to give effect to the 'spirit' of the law, also referred to as the 'equity of the statute', as it applies in changed circumstances	Ch 5, p 85

No.	Rule	Chapter and page reference
69	While the *denotation* of words may change over time, their *connotation* does not	Chs 5 and 7, pp 88 and 120
70	An Act should be read as a whole	Ch 6, p 94
71	It is acceptable for some provisions to be considered 'leading' and others 'subordinate'	Ch 6, p 94
72	Typically a Long Title will be longer and more informative than a Short Title, but this is not always the case	Ch 6, pp 95–96
73	A Preamble may be used both as part of the overall context in which the Act was made and to resolve ambiguity in the wording of a provision	Ch 6, p 96
74	An Objects clause may assist with identification of the purpose of an Act but should not be taken to be exhaustive	Ch 6, p 99
75	Definitions used within an Act prevail over dictionary definitions	Ch 6, p 100
76	A definition in an Act may be disregarded if it is evident from the context in which the word is used that it was not intended to apply.	Ch 6, p 100
77	If an Act has been amended on a number of occasions the various iterations of the Act may be considered to determine whether a definition in the Act should be applied in each instance where that term is used	Ch 8, p 100
78	Definitions are not substantive legislative provisions in their own right—they are explanations to assist in determining meaning	Ch 6, p 101
79	A definition which uses 'means' is exhaustive	Ch 6, p 101
80	A definition which uses 'includes' is non-exhaustive	Ch 6, p 101
81	It is possible for a definition to use both 'means' and 'includes' but the items listed under 'includes' cannot be used to limit ambit of the information under 'means'	Ch 6, p 102
82	It is acceptable for an Act to define a term by reference to a definition in another Act or in an international instrument	Ch 6, p 103
83	In Commonwealth and Queensland Acts, all headings may be used in interpretation	Ch 6, pp 104–105
84	In NSW, Vic, SA, WA, Tas, ACT and NT Acts, only headings to parts and divisions may be used in interpretation—headings to individual sections may not	Ch 6, p 106
85	Schedules are part of an Act and may be applied alongside relevant sections	Ch 6, p 107
86	In Commonwealth Acts, all notes, including margin notes, headnotes and footnotes (but not endnotes) are considered part of the Act and may be used in interpretation	Ch 6, pp 108–109

No.	Rule	Chapter and page reference
87	In NSW, Vic, Qld, SA, WA, Tas, ACT and NT Acts, margin notes, headnotes, footnotes and endnotes are not considered part of an Act but may be used as part of the extrinsic materials to the Act	Ch 6, p 108
88	In Commonwealth, Qld and SA Acts, punctuation may be used in interpretation, but it may not be determinative	Ch 6, p 110
89	Where examples are included in sections to an Act, they may be used in interpretation but cannot override the substantive provision	Ch 6, p 110
90	Unless stated otherwise, all penalties are maximums not mandatory periods	Ch 6, p 111
91	Where a penalty appears below a number of sections, the penalty applies to a breach of any of them	Ch 6, p 111
92	All words have meaning, and a court construing a statutory provision should strive to give meaning to every word of a provision	Ch 7, p 113
93	The meaning of a provision will usually be the meaning of the words in their natural and ordinary meaning	Ch 7, p 113
94	Where a word has several ordinary meanings, courts will apply the most relevant one taking into account the context and purpose	Ch 7, p 114
95	It is not acceptable to disaggregate a phrase, identify the meaning of each word, and then put them back together to work out the meaning of a phrase	Ch 7, p 114
96	A 'technical' or 'legal' meaning of a word or phrase may be used when the context and purpose of the Act in which they are used is taken into account	Ch 7, p 115
97	A 'technical' meaning of a word is the meaning given to it in the area of trade and commerce to which the Act is directed	Ch 7, p 116
98	A 'legal' meaning of a word is the meaning that has been established over a succession of common law decisions	Ch 7, p 116
99	The meaning given to a word in an Act should be the current meaning and not the meaning at the time the Act was passed	Ch 7, p 119
100	It is acceptable to use both Australian and English dictionaries in interpreting Australian legislation	Ch 7, p 120
101	Although in most cases general dictionaries are used, it may be appropriate to use a legal or technical dictionary in the interpretation of a statutory provision	Ch 7, p 121
102	It is assumed that, if a word is used several times within the one Act, the word is used consistently	Ch 7, p 122

No.	Rule	Chapter and page reference
103	It is assumed that, if a different word is used in a place where the same word could have been used, Parliament intended a different meaning	Ch 7, p 122
104	The definition of a word applies equally to variants of that same word, eg use, used, using	Ch 7, p 122
105	Where words such as 'solely', 'primarily', 'exclusively' and 'only' are used, they apply to limit the operation of the provision but minor deviations may be permitted if they are *de minimis* (inconsequential)	Ch 7, p 122
106	Where hendiadys are used (eg 'ready and able'), a court may determine whether they were intended to be read disjunctively or conjunctively	Ch 7, p 124
107	In determining the tense in which words are used (past, present, future) the court will consider the context in which they appear and the overall purpose of the legislative scheme	Ch 7, p 124
108	The words 'deemed', 'shall be taken to be' and 'as if' are used synonymously as deeming provisions	Ch 7, p 127
109	The words 'have regard to' require something to be taken into consideration but is not determinative	Ch 7, p 128
110	Where protean words (such as 'use', 'publish' or 'import') are included in legislation, their breadth will vary depend on the legislative context in which they are used	Ch 7, p 129
111	Extrinsic materials may be used to confirm the meaning is the ordinary meaning, or to determine the meaning where the provision is ambiguous or obscure	Ch 8, p 137
112	There is a discretion as to whether or not to use extrinsic materials—they 'may' be considered	Ch 8, p 138
113	Extrinsic materials may also be used to identify the relevant context and purpose of an Act	Ch 8, p 139
114	Statutory provisions on the use of extrinsic materials do not exclude the common law approach to use of extrinsic materials	Ch 8, p 140
115	No hierarchy applies amongst extrinsic materials although some (Explanatory Memoranda and second reading speeches) are used more than others	Ch 8, pp 141–142
116	The true test for use of extrinsic materials is one of relevance	Ch 8, p 141
117	Delegated legislation may not be used to interpret an Act except where the Act contains an 'as enacted' provision	Ch 8, p 142

No.	Rule	Chapter and page reference
118	Documents that came into existence after the enactment of an Act may not be used in its interpretation	Ch 8, p 142
119	The words of a Minister during debate over a Bill may not be substituted for the text of the law	Ch 8, p 147
120	Where provisions from international treaties are brought into domestic law, the Vienna Convention on the Law of Treaties (1974) may be used	Chs 8 and 12, pp 149 and 229
121	In all cases it is the domestic legislation that gives effect to an international treaty that is applied, and not the treaty itself that is directly applied	Ch 8, p 152
122	Where possible, a uniform interpretation should be given to an international treaty by domestic courts in convention countries	Ch 8, p 151
123	Where possible, national or mirror scheme legislation should be given a uniform interpretation by courts in each jurisdiction	Ch 8, p 158
124	The use of other cases in statutory interpretation is limited to cases on the same Act, as the same provision used in different Acts may have different meanings depending on the contexts and purposes of each Act	Ch 8, p 157
125	In deciding whether to use extrinsic material it is necessary to consider the need to avoid prolonging legal proceedings without compensating advantage	Ch 8, p 158
126	Where more than one interpretation is open it may be appropriate to select the one that is consonant with the common law and/or equity	Ch 9, p 161
127	Parliament has power to make, change and repeal law, and its actions will override judicial decisions except in the area of High Court assessment of constitutional validity	Ch 9, p 161
128	As the construction of statutes is a question of law, it is open to appeal on the basis of errors in statutory interpretation	Ch 9, p 163
129	It is necessary for judges to give reasons as to how they reached a particular interpretation and why they chose one interpretation over another, or to apply one rule over another	Ch 9, p 163
130	Although there is presently little analogical development of statutes, it is open for federal courts at least, to reason by analogy from common law to statutes and vice versa	Ch 9, p 165
131	The common law approaches to interpretation are reflected in textualism (the literal rule) contextualism (the golden rule) and purposivism (the mischief rule)	Ch 9, p 167

No.	Rule	Chapter and page reference
132	Statutory interpretation remains literal, in the sense of the use of the text, but is not literalistic	Ch 9, p 168
134	The Latin maxims, *noscitur a sociis*, *ejusdem generis*, *expressio unius est exclusio alterius*, *expressum facit cessare tacitum* and *generalia specialibus non derogant*, may be used but care should be taken to ensure they do not override a contextual and purposive approach	Ch 9, pp 171–183
135	The meaning of a word or phrase can be determined by surrounding words—*noscitur a sociis*	Ch 9, p 171
136	The meaning of a general phrase is limited by proceeding specific words—*ejusdem generis*	Ch 9, p 174
137	*Ejusdem generis* may not be used where there is only one specific word followed by the general phrase, as it is not possible to identify a genus from a single word	Ch 9, p 177
138	The express mention of one thing is the exclusion of another—*expressio unius est exclusio alterius*	Ch 9, p 180
139	Before using *expressio unius est exclusio alterius*, consideration must be given as to whether it was intended to apply, particularly where a statute has been amended at various intervals	Ch 9, p 181
140	General provisions do not derogate from specific provisions—*generalia specialibus non derogant*	Ch 9, p 182
141	Statutory presumptions may be rebutted by clear and express words, or by necessary implication	Ch 10, p 185
142	Legislation which affects substantive rights does not operate retrospectively	Ch 10, p 186
143	Legislation which affects procedural rights may operate retrospectively	Ch 10, p 187
144	Delegated legislation cannot generally operate retrospectively	Ch 10, p 188
145	Legislation does not apply extra-territorially	Ch 10, p 188
146	References in legislation to places, persons and things are to places, persons and things within that jurisdiction	Ch 10, p 188
147	Courts have jurisdiction to hear disputes arising under law	Ch 10, p 192
148	Where legislation provides an alternative forum for the resolution of disputes, some right to appeal to courts remains	Ch 10, p 192
149	Legislation may bind the Crown even where an express provision does not exist, where an intention to do so is evident from the context and purpose that the Crown should be so bound	Ch 10, p 196

No.	Rule	Chapter and page reference
150	Except in South Australia, re-enactment of a word or phrase which has been interpreted at common law, without a different definition, is taken as approval of the common law meaning	Ch 10, p 198
151	Where a statutory provision creating a penalty is ambiguous, it will be construed strictly in favour of the person facing a penalty unless the context and purpose require otherwise	Ch 10, p 199
152	Where a statutory provision providing for a benefit is ambiguous, it will be construed broadly in favour of the person standing to so benefit, unless the context and purpose require otherwise	Ch 10, p 200
153	It cannot be presumed that taxation provisions should be strictly construed—it depends on the normal application of the rules of statutory interpretation	Ch 10, pp 201–202
154	Legislation should not be construed to remove vested property rights	Ch 10, p 202
155	Where the Crown prosecutes a criminal matter unsuccessfully the Crown should not have a right to appeal that decision	Ch 10, p 204
156	Every offence must contain a *mens rea*, which is imputed if it is not explicitly stated	Ch 10, p 204
157	Legislation does not interfere with fundamental rights, under the principle of legality	Ch 11, p 206
158	Legislation does not interfere with equality of religion	Ch 11, p 204
159	Legislation regularly interferes with basic common law rights, it is only fundamental rights to which a presumption against interference exists	Ch 11, p 207
160	Fundamental rights include free speech, personal liberty, freedom of movement, right to a fair trial, criminal charges to be proved beyond reasonable doubt, right against arbitrary arrest and detention, right to silence to avoid self incrimination, right to legal professional privilege, and right to own and control property.	Ch 11, pp 211–212
161	It may be seen that statutory presumptions have the practical effect of a common law bill of rights	Ch 11, p 214
162	In the ACT and Victoria, once the ordinary rules of statutory interpretation have been applied, consideration should be given as to whether the interpretation breaches a human right, and if so, whether that is justified	Ch 11, pp 215–220
163	Where more than one human right is potentially breached by a provision, the court will need to identify which human right prevails over the other	Ch 11, p 218

No.	Rule	Chapter and page reference
164	Statutes should be interpreted wherever possible to avoid inconsistency with international law obligations	Ch 12, p 222
165	In interpreting domestic statutory provisions in which there is some ambiguity, reference to international law may resolve the ambiguity but cannot effect fundamental change	Ch 12, p 222
166	Parliament has the power to legislate in breach of international law, and if it does so, courts are obliged to give effect to it	Ch 12, p 222
167	Of the three main sources of international law—treaties, custom and general principles—only international treaties are regularly used in statutory interpretation	Ch 12, p 223
168	In some instances an international treaty which has been ratified by the Executive government but not legislated by the Parliament may be used if it can be said there is a legitimate expectation that administrative decision makers will act in conformity with it	Ch 12, p 226
169	International treaties which can and have been used by Australian courts include the *Universal Declaration on Human Rights* (UDHR) *International Covenant on Civil and Political Rights* (ICCPR), *International Covenant on Economic and Social Rights* (ICESCR), *Convention on the Rights of the Child*, *Geneva Conventions*, *Convention Relating to the Status of Refugees*, *Protocol Relating to the Status of Refugees*, *Racial Discrimination Convention*, *Convention Concerning the Protection of the World Cultural and Natural Heritage*, *Convention for the Unification of Certain Rules Relating to International Carriage by Air as amended at The Hague 1955*, *World Intellectual Property Organization (WIPO) Copyright Treaty*, and the *General Agreement on Tariffs and Trade*.	Ch 12, p 229
170	Customary international law may be referred to if it has been embedded in domestic legislation	Ch 12, p 234
171	General principles of law recognised by civilised nations may be referred to in a comparative consideration of the provision being interpreted but cannot override the intended principle in the Act	Ch 12, p 236
172	In the Commonwealth and the ACT, delegated legislation commences on the day after registration of the legislative instrument in the legislative instruments register	Ch 13, p 242
173	In NSW, Victoria and SA delegated legislation commences on the day it is made	Ch 13, p 242

No.	Rule	Chapter and page reference
174	In WA and NT delegated legislation commences on the date of publication in the Gazette	Ch 13, p 242
175	Words used in delegated legislation have the same meaning as in the principal Act	Ch 13, p 244
176	The interpretation of delegated legislation is practical, taking into account its intended, day-to-day lay person audience	Ch 13, p 244
177	Primary legislation will prevail over delegated legislation to the extent of inconsistency	Ch 13, p 245
178	It is not acceptable for delegated instruments to incorporate other instruments on a 'from time to time' basis—only the version of the other instrument or Act in force at the time of the passing of the delegated legislation may apply	Ch 13, p 245
179	The rules of statutory interpretation can be applied in interpretation of constitutions and other documents such as contracts and wills	Ch 13, p 253

Practical methodology

Approaching statutory interpretation problems requires appreciation of the various stages of the interpretation process:

1. *Identification phase*: identifying the relevant Act, checking it is in force at the relevant time and in the relevant jurisdiction, and seeing what the relevant provision says;
2. *Exploration phase*: considering the context and purpose, taking into account the immediate context (the whole of the Act), the broader context (historical, legislative, political, international), the purpose as suggested by intrinsic materials (such as the Long Title and Objects clause) and extrinsic materials (such as second reading speeches and Explanatory Memoranda); and
3. *Application phase*: returning to the text of the provision and considering whether, in the light of the context and purpose of the Act, the ordinary meaning or some other meaning should be applied, taking into account challenges posed by multiple and conflicting purposes, to reach an overall conclusion.

This process is depicted in the flow diagram on the next page.

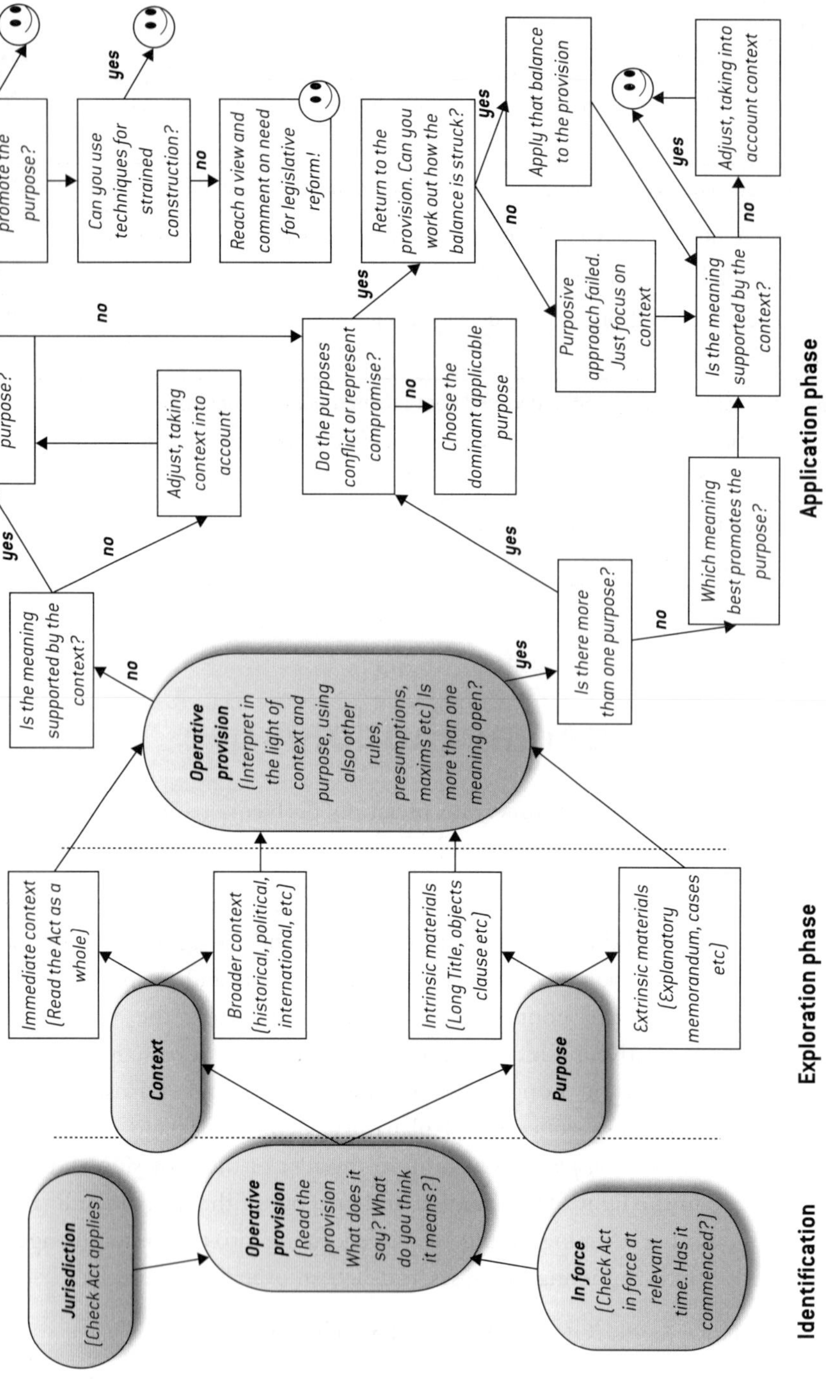

Let us apply this methodology to a specific case situation.

Practical exercise

'John's job has been cut'

Facts

John recently applied for a job with Nicholson's Knives, working in its factory in Dubbo in New South Wales. At the interview he discussed his interest in the industry and his desire to work his way up the ladder, from machine operator to manager. He also expressed a willingness to do a TAFE course to further his skills and qualifications. The human resources staff member who interviewed him was impressed, and told him he could start on Monday, and that there were a number of forms that needed to be completed.

John started work the following Monday, and was shown how to take knives as they came off the machine, hold them in front of a light to identify any imperfections in the metal, and how to use a light sanding machine to remove imperfections. He enjoyed the work and his productivity soon matched those who have been doing the job for a long time. However, since he submitted all the completed forms, it has come to light from John's criminal record check that he has a prior conviction for assault occasioning grievous bodily harm. The circumstances were that he stabbed someone 13 times with a knife during an altercation while working as a removalist. This afternoon John was handed a letter by the human resources manager and escorted from the factory premises by the security guards. The letter says his employment has been terminated forthwith. John considers that he is the victim of job discrimination—he has done his time for the crime, and it should not be held against him for the rest of his life.

The relevant modern award for his workplace provides: 'The employment of any person with a criminal record, or who is convicted of a criminal offence during the period of their employment, will be immediately terminated'.

Law

The *Fair Work Act 2009* (Cth) provides in Part 2-3 for the making of modern awards.[4] Division C of Part 2-3 covers the terms of modern awards, and Sub-division D provides terms that must not be included in modern awards, including:

> **153 Terms that are discriminatory**
>
> Discriminatory terms must not be included
>
> (1) A modern award must not include terms that discriminate against an employee because of, or for reasons including, the employee's race, colour, sex, sexual preference, age, physical or mental disability, marital status, family or carer's responsibilities, pregnancy, religion, political opinion, national extraction or social origin.

4 Proclamation took place on 14 May 2009: see www.comlaw.gov.au/details/F2009L01818.

Certain terms are not discriminatory

(2) A term of a modern award does not discriminate against an employee:

(a) if the reason for the discrimination is the inherent requirements of the particular position held by the employee [...]

Other relevant excerpts from the legislation include:

2 Commencement

(1) Each provision of this Act specified in column 1 of the table commences, or is taken to have commenced, in accordance with column 2 of the table. Any other statement in column 2 has effect according to its terms.

Commencement information		
Column 1	**Column 2**	**Column 3**
Provision(s)	Commencement	Date/Details
3. Sections 41 to 572	A day or days to be fixed by Proclamation. A Proclamation must not specify a day that occurs before the day on which the *Fair Work (Transitional Provisions and Consequential Amendments) Act 2009* receives the Royal Assent. However, if any of the provision(s) do not commence within the period of 12 months beginning on the day on which the *Fair Work (Transitional Provisions and Consequential Amendments) Act 2009* receives the Royal Assent, they commence on the first day after the end of that period.	Sections 41–43, 50–54, 58, 169–281A, 300–327, 332, 333, 334–572: 1 July 2009 (*see* F2009L02563) Sections 44–49, 55–57A, 59–168, 282–299, 328–331, 333A: 1 January 2010 (*see* F2009L02563)

3 Object of this Act

The object of this Act is to provide a balanced framework for cooperative and productive workplace relations that promotes national economic prosperity and social inclusion for all Australians by:

(a) providing workplace relations laws that are fair to working Australians, are flexible for businesses, promote productivity and economic growth for Australia's future economic prosperity and take into account Australia's international labour obligations; and

(b) ensuring a guaranteed safety net of fair, relevant and enforceable minimum terms and conditions through the National Employment Standards, modern awards and national minimum wage orders; and

(c) ensuring that the guaranteed safety net of fair, relevant and enforceable minimum wages and conditions can no longer be undermined by the making of statutory individual employment agreements of any kind given that such agreements can never be part of a fair workplace relations system; and

(d) assisting employees to balance their work and family responsibilities by providing for flexible working arrangements; and

(e) enabling fairness and representation at work and the prevention of discrimination by recognising the right to freedom of association and the right to be represented, protecting against unfair treatment and discrimination, providing accessible and effective procedures to resolve grievances and disputes and providing effective compliance mechanisms; and

(f) achieving productivity and fairness through an emphasis on enterprise-level collective bargaining underpinned by simple good faith bargaining obligations and clear rules governing industrial action; and

(g) acknowledging the special circumstances of small and medium-sized businesses.

12 Dictionary

['Discrimination' and 'Inherent Requirement' are not defined]

26 Act excludes State or Territory industrial laws

(1) This Act is intended to apply to the exclusion of all State or Territory industrial laws so far as they would otherwise apply in relation to a national system employee or a national system employer.

30B Meaning of referring State

(1) A State is a *referring State* if the Parliament of the State has, before 1 July 2009, referred the matters covered … to the Parliament of the Commonwealth for the purposes of paragraph 51(xxxvii) of the Constitution:

  (a) if and to the extent that the matters are not otherwise included in the legislative powers of the Parliament of the Commonwealth (otherwise than by a reference under paragraph 51(xxxvii) of the Constitution); and

  (b) if and to the extent that the matters are included in the legislative powers of the Parliament of the State.

30C Extended meaning of national system employee

(1) A *national system employee* includes:
  (a) any individual in a State that is a referring State because of this Division so far as he or she is employed, or usually employed, as described in paragraph 30D(1)(a), except on a vocational placement; and
  (b) a law enforcement officer of the State to whom subsection 30E(1) applies.

134 The modern awards objective

(1) FWA must ensure that modern awards, together with the National Employment Standards, provide a fair and relevant minimum safety net of terms and conditions, taking into account:
  (a) relative living standards and the needs of the low paid; and
  (b) the need to encourage collective bargaining; and
  (c) the need to promote social inclusion through increased workforce participation; and
  (d) the need to promote flexible modern work practices and the efficient and productive performance of work; and
  (e) the principle of equal remuneration for work of equal or comparable value; and
  (f) the likely impact of any exercise of modern award powers on business, including on productivity, employment costs and the regulatory burden; and
  (g) the need to ensure a simple, easy to understand, stable and sustainable modern award system for Australia that avoids unnecessary overlap of modern awards; and
  (h) the likely impact of any exercise of modern award powers on employment growth, inflation and the sustainability, performance and competitiveness of the national economy.

This is the *modern awards objective*.

Materials

Legislative background

The *Fair Work Act 2009* (Cth) replaces the previous 'Work Choices' legislation, passed in 2005 by the Howard coalition government with the *Workplace Relations Amendment (Work Choices) Act 2005* (Cth) to significantly amend the *Workplace Relations Act 1996* (Cth). That legislation shifted the regulation of industrial matters to the Commonwealth through referring powers by the States. A constitutional challenge to the validity of reliance on the corporations power, as opposed to the conciliation and arbitration power, was unsuccessful: *New South Wales v Commonwealth* (2006) 231 ALR 1. With the change of power, the Rudd Labor government set about reforming the legislation (maintaining, however, a unified federal approach to industrial relations). Transitional legislation was implemented in 2008, and the Fair Work legislation in 2009 under the Gillard Labor government.

Second Reading Speech

Fair Work Bill 2008, Minister for Employment and Workplace Relations, the Honourable Julia Gillard MP, House of Representatives, 25 November 2008:

> I rise today one year on from the election of the Rudd Labor Government to deliver on a promise Labor made to the Australian people. Today we deliver the creation of a new workplace relations system, one that allows Australia to grasp the promise of the future without forgetting the values that made us who and what we are. [...]
>
> The Bill being introduced today is based on the enduring principle of fairness while meeting the needs of the modern age. It balances the interests of employers and employees and balances the granting of rights with the imposition of responsibilities. The Bill delivers:
>
> - a fair and comprehensive safety net of minimum employment conditions that cannot be stripped away;
> - a system that has at its heart bargaining in good faith at the enterprise level, as this is essential to maximise workplace cooperation, improve economic productivity and create rising national prosperity;
> - protections from unfair dismissal for all employees;
> - protection and hope for a better future for the low-paid;
> - a balance between work and family life; and
> - the right to be represented in the workplace. [...]
>
> The bill contains protections against discrimination. [...]
>
> The bill incorporates the current provisions relating to freedom of association, unlawful termination and other miscellaneous protections into a streamlined and easy-to-follow part titled 'General protections'. In doing so, the bill provides more comprehensive protections for workers in some situations.

(www.workplace.gov.au/NR/rdonlyres/53C280C4-17AF-4EED-83BE-418C21E19999/0/fwbill20082rs.pdf)

Explanatory Memorandum

The Explanatory Memorandum to the Fair Work Bill 2008 (Cth) provides, *inter alia*:

> The Fair Work Bill 2008 (the Bill) creates a national workplace relations system that is fair to working people, flexible for business and promotes productivity and economic growth.
>
> Notes on Clauses
>
> Clause 153—Terms that are discriminatory
>
> [591] Clause 153 prohibits a modern award from including certain discriminatory terms.
>
> [592] Subclause 153(1) prohibits modern award terms that discriminate against an employee because of, or for reasons including, the employee's race, colour, sex,

sexual preference, age, physical or mental disability, marital status, family or carer's responsibilities, pregnancy, religion, political opinion, national extraction or social origin.

[593] However, subclause 153(2) provides that a term of a modern award does not discriminate against an employee:

if the reason for the discrimination is the inherent requirements of the particular position held by the employee; or

merely because it discriminates, in relation to employment of the employee as a member of the staff of an institution that is conducted in accordance with the doctrines, tenets, beliefs or teachings of a particular religion or creed, in good faith and to avoid injury to the religious susceptibilities of adherents of that religion or creed.

(www.austlii.edu.au/au/legis/cth/bill_em/fwb2008124/memo–0.html)

Senate Committee Report

Issued on 17 March 2008, the Government Senators' Majority Report recommended passage of the Bill, but made no specific reference to discrimination. The Coalition Senators' Report did not oppose the Bill completely but criticised, *inter alia*, the drafting, consultation and specific areas of detail.

(www.aph.gov.au/Senate/committee/eet_ctte/wr_tff08/report/index.htm)

Other legislation

Section 3(1) of the *Australian Human Rights Commission Act 1986* (Cth) defines discrimination as:

(a) any distinction, exclusion or preference made on the basis of race, colour, sex, religion, political opinion, national extraction or social origin that has the effect of nullifying or impairing equality of opportunity or treatment in employment or occupation; and

(b) any other distinction, exclusion or preference that:

(i) has the effect of nullifying or impairing equality of opportunity or treatment in employment or occupation; and

(ii) has been declared by the regulations to constitute discrimination for the purposes of this Act;

but does not include any distinction, exclusion or preference:

(c) in respect of a particular job based on the inherent requirements of the job; or

(d) in connection with employment as a member of the staff of an institution that is conducted in accordance with the doctrines, tenets, beliefs or teachings of a particular religion or creed, being a distinction, exclusion or preference made in good faith in order to avoid injury to the religious susceptibilities of adherents of that religion or that creed.

Section 21A of the *Disability Discrimination Act 1992* (Cth) provides:

(1) This Division does not render it unlawful for a person (the *discriminator*) to discriminate against another person (the *aggrieved person*) on the ground of a disability of the aggrieved person if:

(a) the discrimination relates to particular work (including promotion or transfer to particular work); and

(b) because of the disability, the aggrieved person would be unable to carry out the inherent requirements of the particular work, even if the relevant employer, principal or partnership made reasonable adjustments for the aggrieved person.

(3) For the purposes of paragraph (1)(b), the following factors are to be taken into account in determining whether the aggrieved person would be able to carry out the inherent requirements of the particular work:

(a) the aggrieved person's past training, qualifications and experience relevant to the particular work;

(b) if the aggrieved person already works for the discriminator—the aggrieved person's performance in working for the discriminator;

(c) any other factor that it is reasonable to take into account; [...]

Cases

At the time of writing no decisions had been handed down which relate to s 153 of the *Fair Work Act 2009* (Cth). However there are some decisions relating to what amounts to an 'inherent requirement'.

Qantas Airways Ltd v Christie (1998) 193 CLR 280

This decision considered whether age was an inherent requirement for Qantas pilots on international routes. It was covered in the case exercise titled 'Too Old to Fly?' in Chapter 6.

Woodhouse v Wood Cofill Funerals Pty Ltd [1998] HREOCA 12

This decision relates to the termination of a funeral business employee because he was found to have a prosthetic foot and there were concerns as to whether he could carry coffins safely. The Human Rights and Equal Opportunity Commission stated relevant factors in determining what are 'inherent requirements' of a job include consideration of the work that is required to be done in practice, not merely what is in the duty statement for the position; the circumstances in which the work is performed; with a focus on the ability to achieve a result more than the ability to use a particular method to achieve a result.

X v Commonwealth (1999) 200 CLR 177

This decision relates to an army officer discharged on account of his HIV-positive status. The High Court held that inherent requirements are not limited to the ability to perform physical tasks, they include being able to perform combat duty requirements with reasonable safety.

KL v State of NSW (Department of Education) [2010] AusHRC 42

The Australian Human Rights Commission reported in relation to an inquiry into a complaint of discrimination in employment on the basis of criminal record by a music teacher. He had convictions across a nine year period for drug possession, illegal use of a motor vehicle, attempt to break, enter and steal, dangerous driving, resisting arrest, shoplifting, dishonesty, and failure to appear. Eleven years later he completed a Bachelor of Music Education and applied for a position as a secondary teacher with the Department of Education and Training. He was advised he would not be offered a position based on his criminal record. DET argued that it was an inherent requirement of the job of a teacher to espouse the highest standards of conduct and integrity. The President of the Australian Human Rights Commission concluded that a person's criminal record does not necessarily render them incapable forever of fulfilling the inherent requirements of such a position.

Application

Identification Phase

The *Fair Work Act 2009* (Cth) is in force, and the operative provision, s 153, entered into force on 1 January 2010. The Act applies to John's employment by virtue of s 26, s 30B and s 30C of the Act.

On an initial reading of s 153, it looks as though we must establish:

1 Whether the term in the modern award that provides for immediate termination of employment where a person has a criminal record or is convicted of an offence during employment, is discriminatory.

2 If the term discriminates, whether the effect of s 153(2) is to deem this discrimination to be not discriminatory, by virtue of it being an 'inherent requirement of the particular position'.

We know that the ordinary meaning of words should be applied unless it is evident from the context and purpose of the legislation in which the words are located that another meaning should apply (Rule 44).

Exploration Phase

The immediate context (Rule 49) of the provision is Part 2-3 of the Act, which is titled 'Modern Awards'. It has three divisions, and s 153 fits within Division 3, titled 'Terms of modern awards'. Division 3 has four subdivisions, the first being preliminary, second being terms that may be included, and third terms that must be included, and the fourth terms that must not be included. Section 153 falls within the fourth subdivision (Subdivision D). It includes six sections, five of which address specific terms, namely payments and deductions, right of entry, long service leave, discriminatory terms, and terms that contain State-based differences. The absence of a definition of 'discrimination' and 'inherent requirement' in the Act suggests that Parliament accepts common law meanings of these terms can apply (Rule 146).

The broader context of the legislation (Rule 50) is an overall government policy towards a national approach to industrial law which is based in fairness in the modern age, balancing interests of employees and employees. It is apparent that the main changes from Work Choices to Fair Work do not relate to discrimination, and there does not appear to be any controversy surrounding the proposition that individuals should not be discriminated against in the workplace.

The purpose of the Act, as revealed by intrinsic materials in circumstances where there is no Long Title, are in the objects clause in s 3. It provides for a 'balanced framework' that will, *inter alia*, provide workplace laws that are fair for employees and flexible for businesses, fair conditions of work and respect for individual rights, and the prevention of discrimination. Paragraph (e) of the objects clause includes '... the prevention of discrimination by ... protecting against unfair treatment and discrimination...'. But an objects clause is not exhaustive (Rule 74). In this case, consideration of extrinsic materials appear to do little to assist with ascertainment of purpose—even the discussion in the Explanatory Memorandum regarding s 153 is merely a regurgitation of the provision and does not explain whether it is intended to adopt or vary existing discrimination law as it relates to inherent requirements. We are looking for an interpretation that best promotes the purpose (s 15AA of the *Acts Interpretation Act 1901* (Cth)) which can be difficult when the overall purpose of the Act is far broader than the intention of the specific operative provision. But we can also look to the result an interpretation may have and consider whether that aligns with the purpose (Rule 64).

Application Phase

Returning to the operative provision, having concluded that consideration of the context and purpose has set the scene but has not revealed any specific debate or issue surrounding the scope of application of s 153, we can consider our questions.

The first question is whether the term in the modern award that provides for immediate termination of employment where a person has a criminal record or is convicted of an offence during employment, is discriminatory. Although there is no mention in s 153(1) of discrimination on the grounds of criminal record, we can see the word 'including' is used which means that discrimination is not limited to the specific examples given (Rule 80). There is no definition of 'discriminate' or 'discriminatory' in the Act, which would otherwise override the ordinary meaning (Rule 75) but the ordinary meaning of the word is the making of a distinction based on some difference in the items being compared. We can use s 15AB(1)(a) of the *Acts Interpretation Act 1901* (Cth) to confirm that the meaning is the ordinary meaning, using a dictionary (using a current dictionary—see Rule 99), which states that 'discriminatory' is an adjective which is characterised by or showing prejudicial treatment, especially as an indication of racial, religious, or sexual bias. The modern award has differentiated, or shown prejudicial treatment, towards John on the basis of his criminal record, so we may conclude that it is, on its face, discriminatory.

The second question, then, is whether the discrimination is justified as an 'inherent requirement' of the particular position. This may be considered a 'deeming' provision (see

Rule 108). In the absence of a legislative methodology for determining 'inherent requirements' and any cases specifically relating to s 153, we may turn (cautiously) to cases relating to other legislation. We can presume that re-enactment of a term such as 'inherent requirement' which has a meaning established by courts, is an endorsement by Parliament of that meaning (Rule 150) given that no express words have been used to rebut this presumption (Rule 141). We can see that being able to work safely can be an inherent requirement of a position, as per *Woodhouse v Wood Cofill Funerals Pty Ltd* [1998] HREOCA 12 and *X v Commonwealth* (1999) 200 CLR 177. But we can also see that a criminal record, which relates to a person's conduct and evidences a disregard for the law, cannot be evidence of an enduring disregard, regardless of how much time has passed and how much a person's conduct reflects rehabilitation, as per *KL v State of NSW (Department of Education)* [2010] AusHRC 42. We may reason that, while absence of a criminal record may not itself be an inherent requirement of a manufacturing position, a demonstrated history of violence, particularly one involving a dangerous object such as a knife, may offend against an inherent requirement that one be capable of working safely with knives. That inherent requirement may cover not only the physical ability but also the emotional ability to maintain self-control around knives. As such, it may be concluded that it is an inherent requirement of a position that involves working with knives that there be no reason to suggest that the person may not conduct themselves safely.

We now ask ourselves whether there is more than one meaning open. It would appear from the above reasoning that there is little doubt that an inherent requirement can encompass both physical and other capacities, and so safety comes within the meaning. We then ask whether this concluded meaning is supported by the context and purpose when considered together (Rule 52), which includes industrial laws that strike a fair balance between employers and employees. Can this not also cover a fair balance as between employees, to work in an environment that is safe? There is an inherent tension between the right of one employee not to be discriminated against, and the right of another employee to work in a safe environment, and the obligation of an employer to provide such an environment. It would be reasonable to conclude that our interpretation of the inherent requirement of John's position is supported by the general legislative context and the purpose of 'fair work', such that the actions by Nicholson's Knives are justified.[5]

5 There is no one right answer, the key is the reasoning followed more so than the result reached.

PRACTICAL EXERCISE A

CRIMINAL LAW

'Demolition Man'

Facts

Brian is a demolition expert. He has worked on a number of projects over the past 25 years, and these days he is mostly called in where a demolition is risky or tricky for some reason—proximity to other buildings, dangerous materials, train tunnels underneath. Recently he was contacted by Matthew, asking for his advice on the safe demolition of a large building that was due for redevelopment. Matthew also indicated that he has businesses overseas and he would like to discuss using Brian's services in relation to those jobs, or otherwise receiving suitable training and advice from him.

Brian met with Matthew at the site. Matthew was accompanied by three other men, whom Matthew introduced as his business associates. Brian gave them a general background briefing to demolition, explaining methods to create an implosion rather than an explosion, which explosives should be used and where in a building's structure they should be positioned. He could see that the men admired his work and were interested in the engineering aspects.

Matthew thanked Brian for his advice, and produced the plans for a building he owns overseas, which is likely to be demolished to make way for a new shopping centre. Brian explained the best strategy and plan for its demolition. He recommended that Matthew leave the plans with him, so that if any issues arise he can call from overseas and Brian can use the plans to further advise him. Months have passed and Brian has not heard further from Matthew. He still has the plans in his office.

Yesterday a terrorist attack caused the Rialto Tower in Melbourne CBD to crumble dramatically to the ground, killing 327 people inside. Scenes were reminiscent of September 11. This morning federal police arrived at Brian's door and arrested him. He has been told that he is to be charged under the Criminal Code in relation to the bombing. He had the following interchange with the arresting officers:

> Officer: 'We will allege that you gave advice to these terrorists on how to demolish the building'.

Brian: 'Well that's right, I did. But I didn't know they were going to demolish a building with people inside it'.

Officer: 'It doesn't matter. You provided training connected with preparation for a terrorist act. There is no requirement that you know the preparation is for a *specific* attack, and as long as you intended the act to occur, and it was a terrorist act, it doesn't make any difference whether you knew the act would amount to a terrorist act or not. You knew the act would occur and that is enough'.

Brian: 'It doesn't seem right'.

Officer: 'Well it's not right. You can't recklessly go around giving people advice on demolishing buildings. You must check their credentials—did you even establish they owned the building, or that the other building overseas ever existed?'

Brian: 'I guess not'.

Officer: 'And the fact is that you have in your possession the plans for the bombing of the Rialto Tower, and they have annotations of where the explosives were to be positioned, and those plans were followed in the attack'.

Brian: 'I can't believe this. What should I do?'

Officer: 'Better get a lawyer son. Better get a real good one'.

Statute

Criminal Code Act 1995 (Cth):

101.1 Terrorist acts

(1) A person commits an offence if the person engages in a terrorist act.
Penalty: Imprisonment for life.

(2) Section 15.4 (extended geographical jurisdiction–category D) applies to an offence against subsection (1).

101.2 Providing or receiving training connected with terrorist acts

(1) A person commits an offence if:
   (a) the person provides or receives training; and
   (b) the training is connected with preparation for, the engagement of a person in, or assistance in a terrorist act; and
   (c) the person mentioned in paragraph (a) knows of the connection described in paragraph (b).

Penalty: Imprisonment for 25 years.

(2) A person commits an offence if:
   (a) the person provides or receives training; and

(b) the training is connected with preparation for, the engagement of a person in, or assistance in a terrorist act; and

(c) the person mentioned in paragraph (a) is reckless as to the existence of the connection described in paragraph (b).

Penalty: Imprisonment for 15 years.

(3) A person commits an offence under this section even if:

(a) a terrorist act does not occur; or

(b) the training is not connected with preparation for, the engagement of a person in, or assistance in a specific terrorist act; or

(c) the training is connected with preparation for, the engagement of a person in, or assistance in more than one terrorist act.

(4) Section 15.4 (extended geographical jurisdiction—category D) applies to an offence against this section.

(5) If, in a prosecution for an offence (the *prosecuted offence*) against a subsection of this section, the trier of fact is not satisfied that the defendant is guilty of the offence, but is satisfied beyond reasonable doubt that the defendant is guilty of an offence (the *alternative offence*) against another subsection of this section, the trier of fact may find the defendant not guilty of the prosecuted offence but guilty of the alternative offence, so long as the defendant has been accorded procedural fairness in relation to that finding of guilt.

101.4 Possessing things connected with terrorist acts

(1) A person commits an offence if:

(a) the person possesses a thing; and

(b) the thing is connected with preparation for, the engagement of a person in, or assistance in a terrorist act; and

(c) the person mentioned in paragraph (a) knows of the connection described in paragraph (b).

Penalty: Imprisonment for 15 years.

(2) A person commits an offence if:

(a) the person possesses a thing; and

(b) the thing is connected with preparation for, the engagement of a person in, or assistance in a terrorist act; and

(c) the person mentioned in paragraph (a) is reckless as to the existence of the connection described in paragraph (b).

Penalty: Imprisonment for 10 years.

(3) A person commits an offence under subsection (1) or (2) even if:

(a) a terrorist act does not occur; or

(b) the thing is not connected with preparation for, the engagement of a person in, or assistance in a specific terrorist act; or

(c) the thing is connected with preparation for, the engagement of a person in, or assistance in more than one terrorist act.

(4) Section 15.4 (extended geographical jurisdiction—category D) applies to an offence against this section.

(5) Subsections (1) and (2) do not apply if the possession of the thing was not intended to facilitate preparation for, the engagement of a person in, or assistance in a terrorist act.

Note: A defendant bears an evidential burden in relation to the matter in subsection (5) (see subsection 13.3(3)).

(6) If, in a prosecution for an offence (the *prosecuted offence*) against a subsection of this section, the trier of fact is not satisfied that the defendant is guilty of the offence, but is satisfied beyond reasonable doubt that the defendant is guilty of an offence (the *alternative offence*) against another subsection of this section, the trier of fact may find the defendant not guilty of the prosecuted offence but guilty of the alternative offence, so long as the defendant has been accorded procedural fairness in relation to that finding of guilt.

PRACTICAL EXERCISE B

TORT LAW

'Sally's Night on the Town'

Facts

Sally Taylor is a law student at Macquwsyduts University. Last weekend she went out with some friends in Sydney city. Sally was dressed in a 'naughty nurse' outfit as they were having a hospital theme to celebrate her friend's graduation from medical school. She's not into getting drunk but did have one Raspberry Vodka Cruiser each hour because she knew you can't get drunk on one standard drink per hour. She left a club on George Street around midnight and headed to Central Station. She entered via the country trains terminal and headed down a long underground corridor towards the suburban train platforms.

Sally noticed a man ahead who was clutching at his chest on the ground, his face was in a spasm and he looked to be in a lot of pain. She rushed to him, desperately looking around for someone to call for help. There was nobody in sight. She grabbed her iPhone from her pocket and found there was no service. She didn't want to leave the man to get help because she was sure he would die.

She then spotted something attached to the wall with a label 'Emergency Use Only: Defibrillator'. Although Sally does not have a first aid certificate, she once saw a defibrillator being used in a TV drama show she regularly watches, and she knows it can be used to restart the heart. She also recalled that there was a voice that gave instructions so she figured it was worth a try. She yanked the box off the wall and took it to the man, undoing his jacket and shirt buttons to expose his chest. She was shaking but managed to open the defibrillator box. Bits fell out everywhere.

The voice from the defibrillator recording stated 'Stick the pad on the person's bare chest'. Sally grabbed a sticky pad, peeled the back off, and stuck it on the man's chest. It then instructed 'Preparing to administer shock. Stand clear'. Sally stood back. The shock was administered but it caused the man's chest hair to ignite. Sally rushed forward, taking off her scarf to douse the flames, but the machine stated 'Preparing to administer shock. Stand clear'. She leapt back just as the second shock was administered. The man started moving, the colour returning to his face. Sally yanked the cord out of the defibrillator and used her scarf to douse the flames. She told the man to remain calm as she was going for help. He moaned with pain.

Sally ran upstairs and called an ambulance as soon as her iPhone came into service, while waving madly to station officers. The ambulance came and took the man to the hospital. While they were getting him onto a stretcher Sally asked what had gone wrong, there must have been a malfunction with the defibrillator. The ambulance officer told her that the shock is only administered when the machine determines the heart has stopped, but that it is supposed to be administered to a bare chest, and the reason for the fire was that she had not shaved his hairy chest before sticking on the pad. Sally said that she didn't realise that, and in the stress of the moment she did not notice the disposable razor that had been in the defibrillator box but had flown out when she opened it.

The man, Joseph Patelli, has now commenced proceedings in the District Court of New South Wales, alleging that burns sustained to his chest, which required skin grafts and several operations, were due to Sally's negligence.

Statute

Civil Liability Act 2002 (NSW)

Long Title

An Act to make provision in relation to the recovery of damages for death or personal injury caused by the fault of a person; to amend the *Legal Profession Act 1987* in relation to costs in civil claims; and for other purposes.

2 Commencement

This Act is taken to have commenced on 20 March 2002.

3 Definitions

In this Act:

'court' includes tribunal, and in relation to a claim for damages means any court or tribunal by or before which the claim falls to be determined.

'damages' includes any form of monetary compensation but does not include:

(a) any payment authorised or required to be made under a State industrial instrument, or
(b) any payment authorised or required to be made under a superannuation scheme, or
(c) any payment authorised or required to be made under an insurance policy in respect of the death of, injury to or damage suffered by the person insured under the policy.

'non-economic loss' means any one or more of the following:

(a) pain and suffering,
(b) loss of amenities of life,
(c) loss of expectation of life,
(d) disfigurement.

Part 1A—Negligence

5 Definitions

In this Part:

'harm' means harm of any kind, including the following:

(a) personal injury or death,
(b) damage to property,
(c) economic loss.

'negligence' means failure to exercise reasonable care and skill.

'personal injury' includes:

(a) pre-natal injury, and
(b) impairment of a person's physical or mental condition, and
(c) disease.

5A Application of Part

(1) This Part applies to any claim for damages for harm resulting from negligence, regardless of whether the claim is brought in tort, in contract, under statute or otherwise. [...]

5D General principles

(1) A determination that negligence caused particular harm comprises the following elements:
  (a) that the negligence was a necessary condition of the occurrence of the harm ('factual causation'), and
  (b) that it is appropriate for the scope of the negligent person's liability to extend to the harm so caused ('scope of liability'). [...]

Part 8—Good Samaritans

55 Application of Part

(1) This Part applies to civil liability of any kind. [...]

56 Who is a good samaritan

For the purposes of this Part, a 'good samaritan' is a person who, in good faith and without expectation of payment or other reward, comes to the assistance of a person who is apparently injured or at risk of being injured.

57 Protection of good samaritans

(1) A good samaritan does not incur any personal civil liability in respect of any act or omission done or made by the good samaritan in an emergency when assisting a person who is apparently injured or at risk of being injured.

(2) This section does not affect the vicarious liability of any other person for the acts or omissions of the good samaritan.

58 Exclusion from protection

(1) The protection from personal liability conferred by this Part does not apply if it is the good samaritan's intentional or negligent act or omission that caused the injury or risk of injury in respect of which the good samaritan first comes to the assistance of the person.

(2) The protection from personal liability conferred by this Part in respect of an act or omission does not apply if:

- (a) the ability of the good samaritan to exercise reasonable care and skill was significantly impaired by reason of the good samaritan being under the influence of alcohol or a drug voluntarily consumed (whether or not it was consumed for medication), and
- (b) the good samaritan failed to exercise reasonable care and skill in connection with the act or omission.

(3) This Part does not confer protection from personal liability on a person in respect of any act or omission done or made while the person is impersonating a health care or emergency services worker or a police officer or is otherwise falsely representing that the person has skills or expertise in connection with the rendering of emergency assistance.

Materials

Second Reading Speeches

Legislative Assembly, 28 May 2002—Civil Liability Bill 2002 (NSW)

Mr CARR (Maroubra—Premier, Minister for the Arts, and Minister for Citizenship) [4.32 p.m.]:

This bill implements stage one of the Government's tort law reform program. I will introduce stage two of the Government's tort law reform program next session. I have already outlined many of the issues that we will address in stage two. Stage two will introduce broad-ranging reforms to the law of negligence. It will ensure that risk warnings can operate as a good defence for risky entertainment or sporting activities—risk warnings should be enough. It will address the test for professional negligence, including medical negligence. Stage two will also ensure that public authorities have a good defence to a negligence claim if they comply with standards set for the particular activity. There will be special protections for good Samaritans.

Legislative Assembly, 23 October 2002—Civil Liability Amendment (Personal Responsibility) Bill 2002 (NSW)

Mr CARR (Maroubra—Premier, Minister for the Arts, and Minister for Citizenship) [12.08 p.m.]:

The bill will also protect the good faith actions of good Samaritans who come to the assistance of a person in danger. This will mean no liability for voluntary rescue organisations, such as surf life saving clubs, if a person is injured in the course of or in connection with a rescue. Individual volunteers will also be protected from law suits where their actions were done in good faith. It is not intended to alter the potential liability of a community organisation by providing the individual members with immunity.

Debate resumed, 30 October 2002

Ms BEAMER (Mulgoa) [12.49 p.m.]:

Many people in the community are appalled that liability attaches to volunteer rescue organisations and good Samaritans. Parts 8 and 9 of the bill provide that members of organisations who are acting in good faith will be protected from liability for acts or omissions. Considerable outcry occurred when surf life rescue organisations and other volunteer groups attracted civil liability claims when they acted in good faith to provide assistance for people who were in danger. Honourable members who are present in this Chamber should applaud volunteers and give them the type of coverage that they deserve.

Mr GIBSON (Blacktown) [12.04 p.m.]:

This nation has been built on the ethos of the good Samaritan, but that ethos has disappeared over the past decade or so. We used to read stories from America about injured people who received no assistance for fear that the good Samaritan would be sued.

Mr TRIPODI: *Seinfeld*.

Mr GIBSON: That is a good example. We thought it would never happen here but unfortunately we have followed that trend. A doctor friend told me that he would have to think carefully before assisting an injured person because if the injury was beyond his capabilities or expertise he could end up in court. People may be reluctant to become involved in an argument, for example, for fear of being sued. This bill looks after good

> Samaritans by protecting the good-faith actions of those who come to the assistance of people in danger. That is one of the most pleasing parts of this legislation. Unfortunately, good Samaritans have disappeared from the Australian landscape in the past few decades, and their return would be most welcome.
>
> The legislation will ensure that volunteer rescue organisations such as surf-lifesaving clubs are free from liability if a person is injured in the course of, or in connection with, a rescue. Those volunteers can continue to rescue and assist people free from the fear of litigation. We have reached the ludicrous situation in this country whereby fear of litigation has halted surf-lifesaving patrols. Those opposite have criticised the Government for taking time to draft this legislation, but if we failed to draft it carefully our Australian way of life could disappear. The bill also protects from lawsuits individual volunteers who acted in good faith.

Legislative Council, 19 November 2002

> The Hon. MICHAEL EGAN (Treasurer, Minister for State Development, and Vice-President of the Executive Council) [2.43 p.m.]:
>
> I move that this bill be now read a second time. I seek leave to incorporate the second reading speech made by the Premier in the other place. [...]
>
> The bill also affords protection to the very special group of people who come to the aid of a person who is apparently injured or at risk of being injured. A good Samaritan does not incur any personal civil liability for any act or omission done or made by the good Samaritan when assisting a person who is injured or at risk of being injured.

Explanatory Notes

Civil Liability Bill 2002 (NSW)

> The object of this Bill is to make the following changes to the law in respect of civil actions for damages. The Bill provides for the proposed Act to commence retrospectively on 20 March 2002.

[The notes are brief and no mention is made of Part 8]
Civil Liability Amendment (Personal Responsibility) Bill 2002 (NSW)
[No explanatory notes]

Dictionary

'injury'—physical harm or damage to someone's body caused by an accident or an attack
'injured'—hurt or physically harmed

'hurt'—to feel pain in a part of your body, or to injure someone or cause them pain; to cause emotional pain to someone; to cause harm or difficulty
'harm/ed'—to hurt or damage something
'emergency'—something dangerous or serious, such as an accident, which happens suddenly or unexpectedly and needs fast action in order to avoid harmful results
'impair/ed'—to spoil something or make it weaker so that it is less effective

PRACTICAL EXERCISE C

CONTRACT LAW

'Getting Sloppy'

Facts

Super Sloppy Joe Sellers Pty Ltd, an Australian company, contracted with Chung Long Textiles, a Chinese company, to have 10 000 tops produced and shipped to Australia in time for winter season of 2011. A dispute has arisen between them. All correspondence between the parties was by emails, which have been reproduced below.

> From: Bruce Arnold <brucearnold@supersloppy.com>
> Date: Fri, 15 Oct 2010 10:27:04
> To: info@chunglong.ch
> Subject: Quote request
>
> Dear Sir/Madam
>
> We are an Australian company specialising in leisure wear, particularly fleece sweaters referred to in Australia as 'sloppy joes'. We are currently seeking quotes from suitable manufacturers for the 2011 winter season.
>
> Can you please provide a quote for 10,000 hooded sweaters, each with tri-colour image on the front, 1,000 sweaters in each of black, navy, light blue, grey, green, brown, yellow, red, orange and white, with 200 of each size XS, S, M, L, XL.
>
> We want a CIF[1] contract. We do not mind if they are shipped, as long as they arrive in Perth by end March 2011. These are for our winter season and we need plenty of time to fill shop orders around the country.
>
> Regards
> Bruce Arnold

1 Cost, Insurance and Freight, a common trade term which requires the seller to pay for carriage and insurance of the goods, with delivery to the buyer occurring at the moment the goods cross the ship's rail at the load port.

From: Sang Cheng<sangcheng@chunglong.ch>
Date: Mon, 18 Oct 2010 08:10:01
To: Bruce Arnold <brucearnold@supersloppy.com>
Subject: Re: Quote request

Dear Mr Bruce

We thank you. We are specialist manufacturer textile garments in China. We do quality for you.

We can make total order US$55,000. This is $5 per sweater plus $5,000 for shipping and insurance. If we ship January 2011 no problem arrive March end. You send us lengths and widths, we make for you. You make 50% deposit on order, pay balance when goods arrive.

We pleased to do business with you.

Regards
Sang Cheng

From: Bruce Arnold <brucearnold@supersloppy.com>
Date: Mon, 18 Oct 2010 16:20:55
To: sangcheng@chunglong.ch
Subject: Re: Quote request

Dear Sang

Thank you for your email.

Your quote is very competitive and, as you have promised us quality sweaters, we will accept your quote. Please find purchase order attached.

I look forward to hearing from you.

Best regards
Bruce

SUPER SLOPPY JOE SELLERS PTY LTD

Purchase Order

Purchase Order No. 1256

Supplier's name:
Chung Long Textiles Co Ltd
A Dist., Kunming Industrial Park
Ruanjiang City, Hunan Province
People's Republic of China (PRC)

Purchaser's name:
Super Sloppy Joe Sellers Pty Ltd
Level 3, 120 St Georges Terrace
Perth WA 6000

Merchandise:	Price per unit	Total price
'Sloppy Joe' style sweaters: Colour: black, navy, light blue, grey, green, brown, yellow, red, orange and white (1000 each) Sizes: XS, S, M, L, XL (200 per colour in each size) Dimensions: XS: 30W 40L; S: 33W 40L; M: 36W 40 L; L: 40W 42L; XL: 44W 42L Affixation: Circles in form of a target with arrow pointing inwards, as per our logo at www.sloppyjoe.com.au	US$5.50 CIF Perth, Australia (Incoterms 2010)	US$55,000
Shipment: Direct from supplier on or before 31 March 2011 (CIF basis)		Included
	TOTAL:	US$55,000

Payment terms $27,500 within 7 days of order confirmation, $27,500 within 30 days of shipment receipt.

OUR PURCHASE ORDER IS SUBJECT TO OUR GENERAL CONDITIONS OF PURCHASE SET OUT ON THE REVERSE SIDE OF THIS FORM. THEY WILL BE THE TERMS AND CONDITIONS OF THE CONTRACT UNLESS YOU SPECIFICALLY OBJECT TO THEM DURING ORDER CONFIRMATION.

GENERAL CONDITIONS OF PURCHASE

[…]

4. Time is of the essence.

[…]

9. The contract is governed by the law in force in Western Australia.

From: Sang Cheng<sangcheng@chunglong.ch>
Date: Wed, 20 Oct 2010 15:02:30
To: Bruce Arnold <brucearnold@supersloppy.com>
Subject: Re: Quote request

Dear Mr Bruce

Thank you for your order. We have pleasure assisting you. We do quality for you. We use best flock fleece, make nice for you.

We attach sales confirmation, with our standard terms and conditions of sale, same as you would have seen on our website. Bank account for part payment:

Acct Name: Chung Long Textiles Co Ltd
Acct No: 153 7960 4538
Bank: Bank of China
Branch: Ruanjiang City Branch

We pleased to do business with you.

Regards
Sang Cheng

From: Bruce Arnold <brucearnold@supersloppy.com>
Date: Wed, 27 Oct 2010 09:11:51
To: sangcheng@chunglong.ch
Subject: Re: Quote request

Dear Sang

Please confirm receipt of USD$27,500 as 50% payment on Purchase Order No. 1256.

Best regards
Bruce

From: Sang Cheng<sangcheng@chunglong.ch>
Date: Thur, 28 Oct 2010 13:12:29
To: Bruce Arnold <brucearnold@supersloppy.com>
Subject: Re: Quote request

Dear Mr Bruce

Thank you we receive your deposit. We make slappy joe for your order, ship January 2011.

We pleased to do business with you.

Regards
Sang Cheng

From: Bruce Arnold <brucearnold@supersloppy.com>
Date: Mon, 17 Jan 2011 10:10:51
To: sangcheng@chunglong.ch
Subject: Purchase Order No. 1256

Dear Sang

I trust you enjoyed a break over the New Year. I hope you have some nice plans for the Chinese New Year. We have dragon boat races here in Perth.

I just wanted to check how our order was coming along. We've received a lot of interest from retailers in this season's sloppy joes, especially with our large logo which is a mark of quality and style.

Best regards
Bruce

From: Sang Cheng<sangcheng@chunglong.ch>
Date: Tues, 18 Jan 2011 14:20:00
To: Bruce Arnold <brucearnold@supersloppy.com>
Subject: Re: Purchase Order No. 1256

Dear Mr Bruce

Order ready and we package nice for you, shipping in one week. We hope you like and your customers like too.

We pleased to do business with you.

Regards
Sang Cheng

From: Sang Cheng<sangcheng@chunglong.ch>
Date: Thur, 31 Mar 2011 08:16:02
To: Bruce Arnold <brucearnold@supersloppy.com>
Subject: Sales Order Sloppy Australia

Dear Mr Bruce

We hope order arrived safe and sound.

Bank account for balance payment, due 30 days:

Acct Name: Chung Long Textiles Co Ltd
Acct No: 153 7960 4538
Bank: Bank of China
Branch: Ruanjiang City Branch

We pleased to do business with you.

Regards
Sang Cheng

From: Bruce Arnold <brucearnold@supersloppy.com>
Date: Wed, 4 May 2011 18:32:01
To: sangcheng@chunglong.ch
Subject: Re: Sales Order Sloppy Australia

Dear Sang

It was April Fools Day when the shipment arrived, and at first I thought there was a joke when my staff told me there were no hoods on the sweaters.

As you would be aware from perusal of our website, and from my original quotation request on 19 October 2011, sloppy joes are hooded leisure sweaters. We cannot sell unhooded sweaters to our retailers. The unhooded sweaters you have sent are not the merchandise we ordered, and we are unable to use them.

As a result of your non-fulfilment of our order, we have had to urgently contract with an Australian supplier to make the sweaters. This cost us $15 per sweater.

We have the sweaters you sent in our inventory store. Please tell us what you wish to do with them. As we are short of space, if we do not hear from you within 7 days, we will onsell them to a clothing wholesaler.

Regards
Bruce

From: Sang Cheng<sangcheng@chunglong.ch>
Date: Thur, 15 May 2011 08:03:11
To: Bruce Arnold <brucearnold@supersloppy.com>
Subject: Re: Sales Order Sloppy Australia

Dear Mr Bruce

We do not understand. You received the shipment five weeks ago on 1 April, yet you say nothing about a problem. If you told us a problem straight away we could have found another buyer for them. Now it is too late for winter season in Australia.

The goods are yours. We made what you ordered. Purchase Order No. 1256 say nothing about hoods. We do not know only sloppy joe with hoods, we think you don't want hoods. We sorry you not happy, we can make price adjustment for you. We keep good relationship for future business. We make balance payable $17,500 instead of $27,500.

Regards
Sang Cheng

From: Bruce Arnold <brucearnold@supersloppy.com>
Date: Fri, 23 May 2011 13:01:48
To: sangcheng@chunglong.ch
Subject: Re: Sales Order Sloppy Australia

Dear Sang

We managed to find a wholesaler willing to purchase the unhooded sweaters for $4 each. This has cost us not only in warehouse space but also in labour and transport, which we calculate totals $5,000.

Therefore the original contract was for $55,000 and we paid $27,500 up front. The sweaters were useless to us, and we were able to recover $40,000 from sale of the sweaters to Overstock Wholesalers Pty Ltd. The replacement sweaters cost us $15 each, which is $150,000. This is $95,000 extra. The total loss to us is $67,500.

Please confirm your willingness to reimburse us for damages, failing which we will commence court proceedings in the District Court of Western Australia. I am sorry it has come to this. I am sure you can understand where we are coming from. Business is tight in this economic market and we just cannot afford the damage to our business reputation in putting the wrong products in the market. A sloppy joe without a hood is no sloppy joe at all.

Regards
Bruce

From: Sang Cheng<sangcheng@chunglong.ch>
Date: Mon, 26 May 2011 14:10:08
To: Bruce Arnold <brucearnold@supersloppy.com>
Subject: Re: Sales Order Sloppy Australia

Dear Mr Bruce

We are taking advice from our lawyers. So far they have said:

If there is a court case it will be in China, as per Chung Long Textiles standard terms and conditions sent to you on 20 October 2011. Although it is apparent that the email did not have an attachment, the standard terms and conditions are clearly marked on the website as being applicable to all sales, and you must have seen this in order to have found out about the company. In any event, you were put on notice by the reference in the email to the terms and conditions. It is not for the buyer to dictate terms—the sellers terms prevail.

Sorry but further comunication on this contract will need be through our lawyer.

Regards
Sang Cheng

Statute

Sale of Goods (Vienna Convention) Act 1986 (WA)

5 Convention to have the force of law

The provisions of the Convention have the force of law in Western Australia.

6 Convention to prevail in event of inconsistency

The provisions of the Convention prevail over any other law in force in Western Australia to the extent of any inconsistency.

Schedule 1—United Nations Convention on Contracts for the International Sale of Goods [excerpts only]

Article 1

(1) This Convention applies to contracts of sale of goods between parties whose places of business are in different States:
   (a) when the States are Contracting States; or
   (b) when the rules of private international law lead to the application of the law of a Contracting State.

Article 3

(1) Contracts for the supply of goods to be manufactured or produced are to be considered sales unless the party who orders the goods undertakes to supply a substantial part of the materials necessary for such manufacture or production.

Article 6

The parties may exclude the application of this Convention or, subject to article 12, derogate from or vary the effect of any of its provisions.

Article 7

(1) In the interpretation of this Convention, regard is to be had to its international character and to the need to promote uniformity in its application and the observance of good faith in international trade.
(2) Questions concerning matters governed by this Convention which are not expressly settled in it are to be settled in conformity with the general principles on which it is based or, in the absence of such principles, in conformity with the law applicable by virtue of the rules of private international law.

Article 8

(1) For the purposes of this Convention statements made by and other conduct of a party are to be interpreted according to his intent where the other party knew or could not have been unaware what that intent was.
(2) If the preceding paragraph is not applicable, statements made by and other conduct of a party are to be interpreted according to the understanding that a reasonable person of the same kind as the other party would have had in the same circumstances.
(3) In determining the intent of a party or the understanding a reasonable person would have had, due consideration is to be given to all relevant circumstances of the case including the negotiations, any practices which the parties have established between themselves, usages and any subsequent conduct of the parties.

Article 11

A contract of sale need not be concluded in or evidenced by writing and is not subject to any other requirement as to form. It may be proved by any means, including witnesses.

Article 14

(1) A proposal for concluding a contract addressed to one or more specific persons constitutes an offer if it is sufficiently definite and indicates the intention of the offeror to be bound in case of acceptance. A proposal is sufficiently definite if it indicates the goods and expressly or implicitly fixes or makes provision for determining the quantity and the price.

Article 18

(1) A statement made by or other conduct of the offeree indicating assent to an offer is an acceptance. Silence or inactivity does not in itself amount to acceptance.

Article 19

(1) A reply to an offer which purports to be an acceptance but contains additions, limitations or other modifications is a rejection of the offer and constitutes a counter-offer.
(2) However, a reply to an offer which purports to be an acceptance but contains additional or different terms which do not materially alter the terms of the offer constitutes an acceptance, unless the offeror, without undue delay, objects orally to the discrepancy or dispatches a notice to that effect. If he does not so object, the terms of the contract are the terms of the offer with the modifications contained in the acceptance.
(3) Additional or different terms relating, among other things, to the price, payment, quality and quantity of the goods, place and time of delivery, extent of one party's liability to the other or the settlement of disputes are considered to alter the terms of the offer materially.

Article 23

A contract is concluded at the moment when an acceptance of an offer becomes effective in accordance with the provisions of this Convention.

Article 25

A breach of contract committed by one of the parties is fundamental if it results in such detriment to the other party as substantially to deprive him of what he is entitled to expect under the contract, unless the party in breach did not foresee and a reasonable person of the same kind in the same circumstances would not have foreseen such a result.

Article 26

A declaration of avoidance of the contract is effective only if made by notice to the other party.

Article 27

Unless otherwise expressly provided in this Part of the Convention, if any notice, request or other communication is given or made by a party in accordance with this Part and by means appropriate in the circumstances, a delay or error in the transmission of the communication or its failure to arrive does not deprive that party of the right to rely on the communication.

Article 33

The seller must deliver the goods:

(a) if a date is fixed by or determinable from the contract, on that date;
(b) if a period of time is fixed by or determinable from the contract, at any time within that period unless circumstances indicate that the buyer is to choose a date; or
(c) in any other case, within a reasonable time after the conclusion of the contract.

Article 35

(1) The seller must deliver goods which are of the quantity, quality and description required by the contract and which are contained or packaged in the manner required by the contract.
(2) Except where the parties have agreed otherwise, the goods do not conform with the contract unless they:
are fit for the purposes for which goods of the same description would ordinarily be used;
    (a) are fit for any particular purpose expressly or impliedly made known to the seller at the time of the conclusion of the contract, except where the circumstances show that the buyer did not rely, or that it was unreasonable for him to rely, on the seller's skill and judgement;

(b) possess the qualities of goods which the seller has held out to the buyer as a sample or model;

(c) are contained or packaged in the manner usual for such goods or, where there is no such manner, in a manner adequate to preserve and protect the goods.

(3) The seller is not liable under subparagraphs (a) to (d) of the preceding paragraph for any lack of conformity of the goods if at the time of the conclusion of the contract the buyer knew or could not have been unaware of such lack of conformity.

Article 36

(1) The seller is liable in accordance with the contract and this Convention for any lack of conformity which exists at the time when the risk passes to the buyer, even though the lack of conformity becomes apparent only after that time.

(2) The seller is also liable for any lack of conformity which occurs after the time indicated in the preceding paragraph and which is due to a breach of any of his obligations, including a breach of any guarantee that for a period of time the goods will remain fit for their ordinary purpose or for some particular purpose or will retain specified qualities or characteristics.

Article 38

(1) The buyer must examine the goods, or cause them to be examined, within as short a period as is practicable in the circumstances.

(2) If the contract involves carriage of the goods, examination may be deferred until after the goods have arrived at their destination.

Article 39

(1) The buyer loses the right to rely on a lack of conformity of the goods if he does not give notice to the seller specifying the nature of the lack of conformity within a reasonable time after he has discovered it or ought to have discovered it.

(2) In any event, the buyer loses the right to rely on a lack of conformity of the goods if he does not give the seller notice thereof at the latest within a period of two years from the date on which the goods were actually handed over to the buyer, unless this time-limit is inconsistent with a contractual period of guarantee.

Article 40

The seller is not entitled to rely on the provisions of articles 38 and 39 if the lack of conformity relates to facts of which he knew or could not have been unaware and which he did not disclose to the buyer.

Article 44

Notwithstanding the provisions of paragraph (1) of article 39 and paragraph (1) of article 43, the buyer may reduce the price in accordance with article 50 or claim damages, except for loss of profit, if he has a reasonable excuse for his failure to give the required notice.

Article 45

(1) If the seller fails to perform any of his obligations under the contract or this Convention, the buyer may:
    (a) exercise the rights provided in articles 46 to 52;
    (b) claim damages as provided in articles 74 to 77.
(2) The buyer is not deprived of any right he may have to claim damages by exercising his right to other remedies.
(3) No period of grace may be granted to the seller by a court or arbitral tribunal when the buyer resorts to a remedy for breach of contract.

Article 46

(1) The buyer may require performance by the seller of his obligations unless the buyer has resorted to a remedy which is inconsistent with this requirement.
(2) If the goods do not conform with the contract, the buyer may require delivery of substitute goods only if the lack of conformity constitutes a fundamental breach of contract and a request for substitute goods is made either in conjunction with notice given under article 39 or within a reasonable time thereafter.
(3) If the goods do not conform with the contract, the buyer may require the seller to remedy the lack of conformity by repair, unless this is unreasonable having regard to all the circumstances. A request for repair must be made either in conjunction with notice given under article 39 or within a reasonable time thereafter.

Article 47

(1) The buyer may fix an additional period of time of reasonable length for performance by the seller of his obligations.
(2) Unless the buyer has received notice from the seller that he will not perform within the period so fixed, the buyer may not, during that period, resort to any remedy for breach of contract. However, the buyer is not deprived thereby of any right he may have to claim damages for delay in performance.

Article 48

(1) Subject to article 49, the seller may, even after the date for delivery, remedy at his own expense any failure to perform his obligations, if he can do so without unreasonable delay and without causing the buyer unreasonable inconvenience or uncertainty of

reimbursement by the seller of expenses advanced by the buyer. However, the buyer retains any right to claim damages as provided for in this Convention.

(2) If the seller requests the buyer to make known whether he will accept performance and the buyer does not comply with the request within a reasonable time, the seller may perform within the time indicated in his request. The buyer may not, during that period of time, resort to any remedy which is inconsistent with performance by the seller.

(3) A notice by the seller that he will perform within a specified period of time is assumed to include a request, under the preceding paragraph, that the buyer make known his decision.

(4) A request or notice by the seller under paragraph (2) or (3) of this article is not effective unless received by the buyer.

Article 49

(1) The buyer may declare the contract avoided:
 (a) if the failure by the seller to perform any of his obligations under the contract or this Convention amounts to a fundamental breach of contract; or
 (b) in case of non-delivery, if the seller does not deliver the goods within the additional period of time fixed by the buyer in accordance with paragraph (1) of article 47 or declares that he will not deliver within the period so fixed.

(2) However, in cases where the seller has delivered the goods, the buyer loses the right to declare the contract avoided unless he does so:
 (a) in respect of late delivery, within a reasonable time after he has become aware that delivery has been made;
 (b) in respect of any breach other than late delivery, within a reasonable time:
  (i) after he knew or ought to have known of the breach;
  (ii) after the expiration of any additional period of time fixed by the buyer in accordance with paragraph (1) of article 47, or after the seller has declared that he will not perform his obligations within such an additional period; or
  (iii) after the expiration of any additional period of time indicated by the seller in accordance with paragraph (2) of article 48, or after the buyer has declared that he will not accept performance.

Article 50

If the goods do not conform with the contract and whether or not the price has already been paid, the buyer may reduce the price in the same proportion as the value that the goods actually delivered had at the time of the delivery bears to the value that conforming goods would have had at that time. However, if the seller remedies any failure to perform his obligations in accordance with article 37 or article 48 or if the buyer refuses to accept performance by the seller in accordance with those articles, the buyer may not reduce the price.

Article 51

(1) If the seller delivers only a part of the goods or if only a part of the goods delivered is in conformity with the contract, articles 46 to 50 apply in respect of the part which is missing or which does not conform.
(2) The buyer may declare the contract avoided in its entirety only if the failure to make delivery completely or in conformity with the contract amounts to a fundamental breach of the contract.

Article 53

The buyer must pay the price for the goods and take delivery of them as required by the contract and this Convention.

Article 61

(1) If the buyer fails to perform any of his obligations under the contract or this Convention, the seller may:
   (a) exercise the rights provided in articles 62 to 65;
   (b) claim damages as provided in articles 74 to 77.
(2) The seller is not deprived of any right he may have to claim damages by exercising his right to other remedies.

Article 62

The seller may require the buyer to pay the price, take delivery or perform his other obligations, unless the seller has resorted to a remedy which is inconsistent with this requirement.

Article 64

(1) The seller may declare the contract avoided:
   (a) if the failure by the buyer to perform any of his obligations under the contract or this Convention amounts to a fundamental breach of contract; or
   (b) if the buyer does not, within the additional period of time fixed by the seller in accordance with paragraph (1) of article 63, perform his obligation to pay the price or take delivery of the goods, or if he declares that he will not do so within the period so fixed.

Article 65

(1) If under the contract the buyer is to specify the form, measurement or other features of the goods and he fails to make such specification either on the date agreed upon or within a reasonable time after receipt of a request from the seller, the seller may, without prejudice to any other rights he may have, make the specification himself in accordance with the requirements of the buyer that may be known to him.
(2) If the seller makes the specification himself, he must inform the buyer of the details thereof and must fix a reasonable time within which the buyer may make a different

specification. If, after receipt of such a communication, the buyer fails to do so within the time so fixed, the specification made by the seller is binding.

Article 74

Damages for breach of contract by one party consist of a sum equal to the loss, including loss of profit, suffered by the other party as a consequence of the breach. Such damages may not exceed the loss which the party in breach foresaw or ought to have foreseen at the time of the conclusion of the contract, in the light of the facts and matters of which he then knew or ought to have known, as a possible consequence of the breach of contract.

Article 75

If the contract is avoided and if, in a reasonable manner and within a reasonable time after avoidance, the buyer has bought goods in replacement or the seller has resold the goods, the party claiming damages may recover the difference between the contract price and the price in the substitute transaction as well as any further damages recoverable under article 74.

Article 76

(1) If the contract is avoided and there is a current price for the goods, the party claiming damages may, if he has not made a purchase or resale under article 75, recover the difference between the price fixed by the contract and the current price at the time of avoidance as well as any further damages recoverable under article 74. If, however, the party claiming damages has avoided the contract after taking over the goods, the current price at the time of such taking over shall be applied instead of the current price at the time of avoidance.
(2) For the purposes of the preceding paragraph, the current price is the price prevailing at the place where delivery of the goods should have been made or, if there is no current price at that place, the price at such other place as serves as a reasonable substitute, making due allowance for differences in the cost of transporting the goods.

Article 77

A party who relies on a breach of contract must take such measures as are reasonable in the circumstances to mitigate the loss, including loss of profit, resulting from the breach. If he fails to take such measures, the party in breach may claim a reduction in the damages in the amount by which the loss should have been mitigated.

Article 78

If a party fails to pay the price or any other sum that is in arrears, the other party is entitled to interest on it, without prejudice to any claim for damages recoverable under article 74.

Article 81

(1) Avoidance of the contract releases both parties from their obligations under it, subject to any damages which may be due. Avoidance does not affect any provision of the contract for the settlement of disputes or any other provision of the contract governing the rights and obligations of the parties consequent upon the avoidance of the contract.
(2) A party who has performed the contract either wholly or in part may claim restitution from the other party of whatever the first party has supplied or paid under the contract. If both parties are bound to make restitution, they must do so concurrently.

Article 86

(1) If the buyer has received the goods and intends to exercise any right under the contract or this Convention to reject them, he must take such steps to preserve them as are reasonable in the circumstances. He is entitled to retain them until he has been reimbursed his reasonable expenses by the seller.
(2) If goods dispatched to the buyer have been placed at his disposal at their destination and he exercises the right to reject them, he must take possession of them on behalf of the seller, provided that this can be done without payment of the price and without unreasonable inconvenience or unreasonable expense. This provision does not apply if the seller or a person authorized to take charge of the goods on his behalf is present at the destination. If the buyer takes possession of the goods under this paragraph, his rights and obligations are governed by the preceding paragraph.

Article 87

A party who is bound to take steps to preserve the goods may deposit them in a warehouse of a third person at the expense of the other party provided that the expense incurred is not unreasonable.

Article 88

(1) A party who is bound to preserve the goods in accordance with article 85 or 86 may sell them by any appropriate means if there has been an unreasonable delay by the other party in taking possession of the goods or in taking them back or in paying the price or the cost of preservation, provided that reasonable notice of the intention to sell has been given to the other party.
(2) If the goods are subject to rapid deterioration or their preservation would involve unreasonable expense, a party who is bound to preserve the goods in accordance with article 85 or 86 must take reasonable measures to sell them. To the extent possible he must give notice to the other party of his intention to sell.
(3) A party selling the goods has the right to retain out of the proceeds of sale an amount equal to the reasonable expenses of preserving the goods and of selling them. He must account to the other party for the balance.

PRACTICAL EXERCISE D

PROPERTY LAW

'Body of Art'

Facts

Bob has 17 tattoos, covering approximately 90 per cent of his body. He is a professional wrestler, whose name in the business is 'Tatters'—both for the tattoos he has, and the way he makes tatters of his opponents. Bouts are all filmed for television before a live audience and are surprisingly popular in Japan.

Bob's two most recent acquisitions are an Aboriginal-looking snake tattoo covering the full length of each arm, and an 'Enjoy Coke' tattoo that covers the whole of his back, complete with the red colour and swirly writing, but without the 'e' at the end of Coke. He thinks they're awesome and has posted a video of himself on YouTube where he twists his arms like a snake and then turns and gyrates with his back to the camera. His video has been an overnight sensation, with 2 467 801 views after just one week. But it seems that not everyone is impressed with his tattoos. He has received an email from David Jumbungalong who says the snake pattern is a sacred image of his people, and is their cultural property. He has also received a letter sent by email from Coca-Cola, saying he has infringed its trade mark.

Statutes

Trade Marks Act 1995 (Cth)

2 Commencement

(1) Part 1 commences on the day on which this Act receives the Royal Assent.
(2) This Act, other than Part 1, commences on 1 January 1996.

6 Definitions

(1) In this Act, unless the contrary intention appears:

'designated owner', in relation to goods imported into Australia, means:

(a) the person identified as the owner of the goods on the entry made in relation to the goods under section 68 of the *Customs Act 1901*; or

(b) if no such entry exists—the person determined to be the owner of the goods under section 133A of this Act.

'goods of a person' means goods dealt with or provided in the course of trade by the person.

'limitations' means limitations of the exclusive right to use a trade mark given by the registration of the trade mark, including limitations of that right as to:

(a) mode of use; or
(b) use within a territorial area within Australia; or
(c) use in relation to goods or services to be exported.

'notified trade mark' means a trade mark in respect of which a notice under section 132 is in force.

'person' includes a body of persons, whether incorporated or not.

'registered owner', in relation to a registered trade mark, means the person in whose name the trade mark is registered.

'registered trade mark' means a trade mark whose particulars are entered in the Register under this Act.

Note: In addition, the regulations may provide for the effect of a protected international trade mark: see Part 17A.

'services of a person' means services dealt with or provided in the course of trade by the person.

'sign' includes the following or any combination of the following, namely, any letter, word, name, signature, numeral, device, brand, heading, label, ticket, aspect of packaging, shape, colour, sound or scent.

'similar goods' has the meaning given by subsection 14(1).

'similar services' has the meaning given by subsection 14(2).

7 Use of trade mark

(1) If the Registrar or a prescribed court, having regard to the circumstances of a particular case, thinks fit, the Registrar or the court may decide that a person has used a trade mark if it is established that the person has used the trade mark with additions or alterations that do not substantially affect the identity of the trade mark.

(2) To avoid any doubt, it is stated that, if a trade mark consists of the following, or any combination of the following, namely, any letter, word, name or numeral, any aural representation of the trade mark is, for the purposes of this Act, a use of the trade mark.

(3) An authorised use of a trade mark by a person (see section 8) is taken, for the purposes of this Act, to be a use of the trade mark by the owner of the trade mark.

(4) In this Act:

use of a trade mark in relation to goods' means use of the trade mark upon, or in physical or other relation to, the goods (including second-hand goods).

(5) In this Act:

'use of a trade mark in relation to services' means use of the trade mark in physical or other relation to the services.

17 What is a trade mark?

A *trade mark* is a sign used, or intended to be used, to distinguish goods or services dealt with or provided in the course of trade by a person from goods or services so dealt with or provided by any other person.

20 Rights given by registration of trade mark

(1) If a trade mark is registered, the registered owner of the trade mark has, subject to this Part, the exclusive rights:

(a) to use the trade mark; and

(b) to authorise other persons to use the trade mark;

in relation to the goods and/or services in respect of which the trade mark is registered.

21 Nature of registered trade mark as property

(1) A registered trade mark is personal property.

(2) Equities in respect of a registered trade mark may be enforced in the same way as equities in respect of any other personal property.

120 When is a registered trade mark infringed?

(1) A person infringes a registered trade mark if the person uses as a trade mark a sign that is substantially identical with, or deceptively similar to, the trade mark in relation to goods or services in respect of which the trade mark is registered.

(2) A person infringes a registered trade mark if the person uses as a trade mark a sign that is substantially identical with, or deceptively similar to, the trade mark in relation to:

(a) goods of the same description as that of goods (*registered goods*) in respect of which the trade mark is registered; or

(b) services that are closely related to registered goods; or
(c) services of the same description as that of services (*registered services*) in respect of which the trade mark is registered; or
(d) goods that are closely related to registered services.

However, the person is not taken to have infringed the trade mark if the person establishes that using the sign as the person did is not likely to deceive or cause confusion.

(3) A person infringes a registered trade mark if:
(a) the trade mark is well known in Australia; and
(b) the person uses as a trade mark a sign that is substantially identical with, or deceptively similar to, the trade mark in relation to:
(i) goods (*unrelated goods*) that are not of the same description as that of the goods in respect of which the trade mark is registered (*registered goods*) or are not closely related to services in respect of which the trade mark is registered (*registered services*); or
(ii) services (*unrelated services*) that are not of the same description as that of the registered services or are not closely related to registered goods; and
(c) because the trade mark is well known, the sign would be likely to be taken as indicating a connection between the unrelated goods or services and the registered owner of the trade mark; and
(d) for that reason, the interests of the registered owner are likely to be adversely affected.

(5) In deciding, for the purposes of paragraph (3)(a), whether a trade mark is *well known in Australia*, one must take account of the extent to which the trade mark is known within the relevant sector of the public, whether as a result of the promotion of the trade mark or for any other reason.

122 When is a trade mark not infringed?

(1) In spite of section 120, a person does not infringe a registered trade mark when:
(a) the person uses in good faith:
(i) the person's name or the name of the person's place of business; or
(ii) the name of a predecessor in business of the person or the name of the predecessor's place of business; or
(b) the person uses a sign in good faith to indicate:
(i) the kind, quality, quantity, intended purpose, value, geographical origin, or some other characteristic, of goods or services; or
(ii) the time of production of goods or of the rendering of services; or
(c) the person uses the trade mark in good faith to indicate the intended purpose of goods (in particular as accessories or spare parts) or services; or
(d) the person uses the trade mark for the purposes of comparative advertising; or
(e) the person exercises a right to use a trade mark given to the person under this Act; or

(f) the court is of the opinion that the person would obtain registration of the trade mark in his or her name if the person were to apply for it; or

(fa) both:

(i) the person uses a trade mark that is substantially identical with, or deceptively similar to, the first-mentioned trade mark; and

(ii) the court is of the opinion that the person would obtain registration of the substantially identical or deceptively similar trade mark in his or her name if the person were to apply for it; or

(g) the person, in using a sign referred to in subsection 120(1), (2) or (3) in a manner referred to in that subsection, does not (because of a condition or limitation subject to which the trade mark is registered) infringe the exclusive right of the registered owner to use the trade mark.

(2) In spite of section 120, if a disclaimer has been registered in respect of a part of a registered trade mark, a person does not infringe the trade mark by using that part of the trade mark.

Copyright Act 1968 (Cth)

2 Commencement

This Act shall come into operation on a date to be fixed by Proclamation.

8 Copyright not to subsist except by virtue of this Act

Subject to section 8A, copyright does not subsist otherwise than by virtue of this Act.

8A Prerogative rights of the Crown in the nature of copyright

(1) Subject to subsection (2), this Act does not affect any prerogative right or privilege of the Crown.

10 Interpretation

(1) In this Act, unless the contrary intention appears:

'*adaptation*' means:

(a) in relation to a literary work in a non-dramatic form a version of the work (whether in its original language or in a different language) in a dramatic form;

(b) in relation to a literary work in a dramatic form a version of the work (whether in its original language or in a different language) in a non-dramatic form;

(ba) in relation to a literary work being a computer program—a version of the work (whether or not in the language, code or notation in which the work was originally expressed) not being a reproduction of the work;

(c) in relation to a literary work (whether in a non-dramatic form or in a dramatic form):
  (i) a translation of the work; or
  (ii) a version of the work in which a story or action is conveyed solely or principally by means of pictures; and
(d) in relation to a musical work—an arrangement or transcription of the work.

'artistic work' means:

(a) a painting, sculpture, drawing, engraving or photograph, whether the work is of artistic quality or not;
(b) a building or a model of a building, whether the building or model is of artistic quality or not; or
(c) a work of artistic craftsmanship whether or not mentioned in paragraph (a) or (b);

but does not include a circuit layout within the meaning of the *Circuit Layouts Act 1989*.

'copy', in relation to a cinematograph film, means any article or thing in which the visual images or sounds comprising the film are embodied.

'drawing' includes a diagram, map, chart or plan.

'engraving' includes an etching, lithograph, product of photogravure, woodcut, print or similar work, not being a photograph.

'infringing copy' means:

(a) in relation to a work—a reproduction of the work, or of an adaptation of the work, not being a copy of a cinematograph film of the work or adaptation;

'literary work' includes:

(a) a table, or compilation, expressed in words, figures or symbols; and
(b) a computer program or compilation of computer programs.

'material form', in relation to a work or an adaptation of a work, includes any form (whether visible or not) of storage of the work or adaptation, or a substantial part of the work or adaptation, (whether or not the work or adaptation, or a substantial part of the work or adaptation, can be reproduced).

'private and domestic use' means private and domestic use on or off domestic premises.

'record' includes a disc, tape, paper, electronic file or other device in which sounds are embodied.

'sculpture' includes a cast or model made for purposes of sculpture.

'sufficient acknowledgement', in relation to a work, means an acknowledgement

identifying the work by its title or other description and, unless the work is anonymous or pseudonymous or the author has previously agreed or directed that an acknowledgement of his or her name is not to be made, also identifying the author.

'to the public' means to the public within or outside Australia.

'work' means a literary, dramatic, musical or artistic work.

'work of joint authorship' means a work that has been produced by the collaboration of two or more authors and in which the contribution of each author is not separate from the contribution of the other author or the contributions of the other authors.

'writing' means a mode of representing or reproducing words, figures or symbols in a visible form, and *'written'* has a corresponding meaning.

13 Acts comprised in copyright

(1) A reference in this Act to an act comprised in the copyright in a work or other subject-matter shall be read as a reference to any act that, under this Act, the owner of the copyright has the exclusive right to do.

31 Nature of copyright in original works

(1) For the purposes of this Act, unless the contrary intention appears, copyright, in relation to a work, is the exclusive right:
  (a) in the case of a literary, dramatic or musical work, to do all or any of the following acts:
    (i) to reproduce the work in a material form;
    (ii) to publish the work;
    (iii) to perform the work in public;
    (iv) to communicate the work to the public;
    (v) to make an adaptation of the work;
    (vi) to do, in relation to a work that is an adaptation of the first-mentioned work, any of the acts specified in relation to the first-mentioned work in subparagraphs (i) to (iv), inclusive; and
  (b) in the case of an artistic work, to do all or any of the following acts:
    (i) to reproduce the work in a material form;
    (ii) to publish the work;
    (iii) to communicate the work to the public; and
  (c) in the case of a literary work (other than a computer program) or a musical or dramatic work, to enter into a commercial rental arrangement in respect of the work reproduced in a sound recording; and

33 Duration of copyright in original works

(2) Subject to this section, copyright that subsists in a literary, dramatic, musical or artistic work by virtue of this Part continues to subsist until the end of 70 years after the end of the calendar year in which the author of the work died.

34 Duration of copyright in anonymous and pseudonymous works

(1) Subject to subsection (2), if the first publication of a literary, dramatic, musical or artistic work is anonymous or pseudonymous, any copyright subsisting in the work by virtue of this Part continues to subsist until the end of the period of 70 years after the end of the calendar year in which the work was first published.

(2) Subsection (1) does not apply in relation to a work if, at any time before the end of the period referred to in that subsection, the identity of the author of the work is generally known or can be ascertained by reasonable inquiry.

35 Ownership of copyright in original works

(2) Subject to this section, the author of a literary, dramatic, musical or artistic work is the owner of any copyright subsisting in the work by virtue of this Part.

36 Infringement by doing acts comprised in the copyright

(1) Subject to this Act, the copyright in a literary, dramatic, musical or artistic work is infringed by a person who, not being the owner of the copyright, and without the licence of the owner of the copyright, does in Australia, or authorizes the doing in Australia of, any act comprised in the copyright.

(1a) In determining, for the purposes of subsection (1), whether or not a person has authorised the doing in Australia of any act comprised in the copyright in a work, without the licence of the owner of the copyright, the matters that must be taken into account include the following:

(a) the extent (if any) of the person's power to prevent the doing of the act concerned;

(b) the nature of any relationship existing between the person and the person who did the act concerned;

(c) whether the person took any reasonable steps to prevent or avoid the doing of the act, including whether the person complied with any relevant industry codes of practice.

41A Fair dealing for purpose of parody or satire

A fair dealing with a literary, dramatic, musical or artistic work, or with an adaptation of a literary, dramatic or musical work, does not constitute an infringement of the copyright in the work if it is for the purpose of parody or satire.

65 Sculptures and certain other works in public places

(1) This section applies to sculptures and to works of artistic craftsmanship of the kind referred to in paragraph (c) of the definition of *artistic work* in section 10.

(2) The copyright in a work to which this section applies that is situated, otherwise than temporarily, in a public place, or in premises open to the public, is not infringed by the making of a painting, drawing, engraving or photograph of the work or by the inclusion of the work in a cinematograph film or in a television broadcast.

68 Publication of artistic works

The copyright in an artistic work is not infringed by the publication of a painting, drawing, engraving, photograph or cinematograph film if, by virtue of section 65, section 66 or section 67, the making of that painting, drawing, engraving, photograph or film did not constitute an infringement of the copyright.

78 References to all of joint authors

Subject to this Division, a reference in this Act to the author of a work shall, unless otherwise expressly provided by this Act, be read, in relation to a work of joint authorship, as a reference to all the authors of the work.

PART IX—MORAL RIGHTS OF PERFORMERS AND OF AUTHORS OF LITERARY, DRAMATIC, MUSICAL OR ARTISTIC WORKS AND CINEMATOGRAPH FILMS

189 Definitions

In this Part, unless the contrary intention appears:

'*act of false attribution*':

(a) in relation to an author's moral rights–has the meaning given by subsection 195AC(2); and

(b) in relation to a performer's moral rights–has the meaning given by subsection 195AHA(2).

'*artistic work*' means an artistic work in which copyright subsists.

'*attributable act*':

(a) in relation to an author's moral rights–has the meaning given by subsection 193(2); and

(b) in relation to a performer's moral rights–has the meaning given by subsection 195ABA(2).

'*attributor*':

(a) in relation to an author's moral rights–has the meaning given by subsection 195AC(2); and

(b) in relation to a performer's moral rights—has the meaning given by subsection 195AHA(2).

'infringing article' means:

(a) in relation to an author's moral rights:
  (i) an article that embodies a literary, dramatic, musical or artistic work, or a cinematograph film, whether or not the article bears or contains other material; or
  (ii) a reproduction of, or of an adaptation of, a literary, dramatic or musical work; or
  (iii) a reproduction of an artistic work; or
  (iv) a copy of a cinematograph film;

being a work or film in respect of which a moral right of the author has been infringed, other than by derogatory treatment not involving the material distortion or alteration of, or the mutilation of, the work or film; and

'literary work' means a literary work in which copyright subsists.

'moral right' means:

(a) in relation to an author:
  (i) a right of attribution of authorship; or
  (ii) a right not to have authorship falsely attributed; or
  (iii) a right of integrity of authorship; and
(b) in relation to a performer:
  (i) a right of attribution of performership; or
  (ii) a right not to have performership falsely attributed; or
  (iii) a right of integrity of performership.

'person representing the author', in relation to a possible infringement of any of an author's moral rights in respect of a work, means a person who, under subsection 195AN(1) or (2), is entitled to exercise and enforce the moral right concerned.

'work' means a literary work, a dramatic work, a musical work, an artistic work or a cinematograph film.

190 Moral rights conferred on individuals

Only individuals have moral rights.

193 Author's right of attribution of authorship

(1) The author of a work has a right of attribution of authorship in respect of the work.
(2) The author's right is the right to be identified in accordance with this Division as the author of the work if any of the acts (the *attributable acts*) mentioned in section 194 are done in respect of the work.

195AJ Derogatory treatment of literary, dramatic or musical work

In this Part:

'derogatory treatment', in relation to a literary, dramatic or musical work, means:

(a) the doing, in relation to the work, of anything that results in a material distortion of, the mutilation of, or a material alteration to, the work that is prejudicial to the author's honour or reputation; or
(b) the doing of anything else in relation to the work that is prejudicial to the author's honour or reputation.

195AO Infringement of right of attribution of authorship

Subject to this Subdivision, a person infringes an author's right of attribution of authorship in respect of a work if the person does, or authorises the doing of, an attributable act in respect of the work without the identification of the author in accordance with Division 2 as the author of the work.

195AR No infringement of right of attribution of authorship if it was reasonable not to identify the author

(1) A person who does, or authorises the doing of, an attributable act in respect of a work does not, because the author of the work is not identified, infringe the author's right of attribution of authorship in respect of the work if the person establishes that it was reasonable in all the circumstances not to identify the author.
(2) The matters to be taken into account in determining for the purposes of subsection (1) whether it was reasonable in particular circumstances not to identify the author of a literary, dramatic, musical or artistic work include the following:
    (a) the nature of the work;
    (b) the purpose for which the work is used;
    (c) the manner in which the work is used;
    (d) the context in which the work is used;
    (e) any practice, in the industry in which the work is used, that is relevant to the work or the use of the work;
    (f) any practice contained in a voluntary code of practice, in the industry in which the work is used, that is relevant to the work or the use of the work;
    (g) any difficulty or expense that would have been incurred as a result of identifying the author;
    (h) whether the work was made:
        (i) in the course of the author's employment; or
        (ii) under a contract for the performance by the author of services for another person;
        (iii) if the work has 2 or more authors—their views about the failure to identify them.

Further Reading

Allen, C 'The Literature of the Law', *Aspects of Justice*, Stevens & Sons Ltd, 1958 at 284.

Atiyah, 'Common Law and Statute Law' (1985) 48 *Modern Law Review* 1.

Bayne, P 'Fuzzy Drafting and the Interpretation of Statutes in the Administrative State' (1992) 66 *Australian Law Journal* 523.

Brazil P, 'Reform of Statutory Interpretation—the Australian Experience of Use of Extrinsic Materials: With a Postscript on Simpler Drafting' (1988) 62 *Australian Law Journal* 503.

Brennan, S 'Statutory Interpretation and Indigenous Property Rights' (2010) 21PLR 239.

Campbell, L 'Legal Drafting Styles: Fuzzy or Fussy?' (1996) 3(2) *E Law Murdoch University Electronic Journal of Law*, www.murdoch.edu.au/elaw/issues/v3n2/campbell.html.

Charlesworth, H; Chiam, M; Hovell, D and Williams, G 'Deep Anxieties: Australia and the International Legal Order' (2003) 25 *Sydney Law Review* 423.

Corcoran, S and Bottomley, S (eds) *Interpreting Statutes* (Federation Press, 2005).

Crawford, E *The Construction of Statutes* (1940).

Eskridge W N Jnr, *Dynamic Statutory Interpretation*, Harvard University Press, Cambridge Mass, 1994.

Evans, C and Evans, S *Australian Bills of Rights* (LexisNexis, 2008).

Evans, H (ed) *Odgers' Australian Senate Practice* (12th edn) at www.aph.gov.au/senate/pubs/odgers/index.htm.

Finn, P 'Statutes and the Common Law' (1992) 22 *University of Western Australia Law Review* 7.

French, R 'The Constitution and the Protection of Human Rights', Speech given at Australian National University, 20 November 2009, http://www.ecu.edu.au/about-ecu/vice-chancellor/distinguished-orator/the-constitution-and-the-protection-of-human-rights (13 June 2011).

Geddes, R S 'Purpose and Context in Statutory Interpretation' (2005) *University of New England Law Journal* 5.

Gleeson, J 'Extraterritorial application of Australian statutes proscribing misleading conduct' (2005) 79 *Australian Law Journal* 296.

Gleeson, M 'The Meaning of Legislation: Context, Purpose and Respect for Fundamental Rights' Address to Victoria Law Foundation, Melbourne, 31 July 2008.

Goode, M 'Codification of the Criminal Law' (2004) 28 *Criminal Law Journal* 226.

Gummow, W M C *Change and Continuity: Statute, Equity, and Federalism* (Oxford University Press, 1999).

Horn, N 'Black Letters: Epistolary Rhetoric and Plain English Laws' (2009) *Griffith Law Review* 7.

Judicial Commission of New South Wales, *Statutory Interpretation: Principles and Pragmatism for a New Age* (2007).

Kelly, D St L (ed) *Essays on Legislative Drafting* (1988) *Adelaide Law Review Association.*

Kirby, M 'Statutory Interpretation: The Meaning of Meaning' (2011) 35 *Melbourne University Law Review* (in press at the time of writing).

Kirby, M 'Towards a Grand Theory of Interpretation: The Case of Statutes and Contracts' (2003) 24(2) *Statute Law Review* 95.

Kirby, M 'The Australian Use of International Human Rights Norms: From Bangalore to Balliol—A View From the Antipodes', (1993) 16(2) *UNSW Law Journal* 363.

Mason, K 'The Intent of Legislators: How Judges Discern It and What They Do if They Find It', in *Statutory Interpretation: Principles and Pragmatism for a New Age* (Judicial Commission of New South Wales, 2007) 33.

Mason, A 'International Law as a Source of Domestic Law' in Opeskin, B and Rothwell, D (eds) *International Law and Australian Federalism* (1997).

McMeel, G 'Language and the Law Revisited: An Intellectual History of Contractual Interpretation' (2005) 34 *Common Law World Review* 256.

Megarry, R 'Administrative Quasi-Legislation' (1944) 60 *Law Quarterly Review* 125.

Mitchell, C 'Entire Agreement Clauses: Contracting Out of Contextualism' (2006) 22 *Journal of Contract Law* 222.

Pearce, D C 'Anticipating Legislation' (2008) 58 *AIAL Forum* 8.

Pearce, D C and Argument, S *Delegated Legislation in Australia* (LexisNexis, 3rd edn, 2005).

Pearce, D C and Geddes, R *Statutory Interpretation in Australia* (LexisNexis, 7th edn, 2011).

Penfold, H 'Legislative Drafting and Statutory Interpretation' in *Statutory Interpretation: Principles and Pragmatism for a New Age* (Judicial Commission of New South Wales, 2007).

Piotrowicz, RW, 'Unincorporated Treaties in Australian Law: the Official Response to the *Teoh* Decision' (1997) 71(7) *Australian Law Journal* 503.

Piotrowicz, 'Unincorporated Treaties in Australian Law' [1996] PL 190.

Pound, R 'Common Law and Legislation' (1907–8) 21(6) *Harvard Law Review* 383 at 384.

Pound, R 'Spurious Interpretation' (1907) 7(6) *Columbia Law Review* 379.

Ramsay, I 'Corporate Law in the Age of Statutes' (1992) 14 *Sydney Law Review* 474.

Sanson, M, Anthony T and Worswick, D *Connecting With Law* (Oxford University Press, 2nd edn, 2010) Ch 11.

Simpson, A and Williams, G 'International Law and Constitutional Interpretation' (2000) 11 *Public Law Review* 205.

Smith, D K 'Interpreting the Corporations Law—Purpose, Practical Reasoning and the Public Interest' (1999) 21 *Sydney Law Review* 161.

Spigelman, J J 'The Intolerable Wrestle: Developments in Statutory Interpretation', Address to the Australasian Conference of Planning and Environment Courts and Tribunals, 1 September 2010.

Spigelman, J J 'The Common Law Bill of Rights', McPherson Lecture, 2008, University of Queensland, 10 March 2008, http://papers.ssrn.com/sol3/papers.cfm?abstract_id=1806775.

Spigelman, J J *Statutory Interpretation and Human Rights*, The MacPherson Lecture Series, Vol 3 (2008).

Spigelman, J J 'From Text to Context: Contemporary Contractual Interpretation' (2007) 81 *Australian Law Journal* 322.

Spigelman, J J 'The Principle of Legality and the Clear Statement Principle' (2005) 79 *Australian Law Journal* 769.

Spigelman, J J 'Statutory Interpretation and Human Rights', Address to the Pacific Judicial Conference, Vanuatu, 26 July 2005, www.lawlink.nsw.gov.au/lawlink/Supreme_Court/ll_sc.nsf/pages/SCO_speech_spigelman260705.

Spigelman, J J 'The Poet's Rich Resource: Issues in Statutory Interpretation' (2001) 21 *Australian Bar Review* 224.

Spigelman, J J 'Statutory Interpretation: Identifying the Linguistic Register', Sir Ninian Stephen Lecture, 23 March 1999.

Stubbs, M T 'From Foreign Circumstances to First Instance Considerations: Extrinsic Material and the Law of Statutory Interpretation' (2006) 34(1) *Federal Law Review* 103.

Sullivan, R 'Statutory Interpretation in Canada: The Legacy of Elmer Driedger' in *Statutory Interpretation: Principles and Pragmatism for a New Age* (Judicial Commission of New South Wales, 2007).

Wilson, R D 'The Domestic Impact of International Human Rights Law' (1992) 66 *ALJR* 551.

Winckel, A 'The Contextual Role of a Preamble in Statutory Interpretation' (1999) 23 *Melbourne University Law Review* 184.

Index